Trade Unions and Arab Revolutions

T0331402

"We started the 2011 revolution and the rest of Egypt followed," say Egyptian workers with strong conviction and passion. Egyptian independent workers' continuous claims of contention and protest repertoires were one of several main factors leading to the January 25, 2011, uprising. After thirty-two years of a Mubarak-led authoritarian regime, massive protests began in January 2011 and forced President Mubarak to step down from his position on February 11, 2011. So, how did Egyptian workers challenge the regime and how did they become one of the factors leading to the January 2011 uprising? These workers were organized into loose networks of different independent groups that had been protesting for a decade and longer prior to January 2011. These regular protests for over a decade before 2011 challenged the Egyptian authoritarian regime.

This book examines the combative role of Egyptian independent workers' formal and informal organizations as a contentious social movement to challenge the regime. It will examine the evolving role of workers as socio-economic actors and then as political actors in very political transitions. Social movement theory (SMT) and its mechanisms and social movement unionism (SMU) will be the lenses through which this research will be presented. The methodology used will be the comparative case studies of two different movements where workers who advocated for their rights for a decade prior to January 2011 experienced significantly differing outcomes. One case study showcases the municipal real estate tax collection workers who were able to establish a successful social movement and then create an independent trade union. The second case study examines an influential group of garment and textile workers, who also developed an effective social movement, yet they were not able to take it to the next step to establish an independent union. I will explore within this research a second question: why one group of workers was able to establish an independent union while the other arguably more influential group of workers, the garment and textile workers, was not able to do so. This had an impact on the overall influence they were able to exercise over the regime in addition to their effectiveness as a social movement for change.

Heba F. El-Shazli is an Assistant Professor at George Mason University's Schar School of Policy and Government, where she teaches undergraduate and graduate courses on International Relations Theory; Politics, Government and Society of the Middle East; Israeli-Palestinian Politics; and Islam and Politics. She is an affiliate faculty to the Ali Vural Ak Center for Global Islamic Studies (AVACGIS) at George Mason University. She is also an Adjunct Faculty at Georgetown University's Master's Degree Program at the Center for Democracy and Civil Society.

Routledge Research in Employment Relations

Series editors:
Rick Delbridge and Edmund Heery
Cardiff Business School, UK

Aspects of the employment relationship are central to numerous courses at both undergraduate and postgraduate level.

Drawing from insights from industrial relations, human resource management and industrial sociology, this series provides an alternative source of research-based materials and texts, reviewing key developments in employment research.

Books published in this series are works of high academic merit, drawn from a wide range of academic studies in the social sciences.

For a full list of titles in this series, please visit www.routledge.com

Trade Unions and Arab Revolutions

Challenging the Regime in Egypt

Heba F. El-Shazli

Routledge
Taylor & Francis Group

NEW YORK AND LONDON

First published 2019
by Routledge
605 Third Avenue, New York, NY 10017

and by Routledge
2 Park Square, Milton Park, Abingdon, Oxon, OX14 4RN

First issued in paperback 2021

Routledge is an imprint of the Taylor & Francis Group, an informa business

Library of Congress Cataloging-in-Publication Data
A catalog record for this book has been requested

ISBN 13: 978-0-367-78629-8 (pbk)
ISBN 13: 978-0-367-14059-5 (hbk)

Typeset in Sabon
by Apex CoVantage, LLC

This book is dedicated to the courageous Egyptian workers, men and women, who continue to struggle for decent work, respect for fundamental worker rights, freedom of association, and for democracy at the workplace and in their homeland. It is also dedicated to my parents, Fawzi M. El-Shazli and Amal Alm el-Hoda Rifaat; sadly, they are not with us today, yet they are always with me and my family in spirit.

Contents

Preface

"Labor history has lost much of its élan, directionality and intellectual purpose."[1] *The goal of this manuscript is to contribute to the return of the study of labor, its history, its political contributions and challenges, and its stature within social science. By studying labor, we are peering into our own lives. Barrington Moore wrote that intellectuals alone could not pursue political goals or initiatives unless they align themselves with massive discontent.*[2] *So this manuscript is also focused on highlighting the "massive discontent" exhibited by the masses, the workers, and their families; without them, change cannot happen.*

Trade Unions and Arab Revolutions: Challenging the Regime in Egypt is comprised of three parts. The first part includes two chapters: first, an introduction to the concept of social movements and civil society and how labor fits into these concepts in Egypt; second, an introduction to industrial relations in Egypt from a historic perspective and pre- and post-1952 historic development of the Egyptian labor movement and its political activism. The second part includes four chapters featuring two case studies that illustrate attempts by Egyptian workers to challenge the regime, starting in earnest in 2006 (several years before the first uprising in 2011). Another two chapters will introduce and explain the role of other sociopolitical actors such as the Muslim Brotherhood (MB), women, and employers, in addition to the socio-economic and cultural framework. The third part includes two chapters that provide a review of labor's role post January 2011 until 2012, and post-Morsi and MB governance from 2013 to the present. The final chapter is the concluding remarks with an epilogue discussing the state of affairs from 2012 to the present (2018).

This book will examine and propose answers to the following two questions: First, what was the political role of the independent Egyptian labor movement leading up to the 2011 uprisings, and how did the workers use repeated contentious collective actions to challenge the regime? Second, the independent labor movement did have a political role, albeit limited and contested—why? The workers valiantly fought many battles but lost the overall war, that being the actual implementation of democratic political reform. Thus, these workers view their efforts as leading to an elusive victory. Historic reviews and lessons learned from other such movements in Poland, Brazil, and elsewhere will provide perspective on the Egyptian movement's role in history.

My research will show that labor's influence was embedded in its acts of defiance from below that challenged the authoritarian state above. Workers used the power of strikes, protests, demonstrations, and sit-ins, which also early on contributed to slowly breaking down the "barrier of fear" within the hearts and minds of many Egyptians. Through their repeated acts of contention and protest over the years, addressed in this research, the workers became a role model for action opposing the regime, thus creating additional cracks within the fabric of authoritarian rule leading to wide breaches in the regime's firm efforts to control. Workers were indeed present in the "infamous" Tahrir Square and elsewhere around the country in the January 2011 uprising, but as individuals, and not under the organized banner of a large independent workers' social movement—why? The independent workers' social movement was still shackled to its past and insecure in the present, leading to an unstable future. Its existence and plans were made all the more confusing by the unambiguous nature of an authoritarian regime. The independent labor movement was not able to achieve a coherent political stance or role, especially post-February 2011 and up to the 2012 presidential elections. They had fallen prey to bureaucratic infighting, leaders' large political egos and quests for power, and the continued authoritarian nature of post-February 2011 rule by the military through the Supreme Council of Armed Forces (SCAF).

Social movements are generally understood as

> challenges to "existing arrangements of power and distribution by people with common purposes and solidarity, in sustained interaction with elites, opponents, and authorities."[3] These movements, ranging from large grassroots organizations to small "principled" groups[4] acting "on behalf of largely silent constituencies,"[5] are all defined by and committed through the contentious activities they implement to achieve a common, collective good. Regardless of their most immediate [short-term] demands, these movements invariably necessitate extensive political changes as the lynchpin of their success.[6]

Extensive political changes were a requirement of the workers' social movement success, thus their elusive victory in Egypt's case.

The Egyptian workers were indeed part of the struggle for political reform and shaped its message. Early on, they voiced the need to change from an authoritarian regime to a democracy. Starting in 2006 and earlier, they initially used an economic discourse, which then changed to a more nuanced political discourse in 2010. The change in the nature and framing of the discourse came about with the debate over instituting a minimum wage for all workers in 2010.[7] However, the workers' contentious collective actions were not able to secure the goal and desired results of a state truly transitioning to a democracy, one that respects fundamental and universal human and worker rights.

Notes

1. Katznelson, Ira. "The Bourgeois Dimension: A Provocation About Institutions, Politics & the Future of Labor History." *International Labor and Working-Class History* 46 (1994): 7–32: 7.
2. Moore, Barrington. *Social Origins of Dictatorship and Democracy—Lord and Peasant in the Making of the Modern World.* Boston: Beacon Press, 1966.

3. Meyer, David S. and Sidney G. Tarrow. "A Movement Society: Contentious Politics for a New Century." In *The Social Movement Society: Contentious Politics for a New Century*, ed. Meyer and Tarrow. Lanham, MD: Rowman and Littlefield, 1998: 1–28.

4. Sikkink, Kathryn. "Human Rights Principled Issue-Networks, and Sovereignty in Latin America." *International Organization* 47 (3) (1993): 411–441: 411.

5. Ottaway, Marina and Theresa Chung. "Toward a New Paradigm." *Journal of Democracy* 10 (4) (1999): 99–113: 107.

6. Grodsky, Brian K. *Social Movements and the New State, The Fate of Pro-Democracy Organizations When Democracy Is Won.* Stanford, CA: Stanford University Press, 2012: 3.

7. www.aljazeera.com/news/middleeast/2010/05/201052161957263202.html: "Hundreds of Egyptian workers have gathered outside Egypt's cabinet building demanding a rise in the minimum wage, which has been set at $6.30 a month since 1984. The protesters were calling for the government to implement a court order that would boost the minimum wage and help millions of poor cope with rising prices. About 500 protesters in central Cairo on Sunday chanted: 'We need wages that are enough for a month!' while some called for an end to the rule of Hosni Mubarak, Egypt's president for more than 28 years. The protest is the latest in a series of demonstrations demanding more assistance for poor Egyptians and greater political freedom in the tightly controlled state."

Acknowledgments

This book could not have been completed without the support, advice, and feedback from my mentors and advisers, especially Professor Joel Peters, the director of the School of Public and International Affairs (SPIA) at Virginia Tech in Alexandria, Virginia. Thank you to Professors Ariel Ahram, Timothy Luke, and Rachel Scott at SPIA at Virginia Tech at the Blacksburg and Alexandria campuses for your continued patience, helpful advice, support, and belief in this research project. Thank you to all my professors from undergraduate to graduate school for all the advice given to me along this lifelong learning journey. In addition, after 28 years of professional working experience with NGOs in the promotion of good governance, empowerment, and democracy, this book is a culmination of both my professional work career with trade unions and political parties in the Central and Eastern Europe (1982–1994), in the Middle East and North Africa (1994–2013), and academic research. Much gratitude goes to the Albert Shanker Institute (ASI) in Washington, DC, for providing the financial support that enabled my field research in Egypt to take place in the summer of 2013. Thanks to Eugenia Kemble (may she rest in peace), the former executive director of ASI, who was instrumental in providing the support and always believed in me. Thank you to the editorial staff at Routledge, Taylor & Francis, and Apex CoVantage for the excellent support, advice and assistance. Finally, I would also like to acknowledge the tremendous support given to me by my family, friends, students, and especially by my husband, Anthony W. Gray, who lifted my spirits from the doldrums when needed (which was quite often), who believed in my ability to complete this project, encouraged me and cheered me on when I wanted to retreat, and who did all of this with a confident smile. I would not be at this juncture in my life completing this research, book, and teaching full-time at the university level if it was not for all his love, support, and encouragement. Thank you and Shukran.

Introduction

An Elusive Victory: How Egyptian Workers Challenged the Regime, and the Rise of the Protest Movement

"We started the 2011 revolution and the rest of Egypt followed," say Egyptian workers with strong conviction. Egyptian independent workers' continuous claims of contention and repertoires of protest were one of several main factors leading to the January 25, 2011, uprising. After thirty-two years of a Mubarak-led authoritarian regime, massive protests began in January 2011 and forced President Mubarak to step down from his position. The first question addressed in this research endeavor is, How did Egyptian workers challenge the regime and how did they become one of the factors leading to the January 2011 uprising? These workers were organized into loose networks of different independent groups that had been protesting for a decade and longer prior to January 2011. However, their regular protests for over a decade before 2011 challenged the authoritarian regime.

This book examines the combative role of Egyptian independent workers' formal and informal organizations as a contentious social movement to challenge the regime. It will examine the evolving role of workers as socio-economic actors and then as political actors in political transitions. Social movement theory (SMT) and its mechanisms and social movement unionism (SMU) will be the lenses through which this research will be presented. The methodology will be the comparative case studies of two different movements, in which workers who advocated for their rights for a decade prior to January 2011 experienced significantly differing outcomes. One case study highlights the municipal real estate tax collection workers who were able to establish a successful social movement and then create an independent trade union. The second case study examines an influential group of garment and textile workers, who also developed an effective social movement, yet were not able to take it to the next step to establish an independent union. I will explore within this research a second question: why one group of workers was able to establish an independent union while the other arguably more influential group of workers, the garment and textile workers, was not able to do so. This had an impact on the influence they were able to exercise over the regime in addition to their effectiveness as a social movement for change.

Part I

A Brief Overview of Egyptian Workers' Revolts and History

1 The Historic Rise of Organized Labor and Its Role in Protest Democratic Movements Globally; and Egyptian Workers' Contentious Collective Action

Chapter Outline:

1. Egyptian Workers' Contentious Collective Action—An Overview

   - Definitions
   - Background: The Rise of Protest Movements in Egypt
   - Protest Events Leading to the January 2011 Uprising
   - Mass Collective Action and the Process of Democratization: Theory and Practice
   - Social Movements, Contentious Politics, and Workers

2. Theoretical Basis for Research

   - Discussion of Social Movement Unionism and Labor Movements in Democratization
   - Discussion of Social Movement Theory and Contentious Politics

3. Literature Review and Context

   Literature Review: Social Movements, Mobilization, and Contestation: Theory and Practice

   Literature Review: How Do We Measure the Impact of Social Movements?

   Literature Review: What Has Been the Role of Trade Unions in Political Life and Revolutions and Its Significance?

   What Insights Does This Literature Offer in the Case of Egypt, and What Are Its Limitations?

4. Concluding Remarks

This chapter introduces readers to the book's intention to study Egyptian workers' protests through two case studies from 2004 to 2011. Workers had been protesting for over a decade before January 2011. The book also examines the following thesis: If workers had not been protesting and thus had not challenged the regime, then the actual uprising would not have taken place in such a massive, effective, and widespread (across societal class/professional lines) manner—a bold assertion, indeed. "Effective" in this context means that millions of Egyptians protested publicly (without the accustomed fear of retribution) against the regime—a victory in itself. Yet, their victory remains elusive so it was a "victory" within limits. With this bold contention, I intend to provide the empirical

evidence to support my hypothesis using the lenses of social movement theory and social movement unionism.

This chapter will also review how independent workers' organizations did indeed play a causal political role in laying the groundwork for the first uprising from January 25–28, 2011, despite several challenges. Yet, their efforts in calling for reforms fell short of success, because Egypt did not transition into a democracy. However, their efforts were not in vain, despite the workers, along with other members of civil society, not being victorious in achieving their ultimate desired goals. The workers' contentious politics and collective action became a role model for other activists and a path of resistance to follow. There will be an overview of the two case studies, background about the Egyptian independent workers' movement, definitions of trade unions and "political unionism," and a review of the rise of protest movements in Egypt. This introduction makes these aims clear while also providing a brief auto-ethnography of what led the author to this topic of study.

Egyptian Workers' Contentious Collective Action—An Overview

For decades since the late 1880s, Egyptian workers have collectively organized and toiled to bring respect for social justice to their work lives and society as a whole. This quest has been eternally elusive, although it has had some success. Pre-1952, there was a more vibrant independent labor movement with strong political alliances to effective political parties. There were still significant disagreements and falling-outs between trade unions and political parties that wanted to take advantage of their mass organizational support. However, post-1952, the state actually initiated labor protections at the expense of the labor movement's freedom of association. The labor movement became an official state entity and thus co-opted a "corporatist" style of organization, accepting government power and control as the norm.[1]

In the post-1952 years, workers acquiesced and were led to believe that they participated in decision-making and policy making.[2] However, as the years passed through the 1990s, Egypt found itself in a "fiscal crisis," and the state was unable to support the public sector and its workers at the accustomed levels. Starting in 1991, Egypt was pressured by the International Financial Institutions (IFIs) to restructure its economy, cut subsidies, and privatize public sector factories. These government policy actions were considered and implemented without societal input.

Trade unions are examples of the "art of presence and active citizenry," according to Asef Bayat.[3] Trade unions and workers are important political actors within the workings of a nation-state. Workers made claims and demands and established themselves as an effective social movement over a period of consistent contentious politics or the intersection between collective action, politics, and contention. However, in Egypt's case, the workers' movement was effective only to a certain extent, thus achieving an incomplete victory.

Definitions

First, as a form of background and introduction, one needs to define certain organizations and concepts such as "trade unions" and "political unionism."

What Are Trade Unions?

Labor unions are a voluntary, grassroots organization/association of workers at a private or publicly owned workplace (office and/or factory). The International Labor Organization (ILO) defines a trade union organization as "an organization of employees usually associated beyond the confines of one enterprise, established for protecting or improving through collective action, the economic and social status of its members."[4] The ILO confirms, "The right of workers and employers to form and join organizations of their own choosing is an integral part of a free and open society. In many cases, these organizations have played a significant role in their countries' democratic transformation."[5] Labor unions are the best-organized grassroots organizations and thus have a direct interest in contributing to political reform.

Free and independent trade unions are civil society organizations (CSO) that contribute to a democratic society. According to labor expert Barbara Fick, trade unions are a stabilizing force for democracy because of their organizational structure and characteristics, i.e. "democratic representation, demographic [and geographic] representation, financial independence, breadth of concerns, and placement within society."[6] There is a direct relationship between free trade unions and a democratic society. In a democratic nation-state, generally freedom of association is respected and promoted, thus paving the way for an independent democratic trade union movement to exist and flourish.

Trade unions have the means themselves to create and protect the space for others to advocate for rights, monitor government activities, and protest when needed. Fick succinctly writes,

> Trade unions are a key element for sustaining a stable democracy. They provide a voice not only for workers within the workplace but also for worker-citizens within the polity [...] trade unions are one of the best mechanisms for providing an authentic and effective voice for worker-citizens. A society concerned about maintaining a vibrant democracy should be concerned about maintaining the conditions necessary for a vibrant trade union movement.[7]

Ideally, trade unions, in cooperation with other civil society (non-government) organizations, can be a positive force to promote democratic principles when the rulers are faltering. Trade unions, however, have to exemplify the aforementioned characteristics and strongly maintain their independence from the government.

Union membership also cuts across gender, ethnicity, religion, and age. Unions do not distinguish between those differentiating human characteristics, but what is binding is that the person is a worker at the same workplace. The organization's financial independence is achieved through union dues that are collected from each member, and these make up the operating budget of a trade union. There is a contribution, generally based on the number of members in the union (per capita), which supports the federation of trade unions on a national level.

Another characteristic of organized labor is their "breadth of concerns," as Samuel Gompers declared,

> Labor wants more school houses and less jails; more books and less arsenals; more learning and less vice; more constant work and less crime; more leisure

and less greed; more justice and less revenge; in fact, more of the opportunities to cultivate our better natures.[8]

This is understood to be a universal demand of labor unions around the world and without exception in Egypt.

Last but not least are trade unions' place and role in society. It is understood that unions can be effective mid-level mediators for conflict resolution. They can mediate between the lower level of the grassroots (rank-and-file members) and the upper-level elite (management) in a conflict situation. Fick writes,

> trade unions, as strategic mid-level actors, can genuinely voice the interests of its grassroots constituency to the high-level actors and, by virtue of their societal position, effectively influence those actors, as well as mediate between conflicting positions within a society both horizontally and vertically.[9]

That position within society can be very valuable for bringing together workers based on where they work and not on their ethnicities or religious affiliations. In several high-conflict areas such as Bosnia, Iraq, Cyprus, and Northern Ireland, trade unions successfully organized across ethnic and religious boundaries to protect their workers' rights. Trade unions were able to play a mediator/unifier role and even become a role model in circumstances plagued by prolonged conflicts.[10]

In addition to the traditional role of trade unions, such as organizing workers, negotiating with employers, and collective bargaining, trade unions do have a political role. Some would argue that in order to protect the "bread and butter" role of trade unions in today's industrial relations, it is imperative for trade unions to have and practice a political role. Particularly, in developing countries and with all the aforementioned characteristics of trade unions, it is irrefutable to recognize and affirm the important political role that trade unions can play.

What Is "Political Unionism"?

Political unionism does differ between developing and developed countries and trade unions do have a history of playing a political role, particularly in developing nations. Bruce H. Millen wrote his book on the political role of trade unions in developing countries in 1963. Although it was published in 1963, Millen's *Political Role of Labor in Developing Countries*[11] is timeless; his ideas, concepts, and conclusions still ring true today. Political unionism is an extension of the economic role of trade unions, and it enables workers to gain their socio-economic demands.

Despite the overall decline in trade unions' role in political democratic societies, in the US model, trade unions do lobby and support politicians who enact legislation favorable to labor. In Western Europe, including the UK in the twentieth century, the trade unions were much more directly involved in politics through their participation in the Labor Party, for example, and developed a tendency to participate in political movement/forces with the goal of acquiring and keeping political power.[12] However, in the last two decades, economic realities have changed and Labor Party politics have also changed, even in the UK.

In the Middle East (similar to the former Soviet Union and countries in Eastern Europe before 1989), the political elites managed to control trade unions instead of being included in mass movements. "As a consequence, the union leadership is likely to engage in maneuvers that are still highly political but uninspired by an ideology."[13] However, during the period of colonialism in the Middle East, trade union organizations played an active role along with other political forces in overthrowing and pushing out the colonial powers, such as in Algeria, Morocco, Egypt, and Tunisia. Egyptian workers first protested in the 1919 revolution, a countrywide uprising against British rule, pushing the nation toward independence in 1922. The largest strike in the nation's history took place in 1947 at El-Mahalla al-Kubra, the nation's largest industrial center and home to the first textile factory in Egypt.[14] And within a few years, in 1952, there was the Free Officer's coup d'état against King Farouk and continued British influence, leading to the declaration of a republic of Egypt; Egyptian workers played a catalyst political role. This will be further detailed in the Chapter 3 on the history of the Egyptian labor movement.

Trade unions are the best grassroots organizations for expressing the needs and interests of a majority of citizens. In countries where the government is going through a transition or appears to be fragile, trade unions have an imperative political role to ensure a more egalitarian program. Millen calls this "political unionism." Political leaders seeking mass approval and support lean on trade union organizations, pre- and post-independence, in developing countries. Before independence in several countries, political forces joined with trade union movements (mass social movements) to push out the colonial powers. After independence, with an increase in nationalism leading the drive for national development (industrialization with more urbanization), political leaders cannot "safely ignore the promises, for the disaffection of the workers cannot be risked. On this fact rides much of the union strength."[15] Trade unions contributed to the national development goals of newly independent nations around the globe in addition to the fight against colonialism. The arguments to support the essential role of workers in democratic transitions continued through Ruth Collier and James Mahoney's research, which established that working class mobilization was key to five of eleven Latin American and southern European transitions in the 1970s and 1980s.[16] They also challenged the widely accepted and unchallenged "transitions paradigm" by Guillermo O'Donnell and Phillippe Schmitter that presents transitions as the sole domain of political elites, "a conversation among gentlemen, with labor protest having relatively little consequence."[17] Labor protests have shown, time and again, with Poland's Solidarnosc in the 1980s as a vivid example, that labor plays an important and consequential role in political transition.

Trade unions contributed to the political development in the newly independent nations in the Middle East and North Africa of Algeria, Morocco, Tunisia, and Egypt. According to Millen, labor organizations possessed the necessary skills and experience to participate effectively in the politics of pre- and post-independence. They provided political education, leadership, and modernization.[18] What is meant by political modernization? Unions are generally moving in sync with the innovations and changes in an economy and industry. In most new governments, they are looking for a consensus on how to modernize the political and economic systems.

Unions are the natural partners of political forces with this goal in mind, partly because they are the intermediary between the political complex and the labor force—and it is on the labor force that a large part of the modernizing effort must depend.[19]

In addition, Millen emphasizes that unions can be that essential democratic modernizing element that counters anti-democratic extremist movements. Before 1952, trade unions in Egypt developed and grew their membership with their members and leaders possessing those afore-mentioned skills and experiences. The hopeful point of departure is that many of these union activists are still active, or they have passed on the knowledge and inspiration to the next generations.

Background: The Rise of Protest Movements in Egypt

Egypt's Prime Minister Nazif's neoliberal economic restructuring policies starting in 2004 gave the impetus to the first of many social movements to organize and to act. Hugh Roberts comments, "[L]ong before the uprisings of late 2010 and early 2011, it seemed to me the extreme accumulation of power that characterized the Mubarak regime [. . .] had at least one definite implication for the future: it couldn't possibly be sustained after Mubarak's departure."[20] Both Roberts and Holger Albrecht[21] believe that Mubarak orchestrated a liberalized authoritarian regime that controlled from the top and allowed venting at the bottom in the form pluralism in the media and other civil society outlets. However, in 2014, we can challenge the opinions stated above with the "extreme accumulation of power" by the current Egyptian ruler.

The Kefaya (Enough) movement, also known as The Egyptian Movement for Change, began with simple, straightforward, small protests in significant public spaces in Cairo (in front of Egypt's Supreme Court of Cassation, the Journalist Syndicate headquarters, or Cairo University) with a simple message: Kefaya. Roberts describes Kefaya as dominated by secularist Arab nationalists and Nasserists attempting to bring back a bygone era—less concerned with democracy and more concerned with getting rid of Mubarak. He also reviews Albrecht's book about opposition movements under Mubarak, which has a good account of Kefaya and its origins, development as a movement, and eventual demise.

The protesters would place large stickers on their mouth with the word KEFAYA in large letters, and they would stand silently for hours for all passersby to see, or they would hold signs and placards with the same word: Kefaya (Enough). Even before the Kefaya movement took center stage, the first Palestinian intifada was reason for many Egyptians to protest in Cairo. Protestors took the opportunity to call for more political freedoms and socio-economic improvements in daily life.

> Kefaya brought together people from across the political spectrum with a simple message, "enough," and was the first movement to call directly for regime change. But few people joined the demonstrations, and the movement suffered internal tensions that weakened its effectiveness.[22]

However, the Kefaya movement captured the imagination of the limitedly independent Egyptian media using different mechanisms, brokers, and processes to

diffuse its message. Kefaya became a regular fixture in the burgeoning opposition to the Mubarak regime.

Interestingly, there was not much heavy-handed state security and police interference—I believe the regime felt that it was a "venting" mechanism that would eventually fizzle and go away. These protests were tolerated by the regime except when they stepped outside of the capital; there was no reason to destroy any social capital already built up to support Mubarak. However, both Roberts and Albrecht present evidence that "Kefaya was essentially an agitation conducted by a dissident wing of the Egyptian elite against Mubarak's monopoly of power and the prospect of his son succeeding him."[23] The pluralism that was allowed by the regime created the space for groups of elites to bicker and argue with each other.

Kefaya also crossed certain "red lines" in terms of violating the Emergency Law's ban on unauthorized demonstrations and criticizing Mubarak and his family. Kefaya would hold protests in Cairo without being harassed when at times the police force outnumbered the protesters. Roberts addressed these issues and wrote that Kefaya was able to get away with these violations unscathed due to their composition (mentioned previously), the military elite's support, and because the Mubarak regime wanted to downplay schisms in the ranks of elites, his supporters. Since the Mubarak regime controlled the top, the "venting" allowed at the bottom did not impact power, control, or longevity in power.

By 2006, the Kefaya movement was still somewhat on the scene, yet it was beginning to exhaust itself. It had succeeded in cracking the hegemony of the Mubarak regime on the civil-democratic movement. However, it was not able to bring workers, peasants, and the informal sector proletariat into its movement. The purely negative political discourse exhibited by Kefaya did not address the socio-economic grievances faced by workers.[24] It continually presented a negative discourse—it did not have a positive agenda or a set of demands to pressure the regime. Cut off from society at large and ridden with internal disagreements, the Kefaya movement began to disintegrate just as the Mahalla workers' strike movement was beginning to grow. Baho Abdul of the Tadamon (Solidarity) organization acknowledges, "Before 2006 no one in the political field was interested in the workers' movement, because there did not seem to be a real movement. The strike of December 2006 changed everything. All [political] parties went to the [workers'] movement."[25] This was a wakeup call to the traditional opposition intellectuals and political elite to return to the working class to find militant action and a challenge to the Mubarak regime.

Hugh Roberts wrote for the International Crisis Group (ICG) in 2005 and argued that Kefaya's mainly negative message was a major reason for its failure to gain a wider audience.

> Outside the legal opposition parties, *Kefaya!* (Enough!) has remained essentially a protest movement without a constructive vision of change. The result is neither wing of the secular opposition has been able to make appreciable gains, leaving the Muslim Brother[hood] despite their illegality, still the most substantial opposition force.[26]

Roberts came to the conclusion that Arab Nationalists/Nasserists' real objection was the abandonment of the pan-Arab vision that Nasser had championed and

not Mubarak's authoritarianism.[27] As a result, the Kefaya movement was not capable of mounting a democratic confrontation involving the public to agitate for their dreams.

The workers began to protest low wages and high cost of living, starting with the garment and textile workers in 2004 and with more frequency in 2006 in various large public sector workplaces in Alexandria, Kafr al-Dawar, Qalyub, and El-Mahalla al-Kubra. Between 2004 and 2011, it has been estimated that there were over three million workers who had participated in one form of a collective contentious action, counting about 3,000 of these instances. Workers had serious contentious claims (grievances) and the means to organize themselves into social movements with a regular repertoire that was often quite creative in methodology and discourse. At times, they were even appealing to the regime for protection from the "savage" private owners who were stripping the workers of their benefits, a clever way to remind Mubarak of the "social contract" made back in the early heady days after the 1952 revolution. This workers' social movement became in one instance an established organization led by a charismatic union leader, Kamal Abu Eita, per the Weberian view or perspective of social movements. Abu Eita led the establishment of the first independent trade union in 2008.

The first independent trade union of civil servants working in tax collection was formed after one year of agitation and protest. In December 2008, the Independent General Union of Municipal Real Estate Tax Collectors Independent Union (IGURETA) was publicly formed, contrary to the laws of the land yet in full accordance with the International Labor Organization's conventions signed by Egypt in 1987 and 1997. These conventions called for the right to freely associate, organize unions, and bargain collectively. Egypt had been placed on the ILO's blacklist as violators of core principles outlined in the Declaration of Fundamental Worker Rights passed by the ILO annual conference in 1998. IGURETA, for example, used international certification by the ILO and sectorial international labor institutions such as Public Services International (PSI) to support and give credibility to their social movement.

Egyptian independent workers became a social movement using mechanisms and repertoires with initially an economic framing of their claims (grievances) against the state. This discourse became increasingly more political as January 2011 approached. The defining moment was during the summer of 2010 when the debate over establishing a minimum wage for workers hit a crescendo. The government was opposed to the proposal and was stalling—the workers' discourse became more and more political, with some even saying, "[I]f this government is not supporting a minimum living wage; then it is time for them to go home."[28] About 500 protesters in central Cairo on May 3, 2010, chanted, "We need wages that are enough for a month!" while some called for an end to the rule of Mubarak, Egypt's president for more than 28 years.[29] This was the transformation to add the "political" to the workers' protest discourse.

The Egyptian "Arab Spring" uprising in January and February 2011 was incomplete. These were heady, exciting, and dangerous times, when a spark hit a powder keg of discontent, bringing together many civil society actors. These actors included independent labor organizations and retiree groups; civil society organizations; youth/student movements (such as the April 6 Youth Movement); professional white-collar associations such as journalists, professors, and judges;

the MB (albeit joining in late—one needs to distinguish between the official MB leadership and that caught between the military and the Mubarak regime and ordinary MB members who were freer to act and participate); and ordinary Egyptians from all walks of life—lower, middle, and upper classes. They all came out to protest the Mubarak regime's policies and actions (or lack of action on several social/economic issues). The revolutionary spirit and zeal spread like wildfire and started in earnest on January 28, 2011, when millions of Egyptians came out to the streets and squares all over the country. They stayed in these public spaces until Mubarak stepped down on February 11, 2011. Mass euphoria, jubilation, and even disbelief that Mubarak stepped down were rampant everywhere, yet this joy and euphoria lasted only for a short time.

Protest Events Leading to the January 2011 Uprising

We have observed with great interest the unfolding developments and coined the "Arab Spring" term to describe events taking place in the Middle East in the early 2010s. Although the new term quickly became fashionable as shorthand for the tumultuous events of 2011, today the "Arab Spring" term is often subject to derision and even ridicule due to the results thus far. So, the use of "uprisings" is frankly more apt and descriptive than "Spring," which evokes a beginning and an ending as the spring season has. These uprisings are still being manifested and quite dramatically in countries such as Libya, Syria, and Yemen. During the Arab uprisings of 2011, subjects became citizens by taking to the streets, shaking off the yoke of authoritarian rule, and demanding the overthrow of the regime. Throughout the region, thanks to the well-developed media and social media networks, the protesters chanted in unison in practically every major city in the Middle East, "El shaab yurid isqaat el nizam/ الشعب يريد اسقاط النظام," meaning the people demand the overthrow of the regime. In the early days and months of 2011, the same Arabic chants, slogans, placards, and tactics were used throughout the region from Morocco to Yemen and as far as Syria. These demonstrations, impressive for their audacious courage, have changed the political structure of several of the Arab regimes, but did they create the foundations for fundamental positive political change and reform? What was the role of social movements and especially the workers through their trade unions? Egypt's labor force makes up nearly a third of the nation's population,[30] and it played an important role in the years leading up to the still-unsecured revolution. "Dr. Joel Beinin sees the last decade of mobilization by various political and social groups—many of them workers—as one of the driving forces behind the revolution. This was a huge laboratory for democracy."[31]

Ann Lesch[32] outlines the varying protests starting in 2000 and earlier—a continuum of events, one after another, led to the massive January 2011 uprising. One has to look at this major uprising in 2011 as part of a larger continuum and not as an event that came out of nowhere. There was a building up of anger against the Mubarak regime over a period of many years; it just needed a tipping point, a spark to ignite into a full-blown uprising, breaking down the barriers of fear. The independent Egyptian workers' movement and protests led the way.

Initially, there were protests against the Israeli reinvasion of the West Bank from 2000 to 2002, supporting the Palestinian intifada. Traditionally, the regime

allowed such demonstrations—anything to deflect from Egyptians' worries and concerns about their daily lives. These protests initially began against Israel and then became more and more of a reflection of anger against Mubarak, with the tearing down of many of the large downtown Cairo billboards featuring his face. In 2003, there were large demonstrations against the US invasion of Iraq, and Lesch states that these demonstrations were larger than the famous bread riots of 1977. Soon thereafter, two major social protest movements were created:

> The March 9 Movement, formed in 2004 to call for university and academic independence. [. . .] Kefaya was [also] founded in 2004 by intellectuals and community activists concerned about the upcoming presidential and parliamentary elections. They spoke out on the intertwined issues of corruption, the state of emergency, Mubarak's running for a fifth term in September 2005 and dynastic succession. [. . .] Kefaya brought together people from across the political spectrum with a simple message, "enough," and was the first movement to call directly for regime change. But few people joined the demonstrations, and the movement suffered internal tensions that weakened its effectiveness.[33]

Meanwhile, collective action protests based on labor grievances earnestly began in the fall of 2004. The Egyptian government, led by Prime Minister al-Nazif (his surname name means "the clean" in Arabic, which is indeed ironic), pushed implementing a neoliberal economic policy of selling public sector factories to private investors. "Public-sector workers were deeply concerned at the loss of benefits, forced retirement with inadequate (or unpaid) compensation packages, and the shrinkage of job opportunities in both the public and private sectors."[34] Workers were relatively well organized and had the necessary structure to protest and speak out, unlike other sectors of society. From 2004 to 2009, there were approximately 2,623 protests (strikes, gatherings, sit-ins, and demonstrations).[35] The most significant in size and prestige was the strike by the crown jewel of Egypt's public sector, the Al-Mahalla al-Kubra's giant textile and garment factories, in December 2006.

Over 25,000 workers were on a strike for one week, occupying the huge factory complex. They demanded payment of year-end bonuses; implementation of a minimum wage; and dismantlement of the official, corrupt, trade union federation, Egyptian Trade Union Federation (ETUF), and they protested the lack of reinvestment in the factories' infrastructure and equipment, as well as poor working conditions.

ETUF, created in 1957, has functioned as the principal means by which the government has exerted control over the country's workforce. The ETUF monopolized all labor union activities and funding provided by the Trade Union Act of 1976. This draconian legislation limited the nomination of union heads to regime-approved candidates and mandated prison sentences for striking workers.

> Egyptian law states that strikes can only be declared with the ETUF approval, which is almost never given. Workers who defy the de facto ban on labor stoppages to protest low wages and deplorable labor conditions invariably find their union heads have sided with the government and company managers.[36]

A union is supposed to protect, defend, and advocate for workers' rights. Then, the Unified Labor Law of 2003 was enacted, which preserved ETUF's monopoly on trade union organization. It allowed for temporary worker contracts that could last for many years and become "permanent-temporary." This further eroded worker rights in Egypt and added to the slow demise of the social contract between government and workers that started with the 1952–56 legislation.

The independent labor movement for many years prior to January 2011 regularly contested the regime's power by protesting and going on strike, especially in enterprises still owned by the government. By having the courage to protest, these workers were indeed challenging the regime and its allies. Workers protested working conditions, low wages, loss of benefits, closures of their workplaces, and the loss of their pensions—and many times, loss of their jobs. The unexpected selling of factories in the dark of night to private entities without making proper accommodations for workers' benefits and wages was another major issue of contention. This movement was disparate and not necessarily united under one umbrella organization, disputing classic social movement theory, which emphasizes mobilizing structures.[37]

> Thus, years before the "January 25 Revolution," a social movement of workers, their families, and their neighbors established its presence. Through strikes and other collective actions, workers had made substantial economic gains, teaching many Egyptians a crucial lesson: Engaging in collective action, previously regarded as a losing game by all but committed middle-class activists, could achieve something of value.[38]

This further adds to the argument that the January 2011 uprising was a culmination of over ten years of contentious politics and social movements led by workers.

Mass Collective Action and the Process of Democratization: Theory and Practice

The process of democratization is highlighted and understood through the field of comparative politics and the study of transitions. The paradigm, or framework, of academic scholarship tends to focus primarily on the role of elites in democratic transitions, while the role of mass collective action demanding political reform and workers' organization are most often ignored. The focus of this research is to show how empirical facts point to the important, yet most often overlooked, role of organized workers in the transition process in Egypt. There has been a "privileging" of elites as the leaders and masters of political change. Mahoney and Collier, who wrote about Latin America, argue,

> [T]he labor movement often played an important role in recent transitions. Labor was not limited to an "indirect" role, in which protest around workplace demands was answered through coopted inclusion in the electoral arena. Rather, the labor movement was one of the major actors in the political opposition, explicitly demanding a democratic regime. In some cases, union-led protest for democracy contributed to a climate of un-governability and de-legitimation that led directly to a general destabilization of authoritarian regimes.[39]

Labor's continued collective action of protests also keeps the process going forward and monitors any backsliding. Therefore, the best course of scholarship and study is to not separate the workers' movement from the elites' movement for democratic change.

Labor became part of the political opposition in the case studies presented by Collier and Mahoney in Latin America. However, did this happen in Egypt? Did labor sit at the national political negotiations table? Did labor play an effective political role for reforms and democratization of the state? From the case studies in this research endeavor, it will be made clear that independent labor organizations paved the road for the major upheaval starting in January 2011 by removing barriers of fear and served as a "political training school." There were several illustrative examples from different economic sectors of how the workers challenged the regime in earnest starting in 2006. This is well documented in the publication *The Struggle for Worker Rights in Egypt*; between 1998 and 2008, a total of 2,623 strikes, gatherings, sit-ins, and demonstrations took place in Egypt. These contentious actions took place in the governmental (public) and private sectors.[40] Participating in these collective contentious actions were approximately 1,741,870 workers.[41] Workers, through their collective action, persistence, and courage (repertoires of contention), confronted the regime's business cronies and state institutions. However, labor's role as part of the political opposition became mired in its legacy, history, and lack of trust, perceptions and baggage inherited from the past.

In the Latin American cases studied and presented by Collier and Mahoney, "the collective action of labor movements thus played a key democratic role not only in propelling a transition, but also in expanding political space and the scope of contestation in the new democratic regime."[42] If we are to take these experiences and compare and contrast them with the Egyptian case, we are then able to see the potential role of labor, the limits of its abilities, and its vulnerabilities. The potential role of labor in Egypt is great, yet the actual role is severely hampered. This will be presented in the case studies in the succeeding chapters. In Egypt's case, the workers definitely propelled the call for transition and political change, contributed to the expansion of political space, and broadened the scope of contestation, but they failed to achieve the desired results of a democratic government.

Social Movements, Contentious Politics, and Workers

Egyptian workers' social movement of protests was successful in bringing their grievances (claims) to the forefront, forcing the government's concessions to many of their demands. This was indeed a political action when it was considered dangerous to confront the regime. Their success was in tearing down the barriers of fear and leading the discontented masses from the factories to the streets— taking it from the realm of special interest to the public street and square protests, including the iconic Tahrir Square and beyond.

A social movement is the campaign of continuous claim-making using mechanisms of brokerage and processes of diffusion in repertoires (regular performances) based on solidarities, networks, and organization (also known as social movement bases).[43] What is contentious politics? It is the intersection between politics, collective action, and contention. The following figure shows the components of contentious politics:

Contentious Politics

Classic social movement theory has evolved over the years from having several drawbacks, including static versus dynamic analysis, and originates from the context of America's civil rights movement in the 1960s. It has also evolved from a political processes mechanism to a more dynamic political opportunity structure (POS) that considers opportunities into its analysis.[44] Another important development has been to focus on repertoires, i.e. what people do when they protest, which is much more dynamic, insightful, and relational. In addition, there is now improved research and understanding of inducements, types of brokerage, diffusion mechanisms, and framing. Framing is a concept that was developed early on by Goffman[45] and further refined by Snow and Benford[46] in their writings. The framing of claims or grievances is critical for the cohesion of a social movement, uniting their claims/grievances within a familiar voice, vision, and discourse to express their demands.

Collective action has been described and analyzed by several scholars; the most notable is Olson.[47] He wrote that the self-interest (individual or group) is the only way for collective action to succeed. He argues that individuals in any group attempting collective action will have incentives to "free ride" on the efforts of others if the group is working to provide public benefits, such as trade unions are. Individuals will not "free ride" in groups that provide benefits only to active participants. So, if it is stipulated that you have to be an active member to receive benefits, then such groups will not have free riders and thus will succeed. Again, using the trade union example, if only dues-paying members will receive benefits, then the organization/union will be successful and there will not be free riders. We need incentives to motivate active participation in collective action/collective organizations. Yet, Olson argues that large groups are more costly when attempting to act collectively and will have difficulty even if they have common interests. Minority groups within a large organization could overtake the overall mission and could dominate the majority.[48]

He believed that coercive, mandatory membership in trade unions, for example, is the only way for the organization to survive. He also points to the "free-rider" problem, which cannot be overcome. The free-rider problem is that there will always be people who will not take a risk but gladly will let others lead the way. Lichbach,[49] on the other hand, disagrees with Olson in "the rebel's dilemma." He states that extreme anger, frustration, and feelings of inequality and injustice will lead a person or persons to collective action. Deprived actor theory takes deprivation, such as discrimination, for example, and turns it into dissent. However, Olson's seminal work, *The Logic of Collective Action*, challenges the deprived actor theory and questions the extent extreme anger will lead to dissent and collective action because of the free-rider problem; it can hamper the level and intensity of protest against the employer, or in this case the government.[50] Lichbach continues to explain, "Rebels, in sum, face dangers and risks, possibly disastrous costs and certain benefits, and hence rational people will almost never rebel."[51] Using this understanding, we can infer that those who dissent and protest are irrational actors, thus a small minority of the overall discontented population.

How can the application of the above synopsis and overview of social movement theory and principles apply particularly to the Arab Spring and to Egypt? Starting with collective action, whether it was in Bahrain, Egypt, Libya, Syria, Tunisia, or Yemen, a significant level of collective action took place but with varying differences. In Egypt, Tunisia, and Yemen, all sectors of society protested, signaling the masses' discontent with the ruling regimes—a form of collective action. With each day of these protests, more and more of the concrete barrier of fear came falling down, piece by piece, which is significant for these societies. The barrier of fear refers to the many years of fear of retribution and punishment by the state security apparatus. The throngs of persons protesting, starting initially on January 25, 2011, and then in earnest on January 28 in Egypt, brought this barrier tumbling down. Also, the military in Egypt initially did not attack the citizenry in the streets and either stood by, protected, or actively took part in these protests. The military's role escalated and took on an increased political role in the months after February 2011. The Egyptian military is a central actor, in addition to civil society organizations such as the labor movement. The military, through the Supreme Council of the Armed Forces (SCAF), was effectively the beneficiary of the January 2011 uprising, with its greater political and economic powers. Their stance against workers is well documented:

> The army has been diligent in disciplining striking workers, while the SCAF has dragged its feet on draft laws setting minimum and maximum wages and legalizing independent labor unions. These moves might also be seen as invoking the spirit of Nasser, who himself hanged two strike leaders less than a month after the coup that brought him to office, except that the army has paired the crackdown with other measures that were preached by the IMF and World Bank.[52]

The role of the Egyptian military was not modest in any way, shape, or form. It appeared sympathetic with the protesting masses and neutral; however, that was not the case.

Kandil's[53] work on the role of the military and state security/interior ministry is also enlightening regarding the causes of the January 2011 revolt. Mubarak had a

blinding penchant for wanting his son, Gamal, who was not remotely connected or related to the military, to succeed him, so for many years prior to 2011, he had been slowly winnowing the best and brightest military cadres into early retirement. Because state funding for the military was decreasing, given their large income from military industries and financial support from the US and elsewhere, there was no love lost between the military and the Mubarak family. That is one reason that the military initially intervened on the side of the people versus the state security apparatus.

Contention was another serious and important factor underlying the Arab Spring uprisings. The main overarching thread among all the Arab countries was the following: sharp increase in unemployment; large unemployed youth population with little hope for a future; bloated state apparatuses, especially state security with heavy-handed tactics; decline in overall economic performance; sharp price increase in daily consumer goods; high levels of corruption and lack of transparency; serious endemic human rights violations; fraudulent electoral practices; and excessive controls over civil society organizations. The picture of daily life was dismal, and for many observers it was a matter of when contention would explode.[54] As Tilly, Tarrow, and McAdam wrote, social movements' contention could take the imagery of a "steam boiler about to explode." Since the uprising, each country has evolved into different states of affairs with varying degrees of success and failure, one being that Syria is now in a full-blown civil war with the end nowhere in sight.

In the Arab world, politics took on an "unnatural" scope within civil society outside of its proper place in the political arena of political parties, elections, parliaments, and regular change in political leadership, which alternates between ruling party and opposition, as in most Western democracies. Politics became ensconced in "civil society organizations," thus corrupting its behavior and derailing it from its true mission. Everything became political, whether it was environmental issues, women's causes, children and youth's concerns, senior citizen's affairs, pollution, or defense of human rights. In the intersection of the three circles of politics, contention, and collective action, we find contentious politics exhibited or carried out via social movements. What are essentially social movements in contentious politics? It is the opportunity for "challengers" to demand of the "elite," who already have access to power, to make changes/reforms. That is precisely what the protesters were attempting to do, whether it was in Tahrir Square in Cairo; Benghazi and Tripoli in Libya; Tunis in Tunisia; Sana'a in Yemen; or elsewhere in the Arab world.

Theoretical Basis for Research

I will analyze the Egyptian independent workers' formal and informal organizations' contentious actions and protests through both social movement theory's (SMT) mechanisms and processes and social movement unionism (SMU). SMU is a trend of theory and practice in contemporary trade unionism. It is strongly associated with the labor movements of developing countries, and it is distinct from many other models of trade unionism because it concerns itself with more than organizing workers around workplace issues, wages and terms, and conditions. It engages in wider political struggles for human rights, social justice, and democracy.

It is important to note that in the "classical social movement agenda," the following factors are considered: "social change processes, political opportunities and constraints, forms of organization (large correlation between strong organization and ability to gain concessions), framing, and repertoires of contention."[55] McAdam, Tarrow, and Tilly identify four major defects with this model as a tool for the analysis of contentious politics. First, a defect is the focus on static rather than dynamic relationships; second, the model does not work well for broader episodes of contention; third, it was rooted in the open politics of America's 1960s, which emphasized opportunities over threats and increased confidence in organizational resources; and fourth, it focused exceedingly on the origins of contention rather on its later phases.[56] Thus, referring to social movement unionism will complement and add to the more dynamic mobilization model detailed later.

I will examine two congruent case studies, going beyond the classical definition to a more dynamic mobilization model in order to fully understand their movements and impact. I will use McAdam, Tarrow, and Tilly's proposal to employ "a new path to the analysis of contentious politics: neither through the stamping of the same general laws onto all the world's contention, [. . .] but through the comparison of episodes of contention in light of the processes that animate their dynamics"[57] while including the historical and social context. This model leads to a much broader set of interpretative processes, leading to a more innovative collective action.[58] Classical SMT focuses on mobilizing structures, framing processes, opportunity and threats, and repertoires of contention—a structuralist approach.[59] I intend to push beyond the classical structuralist SMT toward an interactive dynamic model, and I will review the interaction between mechanisms and processes, or "actions, actors, identities, trajectories or outcomes."[60] My focus will be on investigating the repertoires of collective action within these two case studies: What were the shared values, interests, and goals that led to mobilization? What did workers do when they protested? How did they frame their grievances and demands? What were the internal structures of these formal and informal organizations and networks of workers? What were the decision-making processes? Who were the leaders and how did they (positively or negatively) influence the movement? What were the roles of men and women workers in these repertoires of collective action, were these roles different, and why? "[A]nalyzing repertoires allows us to examine the anticipations, perceptions, and self-definitions of contentious actors and how they take up a position in the political field."[61] I will also examine the nature and role of these "informal" networks created by workers because in authoritarian regimes, such as Egypt, and with high levels of poverty and lack of essential services, networks become vital for survival and collective action.

The Egyptian independent workers' movement highlights the following:

> 1) the importance of perceived threats, as opposed to opportunities, in motivating collective action; 2) possibilities for collective action and movement-building in a resource-poor, authoritarian environment; 3) local networks' capacity simultaneously to enable local mobilization while disabling mobilization on a national scale; 4) the differential effects of political change ("opportunities") on the urban intelligentsia compared to workers; 5) the continuing relevance of class; and 6) the agency of insurgent workers in expanding their repertoire of contention.[62]

This explains sustained action and protest but without the formation of a strong, national organization, although working class consciousness is still alive and well in Egypt. Why? Therein lies the puzzle that despite the lack of a strong, national labor organization, these disparate worker groups and networks were able to hold successful protests and increase the political pressure on the Mubarak regime, thus leading up to the January 2011 uprising. In hindsight, I would argue that several "dress rehearsals" took place, for example the massive strike by workers on April 6, 2008, in El-Mahalla al-Kubra (a large industrial city) when several thousand workers protested the low wages and high cost of food. Yet Egyptian workers' independent organizations were unable to form coalitions with other civil society organizations and activists to bring about a complete victory: a revolution against the authoritarian regime.

There are several assumptions to be examined: Is the perceived weakness/lack of a strong organizational structure due to the nature of functioning in an authoritarian regime? Do these networks of workers succeed only on a local level and not a national level? These protest movements were based on "bread and butter" issues, demanding the regime to protect their gains instead of democracy and regime change per se. Is the problem the workers' ability to lead a more universal revolt? In addition, the question of threat as defined by Tilly and Goldstone as "the costs a social group will incur from protest or that it expects to suffer if it does not take action"[63] is applicable to the Egyptian workers' movement. I will examine whether no action (i.e. no protests) was considered a higher cost to be paid than protesting and that this threat propelled workers (men and women) and influenced their motivation to join these independent trade unions and worker networks.

There is a consensus that today's labor and workers receive less attention in social and historical research than they did in the heyday of the early twentieth century. It seems that it is no longer fashionable to have social mobilizations based on class grievances. We often read about the "death of the labor movement," not just in the US but in the globalized economy as a whole. In Egypt, the situation begs to differ, and labor's class struggle is not yet completely irrelevant. According to Beinin, "Egyptian workers have not received the message that class struggle is unfashionable. From 1998 to 2009 over two million workers participated in more than 3,300 factory occupations, strikes, demonstrations or other collective actions."[64] Tilly and Tarrow's definition of a social movement is "a sustained campaign of claim making, using repeated performances that advertise the claim, based on organizations, networks, traditions, and solidarities that sustain these activities."[65] The creation of the Egyptian independent trade union movement is a social movement according to this definition.

It has been a sustained campaign of protests and making demands that the authoritarian Egyptian government make economic and political reforms to address workers' grievances. Any action in this environment against an authoritarian regime would be considered a potential threat and not necessarily an opportunity for positive change. Despite the high level of potential threats, Egyptian workers took to the streets and used this peaceful repertoire: to march, chant, sit-in, and make verbal and written demands addressing their serious "bread and butter" grievances. However, these grievances eventually gravitated from purely socioeconomic to political demands.

The perceived threat defined by Beinin is broader than Tarrow's (2011): "the costs a social group will incur from protest, or that it expects to suffer if it does

not take action" is more relevant to the Egyptian independent workers' movement.[66] Interestingly, workers rarely called directly for democratic reform and political change throughout their protests leading up to the major uprising in January 2011. Their demands were primarily "bread and butter" socio-economic needs. With the increase in the number of protests over the years and the development of support by other sectors of civil society, such as students and several sectors of professional white-collar workers, the movement started to develop into a more traditional social movement with political demands. The worker movement's full participation in the January 2011 uprising further adds to its portfolio the call for political change. One can argue that demands for economic and social justice are another form of calling for political change or even a first step. This argument will be expanded upon in later chapters.

Political opportunity analysis is the strategy of assessing the potential of a change to achieve a goal. Undergoing an opportunity analysis helps to provide an understanding of what effects, positive and negative, are likely to take place if a particular approach is implemented.

> It emphatically includes not only opportunities but also threats [. . .] it leads us to pay attention to changing opportunities and threats. It helps people decide whether to mobilize, make decisions about optimal combinations of performances to use and which are likely to succeed or fail.[67]

The leaders of the employees of the Real Estate Tax Authority (RETA) used this approach to support their strategies for each protest event. They had to weigh the opportunities and perceived threats and evaluate how they could minimize the threats from state security and other government forces. They had to consider what the minister would or would not do and how they could bring about external influence to affect his decision-making. They had to determine when to step up the pressure and escalate their actions, such as organizing massive demonstrations with thousands of protesters at strategic places in Cairo for media and government officials' attention. It was all done peacefully with clever repertoires, including chants and slogans highlighting their demands.

The overarching hypothesis that frames the relationship between the independent and dependent variables[68] of my research is that workers' consistent collective action for a decade before January 2011 contributed to the mass uprising, yet it was an incomplete victory. The key variables in my research are as follows. (1) The independent variable is the Egyptian independent workers' organizations and non-governmental organizations that supported workers. The independent workers are the two cases in my research: real estate tax collectors and garment and textile workers. The non-governmental organizations that supported workers include the Center for Trade Union and Worker Services (CTUWS), The Land Center, the Egyptian Center for Economic and Social Research (ECESR), and others. (2) The dependent variable is the Egyptian "Arab Spring," starting with the January 25, 2011, uprising and culminating with the first "post-Mubarak" presidential elections in May 2012 as an outcome, an explanation, and a result of their activism, i.e. the sustained collective action by the workers. The theory is that through sustained collective action, i.e. a social movement, the working class can and will contribute to political change. A good theory's "independent variable has a large explanatory power with an effect on a wide range of phenomena under a wide range of conditions."[69] I hope to add

evidence to the already existing literature that massive groups, i.e. workers with significant grievances (whether organized into institutions or informal networks as in Egypt's case) in authoritarian regimes can effect political change. Yet in this case, their influence was limited and incomplete.

A complementary set of theoretical lenses can also be found in SMU theory. SMU has four dimensions or key aspects: (1) locally based and rank-and-file member mobilization, (2) use of different collective action tactics beyond work-place strikes, (3) building alliances and coalitions with others in civil society, and (4) embracing a socio-political discourse beyond the "bread and butter" economic, i.e. developing a political vision for all and not just for workers.[70] I will show within this research endeavor how the Egyptian workers' independent movement did indeed exhibit all, if not many, of these key aspects in the years prior to January 2011. SMU also helps us to further understand how worker ac-tivists can build support for labor's demands using varying tactics to include the community at large. Waterman (1979) first used SMU to describe striking trans-port workers in India.[71] These workers were excluded legally from the national industrial relations system, so they were not covered by the traditional collective bargaining agreements. They challenged the authorities in a creative, different, and unpredictable manner; for example, they called on their community, reli-gious leaders, and neighbors to support their strike. They were acting more like social movement activists than union organizers and negotiators.[72]

SMU began to be used more widely to explain how workers were reacting to the globalization of the economy, particularly to neoliberal economic restructuring policies. Workers in the developing world began to face newly structured work-places, thus their traditional trade unions were not able to advocate for or protect their rights using the traditional methods. In the global south, SMU was able to capture the mood and action of labor militancy, demanding a greater share in the country's wealth. For example, "in authoritarian Brazil as well as apartheid South Africa, factory workers backed up broad demands for political democratization with shop-floor militancy, disrupting production in support of both workplace and political goals."[73] There are additional examples in the Philippines; a militant alliance took place between the workers and community groups to topple the Marcos dictatorship. In South Korea, the term was used to describe the militant activist movement to include women and migrants in calling for inclusion and democracy.[74] Post-colonial militant labor movements adopted a broader view be-yond their members' interests and developed a broader base of support among the community at large. Marshall, in his work *Citizenship and Social Class: And Other Essays* (1950), had predicted that the new unionists saw democratic citizen-ship as a key step toward gaining the economic and social rights that their mem-bers were denied under colonial rule. He gave us an important conclusion: The working class truly earned the right and position in society to participate fully in political life.[75] Labor movements are not of the past, and class-based social move-ments are not to be dismissed as stale, limited, or restrictive.[76]

Literature Review and Context

The literature describing the independent variable in my research (the char-acteristics, role, and development of the Egyptian working class, independent

trade unions, and worker non-governmental organizations) includes journalistic reporting endeavors (especially regarding strikes), interviews with leaders and activists, scholarly journal articles, and several books that cover the history of workers and the working class. There are historical and socio-economic accounts of the Egyptian working class highlighting the dynamic relationship between workers, union leaders, managers, and government. These studies also give a more accurate picture of developing countries that are increasingly becoming the manufacturers of exported goods in a more globalized economy. The main and most thorough research study on Egypt's history of workers was conducted by two history scholars, Beinin and Lockman, published in 1988 as *Workers on the Nile: Nationalism, Communism, Islam, and the Egyptian Working Class, 1882–1954*. There are also several scholars who took on certain aspects or angles and particular time periods of Egyptian workers' modern history and current challenges, such as Vitalis, Issawi, Goldberg, Shehata, Bianchi, Alexander, and others. Scholars such as Goldberg and Posusney, among others, focused their research on beyond the 1950s until the present day. They took Beinin and Lockman's work and added contemporary modern issues intertwined with changing political, economic, and social realities.

The first important historical work to set the stage is *Workers on the Nile: Nationalism, Communism, Islam, and the Egyptian Working Class, 1882–1954* by Beinin and Lockman. Posusney's *Labor and the State in Egypt* continues this genre of writing on labor and labor relations, then it is continued with Goldberg's *Tinker, Tailor and Textile Worker: Class and Politics in Egypt*, Bianchi's *Unruly Corporatism: Association Life in Twentieth-Century Egypt*, Vitalis' *When Capitalists Collide: Business Conflict and the End of Empire in Egypt*, Lockman's *Workers and Working Classes in the Middle East*, Paczynska's *State, Labor, and the Transition to a Market Economy: Egypt, Poland, Mexico, and the Czech Republic*, Alexander's journal article "Leadership and Collective Action in the Egyptian Trade Unions," and more recently, Shehata's *Shop Floor Culture and Politics in Egypt*. There are also studies that give a more dynamic societal description to highlight the importance of networks, family, kinships, and friendships, including neighborhood connections, such as Singerman's *Avenues of Participation: Family, Politics, and Networks in Urban Quarters of Cairo*; all play an important role in social movements and add to the literature on the working popular (*sha'abi*) class in Egypt. Labor as a social movement is covered well in various writings by Beinin, Tarrow, Tilly, McAdam, and Zald on social movement theory, contentious politics, mobilization, and contestation.

However, in order to gain a full understanding of the situation in Egypt, one has to review the literature on the political role of trade unions in developing countries. This is in addition to comparative studies on the role of trade unions in political change in Latin America and Central and Eastern Europe, with Poland as a prime example. Egypt is an interesting case study for examining the political role of trade unions in developing countries, especially in transition from authoritarianism to democracy. The Egyptian labor movement has a long history of activism, yet this can be an educational case of how labor was corporatized (co-opted) by the state and became a reluctant democrat. This is also a case of how workers found their voice and power through consistent collective action due to serious economic difficulties (neoliberal policies), thus creating a social movement to move away from the corporatized status to an activist one. *Trade Unions*

and Democratic Participation in Europe: A Scenario for the 21st Century, edited by Kester and Pinaud (1996), is one example of how much has been written on the historical development of trade union democratic participation in Western, Central, and Eastern Europe. Collier and Collier present the most comprehensive study of the political history of labor in eight countries in Latin America over a period of one hundred years to attempt to understand the political trajectories of state-labor relations. Collier and Collier use "the concepts of 'critical juncture' and 'legacy' in order to make sense of the process of labor's incorporation into a hegemonic capitalist regime and its political and institutional aftermath."[77] Unfortunately, Collier and Collier adopt an "elite political approach" in which workers are considered ignorant of their own interests and are therefore easily manipulated by their leaders. Valenzuela presents cogent arguments in his journal article in *Comparative Politics* (July 1989) titled "Labor Movements in Transitions to Democracy: A Framework for Analysis." Labor movements have significant input into democratic transitions through increased strikes and protests, yet they cannot necessarily alone trigger a successful transition as part of a "resurrected civil society" (O'Donnell and Schmitter) in conjunction with a broader upsurge of mobilization by a variety of other civil society groups.[78] Independent workers' organizations in cooperation with the rest of civil society organizations can play an important catalytic role in transition to democracy.

Bruce Millen's short monograph titled *The Political Role of Labor in Developing Countries* (1963) clearly outlines that countries where the government is going through a transition appear to be "uneasily fragile." Millen wrote that trade unions have an imperative political role to ensure a more egalitarian program, and he calls this "political unionism." Political leaders seeking mass approval and support will lean on trade unions pre- and post-independence in developing countries. Before independence, political forces join with trade union movements (mass movements) to push out colonial powers. After independence, with an increase in nationalism leading the drive for national development (industrialization with more urbanization), political leaders could "not safely ignore the promises, for the disaffection of the workers cannot be risked. On this fact rides much of the union strength."[79] Millen builds upon Lipset and Galenson's work on how trade unions are a major component of community power and a key institution that sustains democratic process in the larger community.[80] Coleman, in the same volume, wrote that labor unions and their leaders give "lip service" to democracy, and their behavior is affected or influenced by the democratic values at large in the community.[81]

There are several studies on the authoritarian state in transition to democracy regarding political-economic development, autocratic regimes, and neoliberal policies adopted by developing countries, including Egypt; these studies help us understand the realities in the context of Egyptian workers and their claims. O'Donnell and Schmitter[82] wrote the seminal work in 1986 showing the diverse transition paths from authoritarian rule to the prospects of democracy. The literature on the connection between the need for economic stability and political legitimacy as prerequisites for democracy (Lipset 1959) and political transition is also helpful in understanding the context. Linz and Stepan show in their research, published as *Problems of Democratic Transition and Consolidation* (1996), why and how democracies need five interacting arenas to become consolidated: (1) a lively civil society, (2) a relatively autonomous political society, (3) rule of law,

(4) a stable state, and (5) an economic society. In addition, they offer a definition of democratic transition, which entails liberalization, but it is a wider and
more specifically political concept. Tilly, in *Democracy*, wrote of democracy's
global advancement, its retreat, and the process of "de-democratization." Tilly
describes the general processes that cause democratization. He makes the claim
that prospects for democracy hinge on three-large scale processes within a country: (1) interpersonal trust networks into politics, (2) the insulation of politics
from economic and social inequalities, and (3) the elimination or neutralization
of the coercive power of autonomous power centers such as clans, war lords, or
military elites.[83] Brumberg contributes to the literature of authoritarian regimes
in the Middle East. He wrote in 2002,

> Over the past two decades, the Middle East has witnessed a "transition"
> away from—and then back toward—authoritarianism. This dynamic began
> with tactical political openings whose goal was to sustain rather than trans-
> form autocracies. Enticed by the prospect of change, an amalgam of political
> forces—Islamists, leftists, secular liberals, NGO activists, women's organiza-
> tions, and others—sought to imbue the political process with new meanings
> and opportunities, hoping that the 'inherently unstable' equilibrium of *dic-
> tablandas* [definition: a word used by political scientists to describe a dicta-
> torship in which civil liberties are allegedly preserved rather than destroyed.
> Origins are from Spanish *dictadura* = dictatorship and *blanda* = soft] would
> give way to a new equilibrium of competitive democracy.[84]

He confirms the strong durability of "liberalized autocracy" and this continued
trap engulfing the Middle East.

Neoliberal policies and the demise of the "social contract" in Egypt are important lenses through which we can and need to analyze the events in Egypt.
"Bresser, Pereira, Maravall, and Przeworski see neoliberalism as having a natural
inclination toward such autocratic and technocratic forms of rule, given the need
to override or evade the political opposition"[85] of interest groups that would be
harmed by such structural adjustments. They argue that autocratic neoliberalism weakens social and political institutions that could play a mediation role.
Heydemann also contributes to the notion of an urgent need for a new social
contract—

> the unprecedented labor crisis confronting the Middle East and North Africa
> (MENA) region underscores the urgent need for both a new social contract—
> the basic laws and understandings that define the relationship between the
> state and labor—and for political reform.[86]

The old social contracts favored strong state intervention in the economy while
providing workers with stability, employment, and welfare in return for alle-
giance to the state.

In order to fully grasp the long-term economic roots of the 2011 uprising for
political change, Soliman's book, *The Autumn of Dictatorship: Fiscal Crisis and
Political Change in Egypt Under Mubarak*, presents a thoughtful analysis of
Egypt's political economy. He argues that both the state and civil society were
weak, and the way out is to strengthen both based on a rule of law framework.

Soliman analyzes how the Mubarak regime functioned like all authoritarian regimes, using the carrot and stick method by distributing benefits to select segments of society (primarily elites) and using harsh repression whenever needed. The regime used public monies to impose political stability. He describes how Mubarak's regime dealt with the steep decline in state revenue in the 1990s by allowing state institutions to degrade over time (except military and security institutions) and by allowing business elites to circumvent the law and prosper on the backs of workers and the society at large.[87]

The dependent variable, the Egyptian "Arab Spring," or the January 25, 2011, uprising, has several causes (equifinality) that contributed to the mass uprising, including independent workers and their organizations. The literature that has been written since these events has not given labor and workers a prominent role except work by a handful of scholars, including Beinin, El Mahdi and Korany, Haddad, Lynch, Ali, Paul, El-Hamalawy, Dabashi, and Shehata. The popular narrative attributes the main leaders of the Egyptian uprising to be the students, youth, and intellectuals fighting for political freedom using social media. History indicates the opposite, that many years of labor organizing laid the foundation for the January 2011 uprising.[88] Ali's "Precursors of the Egyptian Revolution" argues "that there had been sustained protests for at least a decade before the January 25th [2011] uprisings, which functioned as political incubators that nurtured the forces of the revolution, shaping people's consciousness and organizational capacities."[89] The Arab Spring ushered in these "open-ended revolutions," and some experts argue that these are not revolutions in the classical meaning of the word and deed. These are uprisings that have yet to develop into full-fledged revolutions (for example in Egypt) that will truly upend the regimes thoroughly without just removing the top leadership, its supporters, and its benefactors. "The uprisings are an exceptionally rapid, intense, and nearly simultaneous explosion of popular protest across an Arab world united by a shared transnational media and bound by a common identity,"[90] writes Lynch in *The Arab Uprisings*. After the initial euphoria calmed down, observers around the world recognized the gravity of these uprisings and how they are still in process. These are still "open-ended," unfinished revolutions. Several years later, the manifestation of a deeper political, social, and economic transformation is still in process. Lynch further contributes to this literature with his most recent publication *The Arab Uprisings Explained— New Contentious Politics in the Middle East*, edited by him. The main puzzle of interest is "the speed and magnitude of mobilization across multiple countries and the divergent political outcomes."[91] Authoritarian resilience in the Middle East and North Africa was proven many times over by resisting the major pressures in the region, including an employment crisis, a young population, Islamism, globalization, and a civil society that was spearheading a call for democracy.

Why focus on labor unions? Dabashi argues in *The Arab Spring* that until voluntary organizations, i.e. labor unions, women's rights organizations, and student assemblies, are institutionalized and allowed a legal framework respecting freedom of association to continue to organize from a grassroots level and are enabled to fully participate and influence policy makers, "the state will be able to build itself again on a societal foundation, and hence will have legitimacy."[92] So the state's legitimacy depends on respecting freedom of association, allowing grassroots organizations like labor unions to develop and prosper in order to contribute to national policies and protect workers' rights.

Literature Review: Social Movements, Mobilization, and Contestation: Theory and Practice

The Egyptian case, according to Beinin and Vairel's (2011) book on social movements, mobilization, and contestation in the Middle East,[93] had certain characteristics. First, this was a situation of a resource-poor movement within an authoritarian regime context; second, the threat of no action was greater than any available opportunity; third, class designation still matters; fourth, informal social networks played a critical role when organizations could not be formed; fifth, within the Egyptian context, there were creative continuous repertoires; and sixth, the workers' social movement remained on a local level and did not always blossom into full-fledged national organizations (with the one exception of the IGURETA union).

The first to take informal social networks into consideration in their research were Denoeux (1993) and Singerman (1995). Singerman's extensive ethnographic research on Egypt's popular quarters (*sha'abi* neighborhoods) in Cairo, *Avenues of Participation*, highlights the importance of taking into consideration the social, informal, and familial relationships as well as workplace, neighborhood, and friend networks, especially under an authoritarian regime. Diani with McAdam in an edited volume, Social Movements, Contentious Actions and Social Networks: "From Metaphor to Substance" (2003), also focused on and pleaded the case of the importance of social networks in social movement analysis. Diani argues the need to reorient social movement research along network lines. Looking at networks as a powerful pre-condition of collective action has proved to be a fruitful exercise. We would then be better able to specify the relationship between movements and coalitions, solidarity campaigns and political organizations. Social movements are strings of connected events, scattered across time and space, consisting of groups and organizations with varying levels of formulized, linked-in patterns of interaction, from centralized to decentralized and from cooperative to hostile. This harks back to Tilly's initial work[94] focusing on dynamic inter-relationships, particularly within networks. Within that edited volume, there is an interesting chapter by Broadbent[95] highlighting the importance of "thick" analysis of networks within social movements. Broadbent analyzes Japan's environmental movement, for example, and how the focus on networks needs to be viewed as a bridge between resources and cultural attitudes.

Lapidus, Abrahamian, and Burke, *Islam, Politics and Social Movements* (1988),[96] also offer interesting insights into social movements from secular and religious perspectives and with a focus on the resurgence or revival of Islamic activism. By reading their edited volume today, particularly given the events of the Arab Uprisings, one can further understand the motives of workers making contentious claims and the MB (in Egypt's case). Beinin wrote one chapter in the Lapidus and Burke book from his neo-Marxist perspective on workers' activism and class struggle in a sugar production factory. Goldberg wrote another chapter from a corporatist perspective discussing how the MB initially was not interested in building blue-collar trade unions and was more interested in promoting its religious principles and ideology. Goldberg's case studies of trade unions in the 1940s presented a more nuanced MB and a far clearer picture of the limitations on the leaders' abilities to turn ideological sympathy or formal membership intro practical political consequences. Islam appears more like other ideologies, which claim a broad hold on their members, but in reality, the control is not so

complete.[97] Goldberg discussed how union leadership (MB members) attempted to fuse Islamic vocabulary with a movement for social change. Since that era, starting in the 1990s, the MB became more involved in the professional associations, known as syndicates, for white-collar professions such as doctors, dentists, engineers, lawyers, and journalists.

Literature Review: How Do We Measure the Impact of Social Movements?

In what way do social movements matter? Social scientists are still struggling with this task on how to measure the impact of social movements. Giugni and fellow travelers Tilly and McAdam in an edited volume, *How Social Movements Matter* (1999), emphasize the need for more research and exploration on how to measure the impact of social movements in promoting and actually achieving change. How do social movements relate to the processes of social change, and does it matter? Giugni et al. examine what has been done so far in scholarship: (1) disruption versus moderation, where the capacity to achieve goals depends on the ability to create innovative and disruptive tactics; (2) internal versus external explanations, where success depends on the POS (social movements can succeed only insofar as they act disruptively and as political circumstances lead the rulers to make concessions); and (3) defining and determining the consequences of social movements by looking at successes and failures and focusing on policy outcomes.

Davis, with McAdam, Scott, and Zald, in *Social Movements and Organization Theory* (2005),[98] expands our views in the world of social movements' analysis and research. The application of religion, space, voice, discourse, and culture to the analysis can further expand our understanding and also the ability to apply the theory to varying situations and conditions, including in the Arab world. It is of interest to examine spatial analysis of social movements as one of the processes and mechanisms that can be "spatially situated" to achieve impact. In the past, protesters followed those who were committing the grievance, so the protests moved from one World Bank or WTO meeting location to another.

Today, it seems that these social movements are staying in one physical place to highlight their claim, and with each day the number of protesters increases. In Egypt, Tahrir Square has become an iconic, well-recognized symbol and space of the uprising as well as a physical, open space for protest, even though the government at times has attempted to clear out the square. The impact of social movements in the Arab world on social interaction starting with social media, varied public discourse, public art and graffiti, blogs, and chat venues have been immense but not quantifiable. We are just at the cusp of beginning to see, analyze, and fully understand the full impact of social movements in the Arab Spring uprisings. Scholars will have to monitor social movements over a period of time to effectively evaluate the full impact.

Literature Review: What Has Been the Role of Trade Unions in Political Life and Revolutions and Its Significance?

Throughout history, the role of trade unions in revolutions and transitions to democracy has been heralded with much praise and fanfare as the main engine

behind the success of a revolt or denigrated, given a back seat, and even blamed for the failure of a revolution.

> Unions have been hailed as defenders of democracy and equality, and damned as preservers of privilege and corruption [. . .] both sides of the debate have merit with reference to particular currents within the labor movement of each country. The relationship between unions, democracy and equality is mixed and complex.[99]

I adopt in this research endeavor Tilly's definition of a democratic regime, which is the "degree that political relations between the state and its citizens feature broad, equal, protected, and mutually binding consultation."[100] Labor's impact on democratization has been determined in Latin America and elsewhere by the depth of its relationship or connection with the ruling political party, the level of internal democracy within trade unions, the degree to which unions advocate for the broader majority's interests and concerns, the degree of unionization at the workplace, and if there has been a long history of this as a democratic voice at work. If the regime has the mechanisms and adopts broad consultation with citizens (through their institutions like trade unions), and these institutions prize and value democratic structures and behavior, then there is a democratizing impact by unions on the state/regime.

Rueschemeyer, Stephens, and Stephens have presented through their research that organized labor is a consistent advocate and champion of democracy and that, as a result, strong labor movements support a more-likely democratic outcome.[101] However, evidence presented by Levitsky and Mainwaring challenges this argument.[102] Latin American labor movements have played an important and leading role in the struggle against dictatorships, yet their record regarding democracy has been mixed at best, they say. In Argentina, Mexico, Nicaragua, and Peru, the labor movement actively supported nondemocratic regimes. In Argentina and Bolivia, the unions supported military coups against elected governments. In Chile, Bolivia, and Peru, they were involved in maximalist strategies (no compromise) that put democratic governments in peril. Levitsky and Mainwaring focus on labor's self-interest in maintaining power and benefits as their primary goal in the latter half of the twentieth century (1945). They also point to the distance, or "autonomy," of union leaders from their rank-and-file membership. Unions supporting political parties would satisfy their self-interest (especially union leaders) in continuing to exist and maintaining power rather than the main principle of democracy and democratic governance. Latin American labor movements were contingent democrats, a term borrowed from Bellin's research and writings.[103] In the Latin American cases, two factors determined labor's role: the nature of partisan alliances and perceived regime alternatives.[104] The contention here is that if labor witnesses an alternative to democracy that would still guarantee its privileges and benefits, it would lend its support to the alternative. This is a view that needs to be considered when examining the Egyptian situation. However, I do contend that independent and democratic trade unions need the respect and institutionalization of freedom of association, and that can only exist in a democracy. Independent and democratic trade unions cease to exist without freedom of association, and only those that are controlled or co-opted by the regime can exist.

In the Egyptian case study, workers played an important role as a catalyst to the 2011 uprising to bring down the Mubarak regime, yet they rarely made the international headlines. Their contentious voice only became a "national" voice starting in 2010, while before it was mainly focused on local workplace issues. Beinin points to how "strikes played a major role in delegitimizing the regime and popularizing a culture of protest."[105] Still today, there are those in the daily media who believe that the independent workers' movement in Egypt, for example, came late to the scene and did not throw its full support for the uprising until later. Mostafa Bassiouny, a journalist with expertise about the labor movement who writes for *El Nahar* and *El Tahrir* newspapers, and Khaled Ali, former presidential candidate and labor lawyer, communicated this "myth" to me during field research interviews. They also told me during field interviews in 2013 that it was not until February 8 or 9, 2011, when the disparate groups of independent workers announced a general national strike that they fully came to support the January uprising. Again, that is incorrect;

> one of the less noticed events of the popular uprising was the formation of the Egyptian Federation of Independent Trade Unions (EFITU)—the first new institution to emerge from the revolt. Its existence was announced on January 30, 2011, at a press conference in Cairo's Tahrir Square.[106]

It was a revolutionary act since it violated the law that gave the official government organization, ETUF, the legal monopoly. Those who still contend that they were late to protest have fallen for the banal theory that "social media" was the main cause of the uprising, and they have not taken heed of historical facts starting ten years before January 2011.

There continues to be a debate on the role of the intellectual elite versus the mass-based workers' organizations, the trade unions, in pushing for political reform and democratization. In Egypt, this continues to be a heated debate among intellectuals and media journalists; it has not subsided and the workers' collective action is taking the back seat, sometimes even discredited. Collier and Mahoney argue that

> union-led protest in South America and Southern Europe [Peru 1980, Argentina 1983, Uruguay 1984, Brazil 1985, and Spain 1977] was much more central to the democratization process than implied by an elite-centric perspective, which sees labor's role primarily as altering the strategic environment of elite negotiators and theoretically underrates the role of mass opposition, labor protest, and collective actors generally.[107]

The role of mass collective social actors (workers) is effective at pushing for political transition despite being underrated by the elites and the scholars who write about political transition. Collier and Mahoney studied several countries and concluded that there were two patterns for political transitions. "Both patterns suggest that the labor movement was more central to the politics of democratization than has been recognized, and that its role often began earlier and continued to the end."[108] This supports the events in Egypt leading up to January 2011 because their protests were consistently taking place for several years prior. The Egyptian independent workers' movement de-stabilized the regime and

highlighted its weaknesses, paving the way for the upheaval of January 2011. There was then a forced retreat by the regime instead of a negotiated settlement for transition. It is undeniable that Egyptian workers' continued repertoires of contention lasting for several years prior to 2011 pressured the regime to retreat. Shadid wrote on February 17, 2012, in the *New York Times*,

> The labor unrest this week at textile mills, pharmaceutical plants, chemical industries, the Cairo airport, the transportation sector and banks has emerged as one of the most powerful dynamics in a country navigating the military-led transition that followed an 18-day popular uprising and the end of Mr. Mubarak's three decades of rule.[109]

However,

> As Khalid Ali explained, the workers did not start the January 25 uprising because they had no central organizing structure [. . .] but one of the important steps of this [uprising] was taken when they began to protest, giving the [uprising] an economic and social slant besides the political demands.[110]

"The Egyptian Opposition: From Protestors to Revolutionaries?" is the title of an article that was published on an online website journal, *Open Democracy*, on April 22, 2013, by Maha Abdelrahman,[111] a lecturer at the University of Cambridge. Its title and subject matter are apropos to the question at hand: the role of trade unions in revolutions. Abdelrahman asks many questions primarily focused on why there has not been a continuing momentum from protest to revolution in Egypt. Why has there not been a sustained revolutionary movement that transformed from those intoxicating, amazing, and inspiring eighteen days of protest in Tahrir Square starting in January 2011? She writes that simply these protesters were not equipped or skilled in becoming revolutionaries to overthrow and take over the state apparatus.

> Their focus was on perfecting tools and tactics to change the nature of traditional politics. Along this journey, they did not develop the kinds of skills, including organizational ones, that could one day equip them to match the might of the military establishment or the iron discipline and mass base of the Muslim Brotherhood.[112]

Al-Aswany, a prominent Egyptian novelist (most famous for *The Yacoubian Building* novel among several others), journalist, activist, and commentator, wrote that the problem with the Egyptian revolution is that even if you cut off the "head of the snake," the body continues to be alive. The removal of Mubarak was only the "head of the snake," and the entrenched bureaucracy of the state still continues to function for better or worse.

Abdelrahman quotes Wallerstein's article in *The New Left* (1972) on anti-systemic movements where activists reach stage one, achieve control of the state, and then those activists become part of the problem. They become part of the state they are trying to change and therefore are never able to reach stage two of the revolution. The anti-systemic movements, a version of social movements according to Wallerstein, are not interested in taking over the state. Wallerstein

wrote that from 1968 to the World Social Movement Porto Alegre conferences starting in 2000, there have been many changes in outlook on how change takes place and how effective social movement protest can be.[113] In Egypt, Abdelrahman believes that the protesters were not equipped, trained, or interested in taking over the state, thus the dismal state of affairs today. The only ones who were and remain well equipped and organized were the MB, founded in 1928; they were waiting for this moment in history.

There are two groups of protestors with the potential to be revolutionaries in Egypt according to Abdelrahman,[114] the independent workers/labor movement and the pro-democracy human rights movement. The Egyptian workers have been protesting in a variety of ways since 2004, with over three million workers participating in hundreds of protests, strikes, sit-ins, and demonstrations from 2004 to January 2011. Primarily, the workers had socio-economic demands, yet these evolved into political demands, especially with the issue of the minimum wage surfacing in the political arena in 2010. Then the workers' discourse became, "Well, if this government is not willing to set a minimum national 'living' wage, then this government needs to go home!" Abdel Rahman outlines the achievements of the Egyptian independent workers using creative social movement mechanisms and processes but still being hampered by state security, arcane laws forbidding freedom of association, and the government-controlled ETUF, which still exists today. Within days of the beginning of the revolt in January 2011, the independent workers' movement and trade unions formed an independent federation of trade unions. It was established in Tahrir Square among the protesters. Despite this development and others, the workers have not been able to effectively exert their pressure for serious systemic changes in Egypt. Despite the pessimistic tone of Abdelrahman's article, there is still hope and potential for civil society organizations, including trade unions, to be respected and allowed to freely associate and operate in order to truly achieve a more legitimate, credible, and respected state.[115] The only avenue forward for Egypt is to initiate the transition to democratic rule.

According to Lynch, author of *The Arab Uprisings: The Unfinished Revolutions of the New Middle East*, in Egypt's case the literature gives many reasons for the desperate need for a true revolution to change the culture of political behavior from autocratic to democratic, but the reality on the ground left much to be accomplished. The only well-organized opposition was the religious MB, and the secular opposition continues to be in disarray without a vision for the future to galvanize and bring Egyptians together for a full revolution or a grassroots change in the state and its institutions.

Stepping back in the early twentieth century with the 1917 Russian revolution and the rise of the proletariat, the working class was the hero implementing Lenin's *State and Revolution* with the proposed dictatorship of the proletariat and eventual withering away of the state apparatus, which in Lenin's writings was considered a tool of control. We learned quickly that the Communist rule in the Soviet Union did not eventually lead to a withering away of the state and a paradise for the workers. We are presented with Marx's "dictatorship of the proletariat" signaling hope compared to de Tocqueville's "rule of the majority" signifying disaster. Trade unions as movements regained their place as a poignant, reform-oriented, and vital force in the late twentieth century with the protest against Solidarnosc in Poland after ten years of struggle and then the "pact negotiations" overthrow of the Communist regime led by General Jaruzselski in 1989.

As the working class organized into trade unions, their structure and organization must be fully understood to fully comprehend the establishment of democracy, write Rueschemeyer, Stephens, and Stephens.[116] Customarily, such a statement or an analysis from a working class/trade union perspective is given the label of Marxist analysis. Such analysis is accepted in limited political circles in the West and carries a more popular stigma. In the developing world, this statement would not at all befuddle or upset academe or political forces, since Marxist analysis is much more widely accepted and considered an important part of the discourse and narrative. Rueschemeyer, Stephens, and Stephens' work with other scholars is important and gives my research the underlying essential framing that the study and role of trade unions are fundamental to the examination of society, especially a society that is in transition from authoritarian to democratic (or at least the hope of a more open system).

One cannot discuss trade unions and revolution without having to present the theories on the reasons for revolution so well articulated by Brinton, Dunn, Lipset, Moore, and Goldstone (just to name a few). In addition, there are scholars who have spent their life work on the socio-economic reasons for revolution and criteria for democratization, particularly linking wealth and democracy (Lipset, Linz, Stepan, and Przeworski). Brinton, in his 1934 *The Anatomy of Revolution*,[117] presented the uniformities between the four "great" revolutions: British, 1640; American, 1776; French, 1789; and Russian, 1917. He later revised his book in the early 1960s and it became the bible for later US administrations' view of Vietnam, Cambodia, and other conflicts. Goldstone wrote that revolutions have a distinctive role in history because they combine "all the elements of forcible overthrow of the government, mass mobilization, the pursuit of a vision of social justice, and the creation of new political institutions."[118] It is the combination of revolts, strikes, social movements, coups, and civil wars that Goldstone considers a process by which leaders with vision harness the power of the people, the masses, to forcibly bring a new political system.[119] In Egypt, there were a few of these elements in play, yet the crucial one missing was the will or intent to create a new political order. Therefore, the 2011 uprising was not a revolution.

Moore[120] would emphasize the change from agrarian society to modern industrialized society and how peasant revolutions generally led to Communist regimes and bourgeois revolutions led to fascist regimes. His student, Skocpol,[121] emphasized state rules' actions over human agency in her analysis of revolutions and their results. Dunn wrote that post-revolutionary states are even more brutal and incompetent than what preceded.[122] Scott agrees with Dunn that post-revolutionary government can be even worse than what was removed. Dunn's writing also parallels Scott's,[123] who wrote that there is an important need to listen and understand citizens' needs in order to develop coherent and legible policies. Scott wrote that the hubris of not attempting to understand people's needs is detrimental to any democratic project. Scott also believes, like Rueschemeyer, Stephens, and Stephens, in the importance of understanding trade unions and their role. Trade unions have an important role: to diffuse the anger and frustration of the workers and turn it into legible policy recommendations for legislation.

Marshall, in his work on society and citizenship (1950),[124] gave us an important conclusion that the working class has truly earned their right and position in society to participate fully in political life. Millen, in his short monograph,[125] also supported the notion with evidence that trade unions played an important

role, particularly in the fight against colonialism and in the rebuilding of these nation-states afterwards. Workers fought alongside militants, freedom fighters, and militias to secure independence from colonial powers such as in Algeria, Morocco, Tunisia, and even in Egypt.

David Collier[126] adds to this literature with a significant body of work about how trade unions found themselves in the nexus between economic and political transformations in Latin America. Collier does not always attribute positive traits to trade unions' role in revolutions. In a survey of twenty-one countries in Latin America, trade unions often were in collusion with the state authority for power and securing their place in society. Collier has an "elitist" view of labor in the sense that the leaders are those who make the decisions for the workers, because the workers themselves do not necessarily know where their interests lie. However, one still cannot deny that in several countries, workers' and their organizations played an important role in uprisings and revolutions in Latin America, such as in Chile, Argentina, and Cuba.

However, Bellin (2000)[127] points out an interesting caveat referring to both labor and capital as "reluctant/contingent democrats," especially in late-developing economies—why? Late-developing economies are developing nations that were colonized or did not have an industrial revolution similar to what took place in the West. The "reluctant democrat" behavior depends on how the state deals with and treats labor and capital. The authoritarian state has two strategies that put labor and capital in this "reluctant" position. If the state adopts a corporatist policy where it provides funds and co-opts the leadership of the trade unions, as is the case in Egypt, and labor finds itself in a privileged, "aristocratic" position, then it has no incentive to promote change or revolt against the status quo. The same goes for the capital (business) class when they are given privileged access to credit, investment, and monopoly of ownership leading to massive profits; then, again, changing to democracy is neither lucrative nor of interest. If the state adopts a "market approach" to both labor and capital, i.e. let the market decide, divide and conquer strategies, or instead of one trade union federation there are nineteen (as in the case in Morocco), then the trade unions are so weakened that they have no power or ability to start or support change. They remain under the state's control.

Bellin makes a cogent argument in her writings with examples from Egypt, Indonesia, Mexico, South Korea, and Tunisia. She writes of the state sponsorship paradox, which can fatally limit class commitment to democracy.[128] In Egypt, the ETUF was dealt with by the state in the corporatist manner (Vitalis and Bianchi write a great deal about this situation), so the ETUF had absolutely no incentive to promote change or even advocate for workers' rights. This was an institution that was part and parcel of the state apparatus and benefitted greatly from the state's patronage and largess. ETUF and its leaders were co-opted to carry out the state's bidding, which was to keep the workers in check, under control, and definitely keep them from revolting against their employer, which in most cases was the government itself. With the increase in privatization and loss of jobs and benefits under the Mubarak regime, Egyptian workers took to the streets with more and more "wildcat strikes" against the employer and the ETUF.

O'Donnell and Schmitter's work has spanned twenty-five years and gives us informative theories on revolution, transition from authoritarian to democratization states, and the concept of liberalization. It is noteworthy to emphasize

the difference between liberalization and democratization—one does not necessarily lead to the other. Liberalization was implemented in Egypt during certain times under the Mubarak regime, yet it was a calculated opportunity to give the opposition venting space without necessarily leading to significant, real democratization. Twenty-five years after their magnum opus work, Schmitter wrote a retrospective in the *Journal of Democracy* (2010).[129] In this, he notes that civil society organizations (including trade unions) were given far too much attention (including funding and international support) and did not deliver as much as was hoped for. There were many revolutions without "democrats" and many transitions (more than fifty) that serendipitously took place without much fanfare. Tilly has also given us much to ponder in his book, *Democracy*, regarding regression or de-democratization.

Goldstone[130] presented several important reasons for revolution and the need for changes, which are indeed applicable to Egypt. Soliman's book published in English, *The Autumn of Dictatorship* (2011), adopted arguments similar to Goldstone's. First, a decline in the revenue of the authoritarian state leads to revolt. In Egypt's case, this meant a decline in funding for the basic services that affected people's welfare and future, including education, health services, vocational training, and certain subsidies for consumer goods. These changes were in accordance with the neoliberal economic restructuring policies implemented in earnest with the appointment of al-Nazif in 2004. Second, an increase in the fissures between elites leads to revolt. This did indeed take place in Egypt, especially in the business class, where the Mubarak regime, particularly his sons Gamal and Ala'a, orchestrated several "business coups" of large successful businesses and would favor one businessman over another (e.g. the Aboul Foutouh BMW dealership incident or the incident involving Ahmed Ezz, the steel magnate, and the list continues). Third, a significant increase in the level of poverty leads to revolt. In Egypt, this is a result of neoliberal economic restructuring policies; the decline in employment opportunities; more privatization of the public sector, leaving many workers without work and pensions; and early retirement schemes that were not in the workers' favor, just to name a few causes. Fourth, an increase in the security crackdowns by various security apparatuses leads to revolt. In Egypt, there was jailing of human rights activists and journalists and a curbing of civil society organizations' ability to function freely and receive international funding to carry out their programs. An additional reason for revolt in Egypt was the parliamentary elections in 2010 that were fraught with corruption and outright fraud. The reasons outlined here parallel with Goldstone's research, theories, and writings.

What Insights Does This Literature Offer in the Case of Egypt, and What Are Its Limitations?

Limitations up to this point are that the historical accounts and theories have not yet fully encompassed the neoliberal economic restructuring experiment in developing countries such as Egypt and the role of trade unions. Trade unions are not generally considered, and there are only a handful of scholars who focus on trade unions and their role in society overall. The lack of equity and social justice in neoliberal economic restructuring literature is a harbinger for revolution and for the active role of trade unions. Most of the contemporary theoretical

literature that I have reviewed thus far starts with revolts against Communist regimes, particularly in the contexts of Europe, or authoritarian regimes in Latin America, which are not fully comparable to Egypt. Independent political parties are not the norm in post-1952 Egypt, so labor's alliance with political parties is not a cognizant force that can impact politics. Both labor and political parties have been neutered over the years. While the nature of authoritarian rule is a common point and the context is similar, the mechanics/tools of societal forces, such as mature and independent political parties and labor movements, are not.

Trade unions are naturally suited to play an important role in society, including when society is in an upheaval. Trade unions are grassroots organizations based locally and nationally that can organize significant numbers of persons to act, revolt, and demand change. Trade unions bring workers, both men and women, from all sectors of the economy, including professionals and blue-collar factory workers. They can be a force to be reckoned with, and that is precisely why when one revisits history and looks at Communist and fascist regimes in the early twentieth century, one of their first actions is to neutralize the democratic nature of trade unions immediately through violent means and control them.

Concluding Remarks

To conclude this chapter, my goal is that this research will add to the body of knowledge and scholarship about the causes leading up to the January 25, 2011, uprising in Egypt. The purpose is to further explain and add to our understanding the important causal variable of the independent workers with other facets of civil society and how they served as a tipping point for the January 25 uprising. In addition, the research provides a critical review of the "lost opportunities" because these workers were organized in their varying groups without a central coordinating organization and of their contentious protest actions. The workers took many courageous steps, yet there were also critical missteps. In order to understand lessons learned and best practices, one needs to examine, for example, the leadership characteristics of these disparate workers' groups using Weber's "routinization" of charisma. Gramsci wrote of a "crisis of authority" when in the short run the ruling classes are able to reorganize quickly and regain the control that had slipped from their grasp.

> At a certain point, social classes become detached from their traditional parties. [. . .] When such a crisis occurs, the immediate situation becomes delicate and dangerous, because the field is open for violent solutions, for the activities of unknown forces, represented by charismatic "men of destiny."[131]

He wrote that when the ruling class loses the consent of the broad masses, it is a crisis of authority and hegemony. Over seventy-six years ago, Gramsci gave a most appropriate description of the Egyptian situation pre-January 2011. Post-February 2011 and leading to the first presidential elections in May 2012 (when this research endeavor ended), we witnessed a reassertion of the authority of the "deep state" through the strong-arm tactics of the military.

There were several other smaller groups of independent workers who took the lead from these two case studies and joined the growing social movement of labor

protests. These workers came from various blue- and white-collar professions, holding positions such as bakers, cement workers, steel workers, mechanical engineers, Suez Canal and port workers, professors, health technicians, and sugar processing plant workers. The width and breadth of types of workers shows how deeply entrenched the grievances were in many, if not all, professions and workers in Egypt.

Social movements use repeated repertoires of activities, events, and brokers while framing their claims into a clear discourse with the goal of appealing to more and more people—to the masses. The independent Egyptian workers employed these mechanisms and also took advantage of POS. They consciously examined the political power of the Mubarak regime and assessed its strengths, weaknesses, threats, and opportunities available to them. They repeatedly tested the regime, bringing confrontation to the brink of violence. Thankfully, the state's security apparatus and the regime retreated and sought negotiations. Then, it was clear to see how the character of the workers' contentious political and economic actions interacted, or more correctly collided, with the regime. Did they succeed to get their claims heard? Yes. Did they succeed in getting their claims resolved? Yes, partially. Did they succeed in politically influencing the process of reform in Egypt? Yes and no; it was an incomplete, limited, and qualified victory within constraints. Why? The reasons are varied and many and will be examined in more detail in the chapters to follow.

Using the theoretical lenses of social movements and social movement unionism and with the comparative case studies methodology, I will examine the "mixed contribution" of Egyptian workers toward political reform leading up to the 2011 uprising. Undoubtedly, the millions of workers who participated in repeated forms of protests had an impact on several trends contributing to the downfall of the Mubarak regime. This was a movement that had been building and growing in earnest over the years since the early 2000s and before. There was a continuum of protest events, each breaking down bit by bit the wall of fear. The fear of retribution by an authoritarian regime waned thanks to the workers. Egyptian workers stepped out into the streets to demand dignity and universally respected rights when it was not in vogue. At times, they were simply asking to be paid their wages and other such fundamental demands.

I will examine the theories of democratization and the process of change and democratic transition as well as the role of trade unions. The role of workers' organizations in this transition has many precedents, with Poland coming first to mind and then Latin America. With these lessons learned, how do the Egyptian workers' efforts hold up or compare? Where were the major gaffes, and how did their efforts to impact political reforms come up short or incomplete? Is it the historical baggage that the Egyptian labor movement carries? Is it the issue of leadership? Is it the Egyptian society and the "deep authoritarian state" views on labor undercutting their efforts? Or is it that no matter how many millions rose up against the Mubarak regime, no one group or groups could ever stand up to the entrenched deep state apparatus, the military, or the most organized social/political group in Egypt, the MB?

Today, Egyptian workers are still struggling for respect and dignity. They are still demanding respect for freedom of association, a fundamental human and worker right. Indeed, it was an incomplete, qualified limited victory for workers, yet they are still the victims of undemocratic autocratic policies.

Notes

1. Posusney's *Labor and the State in Egypt*, Goldberg's *Tinker, Tailor and Textile Worker: Class and Politics in Egypt*, Bianchi's *Unruly Corporatism: Association Life in Twentieth-Century Egypt*, and Vitalis' *When Capitalists Collide: Business Conflict and the End of Empire in Egypt*.
2. Bianchi (1989), Vitalis (1995), Beinin and Lockman (1987).
3. Bayat, Asef. *Life as Politics, How Ordinary People Change the Middle East*. Stanford, CA: Stanford University Press, CA, 2010.
4. www.ilo.org/public/english/iira/documents/congresses/regional/lagos2011/2ndparallel/session2b/tradeunionleadership.pdf
5. www.ilo.org/global/topics/freedom-of-association-and-the-right-to-collective-bargaining/lang--en/index.htm
6. Fick, Barbara J. "Not Just Collective Bargaining: The Role of Trade Unions in Creating and Maintaining a Democratic Society." *Working USA* 12 (2) (2009): 249–264: 249.
7. Ibid.: 259.
8. Gompers, Samuel. What Does Labor Want? In *The Samuel Gompers Papers*, vol. 3, ed. S. Kaufman and P. Albert. Urbana: University of Illinois Press, 1893: 396.
9. Fick 2009: 11.
10. Ibid.
11. Millen, Bruce H. *Political Role of Labor in Developing Countries*. Washington, DC: Brookings Institution, 1963.
12. Ibid.: 9.
13. Ibid.
14. Lynch, Sarah. "Key Force in Tahrir Square: Egypt's Labor Movement." *The Christian Science Monitor*, July 8, 2011.
15. Millen 1963: 95.
16. Collier, Ruth Berins and James Mahoney. "Adding Collective Actors to Collective Outcomes: Labor and Recent Democratization in South America and Southern Europe." *Comparative Politics* 29 (3) (1997): 285–303.
17. Ibid.: 299.
18. Ibid.: 113–116.
19. Millen 1963: 117.
20. Roberts, Hugh. "The Revolution That Wasn't." *London Review of Books* 35 (17) (2013): 3–9: 4. www.lrb.co.uk/v35/n17/hugh-roberts/the-revolution-that-wasnt.
21. Albrecht, Holger. *Raging Against the Machine: Political Opposition Under Authoritarianism in Egypt*. Syracuse Press, Syracuse, NY, October 2012.
22. Lesch, Ann M. "Egypt's Spring: Causes of the Revolution." Article first published online: 18 (3) (2011): 43, Middle East Policy © 2011, Middle East Policy Council.
23. Roberts 2013: 3–9: 6.
24. Beinin, Joel. *The Struggle for Worker Rights in Egypt*. Washington, DC: Solidarity Center. Published by the Solidarity Center, February 2010: 14. http://www1.umn.edu/humanrts/research/Egypt/The Struggle for Workers rights.pdf.
25. DeSmet, Brecht. "Egyptian Workers and Their Intellectuals. The Dialectical Pedagogy of the Mahalla Strike Movement." *Mind Culture and Activity*, ISSN 1074-9039 19 (2) (2012): 139–155: 148.
26. www.crisisgroup.org/en/publication-type/media-releases/2005/mena/reforming-egypt-in-search-of-a-strategy.aspx
27. Roberts 2013: 7.
28. From various interviews conducted in June and July 2013 in Egypt.
29. www.aljazeera.com/news/middleeast/2010/05/201052161957263202.html
30. http://socialistworker.org/blog/critical-reading/2011/07/09/workers-play-central-role-egyp
31. Lynch 2011.
32. Lesch 2011: 35–48.
33. Ibid.: 35–48: 43.
34. Ibid.
35. Ibid.
36. McGrath, C. "Independent Unions Flourish in Post-Mubarak Egypt." *The Middle East Magazine* (May 2011): 38.

37. McAdam, Doug, Sidney G. Tarrow, and Charles Tilly. *Dynamics of Contention*. Cambridge: Cambridge University Press, 2001: 14–15.
38. Beinin, Joel. "Workers and Egypt's January 25 Revolution." *International Labor and Working-Class History* 80 (2011): 189–196: 192.
39. Collier and Mahoney 1997: 285–303.
40. Beinin 2010: 18.
41. Ibid.: 16.
42. Collier and Mahoney 1997: 301.
43. In *Contentious Politics* by Tilly and Tarrow (2007), social movements are considered part of contentious politics.
44. Tilly, Charles and Sidney G. Tarrow. *Contentious Politics*. Boulder, CO: Paradigm Publishers, 2007. Print.
45. Goffman, Erving 1922–82, American sociologist, b. Manville, Alta. His field research in the Shetland Islands resulted in *The Presentation of Self in Everyday Life* (1956), which analyzes interpersonal relations by discussing the active processes by which people make and manage their social roles. Using metaphors of the stage ("dramaturgy"), Goffman describes how ordinary individuals give performances, control their scripts, and enter settings that make up their lives. This active notion of "role" is often associated with the symbolist interactionist school of George Herbert Mead, which argues that humans manipulate social situations by selecting appropriate roles and by maintaining some distance from these roles. Goffman later studied deviance and the "total institution" in *Asylums* (1961); he later returned to patterns of communication in *Frame Analysis* (1974) and *Forms of Talk* (1981). Widely recognized for his distinctive writing style, he served as president of the American Sociological Association in 1981. The Columbia Electronic Encyclopedia® Copyright © 2013, www.cc.columbia.edu/cu/cup/.
46. Benford, Robert D. and David A. Snow. "Framing Processes and Social Movements: An Overview and Assessment." *Annual Review of Sociology* 26 (2000): 611–639.
47. Olson, Mancur. *The Logic of Collective Action: Public Goods and the Theory of Groups*. Cambridge, MA: Harvard University Press, 1965. Print.
48. Ibid.
49. Lichbach, Mark I. *The Rebel's Dilemma*. Ann Arbor: University of Michigan Press, 1995. Print.
50. Olson 1965.
51. Lichbach, Mark, and Mark Zuckerman. "The Rebel's Dilemma: An Evaluation of Collective Action." *Flood, S. International terrorism: policy implications. Office of International Criminal Justice The University of Illinois at Chicago* (1991), p. 182.
52. Marshall, Shana and Joshua Stacher. "Egypt's Generals and Transnational Capital." *MERIP* 42 (2012). www.merip.org/mer/mer262/egypts-generals-transnational-capital.
53. Kandil, Hazem. *Soldiers, Spies and Statesmen: Egypt's Road to Revolt*. S.l: Verso, 2014. Print.
54. Please note that the United Nations Development Program's (UNDP) Arab Human Development reports are an excellent source of information about the state of freedoms, knowledge, security, women's rights, education, and other critical areas. The reason these reports are so relevant is that they were written by a brave group of Arab scholars, thinkers, and researchers with excellent credentials.
55. McAdam, Tarrow, and Tilly 2001: 41.
56. Ibid.: 42.
57. Ibid.: 314.
58. Ibid.: 48.
59. Ibid.
60. Ibid.: 37.
61. Beinin, Joel and Frederic Vairel (editors). *Social Movements, Mobilization, and Contestation in the Middle East and North Africa*. Stanford, CA: Stanford University Press, 2011: 14.
62. Beinin 2011: 182.
63. Goldstone, Jack A. and Charles Tilly. "Threat (and Opportunity): Popular Action and State Response in the Dynamics of Contentious Action." In *Silence and Voice in the Study of Contentious Politics*, ed. Ronald R. Aminzade et al. Cambridge: Cambridge University Press, 2001: 179–194: 183.
64. Beinin and Vairel 2011: 181.

65. Tilly and Tarrow 2007: 8.
66. Ibid.
67. Ibid.: 49–50.
68. Van Evera, Stephen. *Guide to Methods for Students of Political Science*. Ithaca: Cornell University Press, 1997: 11.
69. Ibid.: 17.
70. Fairbrother, Peter. "Social Movement Unionism or Trade Unions as Social Movements." *Employee Responsibility Rights Journal* 20 (2008): 2013–220: 214.
71. Waterman, Peter. "Strikes in the Third World." *Development and Change* (Special Issue) 10 (2) (1979).
72. Seidman, Gay. "Social Movement Unionism: From Description to Exhortation." *South African Review of Sociology* 42 (3) (2011): 94–102: 94.
73. Ibid.: 95.
74. Ibid.
75. Marshall, T. H. *Citizenship and Social Class: And Other Essays*. Cambridge: University Press, 1950.
76. Seidman: 97.
77. Collier, Ruth B., and David Collier. *Shaping the political arena: critical junctures, the labor movement, and regime dynamics in Latin America*. Notre Dame, Indiana: University of Notre Dame Press, 2002. p. 270.
78. Valenzuela, J. Samuel. "Labor Movements in Transitions to Democracy: A Framework for Analysis." *Comparative Politics* 21 (4) (July 1989): 445.
79. Millen 1963: 95.
80. Galenson, Walter, and Seymour Martin Lipset. "Democracy and Bureaucracy in Trade Union Government." *Labor and Trade Unionism, edited by W. Galenson and SM Lipset. New York and London, England: Wiley* (1960): 203–205.
81. Millen, Bruce H. The Political Role of Labour in Developing Countries. Washington, DC: The Brookings Institution, 1963: 148 pages, Print.
82. O'Donnell, Guillermo A., Philippe C. Schmitter, and Laurence Whitehead. *Transitions from Authoritarian Rule*. Baltimore: Johns Hopkins University Press, 1986. Print.
83. Tilly, Charles. *Democracy*. Cambridge and New York: Cambridge University Press, 2007. Print.
84. Brumberg, Daniel, "The Trap of Liberalized Autocracy." *Journal of Democracy* 13 (4) (October 2002): 56–68.
85. Roberts 2013: 101.
86. Heydemann, Steven, "Towards a New Social Contract in the Middle East and North Africa." January 20, 2004, Carnegie Endowment's Sada publication, http://carnegieendowment.org/2008/08/20/toward-new-social-contract-in-middle-east-and-north-africa/ffyg.
87. Soliman, Samer and Peter Daniel (translator). *The Autumn of Dictatorship: Fiscal Crisis and Political Change in Egypt Under Mubarak*. Stanford, CA: Stanford University Press, 2011.
88. Paul, A. "Egypt's Labor Pains: For Workers, the Revolution Has Just Begun." *Dissent* 58 (4) (2011): 11.
89. Ali, Khaled. "Precursors of the Egyptian Revolution." *IDS Bulletin* Volume 43 Number 1 January 2012 © 2012 The Author, p. 16. *IDS Bulletin* © 2012 Institute of Development Studies. Published by Blackwell Publishing Ltd, 9600 Garsington Road, Oxford OX4 2DQ, UK and 350 Main Street, Malden, MA 02148, USA. Khaled Ali is a labor lawyer, former presidential candidate, and head of the Egyptian Center for Economic and Social Rights.
90. Lynch, Marc. *The Arab Uprisings: The Unfinished Revolutions of the New Middle East*. New York: Public Affairs, 2012: 9.
91. Lynch, Marc (editor). *The Arab Uprisings Explained—New Contentious Politics in the Middle East*. NYC: Columbia University Press, 2014: 5.
92. Dabashi, Hamid. *The Arab Spring: The End of Postcolonialism*. London: Zed Books, 2012: 240. Print.
93. Beinin and Frederic 2011.
94. Tilly, Charles. *Durable Inequality*. Berkeley: University of California Press, 1998.
95. Jeffrey Broadbent, "Movement in Context: Thick Networks and Japanese Environmental Protest." In *Social Movements and Networks—Relational Approaches to Social Action*, ed. Mario Diani and Doug McAdam. Oxford: Oxford University Press, 2003: 204–233, Chapter 9.

96. Burke, Edmund, Ira M. Lapidus, and Ervand Abrahamian. *Islam, Politics, and Social Movements*. Berkeley: University of California Press, 1988. Print.
97. Goldberg, Ellis, "Muslim Union Politics in Egypt: Two Cases." In *Islam, Politics, and Social Movements*, ed. Edmund Burke, Ira M. Lapidus, and Ervand Abrahamian. Berkeley: University of California Press, 1988: 228, Chapter 11.
98. Davis, Gerald F. *Social Movements and Organization Theory*. New York: Cambridge University Press, 2005. Print.
99. Tilly, Chris. "Trade Unions, Inequality, and Democracy in the US and Mexico." UCLA: The Institute for Research on Labor and Employment: 68–83. https://escholarship.org/uc/item/0wt3v445. eScholarship, University of California, 2013: 68. www.irle.ucla.edu/publications/documents/Tilly-Unions-inequality-democracy-inUS_MX-13-45-1-PB-RethinkingInequality_Devel-2013.pdf.
100. Tilly, Charles. *Democracy*. Cambridge: Cambridge University Press, 2007: 12–13.
101. Rueschemeyer, Dietrich, Evelyn Huber Stephens, and John D. Stephens. *Capitalist Development and Democracy*. Chicago: University of Chicago Press, 1992.
102. Levitsky, Steven and Scott Mainwaring. "Organized Labor and Democracy in Latin America." *Comparative Politics* 39 (1) (October 2006): 21–42: 21.
103. Bellin, Eva. "Contingent Democrats: Industrialists, Labor and Democratization in Late Developing Countries." *World Politics* 52 (January 2000): 175–205.
104. Levitsky and Mainwaring 2006: 21.
105. Beinin, Joel. "The Rise of Egypt's Workers." *Carnegie Endowment for International Peace Report*, June 2012: 3.
106. Ibid.: 7.
107. Collier and Mahoney 1997: 286.
108. Ibid.
109. Shadid, Anthony. "Suez Canal Workers Join Broad Strikes in Egypt." *New York Times* newspaper, Published on: February 17, 2011. www.nytimes.com/2011/02/18/world/middleeast/18egypt.html.
110. Kempf, Raphael. "Egypt: First Democracy, Then a Pay Rise." *Le Monde Diplomatique*, March 1, 2011.
111. Abdelrahman, Maha. "The Egyptian Opposition: From Protestors to Revolutionaries?" *Open Democracy*, April 22, 2013. www.opendemocracy.net/5050/maha-abdelrahman/egyptian-opposition-from-protestors-to-revolutionaries.
112. Ibid.
113. Wallerstein, Immanuel, "New Revolts Against the System." *New Left Review* 18 (November–December 2002). http://newleftreview.org/II/18/immanuel-wallerstein-new-revolts-against-the-system.
114. A note: Abdelrahman's book is *Egypt's Long Revolution Protest Movements and Uprisings*, Routledge 2014: 224 pages. "This book intends to throw light on the Arab Spring of 2011 by investigating the specific experience of Egypt. To this end, the revolution in Egypt and its subsequent development are situated within a historical framework of a decade long of protest movements and new forms of opposition politics. The book's main argument is that the proliferation of protest movements and groups since 2000 played a significant role in creating a context in which the 2011 mass revolt and the ousting of Mubarak was possible. The book examines a new generation of political activists that arose in response to ever-increasing grievances against authoritarian politics, deteriorating living conditions for the majority of Egyptians as a consequence of neo-liberal policies, the machinery of crony capitalism, and an almost total abandoning by the state of its responsibilities to society at large."
115. Dabashi 2012.
116. Rueschemeyer et al. 1992.
117. Brinton, Crane. *The Anatomy of Revolution*. New York: Vintage Books, 1965. Reprint.
118. Goldstone, Jack A. *Revolutions, a Short Introduction*. Oxford: Oxford University Press, 2014: 9.
119. Ibid.
120. Moore, Barrington. *Social Origins of Dictatorship and Democracy: Lord and Peasant in the Making of the Modern World*. Boston: Beacon Press, 1993. Print.

121. Skocpol, Theda. *States and Social Revolutions: A Comparative Analysis of France, Russia, and China*. Cambridge and New York: Cambridge University Press, 1979. Print.
122. Dunn, John. *Modern Revolutions—An Introduction to the Analysis of a Political Phenomenon*. Cambridge: Cambridge University Press, 1972.
123. Scott, James C. *Two Cheers for Anarchism Six Easy Pieces on Autonomy, Dignity, and Meaningful Work and Play*. Princeton, NJ: Princeton University Press, 2012. Print.
124. Marshall 1950.
125. Millen, Bruce H. *The Political Role of Labour in Developing Countries*. Washington, DC: The Brookings Institution, 1963: 148 pages, Print.
126. Collier, Ruth B. and David Collier. *Shaping the Political Arena: Critical Junctures, the Labor Movement, and Regime Dynamics in Latin America*. Notre Dame, IND: University of Notre Dame Press, 2002. Print.
127. Bellin, Eva. "Contingent Democrats: Industrialists, Labor, and Democratization in Late-Developing Countries." *World Politics* 52 (2) (January 2000): 175–205.
128. Bellin, Eva R. *Stalled Democracy: Capital, Labor, and the Paradox of State-Sponsored Development*. Ithaca: Cornell University Press, 2002. Print.
129. Schmitter, Philippe C. "Twenty-Five Years, Fifteen Findings." *Journal of Democracy* 21 (1) (January 2010): 17–28. DOI:10.1353/jod.0.0144.
130. Goldstone, Jack A. *Revolution and Rebellion in the Early Modern World*. Berkeley: University of California Press, 1991. Print.
131. Hoare, Quintin and Geoffrey Smith (editors and translators). *Selections from the Prison Notebooks of Antonio Gramsci*. New York: International Publishers, 2010: 210.

2 An Overview of the Egyptian Labor Movement's History (Pre- and Post-1952) and the Shaping of the Current Labor Movement

The Nature of Political Conflict, Contending Elite Factions, and the Institutional Basis of Political Power

Chapter Outline:

Introduction

First in this chapter, I will review the highlights of Egyptian workers' history pre- and post-1952 leading up to the last decade of Mubarak's rule. Second, there will be a presentation of who the Egyptian worker is; and third, there will be a brief overview of the garment and textile industry, particularly the role of cotton in Egyptian history, and the infamous Misr Spinning and Weaving Company factory. This factory is a key part of Egyptian workers' history, and it encompasses one of the major workers' struggles in contemporary Egypt. The reason for the special focus on the garment and textile workers is that this particular group of workers is one of the subjects of this research enquiry (see the case study in Chapter 4 for details), and they have exhibited leadership early on within Egypt's labor movement.

I will focus on workers' history as the development or evolution of a social movement, including the successes, failures, and challenges they faced. One cannot research their recent past (2006–2012) without going back to their history.

Historical Highlights of the Egyptian Labor Movement

The Egyptian labor movement began in the late 1880s with formal organizations, mainly in the railroad and sugar production industries. By 1919, the labor movement played an important role in supporting the Wafd[1] political party and the uprising led by Ahmed Orabi, which led to Egypt becoming nominally (on paper) independent from the British in 1922. The Banque Misr group, as discussed in Vitalis' book[2], was one of the main groups to begin investing in Egypt's economy, despite British objections. Marxist and Communist influences traveled across the seas to make some inroads into the labor movement. By the early 1950s, Egypt's blue-collar workforce had increased, and formal trade unions were established.

The Banque Misr group was "the centerpiece of both triumphalist (nationalist) and exceptionalist (neo-Marxist) accounts of Egyptian economic history [. . .] and the industrial investment group was led by its outspoken nationalist chairman, Tal'at Harb."[3] Harb and his associates symbolized the partnership of an aspiring Egyptian industrial bourgeoisie whose mission was to create a purely Egyptian-owned industrial sector,[4] quite to the dismay of the British, who wanted to keep Egypt primarily an agricultural country with resources to boost British industrial needs. This nationalist group of investors had an ever-lasting impact on local nationalist fervor, even in the 1960s and 1970s. The nationalist investors' efforts such as the Misr Group collided headlong with the privatization efforts that began in the mid-1970s and later on into Mubarak's era. However, the Misr group had to engage in partnerships with foreign capital, primarily British corporations, in order to survive in the late 1930s, at which point the "Misr group ceased to be 'national in character.' "[5] Vitalis helps give context to the writings regarding the radical opposition, currents, and discourses of the late 1940s and early 1950s, "including the writings of al-Barrawi and Maza 'Ulaysh' (1945) and 'Atiya al-Shafi' (1957), among others."[6] Until 1952, the business community held a privileged position within Egyptian government policies and society.

> The power of capitalists as a class in the decades before the 1952 free officers' coup d'état resembles Gramsci's concept of hegemony, [it] is centrally concerned with the contemporary functioning of advanced capitalist democracies, systems where a stable, highly nondemocratic relationship of shared authority between corporate capitalists and government officials is not an issue around which political forces struggle.[7]

Egypt, by contrast, had difficulties reconciling business privileges after the 1952 coup; however, government always had the option to refuse such privileges if it was dissatisfied with the business performance.[8] That is precisely what then took place by the Nasser regime beginning in 1954, when the new government elites began to challenge the main institutions of the private and market-based economy.[9]

Who Is the Egyptian Worker?

This is a critical question that must be explored to put this research project into context and perspective. We need to return to the past to review the development of the Egyptian worker, starting from the nineteenth century and continuing to the present. So, we need to return to 1805 and to Muhammed Ali, the ruler of Egypt under the Ottoman Empire and considered the father of modern Egypt. Industrialization began under his rule, moving Egypt from having a primarily feudal-crafts workforce to factory capitalism in one leap.

> His foundries turned out arms, machine tools, and even steam engines. His factories produced several consumer goods including cloth, paper, glass, oil, and sugar. However, these industries were mainly developed for the military's consumption. They were not protected from the onslaught by foreign products encouraged by the Anglo-Turkish Commercial Convention of 1838. So Egyptian industry fell into ruin and had to wait until around the 1920s for another industrial renaissance with the end of both the Ottoman Empire and British colonial rule.[10]

The limited focus of these industries for the military's consumption laid the groundwork for its demise. The state's development of the consumers' purchasing power, in order to support a more sustainable Egyptian industry, did not come until the twentieth century.

Who was an Egyptian worker during the nineteenth century? According to Goldberg's *Tinker, Tailor, and Textile Worker*, "four main characteristics defined a person as a worker socially and culturally, with a significant bifurcation within a single category":[11] urban male Egyptians who spoke the Egyptian Arabic dialect, worked with their hands, and got them dirty versus those who worked with machines and those who did not work with machines. In the 1930s and 1940s, workers who spoke Egyptian Arabic dialect confirmed their national outlook and were not international in their outlook. In the early part of the century, many of the skilled workers in Egypt were foreigners, Europeans as well as Turks and Arabs from the Levant who spoke Arabic but in a different dialect that was easy to recognize as not Egyptian. Europeans, in particular, had more experience and authority since they tended to hold management positions or have skilled positions at the workplace.[12] Workers used popular culture in the form of songs and poetry, called *zajal*, which is informal, or the classical poetry called *qasidah* to express the challenges they faced at the workplace and solidarity. Fathallah Mahrous, a retired garment and textile worker in Alexandria, recounted during our 12-hour meeting (June 22 and 23, 2013) several of these poems and songs that workers used to recite or sing. "Hardly a major union function or an issue of a union newspaper failed to include at least one poem from a worker in this form."[13] This tradition continues in the present day and shows expressions of workers' nationalist tendency and fervor. Poetry in the folk form of zajal told of workers' daily lives and hardships, so it was translated into nationalist fervor against the colonial rulers and owners. "The textile workers union had a poet laureate in Fathi al Magrabi, who published an entire volume of zajal under the title *I Am a Worker*."[14] This type of poetry is quite informative for learning about workers' political and social beliefs and convictions. In addition, it reflects

the difference among workers in terms of their class, status, and economic conditions, distinguishing between those who work with their hands and those who do not.[15] Such zajal poetry by Al-Magrabi, Bayram Al-Tunisi, and Sayyid Darwish reflected the workers' political beliefs. You will note that being a Muslim was not a readily used characteristic by workers since many workers, like many Egyptians, were Copts. To be Arabic speaking and Egyptian was paramount in the pre-1952 era, particularly in the 1930s when unions began to be formed.

According to Lockman, in 1911, Jean Vallet published *Contribution à l'étude de la condition des ouvriers de la grande industrie au Caire*,[16] where he insists that workers in big industry need to be differentiated from artisans and craft workers in small workshops. On this, Lockman writes,

> Vallet's contribution is a detailed and invaluable study of wage workers in large enterprises. He insists that the state must take this "new class" seriously by promptly enacting labor and social legislation that will ameliorate the terrible conditions these workers endure. For the moment this class is still relatively quiescent and timid; but the strikes and unions that Egypt has witnessed in the previous decade suggest to Vallet that, "if the critical period drags on, who knows of what destructive energy such a mass of workers is capable?"

Lockman sums this up by explaining that collective action, combined with a sort of holy war struggle, gives social struggle that may take place in Egypt an extra violent character.[17] Collective action with a mission of worthiness, unity, numbers, and commitment (WUNC)[18] is distinctively a social movement per Tilly's definition.

The transition to the urban wageworkers in the early twentieth century, as discussed in Nahas'[19] book, comes about as less lucrative work is found in the fields and more industrial factory jobs become available. Yet for Nahas, Egypt essentially was still an agricultural land and was likely to remain so. Hence, it confirmed for Nahas the importance of studying the economic and social situation of the "fallahs" (peasants) and of seeking ways to ameliorate their condition. For Nahas, however, the term "fallah" applies not only to the agricultural population (the peasants in the villages), "but also to the artisans and the lowly [*bas peuple*] in the cities and [. . .] equally to Muslims and Copts."[20] However, "Nahas cites the Egyptian worker's 'marvelous' capacity for emulation, his endurance, and his strength; this would soon make him a serious competitor for the European worker."[21] There continues to be a disagreement on who the Egyptian worker is since the "fallah" characteristics also apply to the urban wage-worker since many, if not all, were and still are "fallaheen," i.e. peasants in their mindset, outlook on life, and psyche.

The nature and character of the Egyptian worker evolved as the country's economy developed. It developed from being primarily an agricultural producer to a more industrialized economy starting in the nineteenth century, and not just for local consumption. Egypt was primarily an agricultural nation for such a long period of time that its main workforce was composed of peasants living off the land in rural areas growing agricultural crops primarily for their own use. A conversion took place among peasants and factory workers due to economic development policies.

Mohammad Ali (1805–1849) attempted to effect a transition from the subsistence economy prevailing at the beginning of the 19th century to a "modern" complex economy. In this he failed, but instead started Egypt on the road leading to an export-oriented economy.[22]

He implemented several policy changes, including taxes, land ownership, communication networks, irrigation, and trade under a monopolistic system, and planting of the long-time staple cotton. Cotton planting started on a commercial scale in 1821, and it found ready markets in Europe. By 1824, over 200,000 kantars of cotton[23] were being exported, and in 1845 the figure of 345,000 was reached.[24] Cotton became synonymous with Egypt, particularly the highly prized long-thread cotton.

A Personal Accounting of the Restrictions on Trade Unions and Eventual Government Control: Interview With Fathallah Mahrous in Alexandria, Egypt

The history of the Egyptian workers' movement is intertwined with the history of the Egyptian Communist Party and the role of the leftist intellectuals. Included in this history are the restrictions on trade union freedoms and the eventual role of the state in controlling workers. The history is full of heroes and martyrs, including Khamis and el Baqari (executed in August 1952 after the infamous Kafr al Dawwar events[25]), who sacrificed their lives for the right of workers to organize independent unions. Leftist leaders continued to influence the broader labor movement, yet it was always a constant battle, especially in the post-colonial and Nasserist periods. The belief in the tool of strikes has been part of the workers' consciousness early on. Marx's explanation is that there is no way to stop or limit this power; it is the sociology of how workers function. If wages decline or jobs are lost, it is a matter of life or death, so there is no other choice but to strike and demand improvements from the employer.

The period from 1918 through the 1940s was the zenith of the Communist Party in Egypt. There were three distinct societal classes according to Lockman, Beinin, and Mahrous (during an interview): capitalists, workers, and peasants. The class struggle developed during that time, and workers began to form trade unions to defend their rights. Foreign workers and Egyptians struggled for these unions, and in many cases foreigners and Christians became the union leaders. Unions became places where tolerance was practiced and there was representation for all, no matter what ethnicity, origin, or religion people had. Starting in 1946, the labor movement joined with political and student forces in the struggle against the government, King Farouk, and the British influence on him. They demanded the Wafd Party end the 1936 agreement with the British. Major strikes took place in 1948 with the police interfering to end them; strife continued until 1952's Free Officers' coup d'état.

Fathallah Mahrous (Figure 2.1) was born in the province of Qena in 1936 and died on October 22, 2016 (81 years old). He started working as a garment and textile worker in Alexandria when he was 16 years old to support his mother and siblings after his father's death. He was imprisoned five times for his political and trade union activism. King Farouk, President Nasser, President Sadat, and

Figure 2.1 Fathallah Mahrous with his books at home
Photo taken by Heba F. El-Shazli on June 23, 2013

President Mubarak all imprisoned him. Fathallah was an active member of the Egyptian Community Party. The following are his insights about the Egyptian labor movement, highlights of its pre-1952 history, and relationship with politics.

Mahrous was openly critical of the left opposition currently and its historic weak role, actually referring to the left as "retarded" or behind the times. To clarify, he is a dedicated leftist, yet he is disappointed in the how the leadership failed to assert itself and have a stronger influence over the Egyptian labor movement. The history of the Communists in Egypt is associated with the rise of industry and capitalism during the 1930s, but they ultimately failed to maintain their influence with the working class. The left, namely the Communists, basically fought with Nasserist/socialist philosophy and were ultimately jailed and killed by Nasser's security forces. Nasser and his policies managed to control labor fully, and therein lay the modern-day struggle and burden that labor still carries. Starting in 1953, Nasser and the military arrested workers for their collective actions, which effectively ended the activist, independent workers' spirit. Mahrous referred to labor's burden as Sisyphus pushing up the mountain the massive rock and then as he reaches the top, it rolls back, again and again. He quoted from Camus' *The Myth of Sisyphus*, pointing out the feeling of futility in the search for meaning and unity of the working class.

Labor's association with political parties, according to Mahrous, was always problematic and rocky. Political party leaders wanted to control labor

without giving them respect and access to the decision-making process. However, workers, starting in the 1900s, recognized that alliances with political parties were necessary to reach policy makers in government. So there were off and on alliances with various parties, most notably with the El-Watani and socialist political parties. It was clear from his recounting of significant events from World War I to 1952 that workers have been fighting for social justice. There were moments of harmony, though, with the political forces/parties when there was a national struggle against British colonial power. In 1939, the campaign for legal recognition of trade unions and independence from political parties began. It was not until 1942 that Law #85 was promulgated to govern trade unions and their legal existence. This law is actually the basis for Law #36, which was in effect until 2003 and controlled every aspect of the trade unions.

In the latter part of the nineteenth century, a large part of labor still worked in small craft workshops, and they could not react and organize in the same way as workers in big factories. The urban Egyptians engaged in production, commerce, and service activities were organized into small guilds.[26] They were spread out geographically, thus getting information and organizing workers into collective action was more arduous. In addition, the skilled, upper-stratum, natural leaders were foreigners and so it was not always easy to cooperate with Egyptian workers. Different language, customs, and traditions got in the way. These foreign workers were mainly Greeks, Italians, Armenians, and Levantine Arabs. Another difficulty was illiteracy; in 1911, it was estimated that more than 90% of the workforce was illiterate. Foreign workers came to Egypt as technicians for the new factory machinery and also as supervisors. They usually had higher wages than the Egyptian workers had. However, these foreign workers brought ideas of socialism and workers' right to improve their wages through collective action. As a result, many of the initial leaders of Egypt's independent unions were foreigners. A Greek led the first trade union organized in December 1899 at the Eastern Cigarette Company, and he led a major strike for three months starting in December 1899. Greek workers taught Egyptians the details of what a strike was and how to use this tool to get their rights.[27]

After 1890, trade unions began to form with friendly societies and associations in the cigarette, transport, and metallurgy industries. World War I (1914–1918) stimulated labor activity, and by 1919 labor was very active in the nationalist Orabi movement against British colonial power. Then labor went into a "quiet mode" until the 1930s when labor, for about six to seven years, was politically active. The number of trade unions increased and established closer relations with each other,[28] and more solidarity developed. A federation of trade unions was established but was not legally recognized until 1942 with the help of the Wafd political party and Prince Halim Abbas. This political involvement with labor was not a positive experience. After 1937, the union reorganized—this time without politicians' assistance.

The year 1938 witnessed violent strikes due to an increase in wheat prices, and El-Mahalla Misr Spinning and Weaving Company's 1,100 workers went on strike, occupying the factory. Trade unions were not initially legally recognized, but the government tolerated them. However, the lack of funds available to these unions limited their activities to primarily passing resolutions. In 1942, more strikes took place again due to an increase in the cost of living. The government

reacted to worker activism and protests with imprisonment of the workers' leaders, but they did ultimately give them raises in wages.

In 1942, trade unions were legalized, excluding state employees and agricultural workers. Yet, unions were forbidden by law to engage in political or religious activities.[29] Issawi's prescriptive conclusions written in 1947 were truly prophetic and are still relevant in 2013:

> [C]learly the struggle of the workers to obtain recognition of their rights is far from ended. And unless the government shows much more wisdom than in the past in its dealings with the working class there is a great danger of this struggle taking a violent form.[30]

1952—Nasser and the Transition to a Public Sector Economy, and the Establishment of the Official Trade Union Federation, ETUF

Egyptian workers have a history for contentious collective action. They were not averse to protesting for their rights and to protect their jobs. There was already a developed working-class movement in Egypt by the early 1900s. The first strike by cigarette rollers at the Eastern Cigarette Company in Alexandria started in December 1899 and lasted for three months into 1900. It was probably the first in any Muslim country. And the first actual trade union to be formed was in the tobacco industry in 1903. In 1908, these workers went on strike again to protest the introduction of new equipment.

> "By 1914, there was an alliance between the Watani (Nationalist) political party and working-class organizations. It was not uncommon to find avant-garde intellectuals cooperating with the workers." By WWI, there were 11 unions in Egypt with a total membership of 7,000. This encouraged the growth of working-class militancy and thus played an important role in 1919 revolution. Trade unions [existed] in 1920s and 1930s [and] by 1930 there were 38 unions in Egypt with a membership of 15,000 workers, [and] three unions having over 1,000 members each.[31]

By the time of the 1952 coup d'état that peacefully overthrew King Farouk and the beginning of the post-colonial period, there was already an active, independent, organized labor movement.

July 1952 marks the beginning of the Revolutionary Free Officers' Movement's rule led by Naguib, Nasser, and Sadat, among several other officers. Nasser formally became president in 1954 and took over from Naguib, Egypt's first president for two years. In addition to the comprehensive land reform legislation that he enacted in July 1956, Nasser announced the nationalization of the Suez Canal in a stirring, fiery speech in Alexandria on the fourth anniversary of the coup d'état. He announced to the world in no uncertain terms that Egypt would not be dominated by any foreign power and could manage its own affairs, including the management of the Suez Canal. This sent a signal that Egypt was embarking on a post-colonial, self-sustaining journey of national development.

The ETUF—The Official Trade Union

President Nasser established the official trade union movement in 1957 under the banner of the Egyptian Federation of Trade Unions (ETUF) with its twenty-eight affiliated unions. It was not an overwhelming grassroots initiative growing from the rank-and-file members. It was Nasser's idea, and it was implemented—plain and simple.

> The ETUF was founded on January 30, 1957, by a meeting of 101 union leaders who affirmed Anwar Salama, the regime's choice, as president. Salama's federation had little independence of the government from the beginning, and it had to engage in bureaucratic battles with the government as well as with employers, administrators, and insurgent workers. The federation had nearly 1,300 local unions in 28 industrial sub-federations with over 310,000 members in 1957.[32]

ETUF continued as a transmission belt of the ruling regime from its foundation until the present day. Its role was to implement government policy regarding workers and their wages and benefits. The ETUF was not an independent advocacy trade union organization committed to defending worker rights.

The unions within ETUF represented the blue-collar factory workers and civil servants of every aspect of the economy—the largest being in the garment and textile industry, which was based in El-Mahalla al Kubra in the Delta region. ETUF

> was essentially an arm of the government that required all trade unions to be members to be legal organizations. The president of the federation [who] . . . served concurrently as the Minister of Manpower until 1986.[33] Governmental control over the terms and conditions of employment and labor organizations crippled efforts to establish an independent labor movement.[34]

In essence, the workers made a pact with the devil, surrendering their fundamental rights.

> The labor movement [. . .] exchange(d) worker restraint for essential material and organizational benefits from the state. Both sorts of benefits spelled aristocracy and dependence for organized labor, and this politically-mediated privilege wedded the trade union movement to the authoritarian status quo, making it unreceptive to democratic reform.[35]

It was an autocratic trade union federation with a thin veneer of "pretend" democratic practices. ETUF's practices continued with an increase in its subordination to the state while its "mandatory" membership grew.

> In 1964 [its membership grew] to almost 1.1 million—[while] workers and leaders became more passive. [. . .] Posusney argued that this passivity occurred as a function of the regime's attack on political opposition (including the left), the entry of more peasants into the workforce, and company unionism.[36]

The ETUF and its leaders operated within the "social contract" norms and led a comfortable, privileged life style. Its mission was to respond to the state, carry out state controlled economic plans, and pretend to negotiate with the relevant ministries over wages and benefits. But everything was already approved and set by the Ministry of Planning and Economy's five-year plans. The parliament, called the People's Assembly, was the mirage by which labor and the peasants "legislated" the laws for Egypt. Two Egyptian social scientists, Mustafa Kamel el Sayyid and Amani Qandil, both argued convincingly that while Egypt's union movement had been subservient to the state on political issues, it has been oppositional regarding economic policies.[37] Bianchi, drawing on their work, found that labor was quite successful in resisting public sector reform in Egypt through the mid-1980s.[38] At the national level, the corporatist union leaders could influence and have the greatest potential to influence government policy, since centralization granted the greatest freedom of maneuvering to unionists at the top of the organizational hierarchy.[39] ETUF's leaders worked to keep the status quo, particularly the large, public sector factories and workplaces from which they gained their political and economic power. These leaders were also quite connected to the ruling party's apparatus and maintained their political power by ensuring "social harmony." The deal maintained that workers would not strike, protest, or conduct sit-ins in exchange for perks from the party and the government.

The social contract between the state and its citizens was born in the post-colonial era in most of the Arab countries. A "social contract" in Egypt was understood as composed of national laws, outlook, and discourse. The social contract was a commitment by the state to provide its citizens with permanent jobs, affordable consumer goods, free education and health care, and defense. In return, citizens, especially workers, made a "pact with the devil," where basic liberties were legislated away, as seen in the labor movement.[40] The notion of a social contract was a response to the substantial inequalities within society that these newly independent nations found themselves facing. The landed aristocracy was in decline and brought down from its privileged position through land reform. There was strong nationalist fervor in response to the fight against colonialism throughout the Arab world.

Until 1986, ETUF's president was the minister of manpower and migration, which clearly shows the subservient role that ETUF played to the state; independence to advocate for workers' and their rights was just not in the vocabulary, let alone the function of leaders. ETUF's leaders were also high-ranking leaders within the ruling party, various committees of the National Democratic Party's (NDP), and in the People's Assembly. However, Egypt has been a member of the International Labor Organization (ILO) since its founding in 1946. Egypt had ratified its major core conventions of 1987 and 1998 covering the rights to freely associate, organize independent trade unions, and bargain collectively with the employers. Throughout the subsequent years, the Egyptian "tripartite" delegation was not in any way tripartite, since all three representatives (government, business, and labor) all came from the state institutions. In 1998, the ILO overwhelmingly adopted the Declaration of Principles, which covers all of its members, whether they had ratified the core conventions or not. The core conventions include the right to freely organize trade unions without state interference, the right to bargain collectively, a ban on child labor, a ban on discrimination, and the right to health and safety at the workplace. Egypt's tripartite delegation voted against this historic declaration.

With the establishment of ETUF came the mandatory membership of workers into one of the twenty-three national trade unions, which were blue-collar workers' trade unions only. Bianchi wrote that associational life in Egypt was controlled "top down" by the state, including the trade unions with mandatory membership and dues. The 1959 labor code, the 1964 trade union law, and the obligation of trade unionists to belong to the ruling party completed the building of corporatist regulations of labor relations (Bianchi 1989).

> In Nasserist Egypt, as in several Latin American countries, a revolutionary elite use corporatism to strengthen working class organizations as junior partners in a multiclass ruling coalition that benefited briefly from ambitious efforts to combine redistributive reforms with import substitution. Moreover, post-Nasserist governments have sought to refashion inherited corporatist structures into more effective instruments for controlling a powerful working class movement that now is perceived as a major obstacle to a more advanced stage of industrialization, requiring greater reliance on imported capital and technology.[41]

The Nasserist view of controlling workers and trade unions was considered part of a national development project to move toward self-sufficiency and out of the colonial period. So to oppose this or call for independent, democratic trade unions would have been considered anti-nation building and anti-development. During the post-Nasserist era, government's policies adopted economic restructuring through neoliberal economic policies imposed by the IFIs. This put ETUF in an awkward position since it was a "cheerleader" for the Nasserist view and could not stop supporting the government without losing its privileges.

The ETUF and its member trade unions became part of a "privileged" class that Bellin would even call "aristocratic," reluctant, or contingent democrats.[42] They had no interest in defending workers' rights because it meant biting the hand that feeds them, the state. ETUF is an example of an organization that was created by the state and not by the workers themselves, thus in this case it is not a democratic entity that truly represents workers' needs and aspirations. It represents the will of the state and its ruling party, the NDP. Posusney argues

> that since 1960s, Egyptian workers have viewed themselves in a patron-client relationship with the state. The latter is expected to guarantee workers a living wage through regulation of their paychecks as well as by controlling prices on basic necessities; the government should also ensure equal treatment of workers performing similar jobs. Workers, for their part, provide the state with political support and contribute to the postcolonial national development project through their labor.[43]

The ETUF's role was to keep every worker and keep production going without disruptions. The state apparatus gave lavish benefits, money, housing, cars, and political access to the ETUF's top leaders, which trickled down to some members or leaders at the local level. No one in leadership would agitate for trade union independence or freedom of association. The rank-and-file and local leaders (on the level of factories and local/regional areas) were more interested in democratic trade unionism and in advocating for basic rights. At the local level, union

elections were generally free and fair. The local leaders were closer to the rank-and-file members, and it was much more difficult to ignore their needs.

> Until 1967, worker protests disappeared, partly because most communist trade unionists were jailed until 1965. State security, factory security, the trade union and the Socialist Union strongly controlled the workers and channeled their claims. The workers accepted this partly because the system provided an increase in their welfare and social position. Real wages increased by 60% between 1952 and 1966 (Posusney 1997).[44]

Starting in the 1980s and continuing into the 1990s, the situation changed due the implementation of Law #203 (1991), which called for privatization of public sector enterprises that ETUF leadership (per instruction of the NDP ruling party) endorsed. This step severely strained the state corporatist mechanisms of control in Egypt, as workers resisted the privatization policies that their national leadership adopted.[45]

In the early twenty-first century, ETUF, with help from the state security apparatus, stepped up their activities to control internal elections of union committees held in 2006. The ETUF held elections for its local/regional leaders every five years, and the 2006 union elections were determined to be the worst in ETUF's history. The CTUWS in Egypt conducted an in-depth election-monitoring program and published a comprehensive report. The report documented the widespread irregularities that characterized the elections and the role played by the ETUF and the Ministry of Manpower and Emigration to "manage" the election results. As a result, in 2007, the government forcefully closed the CTUWS offices in Helwan and around the country and accused the director of the center of several charges that he had to defend in court.

The attacks against the CTUWS offices were linked to the center's active role in informing workers of their rights, including during the trade union elections in October 2006, and in reporting on the widespread irregularities that characterized those elections. For example, the election date was declared less than fifty days before the designated date, which is in violation of the trade union law; the government imposed restrictions for being a candidate not stipulated by the law; there were violations of the candidates' right to communicate with voters and distribute their programs freely; and there was unequal treatment of candidates and violating trade union freedoms.[46] It is important at this point to describe O'Donnell's "populist" vs. "bureaucratic" authoritarianism. O'Donnell's

> elaboration of these [two] concepts were criticized by Alfred Stepan and David Collier. [. . .] The crux of O'Donnell's argument is that populist authoritarianism and bureaucratic authoritarianism are distinct responses to different kind of crises that emerge at different stages of delayed, dependent development. Populist relies on "inclusionary," co-optive forms of corporatism, while bureaucratic relies upon "exclusionary" repressive forms of corporatism.[47]

Populist authoritarianism mobilizes and strengthens the working-class organizations in order to break the power of the traditional landed oligarchy. Bureaucratic authoritarianism deactivates and "conquers" working-class organizations

to insure the political "predictability" that is necessary to consolidate alliances with foreign capital.[48] O'Donnell sees a clear causal relationship between the two—populism sows the seeds of bureaucracy by unleashing political forces that encourage industrialization at an early phase of development, but that then become an obstacle to industrialization at a more advanced stage.[49] This is a perfect description of the Egyptian case.

The first trade union law was passed in 1942 as Law #85, which became the basis of the Nasserist labor policies of corporatism and paternalism. Most of the members of the Revolutionary Command Council of Free Officers (RCC) and then Nasser afterwards exhibited strong hostility towards independent action by the working class, even when in support of the army.[50] There were RCC members such as Khaled Muhyi Al-Din, who were sympathetic to workers and argued for free trade unions and the right to strike, yet the majority of the RCC members dismissed them.[51] The official slogan of the new regime was "Unity, Order, and Labor," which also signaled labor's role, and such a vision did not include initiatives outside the regime's control.[52]

> The successful implementation of this corporatism and paternalism required not only that the RCC eliminate the communists from positions of influence in the working class, but also that it establish a significant base of active support for the regime within the trade union movement.[53]

All labor legislation was revamped, and three new laws were introduced in December 1952 without consultation of the labor movement leaders. These three laws gave workers many benefits within the public sector, including higher wages, pensions, health care, free transportation to factories in remote areas, and much more. However, the workers paid a steep price for these improvements in benefits and wages; the military issued an order banning all strikes.[54] On January 17, 1953, all political parties were banned, and numerous political activists, including many Communists, were arrested.[55] "By January 1953 many of the forces favoring a trade union movement independent of the regime had been stripped of their positions in the unions, and by the end of the year virtually all of the most important communist leaders were in jail."[56]

The crisis of March 1954 set the stage for the years to follow. The political standoff between members of the RCC and General Naguib, Egypt's first president, brought Nasser to power and took down parliamentary democracy and trade union independence.

> It is certainly true that the Free Officers broke the economic and political hegemony of the large landowners, the dominant class in Egypt since the era of Muhammad Ali, through the land reform, the dissolution of the political parties of the old regime.[57]

The labor leaders supported Nasser and made a bargain to support a military dictatorship that was absolutely opposed to a free trade union movement, the right to strike, and any independent labor action or initiative. In return, the regime confirmed the trade union leaders in their positions and agreed to preserve and extend the economic gains that had been achieved so far, particularly the guarantee of job security.[58] This supported the strong nationalist sentiments within the labor movement and Nasser's leadership that could deliver these economic gains.

The RCC was able to completely remove the British troops (an important nationalist demand) and was able to establish a socialist economic agenda to revamp Egypt's economy and industrialize.[59]

The consequences of those early years post-1952 determined the fate of the labor movement for the next fifty-six years until the first independent trade union was formed in 2008. However, the culture of alliance with the state, or entitlement, was still ingrained within those advocating for independent unions. This was apparent in the type of demands they called for, such as that the state continue to provide certain benefits such as housing, access to government-owned holiday resorts, etc. They were willing to accept a

> trade union movement dominated by the government and shorn of the right to strike and a political system which stripped workers of their right to organize independently of government control. This was, in essence, a development of the patron-client model of trade union organization with the state in as the guise of patron. A few years later this would lead to the institutionalization of the corporate conception of society when the trade unions were absorbed into the apparatus of the state.[60]

They gave up independence for perceived economic gains and political power under a system that created a bloated, large public sector, which in many cases was not well funded and inefficient. As a result, there was a decline in worker class consciousness and revolutionary political parties and the destruction of trade union freedoms. These are essential in the maintenance of a social movement that can monitor government and advocate for change. Egypt became an authoritarian-ruled nation with a veneer of "democratic" practices. The regime was clever in co-opting all essential social actors, including the labor movement.

In Nasser's era, free market capitalism was effectively ended, and a mixed system with a strong government role was adopted beginning in the late 1950s. Nasser brought the large factories under state control and established a system of profit sharing and workers' representation in management. This new economic system is state socialism, or state capitalism, because "private enterprise continued to exist in Egypt, the market remained the main means of distribution of goods, and [. . .] state ownership signified little in the way of actual workers' control over the means of production."[61] Workers then had a strong interest in collective action against the state, and this increased after the July 1961 socialist decrees reflecting increasing hostility toward the state. "The evidence for a moral economy in Egypt would be collective action by workers that follow a 'stability-disruption-protest' pattern, with demands that are restorative or exhibit notions of fairness and patron-client relationships."[62] Since the 1960s, Posusney argues that workers have viewed themselves in a patron-client relationship with the state. The state is supposed to guarantee workers a decent living wage by regulating their wages and controlling prices of consumer goods. Workers would in return provide the state with political support and contribute to the post-colonial national development project through their labor.[63]

To counter the rational choice theory,

> Egyptian workers' ability to act collectively at all under severe repression by government should give rational choice proponents pause. Evidence shows that

collective actions had an emotional rather than a dispassionate trigger: anger provided the impetus. And this anger was caused by the violation of workers' sense of justice, by the denial of something to which they felt entitled.[64]

It was understood by workers that the social contract would take care of all their needs in return for their full support of the government's policies in the parliament and public life.

1970s—Infitah (Open Door Economic Policy) Under Sadat and Liberalization

Nasser died in 1970 and was succeeded by his vice president, Mohamed Anwar el Sadat, as Egypt's third president. Sadat embarked on a different approach to the economy, especially after the October 6, 1973, Yom Kippur war with Israel and the Camp David Peace Accords in 1979. In the meantime, blue-collar workers pretended to be paid for pretending to work, and the white-collar workers (journalists, doctors, judges, engineers, and lawyers) organized in professional syndicates (associations) that operated with a little more autonomy and a sense of serving their membership. These were organizations that promoted the profession. Through them, for example, a journalist would get press credentials. They were primarily professional sanctioning organizations, and secondarily they were protecting the profession's position in society. These professional syndicates are where the MB first got their political training. It is also where they were able to infiltrate the membership and achieve some limited power and even credibility. The MB (founded in 1928 and banned during Nasser's tenure) was never able to function or gain acceptance within the blue-collar workers unions.

The change in the economic system crept in slowly at first with the bold policy announcement by Sadat in 1974 calling for the Infitah (the economic opening) of the economy to global markets. After the moral "victory" of the October 6 war, which significantly buoyed Egyptians, and then the Camp David accords in 1979, Sadat became more emboldened to take Egypt out of its economic, political, and social isolation and onto the world's stage—prepared or not. The first shock to the system was which the International Financial Institutions (IFIs) insisted that Egypt must remove or drastically reduce state subsidies on consumer goods; first on the list was bread. Bread is significant in the Egyptian lexicon and in the daily life of every Egyptian. The Egyptian Arabic dialect word for "bread" is "life." January 18 and 19, 1977, in Cairo, which is considered as essentially all of Egypt, witnessed massive protests that shook the country, the state, and Sadat. These changes were rescinded immediately, and from there on the slow, steady decline of the so-called social contract between the state and its people was started. The workers participated fully in those "bread-life" protests.

The labor movement official institution, the ETUF, became an enforcement tool of the state under the so-called social contract. However, the events of January 1977, Beinin argues, were a culmination of several workers' collective action events from 1971 to 1976.[65]

The strong undercurrent of popular indignation over the growing gap between the rich and the poor, the conspicuous consumption of imported

luxury goods, and similar phenomena of the [Sadat] open door era flowed into the demonstrations initiated by these workers to produce the explosive outburst of January 1977.[66]

January 1977 marked a transition point in Egypt's labor movement's advocacy for their rights and possibly the beginning of a slow-simmering revolt against the state institutions, namely the ETUF.

Mubarak's Era: 1980s, 1990s, and 2000s

Sadat was assassinated in 1981, and Mohamed Hosni Mubarak became Egypt's fourth president since 1952. He ruled from October 7, 1981, until February 11, 2011, thirty years. In the 1980s and 1990s, Mubarak and his regime slowly worked on restructuring Egypt's economy, moving away from a "centrally planned" economy to a more market-based economy. The labor movement was still under the state's ETUF control and functioned under the myth of the social contract and in continued support of the NDP. There were several strikes in the late 1980s; the most significant was in the Helwan (industrial area south of Cairo) iron and steel factories, where several union leaders were fired and/or imprisoned. One of them was a welder named Kamal Abbas, who later in 1990 became the founder and director of the CTUWS. Abbas and his followers worked closely with a respected labor advocate lawyer named Yusuf Darwich, who died in 2006. It was under Darwich's tutelage, as well as others from the small Egyptian Communist Party and leftist intellectuals, that the independent labor movement began its long journey.

> From 1984 on, as workers returned from high-paying jobs in the oil-producing countries, unemployment increased, prices rose relentlessly, and concerns about the security of employment spread due to fears that the government was preparing to sell off public-sector enterprises. [. . .] Workers resorted to strikes, protests, and other forms of contentious collective action. There were at least 50 strikes during 1985 and the first third of 1986.[67]

The following were the most notable strikes in the late 1980s:

> the strike at Misr Spinning and Weaving Company in El-Mahalla al-Kubra in February 1986, and the exceptionally militant strike of railroad engineers and stokers in July 1986. The strike and protests at the Egyptian Iron and Steel Company in Helwan in July-August 1989 were also part of this protest movement. Once again, unionized workers in large-scale public-sector enterprises, especially those located in major industrial centers were most prominent in this upsurge of workers' collective action.[68]

Interestingly, local activists led these protests and labor struggles, and they were not necessarily members of the left opposition parties.

There was strong worker dissatisfaction with government policies. The results of the open-door economic policy, which encouraged capitalist investments and opened Egypt's markets to the world, were becoming more disastrous for

the workers. In addition, the ineptitude of the ETUF and their failure to defend workers' interests became well known publicly and ridiculed. The ETUF publicly supported the government privatization policies despite the negative impact on their rank-and-file union members. I agree with Beinin and Lockman's rejection of mechanistic Marxism, which states

> if the consciousness and organizational capacity of Egyptian workers were increasingly enhanced by the spread of capitalist relations of production and growth of large-scale transport and industry, why was the organized working class so easily integrated into the corporatist structure of the Nasserist state after 1954?[69]

Economic determinism is being rejected in favor of class formation as a continual process. Beinin wrote that he and Lockman rejected E.P. Thompson's notion "that the working class made itself and the structuralism of Althusser and his adherents, (and) adopting instead as our guide Adam Przeworski's proposition according to Beinin that class formation is a perpetual process. [. . .] Classes as historical actors are thus the 'effects' of struggles which are structured by the totality of economic, political and ideological-cultural relations."[70] The historical experience of workers was diverse and the political cultural contest persisted. It is thus important to include the voice of Egyptian workers into the historical and class narrative, since Gramsci allows one to be a Marxist and also to be sensitive to culture.[71]

The decade of 2000 saw an increasingly active independent workers' movement rebelling against the state and its institutions, including the ETUF. The political allegiances interestingly remained with the NDP but in name only. Egyptian workers acted against the state from a "moral economy stance" and not necessarily from a rational choice or Marxist principles, according to Posusney's writings. The opposition political parties were weak and disorganized, and they had an "elitist" attitude, especially the traditional Wafd (center-right) political party, and they could not relate to the workers' needs. There were several Nasserist/socialist labor parties with differing names, but they were all small and had minimal influence.

From 1998 to 2010, there were over three million Egyptian workers who participated in 3,500 to 4,000 strikes, sit-ins, demonstrations, and protests—approximately 600 per year in 2007 and 2008. The first major strike in 2004 took place in the garment textile industry in Kafr el Dawar (near Alexandria), and since then workers' strikes and protests have not stopped. In 2004, the political national Kefaya (Enough) movement began its peaceful demonstrations. In December 2006 and then again in September 2007, the 27,000 workers of the Misr Spinning and Weaving Company in El-Mahalla and its affiliated factories went on a one-week strike for economic grievances, including low wages and a decrease in benefits like profit sharing. This shook the labor movement to its core, since the ETUF was a target of the workers' ire in addition to having incompetent management. The workers demanded improvements in "bread and butter" issues like making ends meet with the constant hike in prices of consumer goods. From 2004 until the present, the list of collective job actions is long, with strikes in practically every sector of the blue-collar and white-collar work world—chemical workers, health workers, cement workers, garment workers,

public school teachers, Al-Azhar University professors, pharmacists, journalists, and others all participated in some form of contentious action.

Concluding Remarks

The social contract began to unravel, and the commitments by the government were going unmet. Initially, the influx of renter incomes from the mid-1970s to mid-1980s allowed the regime to manage resources so that it could satisfy the public sector working class. Therefore, as the country made the transition to the market economy, the government could adhere to the social contract Nasser had struck with this class.[72] The social contract provided for job security and a living, and in return the members of this class would remain loyal to the regime, or at least not rebel.

When facing the severe strains of the fiscal crisis of the mid-1980s, the regime knew it would have to terminate the contract or at least amend some of its articles. Above all, it realized that it would have to drastically cut the public sector labor force. This was an action it would never have dared to take until it obtained another huge injection of income following the outbreak of the Persian Gulf War and signed an economic reform deal with the IMF and World Bank.[73] The government was saved financially from ruin by much welcomed infusions of funds. These funds came as a result of the American military interventions in the region and Egypt's assistance and support.

Egypt's labor movement, which had its origins in the late 1880s railway industry and public services, was active and militant, participating fully in the 1919 revolution against the British that led to Egypt's independence (at least on paper) in 1922. Nasser proposed that the People's Assembly seats would be divided between peasants and workers, giving them legislative powers, prerogatives, and political immunity. This is indeed what took place, and in return, labor gave up its rights to strike and negotiate living wages and benefits. They were sold a bill of goods—*a social contract*—that maintained the autocratic manner of rule while convincing them that they are still a part of the ruling class.

Notes

1. *Wafd* means delegation in Arabic, referring to the delegation sent to the 1919 Versailles Peace Conference.
2. Vitalis, Robert. *When Capitalists Collide: Business Conflict and the End of Empire in Egypt.* Berkeley: University of California Press, 1995.
3. Vitalis, Robert. *When Capitalists Collide: Business Conflict and the End of Empire in Egypt.* Berkeley: University of California Press, 1995: 7.
4. Beinin, Joel and Zachary Lockman. *Workers on the Nile: Nationalism, Communism, Islam, and the Egyptian Working Class, 1882–1954.* Princeton, NJ: Princeton University Press, 1987: 10–11. Print.
5. Ibid.
6. Vitalis 1995: 8.
7. Ibid.
8. Ibid.: 11–12.
9. Ibid.: 12.
10. Issawi, Charles. *Egypt an Economic and Social Analysis.* Oxford: Oxford University Press, 1947: 16.
11. Goldberg, Ellis. *Tinker, Tailor, and Textile Worker: Class and Politics in Egypt, 1930–1952.* Berkeley: University of California Press, 1986: 19, Print.

12. Ibid.: 21.
13. Ibid.: 22.
14. Ibid.
15. Ibid.
16. Vallet, Jean. *Contribution a L'étude de la Condition des Ouvriers de la Grande Industrie au Caire*. Valence: Impr. Valentinoise, 1911. Print.
17. Lockman, Zachary. *Workers and Working Classes in the Middle East: Struggles, Histories, Historiographies*. Albany: State University of New York, 1994: 99.
18. Tilly, Charles. *Social Movements, 1768–2004*. Boulder, CO: Paradigm Publishers, 2004: 54.
19. Nahas, Joseph F. *Situation économique Et Sociale Du Fellah égyptien*. Paris: A. Rousseau, 1901. Print.
20. Ibid.: 95.
21. Ibid.
22. Issawi, Charles. "Egypt Since 1800: A Study in Lop-sided Development." *The Journal of Economic History* 21 (1) (March 1961): 1–25: 5.
23. A *kantar* is the official Egyptian weight unit for measuring cotton. It corresponds to the US hundredweight, and is roughly equal to 99.05 pounds, or 45.02 kilograms. It is equal to either 157 kilograms of seed cotton or 50 kilograms of lint cotton. Schanz, Moritz. *Cotton in Egypt and the Anglo-Egyptian Sudan*. Manchester: Taylor, Garnett, Evans &, 1912. Print.
24. Issawi 1961: 5.
25. Beinin and Lockman document the details of the post-coup regime's response to a violent strike and demonstration at Kafr al Dawwar, a textile center 15 miles south of Alexandria, in their book *Workers on the Nile*, 1989: 421–426.
26. Beinin and Lockman 1987: 32.
27. Interview with Fathallah Mahrous, June 22–23, 2013, Alexandria, Egypt. Another excellent source of information is Raouf Abbas' *Al-Harakat-u-Ummalieya fi Masr 1899–1952* [*The Labor Movement in Egypt 1899–1952*], Cairo: Darul-Katib, 1968.
28. Issawi 1961: 96.
29. Ibid.
30. Ibid.
31. Bianchi, Robert. *Unruly Corporatism: Association Life in Twentieth-Century Egypt*. Oxford: Oxford University Press, 1989: 491.
32. Goldberg, Ellis. "Reading from Left to Right: The Social History of Egyptian Labor." In *The Social History of Labor in the Middle East*, ed. Ellis Goldberg. Boulder, CO: Westview, 1996: 180. Print.
33. After 1986, there was a separate head of the ETUF and another person was the minister of manpower (labor).
34. Totonchi, E. P. Laboring a Democratic Spring: The Past, Present, and Future of Free Trade Unions in Egypt. *Working USA* 14 (2011): 259–283.
35. Bellin, Eva. "Contingent Democrats: Industrialists, Labor, and Democratization in Late-Developing Countries," *World Politics*, 52 (2) (January 2000): 175–205.
36. Goldberg 1996: 180.
37. Posusney, Marsha P. *Labor and the State in Egypt—Workers, Unions, and Economic Restructuring*. New York: Columbia University Press, 1997: 12.
38. Ibid.
39. Ibid.
40. Soliman, Samer and Peter Daniel (translator). *The Autumn of Dictatorship: Fiscal Crisis and Political Change in Egypt Under Mubarak*. Stanford, CA: Stanford University Press, 2011: 157.
41. Bianchi, Robert. *Unruly Corporatism: Association Life in Twentieth-Century Egypt*. Oxford: Oxford University Press, 1989: 28.
42. Bellin 2000.
43. Lockman, Zachary (editor). *Workers and Working Classes in the Middle East: Struggles, Histories, Historiographies*. Albany, NY: State University of New York Press, 1994: 215.
44. Clement, Francoise, "Workers Protest Under Economic Liberalization in Egypt." In *Political and Social Protest in Egypt*, ed. Nicholas S. Hopkins, Cairo Papers in Social Science (Book 29). Cairo, Egypt: AUC, 2009: 103.

45. King, Stephen J. *The New Authoritarianism in the Middle East and North Africa.* Bloomington: Indiana University Press, 2009: 97.
46. These are all documented in a full report: www.ctuws.com/uploads/Books/THE-TRADE-UNION-ELECTIONS/English/FACTSs.pdf.
47. Bianchi 1989: 26.
48. Ibid.
49. Ibid.
50. Beinin and Lockman 1987: 431.
51. Ibid.
52. Ibid.
53. Ibid.: 432.
54. Ibid.
55. Ibid.: 433.
56. Ibid.: 435.
57. Ibid.: 443.
58. Ibid.: 444.
59. Ibid.
60. Ibid.: 447.
61. Posusney, Marsha Pripstein. "Collective Action and Worker's Consciousness in Contemporary Egypt." In *Workers and Working Classes in the Middle East Struggles, Histories, Historiographies*, ed. Zachary Lockman. Albany: State University of New York Press, 1994: 239, Chapter 8.
62. Ibid.: 214.
63. Ibid.: 215.
64. Ibid.: 213.
65. Beinin, Joel in Zachary Lockman (editor). *Workers and Working Classes in the Middle East Struggles, Histories, Historiographies.* Albany: State University of New York Press, 1994: 251.
66. Ibid.: 259.
67. Beinin, Joel, "Will the Real Egyptian Working Class Please Stand up?" In *Workers and Working Classes in the Middle East Struggles, Histories, Historiographies*, ed. Zachary Lockman. Albany: State University of New York Press, 1994: 262.
68. Ibid.: 263.
69. Ibid.: 266.
70. Ibid.: 262.
71. Burke III, Edmund. "The History of the Working Classes in the Middle East: Some Methodological Considerations." In *Workers and Working Classes in the Middle East Struggles, Histories, Historiographies*, ed. Zachary Lockman. Albany: State University of New York Press, 1994: 311.
72. Beinin 1994: 261–262.
73. Soliman and Daniel 2011: 157.

Part II

The Two Case Studies, Other Workers' Protests, and Socio-Economic and Cultural Framing

3 First Case Study
The Municipal Real Estate Tax Collectors

Chapter Outline:

1. History and Organization of the Municipal Real Estate Tax Collectors' Movement (Independent General Union of Real Estate Tax Authority Workers—IGURETA)

   Interview With Gamal Oweida, the Secretary-General of the IGURETA (2013)
   The Role of Independent Media

2. Repertoires of This Social Movement

   External Efforts of Support and Internal Mechanisms, Repertoires, Political Opportunities, Brokers, Inducements, Mobilizing Structures, and Collective Action Framing
   Differing Views of Effective Mobilizing Structures: Crowds and Masses
   First-Hand Accounts From RETA's Union Members
   IGURETA January 2011 Activism

3. Factors That Determined the Outcome
4. Concluding Remarks and Lessons Learned

History and Organization of the Municipal Real Estate Tax Collectors' Movement (Independent General Union of Real Estate Tax Authority Workers—IGURETA)

The creation of an independent workers' movement in Egypt set the stage for a new style of collective action, contentious politics, and leadership. These protests beginning in the 2000s were the next step in the continuum of protests against the Mubarak regime; they officially challenged the official trade union federation, ETUF. The creation of the first independent trade union since 1957 was the next step in this continuum of protests. "The mechanisms, processes, events, and episodes provide a flexible explanatory framework for dealing with such questions as how political actors form, how political identities change, and how streams of contention sometimes congeal into sustained social movements."[1] The review of the mechanisms and processes used by RETA workers and their leaders help us understand how they became a sustained social movement leading to an independent trade union.

Interview With Gamal Oweida, the Secretary-General of the IGURETA (2013)

Gamal Oweida, the secretary-general of IGURETA, was eager to share his thoughts and stories about the events leading to the creation of the first independent union since 1957. He was very proud to share a small booklet that he authored about the history of his profession and its struggle for an independent union. He said,

> Originally, within the ETUF union for finance and banking workers, there were nine locals/committees for RETA workers/employees. ETUF wanted to keep it this way since they did not want them to grow or increase in membership numbers. Also, [remaining] at nine committees would keep them weak without bargaining or political power within the larger union. When RETA activists began to organize and the ETUF rejected them, it was a big blow to the heart. Why? Still, there was the feeling that ETUF was their "labor home," even though everyone really knew it was a sham. ETUF never really truly defended their rights; it was a tool of the state.[2]

The organizing within RETA began in the Giza province and then moved on to Ismailia, Menoufiyya, El Behera, El Sharqiyya, and El Daqahliyah.

Figure 3.1 From right to left: "Hussein Megawer [head of ETUF] is chief of the thieves," "Judge those who steal workers' money"[3]

Photo taken by Hossam El-Hamalawy with his permission

On October 21, 2007, there was a protest in front of the Ministry of Finance with about 3,000 people present. A state security official called Gamal Oweida, the secretary-general of IGURETA and chided him for not informing them in advance. So Oweida wrote an open letter with all the details of who, why, when, what, and where, and he sent it to the state security representative in his tax district. "It was important to be in the open and we had nothing to hide," he said.

The protesters came from differing areas and walked to the Ministry headquarters building, and from there they walked to the Council of Ministers building on Hussein Hegazy Street with the police following. The police and the security forces complained that they were getting tired of all the walking—they were not used to walking a lot and were not physically fit.

During November 13–15, 2007, RETA employees held a protest in front of ETUF headquarters on Gala'a Street in downtown Cairo. ETUF would not let them in the building, thus closing the toilets and denying them access to drinking water—another blow. They slept outside the building and would wake up to find their faces and hands covered in black exhaust soot from the heavy traffic on that main thoroughfare and nowhere to clean up. Oweida said,

> Also, we had not learned or implemented the idea of taking shifts to protest, so we were all very tired and felt a sense of doom and gloom and defeat. This experience felt worse than on October 21 for some reason. Our silence enabled ETUF to continue in the charade.[4]

Oweida was keen to share how the social movement of protest made mistakes and learned from those mistakes, and how they used various brokers and repertoires to improve their opportunities for success. They used the independent media, particularly the newspapers *Al-Masry Al-Youm, Al-Badeel, Al-Shorouk, El Youm 7,* and others. Oweida and many other union members reiterated the value of cell phones (in Egypt they are referred to as mobile phones); they were more valuable than computers and social media to most workers. Mobile phones were one of the tools used for diffusing their message and getting members and potential members to participate in protests.

The Role of Independent Media[5]

Independent media outlets, particularly newspapers, were critical in shedding light on the plight of workers and their protests and were an important tool in keeping the independent workers' issues alive in the public eye. During an interview with Mohammed Azzouz, head of the news desk (he covered labor full-time from 2005 to 2011) at *El Masry el Youm* newspaper, he expressed the following views about how independent newspapers supported the independent workers' movement. "The mission of the newspaper, *El Masry El Youm,* as one of the first serious independent newspapers in Egypt, has been devoted to the news/issues of civil society, democracy, progressive issues, and to the defense of fundamental freedoms and liberty. It was established by a group of investors/businessmen who wanted an independent news outlet. They were not necessarily interested in managing the day-to-day operations of the newspaper and did not impose their political views. The newspaper also has an independent and balanced editorial board

that attempts to present each side of a story. Workers'/labor's stories tended to be quite obvious, i.e. present each side, and it was obvious who needed help or who was truly suffering injustice."

In 2005, Azzouz wrote his first newspaper story about a strike of workers at a yeast and glucose manufacturing factory in Maadi, a suburb of Cairo. The newspaper supported Azzouz to cover the events and write the story. Yet, when he was trying to get the owner's side of the events, he was threatened by the owner, and (someone) told him that the owner would call his bosses and get the government to shut them down. He found that the workers were indeed in a bad state of affairs. News reporting and commentary about labor became a regular feature in the newspaper. This added to the improved perception of labor's struggle for decent work and social justice. It began a societal discourse about the hardships faced by the average citizen in being able to live a decent life and provide for their families.[6]

The two big events in the independent workers' (non-ETUF aligned) struggle were the RETA employees and the El-Mahalla garment and textile factories' large strikes. It was a trial run, a rehearsal for the revolution and what would take place in Tahrir Square in January 2011. In our interview, Azzouz stated that he believes that these repertoires of protest and contention by workers had an important influence on societal discourse, the opposition, and the rest of the working class in Egypt. He also thinks that the priority of news reporting should be that of human interest and the worries of the people, and the workers' stories and protests exemplified these issues and the high level of injustice. Actually, *el Masry el Youm* received a prize in 2007–2008 from the Egyptian National Council for Human Rights for their coverage of these types of stories. In 2014, the newspaper will be celebrating ten years of existence and reporting and they hope to publish a retrospective of their history.

Azzouz was clear in his belief that workers are definitely not a special interest—they are a human interest. And to consider workers as a special interest thus marginalizes them, puts them aside, and makes them unimportant. Azzouz said,

> In 2005, another strike by asbestos workers also predicted further upheaval and protests. The workers slept on the street in front of the ETUF headquarters, and they were on strike for a long time. They got their rights and demands, so workers and people got the distinct impression that to get your rights, you have to protest in the streets. This became quite the path to take starting from 2005 to 2011. Also, the government representatives, especially Finance Minister Yousef B. Ghali, spoke with such contempt regarding the workers' state of affairs that it made you want to write headlines about this.[7]

El Masry El Youm newspaper's staff spent many days reporting on RETA's twelve-day sit-in protest in December 2007 at the Council of Ministers headquarters. One reporter actually spent the night on the street pavement with the workers. This was the first time that workers and their families were part of the protest and stayed out on the streets all night. Azzouz said, "There is no distinction or separation between politics and political action and economics—they are all related. So the workers' demands even though the discourse is economic they are speaking politics."

When Azzouz was asked about the post-2011 events and particularly the role of workers, he said, "Before the revolution, it was obvious that there was one

enemy that everyone was united against; after the revolution, it has become very confused, and thus the unity has not been protected or supported." He continued saying that CTUWS[8]

> played a very important role in supporting the independent workers' movement. They wanted and demanded their rights and for social justice so this was a fight between rights, and justice, versus injustice. Before the revolution, the MBs were allies of the Marxist Coordinating Committee of Workers (another NGO that supported independent workers) that was sponsored by the Hisham Mubarak Law Center[9] and made alliances with the political left opposition parties and organization. After the revolution—the MB became fiercer in their quest for power and dropped their alliances with workers' organizations.

Azzouz continued to explain,

> Before the revolution—the workers had the loudest voice of discontent in society and they acted on it. After the revolution, the workers' voice got lost in the din of so many voices of discontent so they are not noticeably on the scene.

Azzouz made comments about the current state of affairs (summer 2013). He said,

> The MB are so eager to take control that they are making so many mistakes! And they are not including the opposition before they make decisions. They have alienated so many persons, lost the trust of so many by their stupidity and hunger for power. They have even failed in pushing the Islamic Nation, or the *"umma"* agenda. That is why the Salafis are so antagonistic to the MB. In one very short year since May 2012, people's condition of daily life has deteriorated so much in a very obvious manner.[10]

Azzouz recommended reviewing the recordings of the (one all-night) session of the Shura Council's Constituent Assembly—CA (to draft a new constitution) during their deliberations on the constitution. The current minister of manpower asked for a clause in the constitution to be included to control, i.e. manage, trade unions. The speaker of the Constituent Assembly, Hossam El Geriyany, said, "No, leave it alone; it really does not matter." According to Azzouz, "the MB has had a history of treachery and alliances with the enemy [perceived enemies of Egyptian nationalism], including the British occupation in the twentieth century. The Muslim Brotherhood are not to be trusted," he said. "They are continuing the Mubarak policies and methods using sterner, more stupid, and more tactless ways," said Azzouz.

Azzouz recounted the famous statement made by a revered Egyptian Islamist philosopher, Mohammed Abdu, in the early twentieth century after his travels overseas. "We need to learn from Abdu," Azzouz said. He continued,

> Abdu said upon his return to Egypt that he saw nations that were not Muslim yet he saw and found Muslims and now back in Egypt, he saw a Muslim nation without any Muslims. So, we need to realize the best practices of

other transitioning countries' experiences regarding the challenges faced and the rewards gained. [. . .] I worry about the Tamarod (rebel) movement day on June 30, 2013.

Azzouz said as we ended our meeting, "there will be blood spilled again in the streets." At this point, one could regard his statements in 2013 as rather prophetic of the ensuing events.

Repertoires of This Social Movement

External Efforts of Support and Internal Mechanisms, Repertoires, Political Opportunities, Brokers, Inducements, Mobilizing Structures, and Collective Action Framing

It can be argued that the Middle East, including Egypt, was a spectator of the trend of protest mobilizations and social movements. However, Egypt has been rich in nonviolent social contestation movements and mobilizations, particularly in the trade union arena. The labor movement does not initially resemble traditional social movements or necessarily fit within the traditional social movement theory. However, it is a social, economic, and political (collective action) movement, and given the opportunity, it did contribute to the uprising that removed Mubarak from power in January–February 2011.

RETA employees were the next major collective protest action in the series of worker protests. The first RETA employees' protest was carried out by one branch located in Giza in September 2007; they were angry over very low salaries and bad working conditions. "They earned 200–400 Egyptian pounds [$32–$64] per month, about one quarter of the pay of sales tax collectors"[11] at the Ministry of Finance in Cairo. It was a small protest, but it gained considerable attention, enabling other branches to contact those activists and slowly develop a following, leading to a nationwide movement. "Two factors enabled this diffusion: the support of independent media and the core activists' extensive experience in political and union organizing."[12] The one-day strike was widely covered on the front page by major independent newspapers, *El Masry el Youm* and *Al-Badil*, which reported 5,000 people participating in the strike. The workers chanted, "Our colleagues[13] earn ten times our salaries, and I cannot afford to buy bread."

The next important internal factor was the significant political and union organizing and leadership skills of this movement. Kamal Abu Eita, the head of the office in Giza who then became RETA employees' union president,

> was a prominent member of the Kefaya movement, a founder of the new-Nasserist Karama Party and president of the Giza local union before losing his seat in the fraudulent ETUF union 2006 elections. His skills in mobilization, negotiations and public speaking were crucial to the tax collectors' success.[14]

Another important advantage these workers possessed was the ability to temporarily suspend tax collection, directly threatening the government's revenue from real estate property taxes, which was quite substantial.

Leadership in social movements is essential if not critical to developing solidarity and mobilizing activists even in well-developed collective action-type organizations and movements such as trade unions. However, there has been a relative inattention to what leaders actually do. Barker, Colin, Johnson, and Lavalette, in their study titled *Leadership and Social Movements*, remind us of a few points to keep in mind: (1) Avoid the "great man" theories that give little proper weight to both circumstances in which movements develop and the part played by members. (2) No one wants to revive conservative agitator theories, which imply that there would be no strikes, no militant movement activity, were it not for the troublemakers who cause them. We must pay attention to the real grievances that cause and motivate movements, and we must avoid treating members as mindless sheep who just follow. Yet, we still have to recognize that a leader has to take up the cause, explain the details, and articulate solutions. (3) Meyer and Tarrow suggest that thinking about movement leadership was once dominated by older movement forms like the "traditional mass organizations of the European left," with their permanent presences, bureaucratic structures, and centralized leaderships. Looser, more decentralized networks of activists and leaders have replaced these traditional mass organizations.[15] (4) Leadership has been associated with a particular type of organization. (5) Underlying patterns of social movement theorizing have tended to divert attention from issues to do with leadership. The collective behavior tradition, stressing irrational movement, could never explore leadership questions well. It was displaced by resource mobilization and political process approaches, which reveal a strong structuralist bias, paying less attention to actors' purposive agency and is thus about leadership.[16]

There are several kinds or types of leadership: unavoidable leadership, leadership as an activity, leadership as a dialogical relationship, and leadership purpose as guiding force. There are also the contexts and resources of leadership: personal and structural resources. Several questions need to be asked: Who actually leads? Can leadership be democratic? Regardless of the type of leadership—democratic and inclusive, bureaucratic, exclusivist, leadership forms and protest cycles—leadership does matter.[17] It is important to recognize for this research endeavor that charismatic leadership in the Egyptian case was present and played a critical role, as indicated previously.

Differing Views of Effective Mobilizing Structures: Crowds and Masses

In terms of how crowds and masses are viewed as effective or not, there are

two main competing theoretical-political interpretations those of Marx and Weber. Weber tended to view crowds and masses with trepidation rather than expectation. They were seen as aspects of social transition, perhaps necessary, but at best temporary. His studies of charismatic authority and styles of leadership point more to the dangers of collective behavior than to any positive potential (Weber 1978:241ff. and 1376–7). Regarding the labor movement, Weber preferred the "mature" politics of organized trade unions

and political parties to the mass politics of social movements (Mommsen and Osterhammel 1987).[18]

Weber also put a lot of emphasis on the role that organization and leadership as strategic actors play in the effectiveness of social movements as strategic actors.

> Focusing on the relations between types of leadership and forms of organiza-tions, [Roberto] Michels argued that the routinization of charismatic leader-ship flowed from the establishment of bureaucratic structures. Both were seen as necessary aspects of the maturation of social movements in modern society, by which dynamic social forces were transformed into stagnant, top-heavy institutions, where an oligarchy of pragmatic "petty bourgeois" lead-ers concerned themselves more with reproducing their own power than with changing society. This particular outcome of the institutionalization of mass movements has come to be called the "Weber-Michels model" (see Zald and McCarthy 1987).[19]

On the other hand, Marxists have tended to view social movements as signs of the eminent decline or even collapse of the repressive capitalist system.

> Marxists have tended to view social movements with expectations and antic-ipation, signs of an impending collapse of an existing (repressive) capitalist order and as the potential source of its replacement by socialism. Move-ments for Marxists were thus taken as collective expressions of discontent and potential bases for social change (Eyerman 1984). The model of the collective actor here was that of the "self-activating class" rather than the faceless mass [. . .] what they represent in terms of their social basis, their class composition. This in turn is related to their political potential. [. . .] What mass movements require, for Marxists, is not so much explanation as evaluation and fundamental social change and about the possibilities for influencing them in those directions.[20]

The connection between social democracy, labor movements, social move-ments and

> the existence of a strong, institutionalized, reformist social democratic labor movement in all the countries of Western Europe affected the way social movements were conceived by social scientists and perhaps more impor-tantly, the very possibility for "new" social movements to take form.[21]

Tilly explains "the collective action typical of social movements as moving from 'organization to mobilization' of resources around shared interests and, finally, to the realization of effective action in specific opportunity structures."[22] The labor movement precisely coincides with Tilly's definition as a collective action/move-ment moving from organization to mobilization with shared interests, resources, and the recognition that they can effectively affect certain opportunity structures that present themselves.

Another internal factor of their success as a social movement was solidarity. There was a strong group identity among the RETA workers—they were aware

and conscious of belonging to the same group with the same grievances. This group identity provided the strength to confront their employer (the government) and make demands. However, group identity is not sufficient for mobilization to take place. "Group solidarity provides the motivation for collective action by linking the welfare of the group to a program of political or social change, and by creating the expectation that the group will act cohesively to bring about that change."[23] The RETA workers believed that they could succeed using collective action because they had a legitimate grievance, a reasonable remedy, and a strong show of solidarity. So, collective action with solidarity and strong group identity are the markers on the road to success.

Diffusion was the next factor that turned the relatively small protest in Giza into a national movement. Leaders in RETA offices in the Delta region, Mr. Abdallah and Mr. Labib, traveled to Giza to meet with Abu Eita and other leaders to learn more about the protest and its goals. Abdallah and Labib became "brokers" after being thoroughly convinced of the mission and goals of the protest movement. Brokers are people who help disseminate ideas to collective action.[24] They were both enthusiastic, and their local branch offices held protest strikes shortly thereafter. These protests then encouraged offices in Fayoum and Minya provinces to contact the main Giza activists. They actively used the independent media to get their message out and to frame their issues of contention. The official Bank and Finance Workers Union, an affiliate of the ETUF, fought them every step of the way and tried to use tactics of fear with threats of firings to dissuade the rank-and-file workers from participating in these protests.

Next, the RETA employees' activist leadership, which now took on the name of the Higher Committee for the General Strike, issued a press release threatening the government if their demands were not met, saying RETA would go on strike in all the municipalities and would gather in front of the Ministry of Finance in downtown Cairo. The nationwide strike took place on October 21, 2007, and a large crowd demonstrated in front of the Ministry of Finance with hundreds shouting, "Hey ya [you] Ghali [minister of finance], come down from your ivory tower." Once they were told that the minister was out of the country, they decided to march to the headquarters of the Cabinet of Ministers to get more publicity for their cause. Both Al Jazeera and the private Egyptian satellite station Dream broadcast images of hundreds of RETA employees marching boldly down Cairo boulevards.[25] The media exposure further added to the diffusion and framing of their message, and it increased participation of many more employees who believed in the cause. They felt that they could legitimately succeed in achieving their goal of significantly increasing their salaries.

Another mechanism that the RETA Higher Committee used was the establishment of a regular newsletter that they called[26] نوبة صحيان a moment/time of awakening. This newsletter [27] was very helpful for diffusing information, news, and updates on the negotiations or lack thereof with the government. This established an open, democratic form of communication with members and future members. Through its distribution, the activists were able to organize and bring in more supporters.

The IGURETA Higher Committee then attempted to negotiate with Minister of Finance Youssef Boutros Ghali. They were repeatedly dismissed by security officers and told that the minister was busy negotiating with the IMF. The leadership tested the resolve of their followers several times by holding sit-ins in front

of the ETUF headquarters, and hundreds came. In early December 2007, after failure of direct negotiations and the ETUF's refusal to support their grievances and fight on their behalf, the leadership called for the large national strike and "sit-in," yet with a slight deception on the location. This deception was done so as to not alert the security forces of the actual location of the intended strike and to not scare off the rank and file. The brokers in each of the RETA branch offices around the country ensured that everyone participating in the large strike was prepared to spend several days in Cairo.

Slogans and chants used by the protesting RETA employees clearly defined their cause and framed their demands. The most commonly used words were "Justice عدالة and Parity تكافؤ" in addition to "Equality مساواة, " referring to their demand for wage equality with the other employees who do the same work at the Ministry of Finance in Cairo and are not associated with the local municipal councils. "We are sitting here, not leaving, and we have justice on our side." Another major theme in the framing of their message and demands was the use of the word "Poverty" and how they were not able to meet their children's needs (which is debilitating to the pride of any Egyptian father and mother). "يا حرام" حكومة، الشعب كله جعان "Shame on you—government; the people are all hungry" was another chant that was repeatedly used invoking poverty and hunger.

Another chant was "we divorce you thrice," which refers to their quest for a free and independent union divorced from the control of government, ministry of manpower, and the ETUF—three. RETA leaders also invoked Allah (God) despite their strong, secular-leftist political ideology and views. This was not a religious versus non-religious debate—it was a matter of culture and appealing to all. "Allahu Akbar الله أكبر" and swearing in the name of Allah "نقسم بالله العظيم" that "we will not return to our homes or our workplaces until our demands are met. We will sit here and not collect taxes until you recognize our demands and fulfill them. We want our rights only and not more or less. That is the will of the people," they would say. When RETA leaders were trying to meet with the minister and he was refusing in December 2007, they chanted, "The minister meets with investors in the 'Smart Village,' so show some intelligence/smarts and meet with us too—or do we smell bad?"[28] In the RETA employees' protests, they often used a mix of economic and political themes: "Free Unions = Free Nation," "Justice and Equity," and "The government is challenging us and we are staying not leaving." They even invoked former President Mubarak by saying, "Ye President, the one who carried out the first air strike, see the mess with your tax authority!"; "Long Live Egypt"; and "We are not begging for anything." It is interesting to note the connection between the economic and political themes; these are workers who still believed in the political system, and even in Mubarak, but were calling for economic relief and improvements in their daily lives. The implications of these statements are that the workers were indeed challenging the regime by holding such protests calling for decent work[29] with decent wages, yet not necessarily challenging the regime's existence—at least not at this moment in time. However, this discourse began to change in 2010 leading to 2011.

In reviewing this social movement's discourse and framing of demands, one has to discuss one of Egypt's influential colloquial poets and icons—Ahmed Fouad Negm. The RETA protesting workers regularly used his work, for example:

Who Are They and Who Are We? هما مين و إحنا مين *(An Excerpt)*
by Ahmed Fouad Negm, Translated by Walaa Quisay

Who are they and who are we?
They are the princes and the Sultans
They are the ones with wealth and power
And we are the impoverished and deprived
Use your mind, guess . . .
Guess who is governing whom?
Who are they and who are we?
We are the constructing, we are the workers
We are Al-Sunna, We are Al-Fard
We are the people both height and breadth
From our health, the land raises
And by our sweat, the meadows turn green
Use your mind, guess . . .
Guess who serves whom?
Who are they and who are we?
They are the princes and the Sultans[30]

A representative of the people's discontent and joy (at times) was the popular poet Ahmed Fouad Negm (1929–2013). He was the people's poet, satirist, and consciousness. He wrote what was in the people's hearts and minds that they could not say out loud. Negm was jailed for several years, and he spoke irreverently through his poetry written in colloquial Arabic for the impoverished underclass.

> Over four decades, Mr. Negm wrote verse in colloquial Arabic that channeled the privations and grim humor that were part of working-class life. His fearless and often mocking critiques of power made him a folk hero, but also earned him a total of 18 years in jail.[31]

The quote from Negm's aforementioned poem is indicative of Egyptian society's view of those who ruled them: the sultans and the princes. This poem was regularly recited in the protest in Hussein Higazi Street in 2007 and then again in Tahrir Square in January 2011.

Galal Amin, emeritus professor of economics at the American University in Cairo and a well-respected commentator, wrote that sociologists were complaining about the increase in corruption and disrespect for the law with an obvious lack of work ethic. Violence was increasing and material values were establishing themselves over socially useful labor that was losing its social status and prestige. The quality of life in the city was declining with an increase in air pollution, overcrowding, and deteriorating health services and education, while the villages were becoming units of consumption, not production. Economists noted the severe imbalances and distortions—a severe deficit, a growing external debt, an imbalance in state budget, high unemployment, an inefficient large public sector, and too much investment by the government in unproductive areas such as luxury housing and import trade. Political observers noted that Egyptians' sense

of loyalty and belonging to their native land had weakened with a high understandable pre-occupation with daily life needs rather than a larger vision of Arab
nationalism or a commitment to national development. There was also a strong
condemnation of increased political and economic dependence on the US and
Europe.[32] Those who monitor intellectual life and national culture pointed to a
decline in societal mores, values, and ethics with the spread of "low culture" and
the growth of religious extremism. However, "cultures are limited, time-specific
constructs that are learned and constantly in a state of flux"[33]—culture changes
or is influenced as a result of the introduction of new forms of mass media and
communication. So, to pinpoint specific cultural impact is difficult since it is ever
changing, particularly popular culture.

Fahmy has documented many changes in the Egyptian cultural landscape. He
confirms that while the literacy rate is quite low, "it was newspapers (especially
the satirical press), [that] recorded and performed colloquial Egyptian songs, and
the vernacular theater that were the principal and most effective mediators and
broadcasters of cultural ideologies, including the idea of a collective Egyptian
identity."[34] Workers were in the heart of this endeavor and used authentic Egyptian cultural icons for cementing solidarity and protest purposes. Their use of
colloquial Egyptian Arabic solidifies the local Egyptian patriotism—*wataniyya*.
Colloquial Egyptian is typically Egyptian and thus nationally exclusive.

> As Joel Beinin notes the mere decision to write in colloquial has often
> been perceived as a political act associated with a nationalist program of
> populism, anticlericalism (not irreligion), and local Egyptian wataniyya as
> opposed to Pan-Arabism—qawmiyya.[35]

Workers embody the heart and soul of colloquial Egyptian Arabic—'*ammiyya*,
which comes from the Arabic word for public. During protests, workers used
leaflets, slogans, hand-held signs with their demands written on them, songs,
chants, and music using drums and *el oud* (the lute). They used the daily vernacular and even jokes to communicate their grievances in a clever and catchy (at
times even funny) manner. They also used props such as coffins, black armbands,
and empty pots and pans to demonstrate a particular point. The workers used
the average person's language to communicate grievances and to challenge the
regime.

In December 2007,

> ten thousand municipal real estate municipal tax collectors and their family
> members held a 'sit-in' for eleven days in front of the Ministry of Finance
> in downtown Cairo. The strike ended when the minister agreed to a bonus
> equal to two months' pay and raised the wages of the municipal tax collec-
> tors by 325%, giving them parity with those employed by the General Tax
> Authority [in Cairo].[36]

Men and women RETA workers held this "sit-in" for eleven days, and for many
of the women, it was the first time they had spent the night outside of their
homes. Beinin points out that this case was exceptional because these workers
were considered white-collar civil servants that were part of the government
service apparatus and not blue-collar factory workers. Also, they had forged a

national movement linked with labor-supporting NGOs such as the CTUWS, opposition political parties such as the Karama Party, and the media. Their leader, Kamal Abu Eita, had many years of practical organizing and political experience and was able to recruit many local activists around the country. In addition, his charisma was infectious, and his ability to listen, organize, and lead was impeccable.

The Egyptian government security apparatus' response was generally measured and different from its dealing with overtly political movements calling for political reforms.

> Strict security measures have always been adopted in Egypt when dealing with any demonstrations seeking political reform. But with striking workers the government has, instead, followed a more careful and tactful strategy. The security approach has been replaced with the intervention of executive officials to meet workers' demands.[37]

Adopting a hard line against workers might backfire, so they were still trying to hold together the myth of workers and peasants together governing or legislating thorough the People's Assembly.

Despite the economic heavyweight El-Mahalla al-Kubra garment and textile workers going on strike earlier in 2006–2007 and making some wage gains, it was the RETA workers that ultimately created an effective social movement leading to an independent union. The El-Mahalla strike committee's leadership became divided, and they were not able to sustain their gains and grow them into a national movement to lead Egyptian workers to massive collective action against the government. "So contrary to McAdam, McCarthy, and Zald's assertions (1996),[38] it was not necessary and in most cases not possible to create an enduring organizational structure to sustain collective action."[39] I concur with Beinin's conclusion that a class-based (worker) social movement had successfully asserted its public presence in an authoritarian state that had imposed severe restrictions on freedom of association.

From December 2007 to December 2008, the RETA workers' social movement had to deal with many legal and verbal attacks in the media leveled at them by the Ministry of Finance, Ministry of Manpower, and the officially sanctioned ETUF. The contentious workers' social movement continued to be active.

In 2008, one year later, the 55,000-member independent trade union of the workers in the Municipal Real Estate Tax Authority was created. After the successful increase in wages, activists around the country took the initiative to begin a petition drive to see if there was an interest to convert the High Committee for General Strike, an organizing committee, to an independent union. The results were overwhelmingly in support of creating an independent union. So on December 20, 2008, drawing on its newly acquired strength, the Independent General Union of Real Estate Tax Authority Workers (IGURETA) was officially formed. It was the first independent union in Egypt since 1957. "IGURETA lawyer Hisham Muhammadayn was not shy about challenging the ETUF's monopoly over labor representation, arguing that 'the Egyptian constitution and the international treaties ratified by Egypt give workers the right to create independent organizations.'"[40] Why was this movement successful? Internally, because of clever and tested political expertise and wisdom; supportive internal networks among Egyptian civil society

organizations, such as human rights organizations, lawyers' groups, and others; and consistent reporting by the media; and externally, international labor support led to its success. The combination and coordination of both the internal and external capabilities worked well in addition to the pressure created by USAID-funded democracy and governance programs. "Once the workers start organizing collectively in a structure that can voice their plight, frustrations, exploitation and oppression, and channel these into a striking force [. . .] then nothing can stand in the face of the labor movement."[41]

After the creation of the first independent union at RETA, several other independent unions were established, inspired by RETA employees. "By the time of the uprising that toppled Mubarak, two other independent unions—one of the health care workers and one of teachers—had been established."[42] In the midst of the January 2011 uprising, Abu Eita, with several other independent unions, formed the first independent trade union federation to rival the officially sanctioned ETUF. The Egyptian Federation of Independent Trade Unions (EFITU) at its founding claimed an affiliated membership of around 1.4 million workers with a membership of one hundred independent unions. In addition, it has an affiliate of an 8.5 million-member retirees' association, and EIFTU's president is Kamal Abu Eita. By August 2011, the number of independent unions had reached around 200, representing about two million workers.[43]

First-Hand Accounts From RETA's Union Members[44]

In several meetings with members of the first independent trade union in Egypt, one gets the sense of great pride and accomplishment. Mahmoud,[45] one of the many members interviewed, spoke a lot about *"tarabot"* ترابط, which in English means "bonding, connection, solidarity" among workers and people. This connection that binds them, he said, "is the common grievance or worry that we share that brings us even closer together and garners deeper solidarity. So, repression is another binding factor that they all shared".

> First, we felt alone and then we found that first, we are bound together in one mission, we are connected; and we share many of the worries, troubles, and grievances. At the beginning, we felt that there was no hope for real change, or to change the regime—maybe we could change one law or one policy at a time. It was small-scale thinking, nothing big since we were not after substantial change all at once [. . .] one step at a time. We just could not imagine a large massive change. We just wanted to eat, feed our families, and live a decent life.[46]

Mahmoud continues to recount the union's history and their feelings:

> At the beginning in 2007, it was the RETA employees who were orphans and left out of the system in the Ministry of Finance. We were relegated to the provinces and with very low salaries. So our first battle was putting us against the Ministry of Finance. In 2007, we discovered the connection (the tarabot) between us, and (it was) that spirit of tarabot that led us to 2011 with many stops along the way. We were working, fighting, and doing all of

this for our children and their future. We were missing "dignity," tarabot, i.e. togetherness and connection with each other. Banding together as a social movement to fight for our principled cause brought us that missing tarabot. During this time from 2007 to 2011, every sector of Egyptian society was present on the protest scene and active, driven by the need for dignity and tarabot with each other.

Mahmoud spoke carefully describing their search for, or the re-establishment of, their dignity as a people, and as a nation created this connection, tarabot, or solidarity.

Another issue of concern was how workers felt that they were constantly being insulted. Let us focus on insult for a moment, since it is an important part of the workers' discourse—in Arabic: إهانة, تحقير, مسبة, شتيمة, أذى and/or an affront إهانة, مذلة; an umbrage إهانة, أغصان ظليلة; an offense إستياء, امتعاض, إهانة, إساءة, جنحة, إهانة, هجوم, إثم جريمة; and an indignity إهانة, إذلال, معاملة مهينة ظل. These are all sentiments expressed to me by Mahmoud and other union members gathered in the room at the union head-quarters, and we talked about those feelings and how they motivated their protests. Mahmoud said,

> When you felt that your own country and its leader [referred to as the father of the nation] treats you with such indignity, in Egypt and outside [stories about bad treatment overseas by others and Embassy], then there is a huge loss of confidence in the ability to get rights.

However, this changed with small steps leading to larger ones of protest and demanding rights until they were able to take the big leap and establish the first independent trade union of workers. Mahmoud continued to recount their story; he outlined the protests (see text box), which contributed to cracks, deterioration, and weakness in the ruling government of Mubarak: "We had the following aspects that helped our cause or contributed to our need to protest," said Mahmoud.

> First, privatization that was conducted in a corrupt manner also played a big role in influencing and inciting the above series of protests. Second, there was the influential leadership under Kamal Abu Eita whose charisma is infectious and his leadership skills are excellent. Third, there was the weakening of the state control mechanisms over us such as the state security (or at least the perception) and that of the police; and we began not to be afraid as much. Fourth, the military would not accept Mubarak's son, Gamal, to take over and inherit the presidency"[47]

2004–2005: The Kefaya movement
2006: El-Mahalla protests and strikes
2007: RETA workers protests
2008: More El-Mahalla garment and textile workers protests
2009–2010: Many more workers' protests/strikes in practically every sector of the economy
2011: Revolution (uprising)

The state security mechanisms that Mahmoud was referring to had indeed not practiced the brutal norm of repression, and this was viewed as a "weakness" of the state starting in 2006 and through their sit-in in 2008. As for his comment regarding the military's non-acceptance of Mubarak's son Gamal as the next president of Egypt, this had been the word on the streets for several years. Gamal was not a military man, and the talk in the coffee shops, or "*qahwas*," where many political discussions take place, was that the military establishment would never accept him. Since 1952, a military man has always ruled Egypt. An article by Roll[48] highlighted how the military would have great difficulty with a Gamal Mubarak presidency, especially with his neoliberal economic ideas. Roll explained that the "new guard" promoted by Gamal and his businessmen allies

> stands for an economic course that benefits the business elite and restricts the role of the state within the economy. This hurts the interests of the old guard, whose most important source of power has been the state, including the inflated public sector and bureaucracy"[49]

The military remained neutral in this battle between the new and old guard and was concerned about protecting its economic power and political position.

> There are several reasons for this neutrality. First, President Mubarak has worked assiduously at cultivating political neutrality and absolute loyalty to the president in the military for 30 years, and it has become an ingrained habit. Second, many officers might share the concerns of the old guard regarding the new guard agenda, which would lead logically to eventual limits on the power of the military and its many economic and other perquisites. Third, there are many personal connections between the old guard and the military leadership. Zakaria Azmi and Safwat al-Sharif, for example, have military backgrounds and are from the same generation as Director of General Intelligence Omar Suleiman, with whom they have worked for decades. Finally, there might well be individual ambitions within the military regarding the presidency; the name most often raised in this context is Air Marshal Ahmed Muhammad Shafiq, the former Egyptian Air Force commander and current Minister for Civil Aviation.[50]

A conversation for several hours with Wael Mohamed Abu Bakr, Mohamed Sayed Ahmed (Sharqiyya province), Salwa Ahmed Abdel Mageed (Ismailia), and Ashraf Abdel Aziz Gehad (Giza) highlighted the following topics: (1) rights and a belief in getting ones' rights was a statement often repeated; (2) knowledge was the basis for every action to get rights and fight for rights; (3) the leadership and charisma of Kamal Abu Eita and was important to the movement; (4) they had no fear in fighting for their rights because it was for their children; (5) what was the worst that could happen? They were already in a bad situation; (6) the independent media played a very good and important role; and (7) the naysayers would say that state security would come after them, no one will hear them from jail, they would not change anything, and here was no hope for change.

The RETA union members mentioned above spent the rest of the time describing the details of the December 2007 sit-in that lasted twelve days in front of the

Figure 3.2 "Megawer & Shehata (leaders of the ETUF) are divorced three times! The Independent union in Aswan, Menoufiyya and Qwessna (provinces)"

Photo taken by Hossam el-Hamalawy and posted on Arabawy blogsite www.arabawy.org; used with his written permission

Figure 3.3 Kamal Abu Eita is the former leader of the RETA independent union, and the (former) minister of manpower (labor)

Photo taken by Hossam el-Hamalawy and posted on Arabawy blogsite www.arabawy.org; used with his written permission

Figure 3.4 RETA workers/employees from Suez (city at the end of the Suez Canal) during the sit-in in front of the Cabinet of Ministers building in Cairo on Hussein Hegazy Street

Figure 3.5 Workers protesting in front of Cabinet of Ministers building on Hussein Hegazy Street, **Cairo**, Egypt

Council of Ministers building on Hussein Hegazi Street in downtown Cairo—the following is a description of this turning point event in December 2007.

They started to recount many details about how they organized themselves and how they got to Cairo for the twelve-day sit-in. Starting on December 3, 2007, "We went to the Council of Ministers and began our sit-in for twelve days, slowly building up our courage in phases until Hussein Higazy Street was full of people chanting, singing, and protesting!" said Ashraf.

In the Sharqiyya province, they started with fifty-three people who boarded mini-vans and buses, and on the road, they picked up more and more people on the way to Cairo. There were hundreds of other workers doing the same thing in other provinces around the country. Abu Eita's role was critical, especially when he was negotiating with the authorities during the sit-in. He would always say he needed to check with his members before an agreement was reached. Wael quoted that a "one-thousand-mile journey begins with one step," and "in unity there is strength." Wael continued with saying, "When we die, Allah will ask us, 'How come you did not fight for your rights and demand your rights?' We would be judged poorly if we did not advocate for our rights."

They further elaborated on the strategy of getting protesters to the Hussein Higazi Street in downtown Cairo. Taking a large bus to Cairo would get attention, so using mini-buses was the best way to move people, plus the bus driver of a large bus would be afraid of being stopped by police checkpoints along the road. They were dropped off several blocks away from the Council of Ministers headquarters and walked the rest of the way. Each group coming from outside of Cairo took a different path to get to Hussein Higazi Street. They came as small groups, which grew and grew in numbers over a few hours.

An interesting anecdote they shared with me was that in the early morning hours when they were conducting their sit-in, bunches of fresh flowers would be delivered to the Council of Minister's building to be displayed in the ministers' offices. They said that in Egypt there are "people who smell the flowers and there are people who are sitting on the ground smelling the dirt."[51] In those early mornings, they watched silently as fresh flowers were delivered to the ministers' offices while protesters were sleeping on the street. There were tremendous differences between workers sleeping, eating, and sitting in the street and the Cabinet Ministers getting fresh flowers for their offices delivered, despite what was going on outside their headquarters. The optics of this did not look good at all and further incensed the protesting workers, whose salaries could not pay for daily fresh flowers and could barely put food on the table for their families. The dichotomy was stark and shameful.

"We want our rights! We are not leaving without our rights!" "We will not be sold," Salwa said. "I would lose my voice from shouting slogans, so I would write them down on paper so others would chant; we would sing the national anthem daily and wave the flag." Salwa continued, "With each day, more and more (people) came to join us, bringing the keys to their offices, which meant the office was closed and no taxes were being collected!" The police surrounded them; however, they did not attack them, and there was even a tacit bit of support. People living in the apartment buildings on the street opened their homes and offered their bathrooms for the protesters, and they helped a lot. They were cheering on the protesters. After the sit-in was concluded, the RETA workers

went to the apartments in every building in the street and presented them with a rose and gratitude.

More slogans chanted by the workers.

"Made of steel/iron, each day we increase in numbers." "Here are the keys, we are closed and no more taxes being collected." The protesters role-played the death of RETA by pretending to have a body wrapped in a shroud and then carried it in a funeral procession (Ahmed played the role of the dead body, and he was very proud to do so). The RETA union members told me with pride that RETA is a very old institution; it was established during the rule of Mohamed Ali in the nineteenth century.

Wael continued,

> the ILO Conventions that Egypt signed have to be respected, and that includes the freedom to create and establish independent trade unions. So, we became a role model for many others in Egypt. This is a responsibility I carry for me, for my children, and for the future generations, to sustain this action and fight corruption in the government.[52]

Salwa added,

> Transparency is needed. There were 42,000 versions of Kamal Abu Eita in the new RETA union (in) all of us. I have become a new, different human being with a feeling of being more powerful—(it's) an increase in faith that translates into an increase in power. We demand, we ask politely for our rights, and I have faith that our demands moved from a specific demand for just one group to a larger demand for all and for more people.
>
> We started small, and then by end of the twelve days we had 13,000 persons on the Hussein Higazy Street. Slowly but surely we were building for the big confrontation in Tahrir Square starting on January 28, 2011; we set the stage. [. . .] We had a tradition that we do not raise our voice to our father (Mubarak), and initially we did not want to remove him, but we just wanted reform and what was owed us, our rights. But that changed! We should have had a new and better constitution before the elections for president in 2012; that was the SCAF's mistake.[53]

In the RETA protests, they decided to stay outside in the street because they were afraid that if they were inside an office building, a mischievous person could set a light to a stack of papers and then it would be blamed on the RETA protesters. The use of cell phones was a double-edged sword. First, the authorities and security forces used cell phones to take photos to intimidate union members and leaders. Second, it was an amazing organizing tool that RETA organizers and workers used regularly to send messages, check on each other, and take videos and photos for social media and blogsites.

The union members I met with told me that RETA management used the technique of moving union activists' and leaders' workplaces to other offices far away from the person's home. "Death is preferable to living as a coward" was the motto for one of the RETA union leaders who was formerly in the army as a ranger. The concept of the individual versus the group or the collective came up again in our conversation. They reaffirmed the need and importance of unifying

large numbers of workers, so when you have a large group, the employer will agree to the demands and needs of workers. Many workers were encouraged when they saw others around them who started talking; they developed the inside energy to overcome being forced down, or the concept of *"El Kabt"* in Arabic.

> We started small and then slowly but surely started to grow while state security was present in each tax collection district. It did not deter or stop us. There are about 350 tax districts in Egypt. The number of tax districts differs per population and amount of real estate property, including agricultural land per province. It is not a uniform number.[54]

IGURETA January 2011 Activism

The Cairo RETA group was the first to participate on January 25, 2011, according to Mohamed Abou Ayyash from Belbees.

> We were concerned with the group welfare versus just the individual. With the garment and textile workers, state security tried to break the workers' cohesion and lured/bribed (them) to [. . .] feed the individual interest [. . .] divide and conquer was the theme. Feed us and we will not complain.[55]

At the beginning, there were a few activists immediately accused of being members of the MB.

> First, I felt that I was just a body they [could] cut up with no feelings or spirit and could not breathe. Jail me, and I will not feel anything. I am just a body with no soul or spirit. Gave up my fate to Allah and appealed to Allah to save us. Allah is with us because he is always with what is just, and what is right. Jews, Christians, and Muslims have belief and faith, so they will succeed. I am talking about jihad within the self to make oneself a better person and far away from taking any bribes.

He began to recount events immediately before January 25, starting on January 18, when there were protests at the journalists' syndicate building. It was much later that the MB came down to Tahrir Square organized as a group. The following interview conducted during my field research in June–July 2013 further supports and highlights the events, mechanisms, and repertoires for collective action used by these workers as a social movement. In our interview, Mahmoud continued to say,

> Then Tunisia gave us the needed push to go forward. Tunis made our revolution come faster. The important events in our revolution were January 25–27, 2011, with no violence in Tahrir by the government; then came 28 January, a big day with protests all over the country, especially in Ismailiya and Suez, the cities along the Suez Canal. The protests started outside of the center Cairo and marched to the center. So, it was decentralized and then became centralized. First, starting in Suez, Ismailia, El Mahalla and then onto Cairo where there were clashes in these cities first.

Please note that from January 25 to 27 there were no MBs to be found anywhere, and then on January 28, the MB decided to join in and thus made their appearance.[56]

Traditionally, social movements function within the sphere of NGOs, political parties, interest groups, and lobbyists. The independent labor movement in Egypt used different tools. It was not allied or associated with a political party per se and was not a savvy adherent to traditional lobbying methods. Its history and social class hamper the labor movement in Egypt. Despite using different mechanisms, brokers, and frames, the independent labor movement succeeded in galvanizing support and attracting student organizations and other civil protest movements to support their cause. The independent labor movement was known to be weak and not well connected to the echelons of traditional social oppositional movements in Egypt.

Traditional social opposition movements included a few political parties with historic roots, such as the Wafd Party, professional syndicates, human rights and legal aid organizations such as the Hisham Mubarak Center, and labor NGOs that supported workers such as CTUWS and the Land Center. "Political parties often played a minor role in a popular upsurge, mobilizations, and pressures. Most of the effort is often borne by unions, professional associations, human rights organizations, religious groups, intellectuals and artists."[57] Opposition political parties were in disarray and too weak thanks to the policies of the ruling party, the NDP. Popular mobilization and pressure against economic and political reform has often been centered at the base of unions, where their members were at odds with the leadership.[58] However, the independent labor movement was often viewed by the opposition elites with derision and as being inept while also ideologically in the Nasserist-leftist camp. These opposition elites included the traditional opposition parties such as the Wafd, whose members were based at university and research think tanks, and the neoliberal businessmen with new-found power in allying with Gamal Mubarak. The contentious movement that led to the creation of the IGURETA was one strong spark to ignite more protests. This spark led the way for broader and larger worker protests, which lead to the mass protests starting on January 25, 2011. It was a social movement in the timeline, or continuum, of several movements and events starting in 2004 and lasting until 2011. It is indeed the time to take the Egyptian independent labor movement seriously as a political force and socio-economic force. This is a movement calling for positive political change and for democracy. The labor movement is an important stakeholder with significant interest in democratic political change.

Factors That Determined the Outcome

Several factors (internal and external) all came together in a serendipitous manner and were not necessarily coordinated or planned. For example, there was the Kefaya movement that began in 2004 with

> dozens of people gathered outside the attorney general's office, making demands far beyond the established boundaries of free expression for the time. Their banners read, "No to power inheritance," "Down with Hosni Mubarak" and "The Egyptian Movement for Change [. . .] Kefaya." That was the first public

appearance of Kefaya, the group that went on to organize a series of protests pressuring the regime to make concessions. Although the protesters in those days were few, their protests were remarkable because they gained heavy media coverage outside Egypt. It was the first time since the 1970s that Egyptians had raised banners demanding the resignation of a president.[59]

Kefaya means "Enough" in Egyptian Arabic, and it represented the fundamental sentiments of many Egyptians—enough and the Mubarak regime must end. Roberts describes Kefaya as

> essentially an agitation conducted by a dissident wing of the Egyptian elite against Mubarak's monopoly of power and the prospect of this son succeeding him. It attracted a range of reformist viewpoints and published a lengthy shopping list of democratic-sounding aims and demands.[60]

Kefaya became a rallying call for opposition to the regime, yet the protests were mostly negative in nature, i.e. they protested without presenting a positive demand or pr   oposal. Roberts believes that this was the reason for Kefaya's eventual demise and failure to gain a broad audience. I would also add that they were fundamentally a group of elites who did not address the average worker-citizen.

The creation of independent trade unions was illegal under labor legislation, emphasized by the monopoly of government-controlled ETUF. Labor-supporting NGOs and committees developed and became more and more active in the Egyptian labor scene.

> Among them are the Center for Trade Union and Workers' Services (CTUWS) and its general director, Kamal 'Abbas, veteran trade union organizers like Saber Barakat and labor lawyer Khalid 'Ali 'Umar of the Workers' Coordinating Committee for Trade Union Rights, 'Abd al-Ghaffar Shukr, a leader of the Socialist Alliance, which seeks to forge a coalition among all the Egyptian socialist forces, Socialist Horizons, the labor studies center affiliated with the Communist Party of Egypt, and Workers for Change, an offshoot of the Kefaya movement for democracy.[61]

In 2010, they were joined by the Egyptian Center for Economic and Social Rights (ECESR). These organizations had strong relations with counterpart organizations overseas in Europe, Asia, and the US. In addition, the CTUWS in particular began to regularly attend Middle East committee meetings held by the International Trade Union Confederation (ITUC) based in Brussels, to the chagrin of ETUF. These relationships became useful when the time was needed to mount a campaign, wage a labor protest, hold a sit-in, and lead a major strike. These local Egyptian organizations could easily send emails and press releases to national and international labor organizations. Then these external organizations would in turn immediately diffuse the information to all their members and request them to send letters of support or condemnation.

The International Labor Organization (ILO) is a tripartite organization of business, labor, and government representatives based in Geneva with several regional offices in the Middle East and around the world. It played an important

role in forcing the Egyptian government to face the realities and accept the creation of the first independent union in fifty years. The ILO's Committee of Experts on the Application of Conventions and Recommendations (CEACR) routinely questioned the Egyptian government about its blatant contravention of the ILO's conventions protecting the fundamental rights of workers. In 2008, Egypt was placed on the ILO's black list of countries in violation of universal worker rights. The CEACR criticized several aspects of the Egyptian Unified Labor Law of 2003. It critiqued the limits on freedom of association, collective bargaining, and the right to strike. The CEACR repeatedly requested that the Egyptian government modify the law.[62] Since the Egyptian government failed to uphold its commitments regarding the ILO's Convention No. 87 on Freedom of Association, Egypt was placed under scrutiny.

This condemnation by the ILO placed the Egyptian government on the defensive. In April 2009, an ILO delegation came to further investigate the government's promises of reforms in the labor sector. During the visit, several hundred members of the newly formed independent union of RETA gathered in the lobby and outside the Ministry of Manpower with bullhorns, pots, and pans.[63] They were chanting for Minister of Manpower, Aisha Abdel Hady, to come downstairs and accept their official registration papers. Under such circumstances, with the ILO delegation hearing all this commotion, the minister had no choice but to personally accept their registration papers. Another political opportunity that worked in favor of the RETA employees was the public feud between Abd el Hady and the president of the ETUF, Hussein Megawer. In April 2009, Minister Abd el Hady "recognized the tax collectors' union, an astounding decision that may be explained by her personal rivalry with the ETUF head as well as a timely visit from the ILO committee."[64]

International trade union organizations also played an important role in mounting an international campaign to support the RETA workers. Their support was particularly crucial after December 2008 and the establishment of the union. These organizations were sectorial, such as the Public Services International (PSI), a global union federation, which is an international federation of national and regional trade unions organizing in specific industry sectors or occupational groups. PSI is a trade union federation of over 500 public sector unions in 140 countries based in France. PSI immediately accepted the RETA union's application for membership at a special executive board meeting. PSI's certification of the new independent union was an important step in recognition and protection against potential threats by the Egyptian security services. The ITUC also strongly supported the RETA workers. The ITUC is a confederation of independent trade union federations. It represents 175 million workers in 153 countries and territories and has 308 national affiliates. During that time, the ITUC's general secretary (who is currently the director-general of the ILO, Guy Ryder) regularly sent letters of support for RETA workers and letters condemning the Egyptian government's blatant violation of freedom of association.[65]

Individual country trade unions and federations in the US, UK, and Europe also played a "certifying," supportive role to the nascent independence of the Egyptian trade union. The American labor movement, along with the international labor movement mentioned earlier, sent letters of support to the RETA organizers during their protests. In addition, members of PSI in Europe and ETUC sent letters of support in addition to petitions to the Ministry of Finance

supporting RETA workers' demands. Additional certification came on March 3, 2010, when the AFL-CIO's[66] Executive Council announced that they would be awarding their annual 2009 Meany-Kirkland Award for Human Rights to the independent union of RETA employees. This was the first time in the history of this award that an Arab labor movement was recognized for its achievements and sacrifices. CTUWS was also honored for their role in support of the independent labor movement. Here is a portion of the statement:

March 3, 2010

In recognition of its extraordinary courage and perseverance in the face of substantial state repression, the AFL-CIO is proud to grant the Egyptian workers' movement the 2009 George Meany-Lane Kirkland Human Rights Award.

Angered by severe economic pressures and frustrated by the inadequate response of "labor" representation in Egypt, workers started to take to the streets in a wave of strikes and other public protests in the early 2000s. More than 3,000 strikes, demonstrations and sit-ins since 2004 have involved more than 2 million workers. The Egyptian government's response to these protests has ranged from attempts to strangle the movement through bureaucratic red tape to more violent responses that have included billy clubs, tear gas, imprisonment and even torture for many of the movement's leaders. Yet Egyptian workers haven't backed down: They are leading the most significant social movement in the Arab world since World War II, and the largest labor unrest in Egypt since the late 19th century. Egyptian workers are continuing to challenge their employers, their unions and their nation's government.

In the fall of 2007, in an effort to achieve wage parity with counterparts employed directly by the national Ministry of Finance, municipal tax collectors organized public demonstrations to publicize their demands. In December of that year, about 3,000 municipal real estate tax collectors held an 11-day sit-in strike in front of the Egyptian Ministry of Finance. The strike ended with the municipal tax collectors being granted a bonus equal to two months' pay and a pay raise of approximately 325 percent. The first nationally coordinated mobilization of public employees in the country, the strike had been organized by democratically elected representatives of the tax collectors.

Buoyed by their success, that strike committee and its supporters—led by Kamal Abu 'Eita—decided to build a new organization that would continue to advocate forcefully for the needs of its members. They gathered 30,000 signatures endorsing a new, independent union and elected local union committees in the governorates (provinces). On December 20, 2008, more than 1,000 municipal tax collectors from all over Egypt met in Cairo and declared the establishment of the Independent General Union of Real Estate Tax Authority Workers (IGURETA).

IGURETA's democratically elected Constituent Council, supported by 300 union members loudly demonstrating in front of the Ministry of Manpower's headquarters in Cairo, [applied] to form a new union to the Minister of Manpower and Migration that was finally accepted after tense negotiations. The first independent Egyptian trade union in more than half a century had

been established. Unfortunately, the 55,000 municipal real estate tax collectors are the only workers so far to have succeeded in winning recognition of their own autonomous workers' organization.[67]

Social and traditional media outlets also played an important role in publicizing the Egyptian workers' activities. They reported on every aspect of their strikes, protests, sit-ins, and celebrations. Overseas, the web-based media outlet based in the UK, *LabourStart*,[68] played an essential role in publicizing all independent Egyptian workers' actions and protests, including the IGURETA protests. In addition, it posted stories and news under the section titled "Act Now," wrote letters, and signed petitions appeals that were circulated all over the world. Messages of support came pouring in, especially from labor movements in the Arab world from Algeria, Bahrain, Kuwait, Morocco, Palestine, Tunisia, and Yemen. Traditionally, some of these "official labor movements" were generally considered allies of the ETUF. The most notable newspapers that consistently reported on the workers' protests were *Al-Masry el Youm*, *El Youm el Sabe'a*, and *Al-Badil*. In addition, Al-Jazeera and the Egyptian Dream satellite channel regularly reported on the events held by RETA workers. Egyptian blogs regularly reported on the RETA workers' protests, such as *The Arabist* and *'Arabawy*, among others.

There was also the US government and IFI pressure that needs to be taken into consideration. The US government, through the US Agency for International Development (USAID) mission in Egypt, was implementing a twenty-five-year-long good governance and democracy promotion program. This program began in 1989 and lasted until 2009, with an estimated total cost of $80 million. Its goal was to provide technical assistance, materials, equipment, facilities, and training. The areas of assistance covered the following: (1) tax and general economic policy analysis and forecasting, (2) tax administration, (3) pension reform, (4) debt management, (5) treasury and budget reform, and (6) institutional and organizational development.[69] The World Bank and the International Monetary Fund (IMF) were also pressuring the Egyptian government, and the regime was complying with proposed significant economic restructuring and neoliberal programs.

> Although the government exerted tight control over political and social life, it privatized the economy. In 1991, Egypt signed an Economic Reform and Structural Adjustment Program with the International Monetary Fund and the World Bank. The government canceled progressive income taxes that year, privatized nearly 200 firms during the decade.[70]

From 2004 to 2008, Egypt was deeply involved in negotiations with the IMF regarding new loans and programs. These programs were in the realm of fiscal and monetary policy and improving governance. According to the IMF's annual economic check report in February 2008, "The reforms have started to tackle critical impediments to private business and investment including: personal and corporate income tax rates were slashed, and tax administration is being modernized, with a move to self-assessment of personal income taxes."[71] This was an additional pressure that the Egyptian government had to contend with in their dealings with the 55,000 employees in the RETA who at one point had stopped

collecting real estate taxes. This could also be seen as an added bonus for RETA leaders to fulfill their demands of an increase in wages.

Both the IMF and the World Bank considered Egypt's Finance Minister Ghali a "poster child" for his efforts in creating a good business and investment environment in Egypt. Bob Davis wrote in the *Wall Street Journal*,

> Egypt has become a Washington economic favorite. In 2007, the World Bank's "Doing Business" report listed Egypt as the world's top reformer because it had hacked apart a regulatory web impeding business. The head of the International Monetary Fund's policy making committee is Egypt's personable finance minister, Youssef Boutros Ghali, who would be on the short list to become IMF chief should Dominique Strauss-Kahn step down.[72]

So another political opportunity in RETA workers' favor was the high profile of Minister Ghali, as well as PSI's connections to the World Bank and the IMF through their participation as a member of the organized consultations processes with civil society and the labor movement.[73]

All the above mentioned factors, actions, and supportive stances are a collective effort that put pressure on the regime. These factors supported the workers' social movement and then the new independent trade union. Those overseas were vocal and strategic in their support, mirroring the actions of the Egyptians on the ground. These actions all came together and culminated in the establishment and de facto recognition of the new independent trade union. In addition, this social movement galvanized the support of the student movement and other social/civic local movements in Egypt. Initially, the creation of the April 6 Youth Movement[74] was attributed to the workers' protests and strikes. However, while the April 6 Youth Movement took its name from the workers' mass protest in El-Mahalla al-Kubra, the movement "had no direct relationship to Mahalla workers or the massive demonstrations that broke out in Mahalla in lieu of the April 6th strike."[75] Initially, according to Mohammed Adel, a leading activist within the movement,[76] they were interested in advocating for the workers' issues, and they took a local event and turned it into a national movement based on a broader political discourse. The April 6 Youth Movement as a social movement, using social media as one of its main tools and prescribing to nonviolence, continued to support workers, yet they became more focused on political, economic, and social reform and challenges, especially those affecting the youth population.

Concluding Remarks and Lessons Learned

Why were the real estate tax collectors successful? What were the ingredients of their success? How did they contribute to the overall Egyptian protest movement and inspire other workers to organize independent unions? Can we say that they contributed to the continuum of events that led to the massive uprising in January 2011? What political role did they play? Did they contribute to positive political change using socio-economic arguments?

It is clear that workers' movements and their organizations, trade unions, have an important political role to play in Egypt. This political role is in addition to their already significant socio-economic role. This role is particularly essential

in developing countries, particularly those transitioning from authoritarian to democratic governance. Workers' protest social movements can play a catalyst role in an overall larger protest/contentious movement as we have seen in Egypt. The RETA workers' social movement was part of a continuum of several protest events taking place one after another over a period of ten years or more.

The combination of internal and external factors was a political opportunity strategically and successfully used by the RETA workers and their leaders. The RETA workers were successful using various mechanisms and processes in starting an effective, contentious social movement making demands from the government. This movement then led to the establishment of the first independent trade union since 1957 in Egypt. The ingredients of their success were varied, organized as well as spontaneous. However, the main recipe was a commitment to independent democratic practices.

Their claims (demands) were clear, and they had suffered for many years from the grievances that affected everyone. They had strong group identity and solidarity for collective action. While their protests started small, these protests grew progressively with more workers joining their ranks. The activist leaders of the branch offices located in every Egyptian governorate (state/county) played an important role as brokers organized more RETA employees to join the protests. The issues were clear—their wages had not increased over a period of several years and remained low in comparison to others doing similar work in the Ministry of Finance. It was a simple message: increase our wages to achieve equity and improve our quality of life. In addition, the RETA workers had done their homework. They produced facts and figures to support their claim that the revenue they collect is important for the Egyptian government and that the government could afford the increase in wages. The leadership (primarily the movement president, Abu Eita) was a main factor in this movement's success. His charisma, commitment, straightforward attitude, and well-developed network within Egypt's political and social arenas all contributed to the movement's success.

The regular independent media and social media (blogs and websites) played important roles in keeping the RETA workers' claims alive by regularly reporting on their events. RETA workers also reached outside of Egypt and received considerable support from various legitimate and certifying international labor and human rights organizations.

The RETA workers contributed to the overall protest social movements against the Mubarak regime. They were in a continuum of events and protests that continued until the major uprising in January 2011. The RETA workers were one spark among many that ignited the larger explosion. Workers are the backbone of any society, especially one that is striving for democratic practices, so their contribution was important.

There was a political role of the independent labor movement in Egypt. Their political role used in socio-economic arguments rang true to the heart and soul of all Egyptians. However, this movement of RETA workers did not achieve the desired political reform; their victory was incomplete. Indeed, they were a catalyst leading up to the mass uprising, but it was after the fall of the Mubarak regime that things fell apart. The Mubarak regime fell, the military took over, and then there was an MB presidency for one year, during which time workers' rights were

still not fully recognized and the political power of the independent workers' movement to effect reform was still weak.

Notes

1. Tilly, Charles and Sidney G. Tarrow. *Contentious Politics*. Boulder, CO: Paradigm Publishers, 2007: 43.
2. Interview with Gamal Oweida June 8, 2013, at the union headquarters in Cairo, Egypt.
3. http://farm6.static.flickr.com/5174/5445496731_dc7c71166a.jpg, taken by Hossam El-Hamalawy (used with his written permission).
4. Interview with Gamal Oweida on June 8, 2013, at the union headquarters in Cairo, Egypt.
5. Interview with Mohamed Azzouz on June 20, 2013, at the Cairo headquarters of *El-Masry el Youm* newspaper.
6. There is evidence of this kind of reporting in several of the aforementioned newspapers over a period of five to six years prior to the January 2011 events.
7. Interview with Mohamed Azzouz on June 20, 2013, at the Cairo headquarters of *El-Masry el Youm* newspaper.
8. CTUWS: an Egyptian NGO that supports workers; Center for Trade Union and Worker Services.
9. http://hmlc-egy.org/english: من نحن: مركز حقوقى مصرى يعمل فى مجال حقوق الانسان من خلال التقاضى والحملات والابحاث القانونية داخل مصر متى اسس: أسس المركز فى غضون عام 1999 كشركة محاماة خاضعة لقانون المحاماة المصري، ويمارس المركز نشاطه من خلال فرعى القاهرة وأسوان.
10. Interview with M. Azzouz, *El Masry el Youm* newspaper, June 20, 2013, in Cairo, Egypt.
11. Lachapelle, Jean. "Lessons from Egypt's Tax Collectors." *Middle East Report* 264 (2012): 38.
12. Ibid.
13. To clarify: their colleagues were those at the main Ministry of Finance based in Cairo, while these workers were under the local municipal councils' supervision and were paid very low salaries for doing the same work.
14. Lachapelle 2012: 38.
15. Barker, Colin, Alan Johnson, and Michael Lavalette. *Leadership and Social Movements*. Manchester, England and New York: Manchester University Press Distributed exclusively in the USA by Palgrave, 2001: 1–2.
16. Ibid.: 2.
17. Ibid.: 1–23.
18. Eyerman, Ron and Andrew Jamison. *Social Movements: A Cognitive Approach*. University Park, PA: Pennsylvania State University Press, 1991: 15.
19. Ibid.: 16.
20. Ibid.: 16–17.
21. Ibid.: 17.
22. Ibid.: 25.
23. Rochon, Thomas R. *Culture Moves—Ideas, Activism, and Changing Values*. Princeton, NJ: Princeton University Press, 1998: 101.
24. Lachapelle 2012: 39.
25. Ibid.
26. نشرة تصدرها النقابة العامة للعاملين بالضرائب العقارية (المستقلة) بمصر، والتي تعد أول نقابة مستقلة منذ ما يقرب من 50 عام شهدت هيمنة وتسلط اتحاد عمال موالي للدولة على النقابات العمالية. وتعد النقابة الجديدة المستقلة الأداة التي اكتشف 55 ألف موظف بالضرائب العقارية حاجتهم إليها عبر نضال طويل خاضوه للمطالبة بحقوقهم.
27. A copy of the newsletter is included in Appendix A.
28. www.youtube.com/watch?v=ByObGdGeV9k&feature=related
29. According to the ILO: Decent work sums up the aspirations of people in their working lives. It involves opportunities for work that is productive and delivers a fair income, security in the workplace and social protection for families, better prospects for personal development and social integration, freedom for people to express their concerns, organize and participate in the decisions that affect their lives and equality of

opportunity and treatment for all women and men. www.ilo.org/global/topics/decent-work/lang--en/index.htm.
30. http://arablit.wordpress.com/2011/07/03/ahmed-fouad-negm-who-are-they-and-who-are-we/
31. www.nytimes.com/2013/12/07/world/middleeast/ahmed-fouad-negm-dissident-poet-of-egypts-underclass-dies-at-84.html
32. Amin, Galal A. *Whatever Happened to the Egyptians? Changes in Egyptian Society From 1950 to the Present.* Cairo: American University in Cairo Press, 2000: 7–8.
33. Fahmy, Z. *Ordinary Egyptians: Creating the Modern Nation Through Popular Culture.* Stanford, CA: Stanford University Press, 2011: 3.
34. Ibid.: 167.
35. Ibid.: 173.
36. Beinin 2011: 198.
37. Shukri, Muhammad. "Backgrounder: Wave of Strikes Rolls Through Egypt." *BBC Monitoring Middle East*, July 10, 2007.
38. McAdam, Doug, John D. McCarthy, Mayer N. Zald, eds. *Comparative perspectives on social movements: Political opportunities, mobilizing structures, and cultural framings.* Cambridge University Press, 1996.
39. Beinin 2011: 200–201.
40. Lachapelle 2012: 41.
41. Blog posting, *Arabawy*, August 15, 2008, www.arabawy.org/2008/08/15/towards_free_unions/.
42. Lachapelle 2012: 41.
43. *Al-Masry Al-Youm* (English), August 31, 2011.
44. Interviews conducted at the Independent General Union of RETA workers headquarters in Cairo, Egypt, in June 2013.
45. Those interviewed requested that I use their first names only.
46. Interview with Mahmoud, RETA union member, union headquarters, Midan Lazghouly, Cairo on June 12, 2013.
47. Ibid.
48. A researcher with the German Institute for International and Security Affairs (SWP) in Berlin.
49. Roll, Stephan. "Gamal Mubarak and the Discord in Egypt's Ruling Elite." *Sada Journal*, Washington, DC: Carnegie Endowment for International Peace, September 1, 2010 http://carnegieendowment.org/2010/09/01/gamal-mubarak-and-discord-in-egypt-s-ruling-elite/6bcv.
50. Ibid.
51. In Arabic, it is such a statement, especially in colloquial Egyptian Arabic.
52. Interview with Wael on June 8, 2013, at the RETA union headquarters in Cairo, Egypt.
53. Interview with Salwa.
54. Notes from interview with RETA workers on 8th and 12th June 2013 at their union headquarters in Cairo.
55. Notes from interview with RETA workers on 8th and 12th June 2013 at their union headquarters in Cairo.
56. Interview with Mahmoud, RETA union member, union headquarters, Midan Lazghouly, Cairo on June 12, 2013.
57. King, Stephen J. *The New Authoritarianism in the Middle East and North Africa.* Bloomington: Indiana University Press, 2009: 97.
58. Ibid.
59. "Kefaya: The Origins of Mubarak's Downfall." *El Masry El Youm* newspaper, English edition, published on December 12, 2011. www.egyptindependent.com/node/545211.
60. Roberts, Hugh. "The Revolution that Wasn't." *London Review of Books* 35 (17) (2013): 3–9: 6.
61. "Strikes in Egypt Spread from Center of Gravity" by Joel Beinin, Hossam el-Hamalawy, published May 9, 2007.
    For background on the ongoing strike wave, see Beinin, Joel and Hossam el-Hamalawy. "Egyptian Textile Workers Confront the New Economic Order." *Middle East Report Online*, March 25, 2007. See also Beinin, Joel. "Popular Social Movements and the Future of Egyptian Politics." *Middle East Report Online*, March 10,

2005. For more on Islamist-leftist cooperation, see Hossam el-Hamalawy, "Comrades and Brothers." *Middle East Report* 242 (2007).
62. Beinin, Joel. *The Struggle for Worker Rights in Egypt*. Published by the Solidarity Center, AFL-CIO, February 2010: 28.
63. A short YouTube video clip of the actual protest: www.youtube.com/watch?v=992BLR STnRA&list=UUIQi8R5ra2_GbUO0mM8wcrQ&index=47&feature=plcp.
64. Lachapelle 2012: 41.
65. Letters from PSI and ITUC can be found in Appendix A.
66. The American Federation of Labor-Congress of Industrial Organizations (AFL-CIO).
67. www.aflcio.org/About/Exec-Council/EC-Statements/The-George-Meany-Lane-Kirkland-2009-Human-Rights-Award
68. www.labourstart.org: LabourStart is an online news service maintained by a global network of volunteers which aims to serve the international trade union movement by collecting and disseminating information—and by assisting unions in campaigning and other ways. Its features include daily labour news links in more than 20 languages and a news syndication service used by more than over 700 trade union websites. News is collected from mainstream, trade union, and alternative news sources by a network of over 500 volunteer correspondents based on every continent.
69. USAID report, 2008, USAID Assistance in Fiscal Reform: Comprehensive Tax Reform in Egypt.
70. Lesch, Ann M. "Egypt's Spring: Causes of the Revolution." Article first published online: September 15, 2011 18 (3) (2011): 35–48.
71. www.imf.org/external/pubs/ft/survey/so/2008/car021308a.htm
72. Davis, Bob. "Egypt: Critical Take on a Model Reformer." *Wall Street Journal*, August 3, 2010. http://blogs.wsj.com/economics/2010/08/03/egypt-critical-take-on-a-model-reformer/.
73. The World Bank engages with trade unions in numerous ways: consultations with union members who are stakeholders in Bank projects; national consultation with unions as members of civil society; international policy dialogue on economic and social issues; research on the economic effects of collective bargaining, and training programs for both Bank staff and trade unions. This site includes reports and other materials from regular, ongoing dialogue between the World Bank, IMF, and the international labor movement. http://web.worldbank.org/WBSITE/EXTERNAL/TOPICS/ EXTSOCIALPROTECTION/EXTLM/0,contentMDK:20223840~menuPK:390633~p agePK:148956~piPK:216618~theSitePK:390615,00.html www.imf.org/external/pubs/ ft/survey/so/2011/pol030411a.htm, Vienna Meeting Reaffirms Cooperation of IMF, ILO, Trade Unions.
74. April 6 Youth Movement is an Egyptian activist group started in spring 2008 to support the workers in El-Mahalla al-Kubra, an industrial town, who were planning to strike on April 6. On March 23, 2008, a small group of young Egyptian activists—calling themselves the April 6 Youth Movement—launched a Facebook page in support of a planned textile workers' strike in the city of Mahalla al-Kobra to protest low wages and high food prices. The group's leaders included 27-year-old Esraa Abdel Fattah Ahmed Rashid and 27-year-old Ahmed Maher. www.pbs.org/wgbh/pages/frontline/ revolution-in-cairo/inside-april6-movement/.
75. Beinin, Joel. "Civil Society, NGOs, and Egypt's 2011 Popular Uprising." *South Atlantic Quarterly* 113 (2) (2014): 396–406: 402.
76. See interview notes with M. Adel in Chapter 4 starting on page 98.

4 Second Case Study

The Garment and Textile Workers at the Misr[1] Company for Spinning and Weaving in El-Mahalla al-Kubra

Chapter Outline:

1. History of the El-Mahalla al-Kubra Workers' Movement

   - Background

     Perception of Workers in Egypt: A "Fi'a"—A Group or Special Interest Group

   - The Egyptian Textile Worker and Bank Misr's El-Mahalla al-Kubra's Centerpiece Factory

     How Did Cotton Become Such a Dominant Feature of Egyptian Economic Activity?

   - Why Was There a Focus on Egyptian Textile Workers in Academic Scholarship?

2. Organization

   - Who Are the Egyptian Garment and Textile Workers, Their Union, and Its Leadership?
   - Militancy of the Textile Workers Starting in 1930s to the Present

3. Repertoires of This Social Movement and What Factors Determined the Outcome

   - The Mahalla Strike Movement—The Development of Workers Into a Social Movement, Its Repertoires, and Its Mechanisms From 2006 to 2011
   - Field Research Findings and Meetings With the Garment and Textile Workers in El-Mahalla al-Kubra
   - Main Strike Actions Leading the Way to the January 2011 Uprising
   - The Art of Presence or Active Citizenry

     Background: The April 6 Youth Movement

     Interview With April 6 Activist and Leader in Cairo, June 2013

4. Concluding Remarks

History of the El-Mahalla al-Kubra Workers' Movement

Background

This case study will outline the repertoire of protests that the workers conducted in building a social movement. Yet, it was a contentious protest movement limited to this factory and to the city of El-Mahalla in the province of Gharbiyya that gave impetus to several social movements around the country. One example was the Tanta Kitan (Linen) Company located in the city of Tanta, the capital of the governorate of El Gharbiyya (see Chapter 5 for more details). They had a mixed national impact of motivating the protest movement to get organized and mobilize.

> Meanwhile, research on textile factory workers [. . .] has found that these supposedly paradigmatic proletarians were by no means the regimented and uniformly exploited masses posited by the classic account; they formed tightly knit, kin-based communities, they prized their skills, maintained remarkable workplace autonomy.[2]

These observations can be applied to the workers in this case study.
   Issawi wrote in 1947 that it was clear that

> The struggle of the workers to obtain recognition of their rights is far from ended. And unless the government shows much more wisdom than in the past in its dealings with the working class there is a great danger of this struggle taking a violent form.[3]

Issawi's statement was prophetic of the years to follow, and the government has fulfilled the prophecy of not acting wisely with regard to respecting workers' rights. In addition, he wrote that in 1947 Egypt's main problems were a fall in income and steady population growth, making the decrease in government revenue even more acute.[4] This clearly reflected Mubarak's regime from the 1980s to 2011. Thus, Egypt has been on a similar trajectory since the early twentieth century and well into the twentieth-first century, despite British colonial rule, monarchical rule, socialist Nasserist rule, and pseudo-capitalist (crony capitalism) open economy (Infitah) Sadat and Mubarak rule.

Perception of Workers in Egypt: A "Fi'a"—A Group or Special Interest Group

Some background explanation of how workers are viewed and regarded in Egypt is needed at this point. Workers are referred to as a "*fi'a*," i.e. a group or special interest group in Arabic. These workers led a movement that contributed to the downfall of the regime, yet they were generally perceived as a special interest with no real power.

The Arabic term *fi'a* simply means group, but has acquired negative connotations and might be compared with how the term "special interest" is used to disparage American labor. In post-Mubarak Egypt, officials have used its adjectival form *fi'awi* in reference to any demonstration, strike or sit-in advancing demands related to distribution of wealth, whether the protesters are blue- or white-collar employees, and whether they are calling for higher wages, greater benefits, improved working conditions or replacement of corrupt management personnel. The term's recent usage seems to encompass the public and private sectors and to apply to collective action as limited as a protest in a single state-owned enterprise and as broad as a national strike by disgruntled members of a professional syndicate.[5]

The use of the term by the media, opposition elites, and the general public was meant to belittle or diminish demands and grievances by workers. By placing the workers into a special interest group, they were not representative of the larger whole, the masses, and the people.

Further explanation of the use and proliferation of the term fi'awi was well explained by Sallam:

> The proliferation of the term "*fi'awi*" to describe Egyptian workers' demands and reduce them to parochial, even counter-revolutionary interests is more than just a denial of the right to a humane living standard. There is more at stake than just the absurdity of the assumptions on which the usage of this term is based. The ubiquity of the term signifies a mounting elite consensus that is rewriting the history of the ongoing Egyptian revolution, its meaning and its goals—with the purpose of sidelining pressing socio-economic problems and the millions of Egyptians who suffer from them. While many believe that Egyptians revolted largely out of socio-economic discontent, the speed with which influential figures clung to the derogatory term *fi'awi* indicates that addressing these grievances in post-Mubarak Egypt—let alone putting them on the national political agenda—may not be as easy as one would have thought. It remains to be seen whether the emergence of new parties and independent unions and syndicates will give workers and their allies among advocates of distributive justice a shot at countering this wave of unreflective elitism. But, in any event, the trends suggest that what awaits Egyptian workers after the end of a decades-long bad romance with Mubarak's authoritarianism is not a happy ending, but new challenges and greater uncertainty.[6]

Sallam points to the difficulty of the workers affecting the political agenda or getting their demands met in post-Mubarak Egypt, especially in an environment of weak political parties that can champion the workers' cause.

The wildcat strikes[7] that took place in many economic sectors were influenced greatly by El-Mahalla al-Kubra workers and RETA employees. They gave them the needed push of support to make their grievances heard and the needed dose of courage. The garment and textile workers and the RETA employees helped the rest of the workers shed their fear of reprisal by the regime. These workers were protesting not only the ETUF, which was interested in protecting the status quo, but also the economic measures and changes in their benefits that were taking place as a result of widespread neoliberal economic reforms. Shokr wrote,

The ETUF counts nearly 4 million members, mostly in public-sector companies and civil service, and until the 2011 uprising, it held a virtual monopoly
on worker representation. From its inception in 1957, the federation regularly undermined independent worker strikes and ensured that regime loyalists
filled top union positions. But the mounting pressures of the last 20 years—low
wages, inflation and the loss of job security—triggered a wave of wildcat labor
protest, the largest and most sustained social movement Egypt had witnessed
in over half a century. Between 1998 and 2010, well over 2 million workers
participated in strikes, sit-ins and other collective actions. These mobilizations
operated on two fronts: The majority protested for improved living conditions
and against privatization, while a smaller group of activists fought to establish
more lasting forms of independent worker organization.[8]

The workers' social movement used an economic discourse, which quickly
evolved into a political one.

The tsunami of labor protests and mobilization had touched a wide range of
economic activities, including textile, cement, railway, shipyard, poultry, mill,
postal, and public utility workers; train, truck, tram, and minibus drivers; tax
collectors, justice, education ministry employees, and other civil servants; and
doctors, nurses, pharmacists, professors, students, and other professionals. Even
Cairo circus workers staged sit-ins to protest low salaries and the proposed privatization of the National Circus.[9]

The government from 2005 until the end of 2010 faced an uphill battle of contentious mobilization of millions of Egyptian workers. The protests were not particularly political, yet they formed a social movement that made regular claims
and demands, while political parties and the MB were relatively silent.

> Labor protests have been locally organized and executed and there has been
> limited contact or coordination between workers across factories. There has
> also been virtually no involvement by the established political parties or the
> Muslim Brotherhood, despite the regime's allegations otherwise.[10]

Egypt's political economic conditions were changing and deteriorating and thus
were directly felt by workers and their families—accelerating neoliberal economic
reforms, rapidly rising inflation, and stagnant wages contributed to these feelings.
This forced workers to use their only weapon against the employers, which were
still primarily the public sector.

> From the regime's perspective, hundreds of thousands of protesting workers
> are potentially more destabilizing than the existing opposition parties or the
> Muslim Brotherhood. The prospect of independent unions is also threaten-
> ing for a regime accustomed to tightly controlling labor. These are some of
> the reasons why the government has responded to workers' protests with a
> mix of accommodation and repression rather than exclusively through force.
> Moreover, it is likely that some government officials believe they can simply
> "buy off" workers, unlike groups that are opposed to the regime's very exis-
> tence, such as the Muslim Brotherhood or *Kefaya*.[11]

The wave of workers' protests that erupted was the largest social movement
Egypt witnessed in more than half a century. These labor actions were amplified

politically because they coincided with a campaign for democracy organized by Kefaya (Enough), The Egyptian Movement for Change, and other groups composed mainly of the urban middle classes and intellectual workers. However, there are only weak links between the workers and these movements.[12] The strike movement started in the center and heart of Egypt's prized El-Mahalla al-Kubra factory and spread into practically every sector of the economy, including white-collar professionals such as teachers, higher education professors, doctors, etc. Even though civil servants (government employees), such as the real estate collectors and teachers, behaved in a militant manner, they were still not considered "militant workers." Despite the perception, these civil servants still were able to force the government's hand by their position within the apparatus. They were able to use their position to make their demands on a national level and thus to be heard. However, the increase in workers' protests was not organized on a national or regional level. They were first initiated on a local level with some copycat actions following large nationally publicized strikes. The Egyptian government was facing a serious legitimacy and credibility crisis. It was unable to deliver its promise of improved benefits to a great majority of the people, and at the same time, the much-advertised democratic reforms were mostly "window dressing." Beinin wrote in 2010,

> The workers movement offers the government an opportunity to listen to the voice of its people and implement long-overdue political and economic policy changes. Failure to do so may well undermine Egypt's internal security, prosperity, and regional influence.[13]

This was quite a prophetic statement in 2010, which foretold the unfolding events starting in January 2011.

However, some observers of the labor movement, such as blogger Hossam El-Hamalawy, noted,

> I believe that labor strikes in the last week of the uprising [2011] were the tipping point that forced Mubarak's resignation. There is no credible account as yet of the exact chain of events that pushed Mubarak out of office. Yet the fact that one of the first things the Supreme Council (of Armed Forces (SCAF)) tried to do after taking power was to bring an end to strikes suggests that work stoppages were a source of deep concern for the generals who surrounded Mubarak in his last days. The claim that these activities hastened Mubarak's ouster is, therefore, quite plausible.[14]

The post-Mubarak government struggled with and against the labor movement. One of the benefits of the January 2011 uprising was the creation of two independent trade union federations and a de facto acceptance of independent unions.

> The ETUF will remain a crucial element in the struggle to redefine labor relations in post-Mubarak Egypt. But just as the burgeoning labor movement was a thorn in the side of the previous administration—and, by some accounts, a factor in its ultimate downfall—it will likely remain so for Egypt's new leadership. Strikes, protests, and workplace mobilizations have only increased since Mubarak's ouster and seem poised to continue.[15]

As mentioned in previous chapters, there has been more egregious government behavior against workers in the post-Mubarak government, giving credence to the theory (Brinton Crane) that post-revolution does not initially engender a more enlightened regime.

The Egyptian Textile Worker and Bank Misr's El-Mahalla al-Kubra's Centerpiece Factory

The Egyptian textile industry was created out of a nationalist fervor to develop the country with Egyptian capital, raw materials, equipment, and workers. In Egypt's history (and present), cotton and the textile industry cannot be separated from each other.

> Under the banner of nationalism and opposition to British occupation and foreign economic domination, Bank Misr established the largest Egyptian-owned textile factories in several locations during the interwar period [World War I and World War II]. Bank Misr itself was established in 1920 to finance Egyptian-owned, large-scale industrial enterprises under the slogan, "An Egyptian bank for Egyptians only." Thousands of male and female agricultural labourers and landless and near-landless peasants of all ages were brought from their villages to work in those factories, thus becoming industrial labourers and urban dwellers.[16]

Thus, is the beginning of this industry and the urban working class.

Business and politics are the pursuit of Vitalis' book *When Capitalists Collide* by its focus on investors as economic and political agents, particularly on post-World War I events and opportunities that shaped Egyptian investors' strategies. Vitalis uses the concepts of interest aggregation, conflict, and the building of industry in the developing world.[17] This model centers on rival coalitions of local investors, or business groups, which are a combination of big landlords, bankers, and manufacturers—a business oligarchy. It is conflict between these oligarchs that is central to understanding Egypt's early industrial development.[18] The outcome of World War I among rival investor coalitions became the politics of business and industrial development in Egypt, which cannot just be reduced to imperialism versus the nation, according to Vitalis.[19] Bank Misr is the story of an investment group led by the infamous outspoken nationalist chairman Tal'at Harb. He is "the centerpiece of both triumphalist (nationalist) and exceptionalist (neo-Marxist) accounts of Egyptian economic history."[20] As historians of the Egyptian labor movement Beinin and Lockman summarize the story, the Bank Misr group "symbolized the organizational consolidation of an aspiring Egyptian industrial bourgeoisie," which allegedly "took on itself the task of creating a purely Egyptian-owned industrial sector."[21] It was a departure from the mostly foreign-owned large, medium, and small business enterprises that had existed and thrived in Egypt.

Egypt's development model was based on joint cooperation between the Bank Misr group and foreign investors, but after 1922, Egyptian capitalists made inroads into local finance, trade, manufacturing, and services. Tignor sees the history of the political economy after 1918 as an attempt by "a dynamic and

farsighted" group of industrialists to "create a vibrant and autonomous Egyptian capitalism."[22] The account of Bank Misr is the colonial-exceptionalist narrative in miniature. "It is the account of an alleged failure of a single institution representing a class—an aspiring Egyptian industrial bourgeoisie."[23] It was more complicated than a tug-of-war over economic development with one side pulling the economy toward independent industrialization and the other straining to keep the economy locked in the grips of foreign capital.[24]

The most notable investment by Bank Misr, particularly in its first years of operation, was in the cotton production business. Bank Misr was a symbol for local capitalist organization from 1880 to 1960. Under Harb's leadership and guidance,

> The Misr Groups' reliance [was] on state business and subsidies in its initial 1920 commercial-banking venture and all subsequent enterprises is well documented. The group's largest sectoral investments during the first years of operation were in cotton trading and textile manufacture.[25]

Harb and his associates had a strong commitment to not only creating and developing but also strengthening Egypt's ties to the world cotton market.[26]

How Did Cotton Become Such a Dominant Feature of Egyptian Economic Activity?

During the last three decades of the nineteenth century and into the early twentieth century, cotton was the main source of income for almost every landowner in the Delta region.[27] As a result, cotton's effect on Egypt's overall economy was profound—land prices tripled; income into the state coffers increased dramatically and became about 70% of the state's income; it attracted more foreign merchants and bankers to Egypt; it transformed agricultural and irrigation practices throughout the country; it improved the system of irrigation in the form of the construction and maintenance of many irrigation canals; it employed many peasants and workers in the whole process; the government erected thousands of telegram miles; it provided opportunities for several young Egyptians to be sent overseas to learn technical skills; the government upgraded Alexandria's port infrastructure; the government increased the number of railroad tracks; and much more.[28] Prior to World War I, there was an abundance of capital in Egypt, with local foreign entrepreneurs bringing expertise and energy and delving into other sectors of the economy. This cash crop improved Egypt's trade accounts by attracting foreign investment. A market for manufactured consumer goods and a need for improved city infrastructure clearly contributed to the need for workers—skilled and unskilled. So Egypt saw an increase in demand for workers to fill those jobs.[29]

However, Owen wrote that the cultivation and export of cotton

> did not lead to the development of a modern sector in the economy. Progress of this kind was inhibited, in part by the unresponsive nature of the traditional [small workshop] sector, in part by certain physical and political obstacles.[30]

Another inhibitor was the presence of a successful and prosperous export sector, but Owen concludes in the final analysis there were many more advantages that Egypt gained from cotton; however, after 1914 this situation changed.

Between 1954 and 1956, Nasser and his revolutionary comrades ended the seventy-year-old regime that had governed capital in Egypt. Nasser successfully got rid of monopolistic capitalism. Starting in 1954, in Nasser's strategy with Argentinian Peronist undertones, he noted how "organized labor has been deliberately and effectively used for political purposes on a nation-wide scale for first time in Egyptian history."[31] Nasser subsequently organized workers (top down) into the one labor federation, ETUF, in 1957. This effort was not a grassroots (bottom up) organizing of workers into the ETUF, because it was a top-down decision; Nasser did this because he saw other countries within his milieu that had national federations for their unions and workers. Then, legislation was passed to include workers into the legislative branch, neutralizing their ability to strike and bargain collectively as organized workers would in a privately held economy. Nasser rid Egypt of most major private investment and replaced it with state-owned public enterprises. He also rid Egypt of independent trade unions and an activist labor movement. Nasser was successful in creating a corporatist style of trade unionism in Egypt.

Why Was There a Focus on Egyptian Textile Workers in Academic Scholarship?

Beinin and Lockman's research focused on the Egyptian "textile workers who assumed the leading role in the labor movement before and after the Second World War, respectively."[32] They focused on textile workers in their study of the emergence of a new group of urban wageworkers from the end of nineteenth century onward. These workers earned their wages solely based on their daily labor. Due to Egypt's social composition, the rural working class also has to be considered since many peasants worked on a casual or seasonal basis in industry and became part of the urban working class.[33] The character of the textile worker is that

> the textile worker exemplified the most complete mechanization of industry in Egypt at the time. Among the textile workers we find large, and even extremely large, concentrations of workers in forms of production requiring heavy capital investment and up-to-date bureaucratic technical structures.[34]

This is an example of Egypt's version of a mini-industrial revolution.

From the nineteenth century onward, initially the town of El-Mahalla al-Kubra, about two hours north from Cairo in the middle of the Nile Delta, emerged as an important textile industry center in Egypt and the Ottoman Empire. In 1927, Harb chose the town as the site for the Misr Company for Spinning and Weaving (MCSW). This is the first large, wholly Egyptian-owned textile factory in Egypt, and it remains one of the biggest today. The MCSW became Bank Misr's flagship company and most successful enterprise, employing the largest number of industrial workers in the country. By the end of the 1930, the factory's products had successfully gone to market, which encouraged the owner of Bank Misr to

continue to expand production. The workforce rapidly increased from approximately 2,000 workers in 1930 to 10,000 in 1938, and then to 27,000 in 1945. Such rapid expansion helped construct the company within Egyptian nationalist discourse as an emblem of national success and progress in the face of foreign political and economic domination.[35] The most famous saying at the time was that every dress worn in Egypt was made by the MSCW. This was associated with the feeling that Egypt's nationalism and freedom was associated with this company.[36]

Harb expressed great admiration for the people of El-Mahalla and their commitment to education and industry, particularly the textile industry. He pointed out that 57% of El-Mahalla's population worked in industry, and almost one-third of the population, worked in the textile industry. The theory was that the textile industry had become so much of a part of the culture of the town that its children were effortlessly predisposed to acquire its skills and traditions, and that consequently the shift from handloom to mechanical weaving should not be difficult.[37] The opportunity to learn new skills helped recruit workers, including landless peasants, *affanddiyya* (middle class professionals), and *umda* (local leaders/mayors), in addition to spreading the nationalist discourse.[38]

Beinin and Lockman wrote,

> The decision of the Misr company to locate its principal textile mills in the Nile Delta and to rely on untrained workers was a direct response to the history of working-class organization and collective action in Cairo and Alexandria, where the textile mills would normally have been located on the basis of economic considerations other than the need to control the labor force. The Misr Company's adoption of paternalism as a strategy of labor control was likewise related to its fear of labor militancy. While this strategy was successful for a limited time, the violence and intensity of the strikes at Mahalla al-Kubra in 1947 and Kafr al-Dawwar in 1952 demonstrated the workers' rejection of paternalism and contributed to the adoption of a new industrial strategy after 1952.[39]

The working-class consciousness developed and bonded despite the origin of the workers. It is clear that the strategy adopted above was successful for a short time. Then, workers' solidarity took over in the face of workplace challenges and the need to advocate for rights.

In the 1930s, the early years of the factory, there was a high level of worker absenteeism and greater interest in working the land even though the income was even more meager than working at the factory.

> Returning to agricultural work whenever it was available was in effect a form of resistance against the company's injustices in the manner that James C. Scott describes as "everyday forms of resistance" among oppressed peasants, and that Asef Bayat calls "quiet encroachment of the ordinary"[40]

among the urban poor. In addition, managers were not trained, treated workers with disrespect, and had no patience for training these new skills. Working conditions in the MCSW were quite bad. "So quitting work was one way of resisting the unjust work relationship with the MCSW, and it exposed the dire lack of a systematic company policy for recruiting and retaining workers."[41] Hammad's

research further shows how workers were divided into competing groups. Geographic origin played a divisive role among the factory workers of El-Mahalla in a manner similar to racial divisions among American workers in the early twentieth century. Kinship was also a significant factor in the creation of a violent atmosphere at the factory and in workers' slums,[42] taking precedence over other bonds among the factory workers. In Egyptian society, geographic solidarity was helpful and important, yet kinship always prevailed.[43]

Urban industrial life developed in Egypt despite strong family, tribal, and, at times, geographic solidarity. "Although familial and communal groupings served to divide workers, these groupings also facilitated their transformation and adaptation to urban industrial life and shaped their social consciousness as a distinctive urban group."[44] Through these natural groupings, workers shared knowledge regarding skills on how to operate machinery safely and reduced alienation by giving them a sense of familiarity in their new lives in El-Mahalla. These groupings also became a job-bank for finding jobs for their kin.[45] During the major strikes of 1938 and 1947, workers living in slums survived on a system of credit. Worker mediation in the company hiring process to secure employment for others empowered laborers in the face of the capitalist factory management, but also created divisions among the workers. Worker empowerment and division formed their consciousness as a distinct community—much like a separate class—in relation to the local capitalist system and their new urban surroundings.[46]

In 1930s Egypt, high recruitment levels and high turnover marked the labor market for factory workers.

> High levels of ignorance about exactly how the machines worked also often led to fatalities, and the textile mills were no exception. Workers were injured and killed by machines throwing off shuttles, gears, or other pieces and piercing the eyes, heads or extremities of workers. Associated with plants managed like Mahalla were the relatively high costs borne by workers in terms of training, job search, and the risk to life and limb as well as long and arduous day in generally very unpleasant conditions.[47]

Poorly trained managers regularly assaulted workers' dignity, and the workers were not organized to act collectively to assert their presence.

> Egyptian firms in the textile industry, especially in el-Mahallah, suffered from low productivity due at least in part to high levels of turnover and absenteeism and the associated costs of an open labor market in the firm, given the low level of qualified workers.[48]

The history of worker/management relations in the industry and especially in El-Mahalla was not positive.

Kafr al Dawwar in 1952 was a significant signpost in the history of the garment and textile workers in Egypt according to labor historians. I had the opportunity to discuss this with Fathallah Mahrous, a retired trade union leader and activist in the industry.[49] He described in great detail the incident of the workers' demands, strike, and the punitive role played by the military. The workers protested for the following reasons: (1) the removal of the much disliked, deposed king's men who were in the management and accused of corruption; (2)

recognition of a freely elected union representation; (3) reinstatement of several dismissed workers; (4) wage increase and an increase in the annual bonus; (5) amnesty for the strikers; and (6) the establishment of the headquarters of their local union outside of the factory.

> On the night of August 12 [1952], some 500 workers at Misr Fine Spinning and Weaving began a sit-down strike and locked themselves inside the mill. Shortly thereafter fires were set to some of the auxiliary buildings inside the complex. [. . .] At 3:00 am on August 13, troops arrived from Alexandria and were met with demonstrations by the workers. The demonstrators supported the revolution and Najib, the leader of the Revolutionary Command Council [RCC]. Shots of disputed origin were fired in the vicinity of the demonstration. [. . .] The army returned the fire, and in the exchange two soldiers, one policeman, and four workers were killed and many others wounded.[50]

The military moved quickly to contain the strike and demonstrations, arrested many workers, and began a military trial to deal with the three principal defendants: Khamis, al-Baqari (rumored to be members of the banned Communist Party), and Shihab (a Muslim Brother). Musa Sabri, a journalist with a law degree, defended them, and the proceedings progressed so quickly that by August 18, Al-Baqari and Khamis were sentenced to death while Shihab got a thirteen-year sentence of hard labor in prison. Khamis and al-Baqari were hanged on September 7.[51] The speed of the trial; the severe, harsh military response; and the dismissal of much evidence that would have exonerated both defendants were all done in the name of "fear of the political effects of the strike rather than their personal responsibility for acts of arson or other violence."[52] The new ruling regime feared Communist-led collective uprisings by workers and a political challenge to the military. This was purely a political decision and not one based on facts of the case, but it left a schism between the regime and workers. It began the slow, step-by-step control of the workers and the elimination of independent trade unionism and collective action.

Over a period of several years starting in 1952, the new regime consolidated its power, and Nasser took over the presidency from the more amenable Mohammed Najib, who was supported by many workers and the MB. From 1952 to 1959, there were several strikes and protests by workers that were quickly put down; of course, the establishment of the ETUF further cemented the subservient role of the trade unions and workers to the state and its centralized policies. Nasser pushed new legislation to control the creation of trade unions; the "notify and accept" علم و خبر method of establishing free trade unions ended, and arguments broke out between nationalists and leftist/Communist supporters, which further weakened the independent labor movement. By the early 1960s, many leftist/Communist trade union activists were rounded up, arrested, and killed. The new Law #91 was the final blow after the Kafr al Dawwar incident and put the final nail in the coffin of independent trade unionism in Egypt. Law #91 canceled local union committees in each workplace, expropriated funds, and mandated one trade union for each type of work with branches in each factory. "So now we need only 26 general trade unions to control the workers—the end of the free independent labor movement as we knew it,"[53] said Fathallah Mahrous with

lament. Mahrous had been in and out of prison during that time period. He was a known activist and member of the Egyptian Communist Party. In 1967, he was officially prevented from trade union or community work, and his campaign for a seat in Maglis el Shaab—the Peoples' Assembly—was ended by the authorities. He gave me several fliers with his platform and campaign slogans. In 1973, he went to prison for twenty-two months, accused of being an active Communist. "We have been greatly missing real trade union structure organizing since 1952," he said. "Real political, cultural, and worker consciousness were missing and not being taught so workers learned to survive the hardships without class consciousness. Trade unions lost their political awareness," he continued. He said that during Nasser's rule there was "the carrot and stick" approach, but during Sadat's era it was just the "stick."[54]

It is well established that collective action in the form of workers' trade unions has positive impacts on the workplace, the workers, and their relation with managers.

> There is good statistical evidence, admittedly drawn from the U.S., that quit rates are lowered more due to union voice than to union monopoly power over wages: that unionized workers quit less and accrue more tenure than otherwise comparable nonunion workers has more to do with the fact that unionism transforms the working places through voice than with the fact that it raises pay.[55]

Organization

Who Are the Egyptian Garment and Textile Workers, Their Union, and Its Leadership?

Since the beginning of the twentieth century, Egyptian workers have been attempting to improve their situation. They were unrepresented in the People's Assembly and faced indifferent or hostile public opinion, so the only open course of action to highlight their grievances was through strikes.[56] As early as 1938, there was record of violent strikes by El-Mahalla workers over the increase in wheat prices, with more strikes in 1942 again due to a rise in the cost of living. Human beings engage in activities to satisfy needs, whereas capitalist exploitation, domination, and alienation replace the development of workers as human beings. Gramsci explains that the working class faces its predicament as a subject of the economic corporate level. The dominant capitalist class will exploit and divide and conquer in order to control the workers, thus atomizing the proletarian forms of organization and consciousness.[57] Gramsci would point out that the only form of organization is the trade union and trade unionist consciousness. Trade unionism organizes the workers for the first time as a class and opens up a new evolving phase "in which consciousness is reached of the solidarity of interests among all the members of a social class—but still in the purely economic field."[58] Workers recognize themselves as political actors through the acquiescence to agreements with the bourgeois state. The will and desire of the proletariat to overcome its subaltern position leads to the workers' movement transcending its economic outlook and developing into a political force.[59] In order to understand how and

why workers engage in collective action, one needs to understand leadership in unions and broader worker movements.[60]

The garment and textile workers adopted the democratic leadership model.

> In the democratic model, the "magical frontier" (Fairbrother, 2005: 259)[61] between union members and leaders is highly permeable: there are many opportunities for members to become leaders (and vice versa), regular dialogue between members and leaders and frequent opportunities for members to hold leaders to account. In the bureaucratic model, communication tends to be one-way: from the top to the bottom.[62]

During the several strikes that took place from 2006 to 2011, it was clear that the workers had adopted the democratic leadership model.

Militancy of the Textile Workers Starting in 1930s to the Present

There have been many accounts written about El-Mahalla's MSCW, and a particularly interesting one is by Carson in the 1957 edition of *The Middle East Journal*. Carson used pseudonyms to protect confidences. The mill (factory) produced more than 20% of all cotton cloth production in Egypt and was an economic pillar in Bank Misr's investment portfolio. "The mill has had serious disturbances about every six years. By 'serious' is meant, for instance, an attempt to murder the General Manager, which took place in 1937."[63] These disturbances were generally a result of poor management exploiting kinship relationships/groupings. In addition, management preferred to hire illiterate peasants rather than workers from urban areas who would demand more wages and benefits.

Beinin and El-Hamalawy wrote an account of the pertinent history of the MSWC as it relates to workers' militancy, activism, and protest. The company had

> a long history of working-class militancy dating back to the 1930s, including a ferocious strike in September-October 1947 demanding an independent trade union. Workers' victories won there have often sent ripples far beyond Mahalla. Since it was established in 1927, the Misr mill has been considered a cornerstone of Egypt's industrialization effort. It has recruited generations of peasants from the surrounding villages, and transformed them into "modern" workers as they turned Egypt's principal agricultural product, cotton, into finished cloth. It is no accident that the Misr conglomerate, of which the Spinning and Weaving mill was the flagship enterprise, was the first industrial firm to be nationalized by the regime of Gamal Abdel Nasser in 1960 as it began to embrace "Arab socialism." Some of the current strikers draw upon an activist heritage in their own families.[64]

In 1927,

> Sayyid Habib's father came from the village of Tala[65] to work in the dyeing department shortly after he was married. His initial monthly wage was 90 piasters (a piaster is a hundredth of a pound). In 1975 he retired with a pension of ten pounds and 80 piasters a month. After the mill was nationalized, pensions were made subject to a cost-of-living increase, so his final monthly

pension when he passed away in 1996 was 182 pounds. Habib's father would regale his little son with stories of the workers' battles of yesteryear. "He did a good job," said 'Attar with a wink. Soon after the Misr firm was nationalized, all textile mills with over 200 workers were brought into the public sector. Nationalization resulted in an immediate wage increase. Workers at the top of the scale earned seven and a half [Egyptian] pounds[66] a month.[67]

Repertoires of This Social Movement and What Factors Determined the Outcome

The Mahalla Strike Movement—The Development of Workers Into a Social Movement, Its Repertoires, and Its Mechanisms From 2006 to 2011

> Muhammad 'Attar and Sayyid Habib were among the leaders of a December 2006 strike at Misr Spinning and Weaving, one of the most militant and politically significant in the current strike wave. This upsurge of labor collective action has occurred amidst the broader political ferment that began in December 2004 with taboo-breaking demonstrations targeting President Husni Mubarak personally, demanding that he not run for reelection in 2005 (he did) and that his son, Gamal, not succeed him as president. An amendment to the constitution permitting the first-ever multi-candidate presidential election generated expectations that the 2005 presidential and parliamentary elections would be fair and democratic. These hopes were frustrated. Nonetheless, a wide swathe of the public, which is mostly engrossed in trying to earn a living, began to take notice of politics.[68]

Posusney discusses the "moral economy" of the 1980s in which the Egyptian workers were deeply embedded or even complicit in this arrangement—an ethical political arrangement that called on workers and the state to respect their reciprocal rights and duties. It was an era where workers respected the corporatist nature of the relationship between their government unions and the state.[69] There was little solidarity among the factories in the same sector due to the nature of the ETUF's "vertical" mediation style, dealing with each factory as a single unit. Solidarity amongst workers would have created a movement, and that is the last thing that ETUF would have wanted or needed. This would have been a movement that would then unite around similar workplace grievances.

The workers used the mechanism of a "work-in," which meant work-in-place and according to the rules (without any creative increase in production)—it is referred to as "work to rule." The workers adopted a "work-in" instead of a "work-stoppage" due to this adherence to the moral economy where workers were part owners of the public sector; they could not harm the production of these factories since they saw the act as harming themselves. Representatives of the workers would leave the factory and make their demands to the management while the remaining workers in the factory continued to work. Kamal Abbas, head of the CTUWS, told me in a conversation[70] that during the famous 1989 "strike" in the Helwan steel factory, they actually increased production. The "strike" was not a stoppage of production but a continuation of work in combination with a sit-in. Workers stayed at the workplace after hours, asserting their role as productive loyal actors (part owners/stakeholders in the public

sector economy) within the patronage activity-system.[71] Beginning with Sadat's Infitah policy in the late 1970s and thereafter, the state gradually and unilaterally withdrew from the moral economy, thereby leaving the workers with diminished bargaining power and the threat of privatization.

The workers initially called on the government to resume its responsibility in the moral economy, not realizing that this model was now defunct. The economic crisis at the end of the 1980s forced the Mubarak regime to turn to the IMF and World Bank to save the economy from bankruptcy.[72] The Egyptian government implemented the neoliberal economic restructuring reforms by cutting state subsidies on consumer goods, privatizing public companies, liberalizing markets and prices, and freezing wages, all to lower foreign debt and inflation.[73] These new economic policies came into effect in coordination with the increased state security apparatus' crackdown on Islamist groups, especially the MB, as well as opposition political parties and workers.

Strikes at El-Mahalla al-Kubra began in earnest after the decline of the Kefaya movement by 2006 (see Chapter 1 for more details on Kefaya). There was a general mood of labor unrest, especially with the economic restructuring being implemented. So in order to calm the workers, the newly appointed Prime Minister, Ahmed Nazif, promised that in 2006 all public sector manufacturing workers would get a raise of their annual bonus equal to a two-month wage. When it came time for the Mahalla workers to claim their raise, they only received their old bonus. This led to a spontaneous demonstration of at least 10,000 workers on December 7, 2006, in front of the factory gates.

> A fighting spirit was in the air. Over the following two days, groups of workers refused to accept their salaries in protest. Then, on December 7, thousands of workers from the morning shift started assembling in Mahalla's Tal'at Harb Square, facing the entrance to the mill. The pace of factory work was already slowing, but production ground to a halt when around 3,000 female garment workers left their stations, and marched over to the spinning and weaving sections, where their male colleagues had not yet stopped their machines. The female workers stormed in chanting, "Where are the men? Here are the women!" Ashamed, the men joined the strike.[74]

When the security guards tried to shut down the factory on December 8, many others from the community at large joined the approximately 20,000 workers, including students, women, and others.[75]

The El-Mahalla workers began a "horizontal" action across factory sections and into the community. They were breaking with the "vertical" tradition employed by the ETUF; creating alliances and organizing workers across sections in the factory was much more effective.

> "More than 20,000 workers showed up," said [Mohammed] 'Attar. "We had a massive demonstration, and staged mock funerals for our bosses. The women brought us food and cigarettes and joined the march. Security did not dare to step in. Elementary school pupils and students from the nearby high schools took to the streets in support of the strikers." On the fourth day of the mill occupation, panicking government officials offered a 45-day bonus and gave assurances the company would not be privatized. The strike was

suspended, with the government-controlled trade union federation humili-ated by the success of the Misr Spinning and Weaving [company] workers' unauthorized action.[76]

In the process, the workers created their own organizational structures to counter the ETUF's discredited local union. The ETUF's local union was actually working against the majority of the workers' demands and against the strike. The strike committee leaders were then recognized as the true leaders of the workers and not the ETUF. What took place next was of great embarrassment to the government and to the ETUF. The Mahalla workers demanded the resignation of local ETUF union leader and its dissolution and for a new and fair trade union election.

> By the end of January [2007], around 12,800 workers had signed a peti-tion addressed to the ETUF's General Union of Textile Workers, demanding impeachment of the El-Mahalla local union committee and the holding of new elections. The MSCW workers gave the ETUF's General Union of Textile Workers a February 15 deadline, by which they would need to sack the local union officials or face mass resignations from the General Federation [ETUF], the workers' first step toward building an independent labor union.[77]

The El-Mahalla workers continued with more strikes in September 2007 and then again in February 2008. The protesters demanded a national minimum wage and also raised political slogans against Mubarak.[78] There were reverberations throughout Egypt's working class and workplaces as a result of the El-Mahalla strike actions.

Field Research Findings and Meetings With the Garment and Textile Workers in El-Mahalla al-Kubra

During my field research in Egypt, on June 9, 2013, I spent several hours with past and present worker leaders, male and female, from the MSCW. We met at the CTUWS office in El-Mahalla. This office is used in lieu of having a local union office in the factory complex. The following workers were present at the meeting/interview:

- Eman (militant labor leader)
- Gamal (old-timer; referred to as the "Nelson Mandela of El-Mahalla")
- El Sayed Habib (old-timer with over forty years' experience)
- Faisal (very active in the movement and a great organizer)
- Eman Ibrahim Gomaa (clothing department representative)
- Essam (forty years of experience)
- Abdel Ghani
- Amm Salah

Our conversation began with an emotional discussion led by Eman, who had walked into the room angry and charged up. She was eager to share a news update about the bakery and bread mafia scandal. She told us of the scandal regarding a bread bakery near MSWC where workers buy their bread on their

way home after their shift is over. It seems that gangs associated with the MB buy all of the bread early in the morning and then resell the bread at higher prices. This is the subsidized government bread that is supposed to be sold for a few piasters (cents) a piece. Now, it is being sold for LE 1[79] for six round breads. She complained to everyone in the municipal government who would listen and she vowed to organize the workers to surround the bakery issue to stop these "mafia thugs" (her words). She said, "These MB thugs threatened to harm me yet I am not afraid."

The workers gathered around a small desk, drinking hot tea, and quite animated recounted the story of how the garment and textile workers attempted to set up a transportation bus co-op through setting up an independent organization. It did not work. They were giving me examples of how it was very difficult to set up an independent union at the factory because there were too many who wanted to be "leaders" and too few followers. There was no agreement on the central concepts and issues, in addition to the issue of worker solidarity funds being managed by the ETUF-affiliated garment and textile workers' union. These "forced savings" funds contain a significant amount of money that a worker would get upon retirement. These funds are taken out of their basic wages and put into a fund that accrues over their years of service. If they formed an independent union, they would not have access to these funds anymore. The law has not changed to allow independent unions' access to these funds or other holdings/assets such as hotels, clubs, and resorts. This is seen as a serious deterrent to establishing new independent unions.

They all agreed that workers' political involvement could lead to getting or at least to demanding their rights. Yet, they did not trust the political parties today in Egypt and felt that the ETUF did not represent their interests. Gamal began to recount the history of the militancy of workers at the factory going back to 1975. He said,

> El-Mahalla workers were and are the leaders of the protest just like in a train—the engine and the caboose. They also supported other workers in Helwan, and there was solidarity. Mahalla has about 23,000 workers in seven departments but with too many leaders within the factory, making it is hard to find a consensus. There is a fear of creating independent unions since because in each of the factories within the El-Mahalla complex there were several leaders. With so many leaders, [he reiterated] is one of the main reasons for a lack of coherent mission, and the worry of being fragmented and not united under one leadership.

The plurality of unions within the factory complex troubled many of the people I met with. I asked them: "Why do they think that there will be so many unions?" They responded, "Too many workers are interested in leadership rather than service."

Faisal felt that he had to comment on the current situation in Egypt. "There was a country with institutions before the revolution, now the MB is taking over institutions and molding these institutions into their image with their own people in charge." Habib then added, "Comparing people of experience with people of trust, the MB go with those they can trust only, and those are their own members—no one from the outside."[80]

Main Strike Actions Leading the Way to the January 2011 Uprising

There were a series of strikes and protests that woke up the workers and people all over Egypt. Before going into the details of these social movement actions with information from the workers themselves, I met with a well-known Egyptian labor journalist and activist, Mostafa Bassiouny, on June 4, 2013, in Cairo, and he gave me additional details that were also mentioned by the workers in El-Mahalla on June 9.

Mostafa is a leftist-activist journalist who focuses his reporting and writings on labor. He writes for major Egyptian and Arab newspapers: *Al-Dostour*, *Tahrir*, and the Lebanese *Akhbar*. When I met with him, he was working on a report for the Al-Ahram Special Economic-Social Reports series edited by Ahmed el Naggar.[81] The title is "The Forgotten Partners in the Egyptian Revolution—The Situation of Workers Before, During and After the 2011 Revolution." He also worked with Dr. Anne Alexander, a professor at the University of Cambridge,[82] on a book regarding labor's role in the Arab Spring that was published in 2014, titled *Bread, Freedom, Social Justice: Workers and the Egyptian Revolution* (Zed Books).[83]

Mostafa Bassiouny told me,

> The garment and textile workers affiliated to the ETUF trade union was one of the oldest, toughest, and well-organized union organizations. It began before ETUF's establishment in 1957 starting in the 1930s/40s and the workers in El-Mahalla were the best organized in the independent labor world in Egypt. So we then have the strongest two groups that are going head to head facing/challenging each other—the local union and leaders today and the ETUF-affiliated general union. The ETUF garment and textile union was the most aware and confident compared to the workers at MSWC, and they had the know-how to fight workers and keep them in place. The RETA experience was much different; their counterpart in the ETUF, the Finance and Banking workers union, was very weak and young, and they were relatively not known or not a player on the scene.

Bassiouny explained the culture of strikes before, during, and after the January 2011 revolution. He also said that he prefers to know the number of workers participating, since it is more indicative than the number of actual strikes or events. Workers have somewhat innate internal organizational tools when it comes to the logistics of strikes and organization of details. When you ask workers and leaders how or why they strike, they are sparse on the details and emphasize that it was the correct and just thing to do. They assume that the listener knows the details of the how and why. They are more interested in the mission and ultimate goal, not in the mechanisms that make it a reality. It is not that they have a prepared checklist when it comes to preparing for strikes, for example. He prefers to "live" with the workers during strikes or protests, since it captures the gravity of the strikes more than relying on reports after the fact. The following are details regarding each of the four major protest events that took place at the factory and in the city of El-Mahalla.

(1) **December 6–8, 2006, Protest Strike**—The workers interviewed in El-Mahalla told me that this event chipped away at the fear that had gripped workers in general, but the younger workers acted too quickly by declaring a strike.

This was the first of a series of strikes that took place, which woke up all Egyptians. In addition, the workers' actions were able to twist the government's arm, and several demands were fulfilled.

On December 7, 2006, the fighting spirit was high and the 24,000-strong local union members of the MSWC went on strike. They assembled in Tal'at Harb Square facing the entrance to the mill. The strike began with 3,000 women workers first, then they chanted, "We are here, we are here, where are you the men?" and prompted male workers to join, making the numbers swell over a few hours to 10,000 workers. The riot police were dispatched to the site, but they were shocked at the large numbers of workers. Workers quickly got the message out to the others who had gone home, and many workers then rushed back to the factory compound. The local state security and police were spreading rumors that there were just a few hundred workers protesting. The numbers of strikers grew to 20,000 and the strike continued for several days. El-Mahalla is a typical company town, and everyone knew of the strike and everyone was involved—each of the protesters had family and friends in town. The strike ended after five days, and the workers won their demands.

However, the women did not sleep in the factory at night to protect the machines, because they were afraid of any harm coming to the women through hearsay. They were worried that the management would spread bad rumors about the perception of women sleeping in the factory and not in their homes. Another indication that the workers were in desperate financial need was the prevalence of the avian flu virus. Many of the workers' and their families still lived in rural areas around the city, and their wives raised chickens and other livestock in addition to growing vegetables to supplement their income. In 2006–2007, the bird flu virus hit Egypt, and the government called for the indiscriminate slaughter of all poultry. This was a catastrophe for many workers' families that decreased their supplementary income. This was another factor in the workers rising up to demand increase in wages and benefits.

Habib said during the interview on June 9, 2013,

> The December 2006 Mahalla strike was significant and then the workers at the Real Estate Tax Authority continued the job and created the first independent union in December 2008 since 1957. Unfortunately, there is the perception that workers are simple minded and thus easy to influence, while at the same time, ETUF is a very entrenched state institution, especially its garment and textile workers' affiliate under leadership of its president Saeed El Gohary, who is now retired. They did try to organize an independent union yet they had to fight state security, management, in addition to the "system" and rumors which can be a deadly combination.[84]

Bassiouny said that the 2006 demands of the workers were very practical, realizable, and goal-oriented. Their wages were very low, so that was the main reason that 25,000 workers went on strike. They initially asked for a bonus of two months' wages, and as we know demands are like an ascending ladder—you start with one that is doable and realizable that you succeed in getting, then once you have that you move on to the next item on the list.[85] "25,000 workers asked for a simple demand of two months' profit sharing wages; their wages were so low that this extra money was much needed."[86] This strike was political under

the social guise (i.e. with social repercussions), and it was a strike and not a sit-in. "In Arabic 'اعتصام!' is a protest/sit-in where the workers still work and they protest in place so the production continues, and it is meant to put political pressure on the government."[87]

Bassiouny continued, saying,

> In Arabic "إضراب" is a strike and it is putting economic pressure and literally means to stop work. Workers chose to immediately strike instead of holding a "sit-in" because privatization had begun in 1991 in agreement with the IMF/World Bank, and fifteen years or so had passed and "killed" the nation-alistic, paternal culture that workers had vis a vis the public sector. It was becoming non-existent.[88]

With that turning point, the government was forced to negotiate, which prompted hundreds of strikes to take place thereafter.

(2) **The September 2007 Strike**—This is the next strike that took place at the El-Mahalla factory where, according to one of the workers interviewed,

> everything happened in El-Mahalla first and then continued on to Tahrir in 2011—the same repertoires and mechanisms such as tents, posters, chants, and discourse and this is also where the older generation met with the younger generation at El-Mahalla and later on in Tahrir Square.

Bassiouny explained,

> By September 2007, the group or bundle [*hizma* in Arabic] of demands grew with the needs by the workers, which encompassed working conditions, meal allowance, etc. They were able to achieve some successes. The Mahalla workers then began the process of removing the confidence in the local ETUF union committee; they gathered 13,000 signatures for a petition to remove the local union committee from representing them. The ETUF bureaucracy killed this move just like the dreaded bureaucracy [deep state] killed the January 2011 revolution. Egypt is a very bureaucratic state. The El-Mahalla workers went to the ETUF union headed by Saeed el Gohari, a trade union-ist skilled in bureaucratic machinations and delay tactics. The workers took the 13,000 signatures to Saeed el Gohari and he said, "Ok, time for the local ETUF to go." His El-Mahalla brothers and sisters[89] welcomed his response. He said, "We are at your service, you are the masters," blah, blah, blah, "but we will need to review all 13,000 signatures to ensure that everyone's rights are protected." So of course, the petition went nowhere but into a drawer to gather dust, and that is where the petition died (ended).[90]

(3) **February 17, 2008**—An important turning point took place on Febru-ary 17, 2008, when the workers in El-Mahalla stole the government's thunder. Twelve thousand workers protested and began the first important step to put "class demand" on the national agenda, calling for a national minimum wage of LE 1,200 per month. The call for a minimum wage was also a national and not a special interest demand. This took place one day before the meeting of the National Wages Council on February 18, 2008.[91]

(4) **April 6, 2008**—This protest was the first time a large billboard with Mubarak's face was brought down, stepped on, and destroyed. April 5 was the last day in the pay period and payday, so they decided to protest on April 6, and on April 8, municipal elections were to be held. On March 30, leaders from El-Mahalla called on ETUF with their demands. ETUF leaders "whispered in their ears" telling them to go ahead and protest. In hindsight, they realized that ETUF leadership was trying to get them caught into a trap of blame for setting the factory ablaze or something like that. About ten workers met with Abbas, the general coordinator of the CTUWS, about ten days before April 6 to prepare for the event, predict various scenarios, and plan on how to deal with each. They met at a public park near el Sayyida Zeinab mosque. There was the distinct possibility that management and state security would set fire to the factory, so the leaders agreed to protest outside the factory gates in the El-Shon Midan (square) away from the factory and in the city center. When they arrived that morning of April 6 to work, they saw many unfamiliar faces within the factory complex. The leaders wondered with much concern about who they were, since they felt that this was going to cause trouble. "On the day of the strike," El-Fayumi said, "State Security agents in plain clothes filled the premises of the company that spans over almost 600 *feddans*.[92] They stood at the gates of the company and escorted whomever finished their shifts to a vehicle that drove them home and escorted any worker standing outside the gates inside," El-Fayoumi said, "preventing workers from assembling outside where they were supposed to demonstrate."[93] El Sayid Habib and Gamal outlined the critical factors that the workers' leaders focused on for this strike: public opinion, awareness, opportunity, and the media.

Bassiouny concluded with the following comments: as a result of the April 6, 2008, event, worker elections in El-Mahalla took place for an independent union, and there was a greater emphasis on involving the society at large; it became a rallying political power tool and a model for general strikes/protests in many other sectors of the economy. It was a huge uprising where for the first time large billboards of Mubarak were torn down. Unfortunately, the labor bureaucracy ended the possibility of a national and even a local garment and textile union starting with El-Mahalla workers. They were not able to organize an independent national union like RETA employees did because of the strength and entrenchment of the ETUF garment and textile affiliate union. The labor bureaucracy killed that idea.[94]

In the *Ahram* newspaper, a retrospective account written on April 8, 2013, stated,

> A planned worker's strike morphed into popular struggle following clashes with the police who used—according to eyewitnesses—rubber bullets, birdshot and live ammunition to disperse crowds. While such unrest is now common in post-2011 Egypt, it was unprecedented at the time, the open defiance of a city to the regime, sending shockwaves across the country. For the first time, images of a tarnished, trampled upon poster of Mubarak circulated on the internet, signaling the beginning of the fall of Egypt's then-feared dictator.[95]

Concluding the meeting in El-Mahalla with the workers, they discussed the issue of privatization. They said that there would be privatization in El-Mahalla over

their collective dead bodies. The government (still the owner) needs to develop the factory, invest in its equipment and workers, and restructure the workflow to take advantage of every inch of space. It should also ask the workers what they would do to improve the factory and make it profitable and competitive. Never privatize, they said. They insisted there was no question as to the importance of labor's independent political role. "Any of labor's demands and needs are inherently political and there is no shame in that." I asked them for their last words of wisdom or what they want to tell others outside of Egypt; they said the following: "The January 2011 revolution was an uprising against injustice; the workers are the basis for this "revolution"; workers must struggle until freedom is reached; social justice is a must; respect for dignity; workers of the world unite against injustice; and workers who are united are undefeated and can fight for everyone."

The Art of Presence or Active Citizenry

Let us first discuss the "art of presence or active citizenry," as explained by Bayat, and then apply this concept to the Egyptian independent labor movement. Bayat describes the

> art of presence or active citizenry as the skill and stamina to assert collective will in spite of all odds by circumventing constraints, utilizing what is possible and discovering new spaces within which to make themselves heard, seen, felt and realized.[96]

Authoritarian governments can clamp down and end movements of contention, but they cannot silence or stifle the entire society or community.

Workers over a period of a decade prior to 2011 had been utilizing the "art of presence," yet their big shortfall was not taking it to the street protests. Why is taking it to the streets important and how can it have an effective impact? Bayat refers to the "streets of discontent" and how millions work in their daily lives and workplaces can bring to fruition these highly complex revolutions.[97] The streets of discontent are where these collective challenges against the invincible power holders are stimulated and where the destiny of political movements is often determined.[98]

The streets today leading to major squares such as Tahrir Square in Cairo, with their location and mass transit, are spaces where people can easily gather and disperse if needed from policy brutality and which hold historic memories and significance of protests.[99] Streets represent the modern urban stage where protesters voice discontent, march, and encourage others to join in. It becomes an epidemic that grows and swells with high numbers of people wanting to raise their voices. Those voices belong to those who have been marginalized for so long under authoritarian rule. The beauty of these streets is that they become the central focal point of politics for ordinary persons, "those who are structurally absent from the centers of institutional powers. [. . .] The Street is the physical space where collective dissent may be both expressed and produced."[100] This space element distinguished street politics from strikes or sit-ins because "streets are not only where people protest, but also where they extend their protest beyond their immediate circle."[101] In the case of Egyptian workers, protests were often limited to

the workplace itself, which in the case of the MSWC factory is practically a large town in itself surrounded by walls so the inside is not seen by passersby.

There is a tradition of workers to stay at their workplace to protest and protect the machines at the same time, especially from vandals sent by the company. This strategy would help the workers avoid arrest and accusation of destruction of public company property. In 2006, 2007, and again in 2008, El-Mahalla al-Kubra witnessed several large strikes and protests. The workers intentionally stayed in the factory compound and they would occupy the large Tal'at Harb Square within the factory compound, by the entrance gate. It was only on April 6, 2008, that the workers went outside the factory to the main square in the city of El-Mahalla al-Kubra.

The textile mill in El-Mahalla al-Kubra witnessed a spate of strikes starting in December 2006, another strike in September 2007, and then another in April 2008 for the second time in less than a year. The workers went on strike occupying the factory and its surrounding space within the compound and won. "Yet this last strike was even more militant than December 2006. [. . .] Workers established a security force to protect factory premises and threatened to occupy the company's administration headquarters as well."[102] They received support from the city's townspeople and other textile mills of Kafr al Dawwar and Shibin al Kom railway workers and urban intellectuals.

Egyptian workers took their protests out of their workplaces, into the streets, and to the seat of the state's power. The garment and textile workers in El-Mahalla al-Kubra went on strike again in April 2008, and this time they took it to the streets.[103] Violence erupted in the city with repressive measures of arrests, tear gas, volleys of rocks, and beatings of workers by hired thugs of the regime. The crowd burned NDP banners with candidate photos for municipal elections scheduled for April 8. "Thousands of demonstrators were out in the streets, throwing stones, chanting anti-government slogans and defying the batons of the riot police, tear gas, and bullets."[104] Dozens of middle-class activists and workers were detained for weeks without charge; some credibly claimed they were tortured (Human Rights Watch 2008).

> "The price of basic foodstuffs rose at rates of at least 33 per cent [for meat], and as much as 146 per cent [for chicken], from 2005 to 2008. The official annual rate of inflation for January 2008 was over 11 per cent, and over 12 per cent for February," says Egyptian labour historian Joel Beinin. The demonstrations at Mahalla Al-Kubra erupted against this backdrop of deteriorating living conditions for the working class and Egyptian poor. "This is a popular Intifada, a scene of street battles for subsistence," said El-Attar on Monday. Hence the demonstrators' chant: "Ye pasha, Ye bey, a loaf of bread now costs a quarter of a pound."[105]

These events gave rise to a student youth movement that was initially created on Facebook, the April 6 Youth Movement.

Background: The April 6 Youth Movement

What was the April 6 Youth Movement? How long had they been organizing? What were the effective tools that they used? And how did the often-maligned

civil society organizations contribute successfully despite the odds against them? A decrepit, hostile environment for NGOs, internal corruption, and a lack of civility, transparency, and accountability were the rule of the day when the April 6 Youth Movement was established. It was an organization of young people that was motivated and tactically adaptive.

The April 6 Youth Movement received assistance and support from abroad, but it was in the form of opportunities for training in and outside of Egypt. The April 6 Youth Movement had a connection with Serbia's Otpor student movement, and they benefitted from the contact.[106] It adopted many of its tactics, mechanism, symbols (the clenched fist and black-and-white attire), and strategies of opposition to the regime while rallying public support. By 2009, it boasted a membership of 70,000 people. The movement was

> part of a diverse gaggle of opposition campaigners in a nation whose size, security apparatus, and strategic importance to the west all complicate efforts to repeat this month's popular uprising in neighboring Tunisia. The group—dubbed April 6 after the date of a strike it was set up to support in 2008—is a social media network of dissenters, coordinated by Ahmad Maher, an engineer.[107]

It was a mismatched group of individuals who boldly took advantage of opportunity and worked at down-to-earth community grassroots organizing. As widely reported, the group effectively employed social media tools.

> The group's prominence in [. . .] protests is partly down to chance: it co-ordinates an annual January 25 demonstration, which this year fell less than a fortnight after the overthrow of Tunisia's president Zein al-Abidine Ben Ali. That helped the protests gather a broad base of support from other activist groups, opposition politicians, and Islamists—the last of whom, according to Ms. Sharaf [one of the leaders], was "very strong but [was] not using their strength."[108]

It is interesting to note that the famed, well-organized, and established opposition, the MB, jumped onto the protest bandwagon several days later.

The leaders and activists within the April 6 Youth Movement were younger and more at ease with cyber networking and using social media tools to create alliances and build a movement. They were college students, recent graduates, young professionals, and young workers who were savvy about the use of social media. The simple decision to make the textile workers' protests at El-Mahalla al-Kubra a broad call for a demonstration on April 6, 2008, and to begin an alliance in support of workers proved to be a stroke of genius that evoked nostalgia from the 1980s Polish anti-Solidarnosc movement, which encompassed workers and civil society.

The traditional NGO scene reflected the feebleness of the official political arena. Weak political parties and election fraud were hallmarks of the political scene. It was no longer an entity that could contest the entrenched Mubarak political power. NGOs, despite the potential for becoming active politically, remained largely divided and fragmented.[109] In addition, there was a "caste system" of the secular elites and intellectuals who claimed to know best, and they would

not associate with the lower classes. There was virtually no solidarity between the established civil society NGOs and the growing independent labor movement. A study by Beinin about the struggle for worker rights in Egypt details this lack of solidarity.[110] This study confirms disconnect among the civil society actors and the workers, despite the workers' regular protests and strikes for fundamental socio-economic rights and against the regime. The saga of the Egyptian 2011 uprising continues, since a revolution, in the truest sense of the word, has not yet taken place in Egypt.

The Mubarak regime had a relatively easy time manipulating its political opposition. The secular leftists were rendered toothless and the more conservative MB was outlawed. It is common knowledge that the Mubarak regime used the "divide, conquer, and rule" theory of politics to cleverly thwart a political alliance where the two rivals—secular intellectual elites and the MB—could cooperate to challenge his rule. It was also commonly believed that Mubarak and his family would continue to rule for the next thirty to forty years, reinforcing the concept of stability at the price of political freedom. However, the Mubarak regime did not count on several other emerging factors that will be discussed in detail later: the resurgence of civil society in the Arab world and its relation to democracy reform efforts; hegemony, consent, and the crisis of the state in Egypt; neoliberal policies and increased economic hardship of daily life for Egyptians; serious financial shortage in the state's budget; and the growing youth movement. Reports on the scene captured the political irony being played out,

> but this enduring and, many here say, all too comfortable relationship was upended this week [January 25, 2011] by the emergence of an unpredictable third force, the leaderless tens of thousands of young Egyptians who turned out to demand an end to Mr. Mubarak's 30-year rule. Now the older opponents are rushing to catch up.[111]

An interesting and almost accidental alliance was formed between the independent workers' movement and the youth of Egypt. This came after several unsuccessful strikes led by the workers in Egypt's largest and most important public sector industry located in the delta city of al Mahalla el Kubra.

> On April 6, 2008, the Egyptian government crushed a strike by a group of textile workers in the industrial city of Mahalla, and in response a group of young activists who connected through Facebook and other social networking Web sites formed the 6th April Youth Movement in solidarity with the strikers.[112]

The early efforts to strike were not successful, but it gave birth to an online network that initially could not be stopped or strategically monitored by the Egyptian security police. "It was an online rallying cry for a show of opposition to tyranny, corruption, and torture that brought so many to the streets."[113] So, the April 6 Youth Movement adopted a local event, the workers' strike in El-Mahalla, and then turned it into a national event[114] (see interview details below). This is significant because normally it would have stayed localized, yet the April 6 Youth Movement's adoption of the workers' strike turned it into a national event. The idea was to call for a general strike throughout Egypt based on the workers'

local protest. The movement asked everyone to stay at home and not go to work via social media, local organizers, and word of mouth. The Ministry of Interior promised that they would use violence to counter any and all protests—these statements further assisted the April 6 Youth Movement's call. It was a perfect gift for their campaign. For the first six months, the April 6 Youth Movement stayed focused on worker issues, but they found as an organization they were not growing in membership. They wanted to grow and highlight additional socio-economic, even political issues, which young people were concerned with. Also, a movement needs numbers in addition to worthy cause, unity of purpose, and commitment in order to be a viable social movement. The following is an inter-view conducted during my field research in June 2013 with Mohamed Adel, one of the main leaders and activists in the April 6 Youth Movement.

Interview With April 6 Activist and Leader in Cairo, June 2013

Mohamed Adel[115] is a leader and activist within the April 6 Youth Movement, who was arrested in December 2013 and was released on January 22, 2017, according to an Ahram Online article:

> 6 April Movement co-founder Mohamed Adel has been released Sunday from Aga police station in Mansoura city, after finishing Saturday a three-and-a-half-year prison sentence on charges of violating Egypt's protest law, his lawyer Sayed El-Banna confirmed to Ahram Online. Adel will remain on probation for three years, and will have to report to Aga police station on a daily basis for 12 hours, from 6 pm to 6 am.[116], [117]
>
> Ahmed Maher, Ahmed Douma and Mohamed Adel, all senior members of the 6 April youth movement that stirred dissent during the final years of the Mubarak era, were also fined for flouting a new law that severely curtails the right to protest. They were accused of organizing an unsanctioned street protest deemed illegitimate by a controversial new law and of assaulting a police officer.[118]

In a meeting with Adel on June 20, 2013, he shared with me his views on the Egyptian labor movement, their role, the April 6 Youth Movement's birth, and its and support of the workers. Astonishingly, their leaders never coordinated or dis-cussed with the MSWC workers activities and actions; instead, they coordinated with the Revolutionary Socialist Movement (as if they were the spokespeople for the labor movement). The following is my transcript of notes from my interview with Adel in downtown Cairo at the offices of the Egyptian Center for Economic and Social Research (ECESR):[119]

> Initially, the 6th April Youth Movement (6AYM) leaders and members were not interested in the Marxist view in the workers' movement—that was not what motivated their involvement or support. This movement started from the fruits of the IGURETA strikes/sit-ins (2007–08) and the Kefaya move-ment that started in 2004. 6AYM began with a stand in solidarity with the Mahalla workers' protest on April 6, 2008. These youth leaders came out of the Kefaya movement and the Youth for Reform and Change organization.

They were intent on involving workers or associating the workers' movement with the political reform movement. There were many workers' protests, such as in Kafr Soul, Sarando, El-Mahalla, and in Damyietta. The idea was to support and call for a general strike throughout Egypt based on the Mahalla protest. We wanted to take a local event and turn it into a national event. A good idea! The 6th April Movement asked everyone to stay at home and not to go to work. They used the internet and activated all social media tools (particularly Facebook) to call for a day at home. The 6AYM also reached out to teachers, private sector workers, and particularly the "couch party" adherents to ask them to stay at home in protest. The Ministry of the Interior announced that there would be violence and attacks on cars on April 6, so it was a perfect gift to further promote and encourage people to stay at home.

Adel continued to say,

For the first six months of 6AYM activism in 2008, it was focused on supporting the workers' strikes and demonstrations. After the first six months, 6AYM moved from just focusing on support for workers to other issues, why? They found that they were not growing in membership; actually, they were losing members. They needed to grow as an organization. There was a division within the 6AYM organization on whether to focus on economic or political challenges/reforms. They moved to address more of a social movement, minimum wage, employment, and challenges facing youth, which was a larger scope for the movement. You need members to become a viable, effective organization able to affect decision makers. So we needed to do widen our scope to organize and include more university students. The 6AYM began to encourage members to enter elections of unions/professional associations where they work.

According to Adel, the 6AYM activists and leaders are centrists politically; they are not leftists/Marxists. This alliance was important to show that the workers were able to align themselves with centrists and not just ideological leftists and Marxists. The center-right wait until the workers come to them, making them the true "couch party." Mohamed explained that they are a version of "American liberal capitalists." He works as a researcher at the Egyptian Center for Economic and Social Rights.[120] When I interviewed him, they had just gathered one million Tamarod (rebel) signed petitions and held a press conference to announce this.

The April 6 Youth Movement led the overall Egyptian youth movement to the forefront, and it became an effective political independence force in Egypt. The Mubarak regime could not derail it. In January 2011, after eighteen days of intense protests at the heart of the capital in Tahrir Square and all over the country, the regime's figurehead stepped down.

Concluding Remarks

The garment and textile industry and its workers are a significant force in civil society activism and they have an important presence in the Egyptian labor

Figure 4.1 Gamal Hussein (on the right) and Sayid Habib (both retirees after forty years of work at MSWC) at the CTUWS headquarters in El-Mahalla al-Kubra

Photo taken by Heba F. El-Shazli

movement. Their militant history and actions have continued from the late nineteenth century through to the twenty-first century. This is one of the most important sectors of the economy, with an independent movement that faced the massive challenge of protesting against the ETUF's strongest and most established union. However, an independent union was not formed, which did not necessarily undermine the role that these workers' played for the rest of Egypt's workers starting in 2006 to the present. This was a social movement that ultimately did not develop into an institution (a trade union organization) similar to the RETA workers. The ETUF's official union for garment and textile workers is still relatively strong and has control of the assets, pension funds, and retirement bonuses that workers have been paying into for many years. It is a difficult choice for the workers to leave their lifelong work investments and begin an independent union without these benefits. However, this does not diminish the political role these workers played or how they became a role model for other workers in Egypt to stand up and challenge their employers, which in many cases effectively challenges the state.

Figure 4.2 Gamal Hussein and Sayid Habib (retirees after forty years of work at MSWC) and Hussein el Masry, head of training and education at CTUWS

Photo taken by a member of CTUWS staff

Notes

1. The word *Misr* in Arabic means Egypt.
2. Sewell, W. H. Jr. "Uneven Development, the Autonomy of Politics, and the Dockworkers of Nineteenth-Century Marseille." *The American Historical Review* 93 (3) (1988): 604–637.
3. Issawi, Charles. *Egypt: An Economic and Social Analysis.* Oxford: Oxford University Press, 1947: 97.
4. Ibid.: 194.
5. Sallam, Hisham. "Striking Back at Egyptian Workers." Published in MER259, 41 (2011) ME Report (MERIP).
6. Ibid.
7. A wildcat strike is a strike action undertaken by unionized workers without union leadership's authorization, support, or approval; this is sometimes termed an unofficial industrial action.
8. Shokr, Ahmad. "Reflections on Two Revolutions." Published in MER265, 265 (2012): 2–12.
9. Shehata, Samer. *Shop Floor Culture and Politics in Egypt.* New revised afterword for the AUC publication in 2010: 253.
10. Ibid.: 268.
11. Ibid.
12. Beinin, Joel. *The Struggle for Workers Rights in Egypt.* Washington, DC: Solidarity Center. Published by the Solidarity Center, February 2010: 14. http://www1.umn.edu/humanrts/research/Egypt/The Struggle for Workers rights.pdf.
13. Ibid.: 15.

14. Sallam 2011.
15. Ibid.
16. Hammad, Hanan. "Making and Breaking the Working Class: Worker Recruitment in the National Textile Industry in Interwar Egypt." *International Review of Social History* 57 (2012): 73–96: 73–74.
17. Vitalis, Robert. *When Capitalists Collide: Business Conflict and the End of Empire in Egypt*. Berkeley: University of California Press, 1995: 4. Print.
18. Ibid.: 5.
19. Ibid.
20. Beinin, Joel and Zachary Lockman. *Workers on the Nile: Nationalism, Communism, Islam, and the Egyptian Working Class, 1882–1954*. Princeton, NJ: Princeton University Press, 1987: 10–11.
21. Vitalis 1995: 7.
22. Ibid.: 10.
23. Ibid.
24. Ibid.: 28.
25. Ibid.
26. Ibid.: 57.
27. Owen, E. R. J. *Cotton and the Egyptian Economy 1820–1914—A Study in Trade and Development*. Oxford at the Clarendon Press, 1969.
28. Ibid., introduction.
29. Interview with Fathallah Mahrous in Alexandria, Egypt, June 22–23, 2013.
30. Owen 1969: 375.
31. Ibid.: 208.
32. Beinin and Lockman 1987: 5.
33. Ibid.
34. Goldberg, Ellis. *Tinker, Tailor, and Textile Worker: Class and Politics in Egypt, 1930–1952*. Berkeley: University of California Press, 1986: 140.
35. Hammad 2012: 76.
36. Ibid.: 77.
37. Ibid.
38. Ibid.
39. Beinin and Lockman 1987: 453.
40. Hammad 2012: 81.
41. Ibid.: 82.
42. Ibid.: 93.
43. Ibid.: 94.
44. Ibid.: 96.
45. Ibid.
46. Ibid.
47. Goldberg, Ellis in Lockman, Zachary (editor). *Workers and Working Classes in the Middle East: Struggles, Histories, Historiographies*. Albany: State University of New York Press, 1994: 117.
48. Ibid.: 125.
49. Interview on June 23, 2013, at his home in the Baqoos neighborhood in the city of Alexandria, Egypt.
50. Beinin and Lockman 1987: 422.
51. Information from the interview and supported by Ibid.: 423.
52. Ibid.
53. Interview on June 23, 2013, in Alexandria, Egypt.
54. Ibid.
55. Lockman 1994: 125.
56. Issawi 1947: 95.
57. Thomas, P. D. *The Gramscian Moment. Philosophy, Hegemony and Marxism*. Leiden: Brill, 2009.
58. Gramsci, A. *Selections from the Prison Notebooks*. New York: International Publishers, 1971: 181.
59. Ibid.
60. Alexander, Anne. "Leadership and Collective Action in the Egyptian Trade Unions." *Work Employment Society* 24 (2010): 241: 242.

61. Fairbrother, P. "Book Review of G. Gall (ed.) Union Organising: Campaigning for Trade Union Recognition." *Capital and Class* 87 (2005): 257–263: 259.
62. Alexander 2010: 242.
63. Carson, William Morris. "The Social History of an Egyptian Factory." *Middle East Journal* 11 (4) (1957): 361–370. Published by: Middle East Institute: 361.
64. Beinin, Joel and Hossam El-Hamalawy. "Egyptian Textile Workers Confront the New Economic Order." *Middle East Report*, MERIP. Published March 25, 2007. www.merip.org/mero/mero032507.
65. Tala is in El Menoufiyya province (governorate), which, incidentally, is also where my father was born and grew up until he left for Cairo to attend university in 1942.
66. About 1 US dollar.
67. www.merip.org/mero/mero032507
68. Ibid.
69. Posusney, M. "Irrational Workers, the Moral Economy of Labor Protest in Egypt." *World Development* 46.1 (1993): 83–120. Print.
70. June 22, 2013, in Helwan (outside of Cairo) at the CTUWS headquarters office.
71. Al-Mahdi, Rabab. "Labour as a Pro-democracy Actor in Egypt and Brazil." Paper presented at the APSA 2009 Toronto meeting, revised September 23, 2011.
72. Farah, Nadia. *Egypt's Political Economy. Power Relations in Development.* Cairo: American University Press, 2009.
73. DeSmet, Brecht. "Egyptian Workers and Their Intellectuals. The Dialectical Pedagogy of the Mahalla Strike Movement." *Mind Culture and Activity*, ISSN 1074-9039 19 (2) (2012): 139–155: 8.
74. Beinin and el-Hamalawy 2007.
75. Ibid.
76. Ibid.
77. Ibid.
78. Hamalawy, Hossam. "Revolt in Mahalla. As Food Prices Rise in Egypt, Class Struggle Is Heating Up." *International Socialist Review* 59 (May–June 2008).
79. LE is the French acronym for *livre égyptienne* = Egyptian pound (currency).
80. A side comment of possible interest: The conversation touched on a Morsi speech given on June 8 regarding water security for Egypt and what he will and will not do. After leaving the conference hall in his massive motorcade, outside of the gates his vehicle stopped and he came out to greet his "fans" that gathered to cheer him on. The workers laughed and reminded each other of the Mubarak days and how not much has changed.
81. This report was published in late 2013.
82. Dr. Anne Alexander, Coordinator, Digital Humanities Network, Centre for Research in the Arts, Social Sciences and Humanities (CRASSH), University of Cambridge. Dr. Anne Alexander's research focuses on leadership, collective action, and social movements in the Middle East. She has a particular interest in Egypt, Iraq, and Syria post-1945 and labor movements across the region. www.csap.cam.ac.uk/network/anne-alexander/.
83. www.palgrave.com/page/detail/bread-freedom-social-justice-anne-alexander/?K=9781780324319
84. Interview with workers in El-Mahalla on June 9, 2013.
85. Interview with M. Bassiouny in Cairo on June 4, 2013.
86. Ibid.
87. A note: Workers in the Egyptian public sector have a culture of nationalism regarding working in the public sector, and it is part of their legacy. Sit-ins were more prevalent since they worried about and cared for the public sector as if they owned it. They did not want to cause any economic pressure by stopping the production, so political pressure was the best path to take.
88. Ibid.
89. Common usage by workers referring to each other as brothers and sisters in solidarity.
90. Interview with M. Bassiouny in Cairo on June 4, 2013.
91. Ibid.
92. A *feddan* is an Egyptian unit of area equivalent to 1.038 acres.
93. http://english.ahram.org.eg/NewsContent/1/64/68543/Egypt/Politics-/Revolutionary-history-relived-The-Mahalla-strike-o.aspx

94. Interview with Bassiouny in Cairo on June 4, 2013.
95. http://english.ahram.org.eg/NewsContent/1/64/68543/Egypt/Politics-/Revolutionary-history-relived-The-Mahalla-strike-o.aspx
96. Bayat, Asef. *Life as Politics, How Ordinary People Change the Middle East*. Stanford, CA: Stanford University Press, 2010: 249.
97. Ibid.: 165.
98. Ibid.
99. Ibid.: 168–169.
100. Ibid.: 167.
101. Ibid.
102. Beinin, Joel. "Militancy of the Mallah el Kubra Workers." September 29, 2007, MERIP.
103. Beinin, Joel. "Egyptian Workers Jan 25 A Social Movement in Historical Context." *Social Research* 79 (2) (2012): 13.
104. Ibid.: 335.
105. Rady, Faiza. "A Victory for Workers." *Ahram Newspaper*. http://weekly.ahram.org.eg/2008/892/eg7.htm.
106. www.pbs.org/wgbh/pages/frontline/revolution-in-cairo/inside-april6-movement/
107. Peel, Michael. "Egypt's Activists See Chance to Drive Reforms." *FT.com*, January 27, 2011.
108. Ibid.
109. Abdelrahman, Maha M. *Civil Society Exposed—The Politics of NGOs in Egypt*. London and New York: Tauris Academic Studies, 2004: 148.
110. Beinin, Joel, *The Struggle for Worker Rights in Egypt*. Washington, DC: Solidarity Center, 2010. http://www1.umn.edu/humanrts/research/Egypt/The%20Struggle%20for%20Workers%20rights.pdf.
111. Kirkpatrick, David D. and Michael Slackman. "In New Role, Egypt Youths Drive Revolt." Mona El-Naggar contributed reporting from Cairo. January 27, 2011 Thursday, Section A; Column 0; Foreign Desk; Pg. 1. www.nytimes.com.
112. Ibid.
113. Ibid.
114. Information from an interview with April 6 Youth Movement leader, Mohamed Adel, in June 2013.
115. "During that period April 6 members also studied the nonviolent tactics of Serbian and Ukrainian youth movements. In the summer of 2009, blogger and April 6 activist Mohammed Adel traveled to Serbia to take a course on strategies for nonviolent revolutions. It was taught by people who had organized the overthrow of Slobodan Milošević in the 1990s." www.pbs.org/wgbh/pages/frontline/revolution-in-cairo/inside-april6-movement/.
116. http://english.ahram.org.eg/NewsContent/1/64/256633/Egypt/Politics-/April--Movement-cofounder-Mohamed-Adel-is-released.aspx by Hadeer El-Mahdawy, Sunday January 22, 2017.
117. www.theguardian.com/world/2013/dec/22/egypt-court-jails-three-leaders-2011-uprising-6th-april-youth-movement
118. Ibid.
119. http://ecesr.com/en: Egyptian Centre for economic and social rights is an Egyptian non-governmental legal and research entity, stems from the values of justice, freedom, and equality, abiding to all treaties, declarations and international conventions concerning human rights, particularly the international charters for economic, social, cultural rights, and all the treaties and recommendations of the International Labour Organisation as a reference on the level of vision and practice.
120. http://ecesr.com/en: "In an escalatory and unjustified step, police forces have raided the premises of the Egyptian Center for Economic and Social Rights (ECESR) at around 11:30 p.m. on Wednesday December 18, 2013, in which they violently assaulted and arrested six of the staff and volunteers: Mostafa Eissa, the Head of the Documentaries Unit; Mahmoud Belal, Lawyer in the Criminal Justice Unit; and Hossam Mohamed Nasr, Mahmoud El-Sayed, Mohamed Adel and Sherif Mansour, volunteers in the Media Unit. The police forces arrested them without legal basis, abducting them to an unknown detention location. Moreover, the police officers destroyed the Media Unit's

equipment, its furniture, as well as stealing computers. Lawyers failed to reach the abductees mentioned above as a result of the abstinence and refusal of police officials in Abdeen and Kasr El Nile Police Stations and the Cairo Security Administration to provide them with any information on fate of the detainees. Consequently, a police report was made outlining details and information describing the raid, the arrest and abduction of the Center's staff and volunteers, including the damage of the Center's furniture and robbery of its equipment. All abductees and detainees were released this morning except for Mohamed Adel, the volunteer in the Media Unit, and his place of detention remains unknown."

5 Other Workers' Protests and How Their Repertoire Mirrored the Protests of Larger Unions and Worker Groups

Chapter Outline:

1. The Quest for Democratization Through Social Movements
2. What Transforms a Group Into a Social Movement?
3. Differing Views of Effective Mobilizing Structures: Crowds and Masses
4. Other Significant Protests by Egyptian Workers
5. Background: The Legal Framework to Control Workers

   The Right to Strike in Egypt

6. An Example—Teachers on Strike: "Education and Learning Are Not Taking Place in Egyptian Schools"
7. Tanta Kitan (Linen) Factory in the City of Tanta, El Gharbiyya Province
8. What Factors and Organizations and Which Players Helped and Supported You?
9. The Information Technology (IT) Centers' Workers: "We Just Want to Live" Is Our Story (November 2010)
10. Concluding Remarks

The Quest for Democratization Through Social Movements

Unfortunately, the study of democratization in the Middle East was conducted through the lenses of the regime: the actors being the state and elites. The role of social movements and marginalized groups (non-elites) were not normally taken into consideration. The emphasis on elites came with the understanding that they would be the ones to lead the change and, in particular, the reforms needed in the political sphere. So using social movement theory by scholars of democratization and transitions to examine non-state and non-elite actors is not common. Social movements bring the average citizen to the forefront—the citizen who is searching for a voice to influence public policy makers. It organizes that voice into a movement calling for changes and reform.

> Social Movement Theory (SMT) has been infrequently used to understand democratization in the region (or its lack) in the Arab world is of utmost importance in order to qualify the prevalent idea of region's "exceptionalism" and push away from restraining cultural explanations.[1]

There are three schools, models, or concepts that make up SMT: resource mobilization, political process, and new social movements. "The political process model looks at three main variables to explain the origins and impact of social movements: mobilizing structures, political opportunity structure, and cultural framing."[2] And in this research endeavor, the same variables are used to explain the origins and impact of the workers' social movement. The mobilizing structures in this research are the independent workers' movement that was organized loosely as more of a network and not under an organized structure such as a federation. The political opportunity is the steady decline of the authoritarian regime's grip on many aspects of society and particularly the financial/fiscal deterioration. The cultural framing is examined through the significant changes taking place within Egyptian society and culture due to globalization and increased access to information technology and the use of social media.

What Transforms a Group Into a Social Movement?

Social movements in the political historical context help us to understand what took place within the specific time and place in order to connect social movements to political and social change. However, a social movement does not necessarily become routinized into an ever-lasting institution. Actually,

> the more successful the social movement in spreading its knowledge interests or diffusing its consciousness, the less successful it is likely to be as a permanent organization. [. . .] Social movements are best conceived of as temporary public spaces, moments of collective creation that provide societies with ideas, identities, and even ideals.[3]

However, they can be significant moments (long or short) that can have a dramatic impact and can morph into something more durable and substantial. Now, how does this relate to the question at hand—the Egyptian Arab Spring and the role of Egyptian workers?

> The "Arab Spring" at first had nothing about it that was specifically "Arab" or "Muslim." The demonstrators were calling for dignity, elections, democracy, good governance, and human rights. Unlike any Arab revolutionary movements of the past sixty years, they were concerned with individual citizenship and not with some holistic entity such as "the people," the Muslim *umma*, or the Arab nation.[4]

The 2011 January Egyptian uprising or "revolution" is an untidy blend of old and new, which then informed what followed until the presidential elections took place in 2012. We are concerned with the interpretation of how, who, why, what, and when the "revolution" happened, but this is a contentious endeavor. Revolution is not a tidy concept, and it does not guarantee or necessarily bring about a new clean slate or a new page of history. It does not even ensure that democratic practices are the results of revolution. Crane Brinton in *The Anatomy of Revolution* reminds us that revolutions replace moderates with radicals who then fall to authoritarians. Revolution also reminds us of Hannah Arendt's observation half

a century ago that the modern concept of revolution is "inextricably bound up with the notion that the course of history suddenly begins anew, that an entirely new story, a story never known or told before, is about to unfold."[5] This is certainly not the case in Egypt. Similarly, the Egyptian workers' movement is also a blend of the old and new. Their actions are bound in the course of history, the constraints placed upon them, perceptions of their place and role in society, and their experiences going forward.

The workers have a unique gift of having their pulse on the socio-economic conditions and as a result can make demands to improve the quality of life. This gift then develops into the political acumen for demanding changes. "Political change is the result of a constant process of learning, and policies evolve in response to a continual monitoring of social conditions and demands."[6] Workers and their organizations (official or unofficial) learn quickly that these tasks of calling for changes and reform is a lengthy process. In addition, calling for reforms can be quite dangerous to undertake in an authoritarian regime.

> There are times when human communities face the need to adapt, and to do so quickly. But adaptation does not occur automatically just because it is needed. The institutions of human society are constructed in the first instance for continuity. As Fernand Braudel put it, a cultural mentality is a "prison de longue durée" (cited in Tarrow 1992:179). [. . .] Social and economic institutions teach entering members appropriate roles and then enforce them.[7]

Political transition is a "longue durée" road full of pitfalls and setbacks.

Social movements are and can be an effective tool to advocate and pressure for change.

> [Social] movements bring the issue and its value context to a wider public and to the political arena. One important part of this task is to organize demonstrations, discussion groups, petition signings, teach-ins, sit-ins [. . .] and other types of collective action that draw attention to new values and show determination to act on them. While the critical community develops a language to express new values, the [social] movement acts so as to create settings in which those values can be expressed.[8]

Social movements are also fundamentally collective action, which is all too familiar to the labor movement. Collective action is the essence of trade unionism fostered by working-class solidarity.

How do social movements achieve their goals? They are a good form of bringing collective ideas to the forefront with public support of the masses. The ability to connect ideas and group identities together brings much strength to the demands the social movement is making.

> Of the primary forms of collective action, movements are most closely linked to critical communities and they are the best channel for the translation of critical values into topics of public discourse. Movements are also distinctive in their ability to connect ideas to group identities. By so doing, they infuse group identities with new political and social meanings, and they strengthen

solidarity among group members. This enhanced degree of solidarity encourages mobilization by making people more willing to accept the costs and risks of collective action for a public good. [. . .] Group identification is thus converted into solidarity and engagement among activists.[9]

This excellent description provided by the scholar Thomas Rochon aptly if not exactly describes the fundamental principles of labor's collective action and then the creation of trade unions.

Social movements are critical in the formulation of public debate over issues. They can be an effective means to influence policy makers particularly in an open society.

[Social] movements bring ideas that are critical to the community to a wider public; these perspectives must also be formatted and adapted in a way that will make them suitable for influence in the social and political arenas. Refine ideology for the purposes of mobilization—a movement must also identify specific targets of action.[10]

The key to social movement's success or failure is "the ability of a movement to stimulate societal debate and political response depends not only on its strategic choices, but also on the social and political institutions that encourage or inhibit reception of the movement's message."[11] However, this can be effective in a society and government that respects public debate over issues and recognizes and respects the mechanism of influencing policy makers. In Egypt, unfortunately, that is not the modus operandi of the authoritarian regime.

Solidarity is a fundamental element in the labor movement, where workers see themselves as part of a much larger movement, one that exemplifies the concept: if one worker is harmed, then all workers are harmed. Within the work world, it is relatively easy to create such solidarity. Yet, mobilizing activists to create solidarity even within the labor movement can be one of the most difficult tasks at hand. Creating a successful movement is even more difficult in an authoritarian regime that controls many mechanisms of expression and organization. The only way to develop solidarity and to diffuse change in cultural values and other issues is to overcome the free-rider problem.

Ever since Olson's (1965) clarification of the barriers to mobilization for collective goods, scholars have understood the necessity for movements to push people out of an individualistic, expected utility calculus and to foster an alternative set of calculations involving the group welfare.[12]

The movement mobilization literature is divided between writings based on rational choice and other work based on networks and solidarity,

consider the range of solutions to the free-rider problem that has been proposed by scholars working within the rational choice models. Olson (1965) proposed that movements organized in small groups will have greater success in mobilizing support because the impact of their efforts is likely to be greater in a small group setting than in a large group.[13]

Workers in their collective trade union organizations exhibit a high level of solidarity. Their solidarity "makes movement mobilization possible by fostering a collective rationality that operates alongside individual rationality (Klandermans 1988)."[14] The labor movement has a strong group identity and solidarity. These characteristics are critically important and are present within the workers' movement. What is solidarity? Solidarity is the belief that the group is capable of unified action in pursuit of the group's goals. You feel solidarity with a group with whom you can identify, so it is the task of the (social) movement to heighten the sense of solidarity within the groups linked to the movement cause.[15] What were the characteristics of this solidarity in Egypt among workers? What brought them together so effectively to create an uprising, a revolution? Hisham Sallam wrote,

> There is considerable consensus that the revolution is—at least in part—a backlash against the exclusionary economic order that the deposed president's son Gamal Mubarak and his associates helped to erect over the last decade. Yet it remains unclear if the new, post-Mubarak Egypt can succeed in addressing the socio-economic grievances that helped to spark the January 25 uprising.[16]

The socio-economic grievances are so intractable and complex that it will take several decades to overcome the effects of the last thirty to forty years of economic policies.

Solidarity exists amongst workers working side by side even if their specific work is different, because their grievances are the same. It is the critical job of the union leaders and organizers to show workers that their lives, work, and sources of their grievances are the same. It is called the language of class per Asa Briggs (1960).[17]

> The elements of solidarity—group solidarity provides the motivation of political or social change, by creating the expectation that the group will act cohesively to bring about that change. As Klandersman (1984) notes, people must decide whether to participate in a movement without having full information on how many others will participate. They must, then, develop expectations about the participation of others based on their belief that the group has a legitimate grievance, has identified reasonable strategy of remedial action, and will act cohesively. These beliefs are the constituent elements of the feeling of solidarity.[18]

The feeling and acting in solidarity are the key elements of success for workers. However, in the Egyptian case, it is not sufficient to achieve the larger overall political reform agenda.

Solidarity movements, particularly by workers, can lead to effective political collective action. Greater participation in movements' signals increased sentiments of political engagement and the hope to achieve change. "As Tarrow (1992:197) has noted, group identities are best observed 'through the study of how people struggle, against whom they struggle, and in the name of which symbols and points of concern they struggle.'"[19] This so aptly describes this research endeavor of studying how Egyptian workers struggle, against whom they

struggled, and their points of contention. Thomas Rochon outlines the foundations of social movement mobilization:

> 1) Group solidarity assist in movement mobilization by connecting individual interests to group interests, leading to a calculus of action based on collective rationality. 2) Movement mobilization is maintained as a function of the participation of others, success in achieving objectives, and a steady flow of the rewards that are associated with movement activism. 3) Movement mobilization expands in part through the ripple effect of protest activity that lead to increased engagement among those who have contact with movement activists (e.g. family and friends) and among those who are members of the group whose interests the movement represents.[20]

Collier and Mahoney's research[21] gives ample examples of how the labor movement in several countries in South America played an important and even decisive role in their countries' political transition. They wrote,

> Focusing on collective action undertaken by unions and labor-affiliated parties, we argue that the labor movement often played an important role in recent transitions. Labor was not limited to an "indirect" role, in which protest around workplace demands was answered through co-optive inclusion in the electoral arena. Rather, the labor movement was one of the major actors in the political opposition, explicitly demanding a democratic regime.[22]

There has been a focus on the study of the role of elites in political transitions. As mentioned before, the prominent paradigm has been the study of leadership and elite interaction (O'Donnell), yet leadership and protest by workers brings into play the paradigm of the role of the masses and its importance.

Other Significant Protests by Egyptian Workers

The research presented thus far has focused on two types or categories of workers' protests—garment and textile workers, specifically at El-Mahalla al-Kubra, and civil servants working as real estate tax collectors in the Ministry of Finance and municipal governments. Their persistent wave of protests that lasted from 2006 to 2009 had an indelible effect on the rest of the working class—white-collar professionals and blue-collar workers. In this chapter, I will review other worker protests often referred to as "wildcat strikes"; their repertoires of contention, mechanisms of diffusion, and framing of their grievances to contribute to an ever-growing worker-based social movement. It is interesting to note that civil servants—government workers—were better positioned to create independent unions given the balance of forces in Egypt. The public feud between the minister of manpower and the head of the ETUF was one factor; other factors included the government's embarrassment over criticism of Egypt and the ETUF at the 2008 ILO conference and in other international forums; and that tax collectors (civil servants) had advantages over industrial workers since they temporarily suspended collecting taxes, thus impacting the government's revenues, that their independent unionization did

not threaten the privatization of the public sector enterprises, and that they were not employed by an institution with such a high degree of historical and political symbolism as El Mahalla el-Kubra spinning and weaving company.[23]

The following are the most significant protests/strikes that took place from 2005 to 2010:

1. ESCO Spinning Company in Qalyub, north of Cairo; strike from February to May 2005
2. Ghazl Shibin Spinning Company, which was sold and became the Indorama Shibin Spinning Company, 2006
3. The struggle of the 526,000 administrative workers in the Egyptian public school system, 2008–2009
4. Postal workers threatened to create an independent union, 2009
5. Strike at the Tanta Flax and Oil Company (Kitan Tanta), 2005–2010
6. Strike of the Port workers at the Canal Company for Ports and Large Projects at the Suez Canal, 2008
7. Train drivers strike, January 2009
8. Omar Effendi Department Store workers on strike, April–May 2009
9. Mansura-España Garment Company workers on strike, April–June 2007
10. Information technology centers' workers strike, 2010
11. Strikes of teachers in elementary and secondary public schools, 2009–2010

Background: The Legal Framework to Control Workers

In 1957, Egypt ratified the ILO convention No. 87 (1948) on Freedom of Association and Protection of the Right to Organize. In 1954, it ratified ILO Convention No. 98 (1949) on the Right to Organize and Collective Bargaining. However, compliance with these conventions was undermined by national legislation, close links between the ETUF and the state apparatus, and intervention in trade union affairs by security forces, typically state security (comparable to the FBI in the US). These state instruments were often involved in resolving "wildcat" strikes and protests and in preventing independent labor organizations.[24] As previously noted, the ETUF is closely aligned with the state apparatus with its leadership firmly under the control of the ruling party.

The Right to Strike in Egypt

It is important at this juncture to review parts of the Egyptian labor law that concerns strikes. Egyptian Labor Law No. 12 for the Year 2003 also provided in Article 191 that

> workers have the right to a peaceful strike which is to be exercised by their unions in order to defend their vocational, economic, and social interests within the limits and according to the regulations stipulated in this law. If workers of an establishment that has a union decide to strike in the cases allowed under this law, the establishment's union—following the approval of two-thirds of the members of the administrative board of the concerned general union—should notify the employer and the concerned government

authority of the strike at least fifteen days in advance in a registered letter. If there is no union in the establishment, workers should notify the concerned general union of their intention to strike. In this case, the administrative board of the concerned general union—following the approval of the majority mentioned in the preceding clause—should make the aforementioned notification. In any case, the notification should include the reasons behind the strike action and its intended period.

Article 195 of Labor Law No. 12 for the Year 2003 considers the period of the strike an unpaid leave for the worker.[25]

An Example—Teachers on Strike: "Education and Learning Are Not Taking Place in Egyptian Schools"

The dismal state of Egypt's educational system, the decline of state investment in infrastructure and personnel, and an increase in class size have all contributed to the overall decline in education and the state of learning in Egypt.

> Abdel Hafiez Tayel directs the Egyptian Center for Education Rights (ECER), an activist organization dedicated to pressuring the government into investing more into the education system. ECER just announced its report on the dismal state of Egypt's education system. The report showed that the current budget in Egypt calls for spending $757 US annually to educate one student, compared to $8,000 in Saudi Arabia and $11,000 in Israel.[26]

Teachers are state employees and depend on the government to allocate enough funds in the state budget for salaries and benefits. As Egypt has been prescribing to neoliberal economic reforms, education has become a scapegoat for government's reshifting of priorities while maintaining the most important state security apparatuses to keep the regime in power. The result has been a slow and gradual decline in the education system, with teachers bearing the brunt. There are about 810,000 teachers from kindergarten to high school and about 28,000 school buildings.

It became apparent that government employees were better positioned than others to establish independent unions. The balance of power tipped towards those employees who could affect the government's performance and by their use of that power could force the government to give in to their demands. This was clear with the real estate tax collectors when they closed their provincial offices and stopped collecting taxes. These taxes are direct revenue for the government and can impinge negatively on government's performance. The same situation describes another group of workers—526,000 administrative workers in the Egyptian public school system. "These administrators—who manage student affairs, order and distribute school books, organization examination materials, and work in accounting, human resources, and legal affairs—demanded wage parity with teachers."[27] If administrators, who threatened to stop administering exams or ordering and distributing school books, had followed through on their threats, it could have had a huge impact on millions of students.

Historically, the salaries of teachers and administrators were the same and very low. In 2007, under pressure, the Egyptian Parliament passed a bill to increase teachers' salaries yet not those of the administrators, since they were not classified as "educational staff."[28] The ETUF-affiliated union for educational services workers did not support their members' grievances. So, these workers formed an independent committee to provide representation for them, instead of being represented by the official ETUF union. "The committee organized local strikes in several schools and local education authorities in February and March 2009, a demonstration in front of parliament [in Cairo] on March 9, and a national school strike on March 29."[29] Their demands included the creation of an independent union in addition to their demand for increase or parity in wages with teachers.

The teachers' advocacy for their rights continued after January 2011:

> 1st March 2011: More than 6,000 teachers went in strike today in front of the premises of the Administration of Education in the Governorate of Qena. They called for permanent jobs for the teachers working according to temporary contracts. The Minister of Education issued a decision yesterday to appoint all the teachers who worked as temporary employees for a period of three years on condition that they pass the "Cadre Examinations" which the Ministry will hold on March 25, 2011. Commenting on the Minister's decision, Mr. Essa Aly Mohamed, a teacher at Abu Mannaa Bahry School said it disappointed all the teachers employed by temporary contracts. He said that the strike will continue until the Ministry responds to their demands.[30]

Several additional workers and government employees threatened to form independent unions to advocate for their rights. They demanded improvements in working conditions, an increase in wages (in many cases wage parity with similar work positions yet at headquarters), and job security. In 2008–2009, protests by postal workers, train drivers, and port workers were additional examples of such actions and how the government used state security and the official trade union, ETUF, to pressure workers to end their protests and accept an inept agreement.

> On May 18, 2009, postal workers in Kafr al-Shaykh governorate went on strike for six days. [. . .] They demanded wage parity with the Egyptian Telecommunications Company (ETC) workers, who earn up to three times as much as the 52,000 postal workers. [. . .] They also demanded that the 5,000 temporary workers employed by the Postal Authority receive permanent status.[31]

Workers at Omar Effendi, Egypt's largest department store chain, also joined the strike wave, reported Sarah Carr in April and May 2009:

> [Workers] went out on strike for three days in April 2009 and again on May 5, 2009. In 2007, the Saudi Arabian-based clothing retailer, Anwal United Trading, bought a 90 percent share of the previously publicly owned firm. Strikers claimed that the new owners violated a contractual commitment that the work force would be cut by no more than 600 and that new employees had been hired at higher wages than more qualified workers doing the same work.[32]

At the Mansura-España Garment Company,

> the great majority of the employees are women. These women were the prin-
> cipal force behind a two-month strike in April–June 2007. In the course of
> the strike at the Mansura-España Garment factory several women went on a
> hunger strike, and five threatened to commit suicide. Even though the strik-
> ers nominally won their demands, management and the government did not
> fulfill their promises. Their culturally supposed "docility" and "traditional"
> background did not inhibit active participation in the strike.[33]

"Women Are Also Part of This Revolution," is the title of a chapter in *Arab
Spring in Egypt* by Hania Sholkamy. She presents the concept of liminality. Moments of solidarity and popular mobilization "are also 'liminal' moments in
which hierarchies and structures of distinction are temporarily suspended (Turner
1969; 1974); they are also moments that [are] impossible to sustain as they are
temporally and spatially bounded."[34] The liminal phase is when anything is possible under particular circumstances, where taboos, rituals, and traditions are
broken. "Liminal moments are wedged between two states of normalcy as they
mark the disruption of one order and clear way the debris of what used to be
the norms [. . .] [i]n order to create a new set of norms."[35] Working women at
the Mansura-España Garment factory, in addition to many other workplaces,
engaged in those liminal moments and broke with traditions to advocate for their
rights. They became "equal" with their fellow male workers and free from stric-
tures and structures that had defined them.[36] This condition is defined by Turner
as one of "communitas,"[37] a necessary condition from which a transformed order
emerges and into which women and others are reintegrated creating a new state
of relations between men and women workers, in this particular situation. This
condition of communitas existed in several worker protests over the period of
2005–2010 and into those eighteen days in Tahrir Square in 2011 and beyond.
    Sholkamy further supports the thesis of this research project:

> [W]ith hindsight it is now clear that the protest movements that had been
> taking place for a decade, and that were initiated by rights activists belonging
> to workers' and civil liberty groups and other social movements, became the
> revolutionary agglomeration that toppled the elite echelons of the regime.[38]

The elements of time (over a decade of organizing and protesting) and the
increase in miserable economic and working conditions made these protest
movements more successful despite the lack of a larger coordinating organizational body.
    Privatization and workers' fear of losing their jobs became a regular occurrence,
and there are several examples. One example is the ESCO Spinning Company in
Qalyub, north of Cairo, where a strike took place from February to May 2005.

> By 2005 the number of workers in the six ESCO textile mills had been
> reduced from more than 10,000 to 3,500 through a combination of attri-
> tion, early retirement, and a long-term hiring freeze following a major strike
> in 1986. When the 400 workers at the Qalyub Spinning mill learned about
> its impeding sale to an Egyptian investor they began a campaign to reverse
> the privatization of their workplace.[39]

They wanted job security or, if that was not possible, to receive adequate pensions. However, as soon as Prime Minister Nazif's government took over in 2005, ESCO Qalyub Spinning Company's privatization process began. This was part of a larger strategy of privatization of the textile industry as a whole. The ethos of the public sector being owned by the workers was still relevant, and so the sale of the company to private hands without the workers' participation and consent was considered illegal by the workers. The ETUF-affiliated union did not stand by the workers and instead supported the government's policies.

> While the ESCO workers did not stop the privatization [. . .] they did receive a pension package according to the Unified Labor Law of 2003. This strike set the tone for many that followed in the public sector [. . .] the ESCO workers conducted an orderly strike and sit-in. They were not subjected to violent repression. And they achieved economic gains well beyond anything that other striking workers achieved in the 1980s or 1990s. As a result, Egyptian workers received the message that collective action might achieve real gains.[40]

Another example of privatization that became a disaster was the Ghazl Shibin Spinning Company, which was sold in 2006 and became the Indorama Shibin Spinning Company. The company employed 4,200 workers and was sold to a private foreign company. The contention between the workers and the new management continued from 2006 to 2009 with the management failing to meet the minimum agreements. The agreement stipulated that workers could take the early retirement package (referred to by workers as the early death plan) in addition to not hiring any new employees until they reached the "optimal" workforce. "In February 2009, the company sent out a letter announcing that due to the international economic crisis it would not be paying workers their annual bonus, equivalent to 228 days' pay. This provoked an 11-day sit-in strike beginning on March 5."[41] In this case, the ETUF-affiliated union supported the workers and after negotiations they did receive their bonuses. However, in May 2009, four of the strike leaders were punitively transferred to the company's warehouse in Alexandria. In addition, the company managers continued to accuse the workers for the company's financial losses. Indorama Shibin has experienced two major strikes and 100 brief work stoppages and other protests since it was privatized.[42]

Tanta Kitan (Linen) Factory in the City of Tanta, El Gharbiyya Province

On Tuesday, June 11, 2013, I met with three workers and trade union leaders from the Tanta Kitan factory, Gamal, Ashraf, and Mohammed, at a local coffee shop in Tanta. Their story is that of struggle and sacrifice—one year right before the January 2011 revolution. They told me that the street called Hussein Higazi in front of the Council of Ministers needs to be renamed Egyptian Workers Street, since it has witnessed so many protests, demonstrations, and sit-ins for days on end, particularly in the last few years. The Tanta Kitan factory workers stayed in that street probably the longest number of days, seventeen days. Tanta Kitan was (and in the workers' minds) remains a public sector factory. It was sold under suspicious terms to a Saudi investor, Abd el Ellahy El Kahky (the same person who built the City

Stars Mall in Nasr City in Cairo). This was a profitable factory that employed hundreds of workers (2,300 workers; today there are 166 plus a few hundred contract workers earning about LE 500 per month). The workers at this factory make use of every part of the linen plant. There are ten factories in the complex that made linseed oil, various types of linen, plywood, and even furniture.

The following narrative is their brave and sad story through a detailed timeline, facts and stories that they shared with me:

2004—This was the beginning of full privatization program (the implementing prime ministers started with El Ganzouri and then Atef Ebid; the final coup de grace was delivered by Ahmed Nazif, who took office in July 2004).

2005 and 2006—Successive problems with the new owners vis-à-vis the workers.

2007—The first strike by workers at Tanta Kitan, in addition to many other workers who also went on strike all over the country in a variety of workplaces, such as building material workers, transport workers, Cairo underground metro workers, food processing workers, bakers, sanitation workers, oil workers in Suez, and many others.[43]

2009—A thirteen-month strike where the infamous nine trade union leaders (union committee) were fired; this was actually the first ever "legal" strike. It was approved by the ETUF-affiliated union (under the magnanimous leadership of Saeed el Gohary, the ETUF garment and textile union president at the time). First, the strike started with five days and then continued to thirteen months. It took the ETUF-affiliated union six months to publicly announce that the strike was legally sanctioned! After those first six months, Minister of Manpower Aisha Abdel Hady, Saeed el Gohary, and the Saudi owner signed an agreement without any consultation with the workers or their legitimate leaders. The agreement stipulated the end of the strike with success, giving the workers six months' leave without pay (the six months of strike time period) and demanding that the workers had to pay back their social insurance payments for those six months. "Talk about a massive slap in the face," said Gamal. Gamal continued to say,

After that incredibly outrageous agreement—nine trade union leaders stayed in the factory for seven days in protest. And no one could move them off of the factory premises. For those six months they were able to get their base wages yet without any of the additional allotted allowances, etc.

Ashraf added,

The factory occupies a large space of land approximately 74 feddans and so it is a huge complex that is worth a lot of money—just the land itself and this is without the buildings, equipment, and raw materials. It was sold for a song and rumor has it that the minister of manpower and the ETUF leadership got quite a bit of money under the table to ensure that all goes smoothly and that the new owner does not have any labor trouble! Ha! In his dreams.

January–February 2010—Another strike that began in mid-January lasted for seventeen days; one year exactly before the January 2011 revolution (uprising) took place. One of their many chants was, "Build the walls/the fences of prison and make them higher; tomorrow is the revolution that will rise and bring down these fences."

All three workers interviewed agreed to the commonly heard statement made by workers that the government early retirement scheme is referred to as the "early death." They usually received a lump sum payment between LE 25,000 to LE 50,000 and then received a monthly "pension of pittance" between LE 250 and LE 300. "Another bit of additional anger against the new Saudi-owned management—they forced those with terminal diseases to leave the factory so not to incur additional health insurance costs," said Ashraf.

June 30, 2010—An agreement was made with the Saudi owner in Beirut, Lebanon, since there was a court order in Egypt against the new owner for two years in prison. He was not able to travel to Egypt or else he would be imprisoned. There is an archaic statute called "attack on the rights of others" that was used in this case by Khaled Ali, the workers' lawyer. Actually, the court in this case, especially Judge Hamdy Yassin Okasha (head of the Judges' Club and in Maglis el Dawla), handed down an amazingly excellent decision (seventy-two pages long) on behalf of and good for the workers, but it has not been implemented. This court decision called for everything to return to the government's ownership as of 2005 and that the sale to the Saudi investor was null and void. "Sadly, the government after the 2011 revolution went to court to say it does not want Tanta Kitan factory back!" said Gamal.

So, Gamal, Ashraf, and Mohammed returned to sharing the details of the Beirut agreement between the Saudi owner and Minister of Manpower Aisha Abdel Hady.

The agreement called for 450 workers to go into immediate retirement on 30 June (end of fiscal year). So, Gamal Oweida, for example, was reinstated back to work on 30 June and then put on retirement on the same day, 30 June—an amazing feat! This deal called for LE 50,000 lump sum payment and then the pitiful monthly pension thereafter. The local ETUF union committee and national union played an incredibly negative role adding more pressure on the workers. There was a lot of "buying time" through delays and wasting time. The next date in court will be 28 September 2013. Today, two factories out of the ten are working and at 1/3 production rate with only one shift of workers at work.

What Factors and Organizations and Which Players Helped and Supported You?

"The independent media played a very important role!" Ashraf said. He continued,

Daily there were news reports, articles, and headlines from *El Masry el Youm* newspaper to Al-Jazeera. There was an independent union at the factory yet

without an official name. They were daily fighting the ETUF-affiliated union for survival and for the workers' rights. There were no profits, no raises, no meal allowances, no promotions since the new Saudi owner took over. It seemed that they were running the factory into the ground on purpose in order to sell it as property and make a mint! The workers were accused by the minister of manpower of being "politicized" in a bad way and influenced by the Communists, Revolutionary Socialists, and others, but not the MB.

They referred to the minister of manpower as often being ridiculed and how she was negligent vis-à-vis the workers.

El Masry el Youm (Egypt Today) newspaper ran a report called "One Night Living on the Street With the Tanta Kitan Workers"[44]

الوزراء المصرى اليوم" تقضى ليلة اعتصام كاملة مع عمال "طنطا للكتان" أمام مجلس : فرشوا الأرض"
"كراتين" وأعدوا ١٢ "صفيحة جبنة.". وقالوا: ننتظر عودة نظيف

Translation: "*El Masry el Youm* spends the night in a full sit-in with the Tanta Kitan workers in front of Ministers' Council; they spread cardboard boxes and prepared 12 large cans of cheese, saying: we are waiting for Nazif's return."

A journalist spent the night with the workers during their sit-in and wrote a wonderful, descriptive story. Gamal recounted parts of the story:

> For about 50 to 70 meters on the pavement in front of the Council of Ministers' building on Hussein Higazy Street [which includes the Prime Minister's office] slept the workers for 17 days. The businesses and inhabitants in the apartment buildings on the street were very supportive. There was one shoe maker/cobbler on the street who did have a hard time getting business—so Hussein el Masry [head of education and training at the Center for Trade Union and Worker Services—CTUWS] asked him to make a pair of shoes for him just to give him some business. The food establishments all benefited from having the workers there day and night. Once the police and state security forces got so fed up with these hundreds of workers not leaving that they decided to cordon off the area and not permit them to leave to go to the bathrooms, so the workers just went to the bathroom at the feet of the security! It sent a message. Then the workers' representatives told the security forces—hmm, the tents are coming tomorrow; and then our wives and children are coming too! The security forces recognized that these workers are not going anywhere—they are staying.

Again, this is a preview of the Tahrir Square events, tactics, and repertoires.

According to Gamal and the others, there were several civil society organizations that helped the 450 striking Tanta Kitan workers for the seventeen days sleeping in front of the Council of Ministers building on Hussein Higazi Street. They were the National Organization for Change; Dr. Abdel Galleel; the CTUWS; the Kefaya movement, especially George Ishak, who brought thirty-seven blankets for the sleeping workers on the street; Hisham Fouad, representing the Revolutionary Socialists organization; the Lawyers Syndicate's human rights committee; El Hillali Center; and the Solidarity Workers' Group, led by Fatima Ramadan. They began a "living support fund" with each organization contributing about LE 1,000 to feed the workers. Tents were also brought in so that they could sleep in a bit warmer area, since this was January and it got

cold at night. The tents caused lots of discomfort and anxiety for the police and state security forces, since it meant that the workers were staying and not going anywhere. The state security apparatus did arrest for a few hours some of the supporters of the striking workers, including Fatima Ramadan and other activists. The workers got very irate and threatened to attack—the police then quickly released them. "Al-Jazeera news, written and television, also played an excellent role in keeping the issue alive," said Mohammed.

Gamal continued to say,

> Daily the workers would release a press release so they had seventeen in all; one for each day. They bought whistles and used them which drove the Council of Ministers building employees nuts! Prime Minister Ahmed Nazif got married during that time and so they chanted: *Ya Nazif, ya aarees* [new groom], we are sitting on the pavement; *Ya Aisha* [minister of manpower] the blind, you burned the okra [*bamya*]. The Ghazl el Mahalla factory [Misr Spinning and Weaving factory in El Mahalla el Kubra] workers stood in solidarity with us [Tanta Kitan workers] and the Amonscito factory workers too—they protested in front of the Shura Council and each day they removed one piece of clothing to protest!

They had very creative mechanisms of protest, slogans, songs, and repertoires.

Ashraf shared information about another workers' protest movement at the Amonscito factory. He said,

> Mohamed Farid Khamis, [a] big Egyptian investor in 10th Ramadan industrial city wanted to buy Amonscito yet the workers' knew his terrible bad reputation and actions. So having knowledge played a good, important and positive role confirming the old adage that knowledge is power. Workers of the information centers, disabled workers, and the Amonscito workers all protested in front of the People's Assembly too. So, the government was under siege—protests and sit-ins at many of its institutions! Hamdeen Sabahi [political figure, leader of Karama political party and ran for president after revolution] came very often to check on and see how to help the striking Tanta Kitan workers. There was and still is a strong feeling that those industries that were nationalized under Nasser should never be privatized. The Tagamu political party also supported the workers. In the report of the manpower (labor) committee in the People's Assembly, there is great stuff! including Saeed el Gohary [president of the garment and textile workers affiliated to the ETUF] supposedly "crying" for the workers. All the while Yusri Bayoumi, an MB member of Parliament, quietly advised the workers to go against the management and to oppose the government. They were not upfront in their support at all.

"So, 25th January 2011 was not a surprise at all," said Gamal. I asked, "Why were the workers not 'obviously' present in the first few days?" He responded,

> (1) anything that threatens their daily bread they are cautious and not always eager to not get paid; (2) bad to poor organizing and they did not come down to Tahrir as a block/group; they came as individuals—this changed

as the days went on and Mubarak gave them one-week paid vacation [first week of February 2011]. Afterwards, they came in droves.

On May 1, 2011—there was a huge worker presence in Tahrir Square. Public sector ideology needs to be understood and included in analysis—it is very hard for workers growing up under the Nasser days to give that up. So, privatization has to be done very very carefully, etc. [. . .] with the workers' participation and understanding. We need a true labor and trade union law that is correct and fair. The public sector did play a good role—this cannot be ignored—it provided employment for so many persons, health insurance, and a living wage to eat and raise our families. With the sale of public sector companies—there are many unemployed workers; wages are still low and consumer prices of goods are going higher daily! What is needed is good expert management to make these public sector factories profitable and competitive.

Gamal, Ashraf, and Mohammed, who graciously took several hours of their time to speak with me, worked between twenty-three and thirty-one years at the Tanta Kitan factory and now get a pension of between LE 200 and LE 400 per month. It is clear that for these workers and many others (not just at Tanta Kitan), privatization is a dirty word. Pension reforms have been very negative for workers and government employees. They were also very keen to mention the incredible role of cell phones and how cell phones (mobiles) were such an excellent and effective organizing tool. There was no mention of Facebook or Twitter.

The Information Technology (IT) Centers' Workers: "We Just Want to Live" Is Our Story (November 2010)[45]

The number of workers in these centers for information technology (IT) is around 32,000, and they are located all over Egypt. The employees were hired as a result of a national contest held in 2001 and 2002 based on their academic achievements and their cumulative grades in college. These employees signed a document that they would not take on part-time additional jobs so that they could be focused full-time on this work. Their salaries were LE 150 per month for those with a university degree, LE 120 per month for those with a technical/vocational college degree, and LE 100 for those with a two-year associate's degree. These workers worked on several national projects gathering information and inputting data— such projects included a national literacy program, creation of tourist maps for the governorates, gathering data on the bread crisis and the bird flu epidemic, and field research on gathering data on the numbers of street lights and the numbers of water pumps and wells in rural areas, in addition to initiatives for improving girls' education, the population census in 2006, and a census of disabled persons. These workers started their strikes and protests in March 2010, raising the following demands: (1) receiving their unpaid salaries past due for several months and for some who had only been receiving LE 99 for the last eight years; (2) ending of contractual arrangement and making them full-time workers with benefits given to other civil servants, increase in salaries and bonuses, clear job descriptions, health insurance, and social security; and (3) regularly paying their salaries every month instead of getting paid every three months based on the agreement made between the Ministry of Finance and the Ministry of Local Development.

In March 2010, around 4,000 workers participated in a sit-in protest in front of the Council of Ministers' headquarters in Cairo (a favorite and effective gathering place for worker protests). They came from the following provinces (governorates): Beni Suewayf, Damietta, Kafr el Sheikh, Port Said, Alexandria, Sharqiyya, El Gharbiyya, Ismailia, El Minya, El Fayoum, Sohag, Menoufiyya, Qena, Cairo, Giza, and El Behera. This protest included a large number of women who set up "picnic-style" blankets on the pavement facing the building, many of whom brought their children, including babies. One of the female protesters said, "What can we do? The house is empty without food and money and we cannot leave our children alone at home and we just cannot continue living this way." Many suffered from a lot of pressure by the governors to produce information and refused many requests for days off or vacations, especially in Menoufiyya province. In Kafr el Sheikh province, the governor threatened the workers with firing if they did not comply with his order to open literacy classes and work there, even though this project was considered voluntary. So fifty-three workers from all the IT centers in the province held a sit-in protest in front of the city council building. In El Minya province, security forces prevented a bus with IT center workers from leaving for Cairo to participate in the larger protest, based on the instructions of the governor, and in Sohag province, 380 workers conducted a sit-in protest with their families in front of the governor's office building as a result of the unreasonableness of the governor's actions and decisions.

One of the protesters reported that they presented more than three official signed petitions to the member of the Parliament on the committee of grievances, Ehab Othman, and each time he told them to be patient and that he was working on their situation. Many Parliament members took an interest in their situation, so they presented a formal request on March 29, 2010, to the parliamentary committee for labor and social issues to discuss this problem. The members of the committee agreed to solve the problem by making all the IT center employees permanent civil servants and ensuring that they received their owed salaries and that it all needed to be done in two weeks. So, based on the committee's decision and declarations, the workers suspended their sit-in protest that had been taking place for nine days. However, the workers never got these basic demands met despite the parliamentary committee decision and returned to protest yet again on April 17, 2010. This time over 1,500 workers protested in front of the parliament building, and this continued for thirty days. It resulted in repeated sessions of negotiations until finally an agreement was signed providing for the following: increase in salaries so that the minimum wage was LE 320 for those with technical college degrees and LE 381 for those with four-year university degrees; yearly raises; and to transfer their current work contracts to permanent employment civil servants' contracts. At the same time the government announced the allocation of LE 150 million from the state budget to raise salaries in the IT centers, which meant an increase of LE 100 million from the current allotment in the budget. The increase in wages would begin from July 2009. The story does not happily end here, for on September 14, 2010, over 4,000 workers returned to a sit-in protest in front of the Cabinet of Ministers' building to demand that the aforementioned signed agreement be implemented.

These workers continued to push for the implementation of the signed agreement. They faced many threats of firings, actual transfers to other IT centers far from their homes, implementation of rigid work rules by their supervisors,

and threats of reporting workers to state security. Then came another insult in which the salaries were paid, but at the old rate. These protests continued again in October and November 2010 without serious resolution or implementation of the negotiated agreement. One female protester said,

> My husband does not work regularly and when he does he brings home LE 300 and my salary is LE 119, we have three children and two of them go to school. Our combined salary is around LE 400 and we cannot afford to buy two kilos of meat [cost of one kg of meat is around LE 80] in one month, and after we slept on the pavement and they promised us that our salaries would increase to LE 300 which is really not enough money but it is at least something a little more to help us live. [. . .] That is all we are asking for, we are not asking for more, we just want to live.

As mentioned in previous chapters, there has even been more egregious government behavior against workers in the post-Mubarak government, giving credence to the theory (Crane Brinton) that post-revolution does not initially engender a more enlightened regime.

Concluding Remarks

It seems that what the labor movement has achieved with limited success was pushing for and taking large steps towards imposing trade union freedoms and the right to organize. The workers have come very close to achieving these momentous goals, and the government's offer of simply reorganizing the ETUF executive board, for example, is considered an insult. One has to recognize that building a trade union or a federation or tearing it down has to be done by the workers themselves and not the government. The government's role is to set, protect, and implement the legal framework to enable workers to form independent democratic trade unions. Mostafa Bassouini, a noted labor advocate and journalist, said in my interview with him,[46]

> the official trade union ETUF is the one that supported Nasser's nationalization project in the 1950s and 1960s; ETUF supported Mubarak's privatization, supported Nasser's wars and ETUF's representatives traveled with Sadat to Jerusalem and for the signing of the 1979 Camp David peace agreement with Israel. The only way for a real honest trade union organization to be created is by only the workers themselves and that is the road upon which the workers today are traveling.[47]

In examining the labor movement's role in leading up to the Egyptian uprising, it is the case of missing of the big picture, the bigger story.

> While Western and Egyptian media have been preoccupied in recent years with small demonstrations in downtown Cairo protesting the widely-held belief that President Hosni Mubarak is grooming his son Gamal for the presidency, they have missed the bigger story: a rising labor force has become the country's most effective political force. Since the massive strikes of 27,000 Ghazel

el-Mahalla Textile Company workers in 2006 and 2007, Egyptian workers have started to shift their demands from strictly economic—salaries, bonuses, and industrial safety—to the more political question of re-configuring their relation to the state. For half a century, the state-controlled Egyptian Trade Unions Federation (ETUF) has monopolized workers' representation. The Ghazel el-Mahalla workers called for dissolving their factory's union committee, which they deemed "undemocratic and unrepresentative."[48]

The cases of workers' protests presented in this chapter definitely highlight labor's decisive role in putting pressure on the authoritarian ruler that ultimately brought Mubarak down. However, labor was not necessarily considered at the forefront of the pro-democracy movement and did not directly use democratic and political discourse. They used a socio-economic discourse through their demands for increased wages, improved benefits, better working conditions, and wage parity and their desire to create an independent trade union. I would argue that these are very political actions and demands that were made under an authoritarian regime, where any form of opposition is political. Second, these cases also show that large groups or organizations need not coordinate labor mobilization in order to be effective.

Egypt had maintained a tight grip on workers through state-controlled labor organizations, which led to a growing discontent between rank-and-file workers and union leaders. [. . .] Egypt nonetheless witnessed a great deal of sustained workers' mobilization, organized independently of the official union structure.[49]

The question examined is how these mobilizations took place despite their disparate fragmented nature, i.e. not all coordinated by one umbrella trade union organization (federation or coordinating body). The role of independent NGOs concerned with labor issues is critical in responding to this question. These NGOs played that most important coordinating role. In addition, these workers' protests further added to the breaking down of the barriers of fear and were "training schools" for repertoires, mechanisms, and brokers of contention. They used the independent media (newspaper, radio, and television) to further bring their cause into the home of every Egyptian. These workers took the many brave first steps for several years on the road to the January 2011 uprising. They created an effective social movement to highlight many issues that concerned the overall population. However, it was effective initially, but was not necessarily sustainable for the long term.

Notes

1. El-Mahdi, Rabab. "Enough! Egypt's Quest for Democracy." *Comparative Political Studies* 42 (8) (2009): 1011–1039: 1016.
2. Ibid.
3. Eyerman, Ron and Andrew Jamison. *Social Movements: A Cognitive Approach.* University Park, PA: Pennsylvania State University Press, 1991: 4.
4. Roy, Olivier. "The Transformation of the Arab World." *Journal of Democracy* 23 (3) (July 2012): 5.

5. Arendt, Hannah. *On Revolution*. London: Penguin, 2006: 18–19.
6. Rochon, Thomas. *Culture Moves—Ideas, Activism, and Changing Values*. Princeton, NJ: Princeton University Press, 1998: 5.
7. Ibid.
8. Ibid.: 240.
9. Ibid.: 241.
10. Ibid.: 242.
11. Ibid.: 243.
12. Ibid.: 95.
13. Ibid.: 97.
14. Ibid.
15. Ibid.: 98.
16. Sallam, Hisham. "Striking Back at Egyptian Workers." Published in MER259 41 (2011) ME Report (MERIP).
17. Briggs, Asa. "The Language of Class." In *Essays in Labour History in Memory of G.D.H. Cole*, ed. Asa Briggs and John Saville. London: Palgrave MacMillan, 1960: 43–73.
18. Rochon 1998: 101.
19. Ibid.: 102.
20. Ibid.: 161.
21. Collier, Ruth Berins and James Mahoney. "Adding Collective Actors to Collective Outcomes: Labor and Recent Democratization in South America and Southern Europe." *Comparative Politics* 29 (3), Transitions to Democracy: A Special Issue in Memory of Dankwart A. Rustow (April 1997): 285–303.
22. Ibid.: 285.
23. Beinin, Joel. *Justice for All—The Struggle for Worker Rights in Egypt*. Washington, DC: The Solidarity Center, 2010: 32.
24. Beinin, Joel. *Struggle for Worker Rights in Egypt*. Washington, DC: Solidarity Center, 2010: 27.
25. http://egypt.electionnaire.com/issues/?id=8 and www.egypt.gov.eg/arabic/laws/labour/default.aspx.
26. Paul, A. "Egypt's Labor Pains: For Workers, the Revolution Has Just Begun." *Dissent* 58 (4) (2011): 11–14.
27. CTUWS report, "Subject to Discrimination" April 2009.
28. Beinin 2010: 33.
29. Ibid.
30. CTUWS press release; http://ctuws.com/labour_movements/?item=836.
31. Beinin 2010: 34 and www.arabawy.org/2009/06/08/disgruntled-postal-workers-call-for-independent-union/.
32. Carr, Sarah, *Daily News Egypt*, April 2 and May 7, 2009 and from Beinin 2010: 52.
33. Beinin 2010: 72.
34. Sholkamy, Hania. "Women Are Also Part of This Revolution." *Arab Spring in Egypt*, ed. Korany and El Mahdi. Cairo, Egypt: American University in Cairo Press, 2012: 154.
35. Ibid.: 155.
36. Ibid.
37. Ibid.
38. Ibid.: 153.
39. Beinin 2010: 48.
40. Ibid.
41. Ibid.: 52.
42. Ibid.: 52–53.
43. Beinin, *The Struggle for Worker Rights in Egypt*, 2010: 14.
44. A report by and *El Masry el Youm* journalist, who spent one night with the workers on strike at a sit-in in front of the prime minister's office: http://today.almasryalyoum.com/article2.aspx?ArticleID=244156.
45. Information obtained from the CTUWS, Arabic press releases, and personal interviews in June and July 2013.

46. Interview with Bassouini in Cairo in June 2013.
47. Ibid.
48. Nasrawi, Saif. "The Political Edge of Egyptian Labor Protests." November 2009. http://carnegieendowment.org/sada/2009/11/10/political-edge-of-labor-protests-in-egypt/95fi.
49. Bishara, Dina. "The Power of Workers in Egypt's 2011 Uprising." In *Arab Spring in Egypt—Revolution and Beyond*, ed. Korany and El Mahdi. Cairo: American University Press, 2012: 101.

6 The Cultural Framing

Socio-Economic, Political, and Cultural Changes in Egypt Leading Up to the January 2011 Uprising

Chapter Outline:

1. Egyptian Society—The Changing Cultural Landscape
2. The Relationship Between the State and the People—The Authoritarian Boot on the Neck?
3. Popular Culture and Workers

   Egyptian Workers Used Street Politics to Highlight Economic and Political Mobilizations

4. The "Soft State" and Impact on Workers and Society at Large
5. The Question of Justice vs. Democracy in Egypt
6. Concluding Remarks

Egyptian society had been undergoing rapid change that has not been reflected in political change. The authoritarian system of governance remained fossilized with an aging leadership and a "youthening" of the population. It did not allow for these changes in the population's needs or discontent to be manifested in the political choices that Egyptians made. Ultimately, there were no choices for Egyptians except for the referenda that took place every five years with the over 95% approval for the president and the parliamentary elections that were pretty much controlled by the ruling NDP. For several years leading up to the twenty-first century, "Egyptians had been expressing a feeling of discontent, whether on the subject of the performance of the economy, the state of culture and intellectual life, social relationships, morality and political developments."[1] The slow decline of a middle class was becoming a bitter reality, and comparisons with other Middle Eastern countries were becoming a matter of laughter or dismay.

   Let us review some fundamental characteristics of Egyptian society, then examine the rapid changes that started with Sadat's era leading up to 2011, and finally put into historical context the protest movement, including the workers' role.

Egyptian Society—The Changing Cultural Landscape

One cannot begin to write about Egyptian society without paying homage to the many popular writers, artists, singers, cartoonists, comedians, journalists, and the like. A representative of the people's discontent and joy (at times) was

the popular poet Ahmed Fouad Negm (1929–2013). He was the people's poet, satirist, and their consciousness. He wrote what was in the people's hearts and minds, things that they could not say out loud. Negm was jailed for several years, and he spoke irreverently through his poetry written in colloquial Arabic for the impoverished underclass.

> Over four decades, Mr. Negm [pronounced NEG-em] wrote verse in collo-quial Arabic that channeled the privations and grim humor that were part of working-class life. His fearless and often mocking critiques of power made him a folk hero, but also earned him a total of 18 years in jail.[2]

The quote from Negm's poem that begins this chapter is indicative of Egyptian society's view of those who ruled them—the sultans and the princes. This poem was regularly recited in Tahrir Square in January 2011.

The economists, political observers, sociologists and those concerned with in-tellectual life and national culture were all complaining. Galal Amin, emeritus professor of economics at the American University in Cairo and a well-respected commentator, wrote that sociologists were complaining about the increase in cor-ruption and disrespect for the law with an obvious lack of work ethic. Violence was increasing and material values were establishing themselves over socially useful labor that was losing its social status and prestige. The quality of life in the city was declining with an increase in air pollution, overcrowding, and dete-riorating health services and education, while the villages were becoming units of consumption, not production. Economists noted the severe imbalances and distortions—a severe deficit, a growing external debt, an imbalance in state bud-get, high unemployment, an inefficient large public sector, and too much invest-ment by the government in unproductive areas such as luxury housing and import trade. Political observers noted that Egyptians' sense of loyalty and belonging to their native land had weakened with a high understandable pre-occupation with daily life needs rather than a larger vision of Arab nationalism or a commitment to national development. There was also a strong condemnation of increased political and economic dependence on the US and Europe.[3] Those who monitor intellectual life and national culture pointed to a decline in societal mores, values, and ethics with the spread of "low culture" and the growth of religious extrem-ism. The daily discourse had even taken an additional tinge of religiosity. The simple greeting in Egyptian daily dialect of "Ahlan" = Hello is being replaced with the more formal "Islamic" greeting of "Alsalam Aleikum" = Peace be upon you, which then separates the Egyptian Copts and the Muslims even in their daily greeting. However, "cultures are limited, time-specific constructs that are learned and constantly in a state of flux"[4]—culture changes or is influenced as a result of the introduction of new forms of mass media, and communication. So to pinpoint specific cultural impact is difficult since it is ever changing, particularly popular culture.

Fahmy has documented many changes in the Egyptian cultural landscape. He confirms that while the literacy rate is quite low, "it was newspapers (especially the satirical press), [that] recorded and performed colloquial Egyptian songs, and the vernacular theater that were the principal and most effective mediators and broadcasters of cultural ideologies, including the idea of a collective Egyp-tian identity."[5] Workers were in the heart of this endeavor and used authentic

Egyptian cultural icons for cementing solidarity and protest purposes. Their use of colloquial Egyptian Arabic solidifies the local Egyptian patriotism—*wataniyya*. Colloquial Egyptian is typically Egyptian and thus nationally exclusive.

> As Joel Beinin notes the mere decision to write in colloquial has often been perceived as a political act associated with a nationalist program of populism, anticlericalism (not irreligion), and local Egyptian wataniyya as opposed to Pan-Arabism—qawmiyya.[6]

Workers embody the heart and soul of colloquial Egyptian Arabic—*'ammiyya*, which comes from the Arabic word for public. During protests, workers used leaflets, slogans, hand-held signs with their demands written on them, songs, chants, and music using drums and *el oud* (the lute). They also used props such as coffins, black armbands, and empty pots and pans to demonstrate a particular point. The workers used the language of the average person to communicate and challenge the regime.

The Relationship Between the State and the People— The Authoritarian Boot on the Neck?

The relationship between the state and the people is particularly helpful to understand the nature of Egyptian society and how it impacts political behavior. For the mass of Egyptians, "*al-nizam*" (the order/system) is the controlling influence seen in everyday life. However, Egyptians were ruled by an authoritarian, inept, inefficient regime that was failing to fulfill its basic role. "Egypt is an unequal society in which more people are poor and insecure, and in which problems of daily survival are more pressing. The people and 'the order' are joined by little except mutual fear and hostility."[7] This was the state of affairs leading up to January 2011. The Mubarak government, picking up the baton from the previous Sadat regime, was characterized by low-intensity "window dressing" democracy, more income inequality, a clever combination of repression and co-optation, several electoral travesties with pointless political parties, corporatism within the normally vibrant workers' movement—leading ultimately to a divided, unequal society with increasing religiosity as a form of protest more than true religious fervor. So protests by the subaltern classes, i.e. the workers were not a surprise.

Jason Brownlee shows through his field research and studies that the regime maintained its power through the ruling political party, the NDP, which bound elites together into a ruling coalition. It was then difficult for the opposition to mount a significant campaign to counter the power of the ruling party. The ruling party shielded their members of parliament, and there was never a possibility of influencing or lobby the members.[8]

Amin believes that so many of the social, cultural, and political problems in Egypt are associated with the growing inequality in income distribution. This phenomenon started with Sadat's open-door policy, "Infitah" (opening), in the early 1970s. This entailed the slow and deliberate removal of the state's role in the economy, abandoning active investment in agriculture and industry, and not regulating the growing private sector investments. In essence, the state used to play an "equalizing" role in society through the economy, but with its removal

from that role, the inequalities were exposed. In addition to the liberalization of imports, the decline in social welfare provided by the state along with inefficient tax collection thus resulted in reduced revenues for the state.

The fear of the rising up of the masses was definitely a part of Mubarak and his lieutenants' worries and anxieties. "In 2007 Finance Minister Youssef Boutros-Ghali confided that the plight of the poor was 'a basic challenge that keeps me awake at night.' "[9] I do not believe that he was genuinely worried about how the poor fared; instead he worried about them rising up and rebelling against the upper classes, the elites. For long periods of time, the majority of the people were excluded from political life, yet the regime still feared them. Why? They still believed that even these disenfranchised, voiceless masses with the growing grievances could manifest themselves into outbursts, protests, and strikes in workplaces that would be successful and capture the masses' attention. The allowance of some liberal independent media contributed tremendously to the diffusion of claims and grievances in addition to reporting and documenting the repertoires of contention by the workers' as a social movement—bringing to light the larger than just "bread and butter" workplace issues.

The following review further confirms that previous regimes had to bow down to the masses' grievances and that the Mubarak regime's fears were legitimate. Examples such as the 1968 protests in Helwan's industrial complex, the 1977 bread intifada, the 1984 strikes in Kafr al Dawwar, the 2007 shortage in drinking water precipitating months of demonstrations across the country, and several more all had in common cuts in benefits, wages, basic services, and then resorting to the use of force by the regime to maintain control further fueling anger among the population. "With each eruption of anger threatens to become another intifada, drawing in millions whose frustrations have reached a boiling point."[10] It might seem that Egyptians had been "docile" and accepting of the authoritarian regime, yet when life's essentials—bread and clean water, for example—were in jeopardy, Egyptians went to the streets to protest as a form of political action.

Under authoritarian regimes, the nature of popular participation in political life, let alone economic and social life, is erratic and not necessarily encouraged. "The political participation of ordinary men and women [who are not part of formal organizations] is even more circumscribed as repression and fear work to intimidate their voices and their leaders."[11] As power is concentrated in a few hands, the study of the elites becomes more interesting and important than the power of the popular masses. Yet Singerman argues that these popular classes under authoritarian regimes are far from being unimportant, politically apathetic, or acquiescent. "They are part and parcel of the overall political dynamic in a nation and cannot be left out of political analyses"; whenever there is an outbreak of political expression—a demonstration, a strike, or a social movement—analysts scramble to learn about the popular masses' sector and what their demands are.[12]

The prevalence of authoritarian regimes in the Middle East has not changed despite the "third wave" of democratization that began among developing countries, starting in Latin America in the 1970s and spreading to Eastern Europe in the 1990s. The region has witnessed stalled liberalization efforts and even reversals—not one authoritarian leader left office through competitive elections. The "Arab Spring" (now a mostly discredited term) starting in late 2010 has added a new dimension but no guarantees of democratic reforms and practices.

It has unleashed a concept of the power of the people and brought down the barrier of fear by the people of their authoritarian masters. However, this "people power" we saw during the Arab Spring has not been routinized into sustainable institutions to further cement the steps and institutions towards democratization. Therein lies the crux of the problem in Egypt, and the only well-organized institutions and movements were and still are the military and the MB.

Why has the Middle East region remained so isolated from the "third wave" of democratization? asked Eva Bellin in her essay "Coercive Institutions and Coercive Leaders" in Posusney and Angrist's *Authoritarianism in the Middle East* (2005). She shares various analysts' conclusions that the region, including Egypt, lacks the prerequisites of democratization. The lack of a strong civil society, a market-driven economy, adequate income and literacy levels, democratic neighbors, and democratic culture explains the region's failure to catch the third wave.[13] However, these explanations are not satisfactory for Bellin. Conditions that foster robust authoritarianism are these politically tenacious and coercive apparatuses such as: (1) prevalence of coercive patrimonialism in state structures and (2) low level of popular mobilization. There were multiple Western security concerns that provided support for authoritarian regimes especially during the Cold War era. In this context, regime elites are able to maintain the will and capacity to suppress democratic initiatives.[14] Bellin actually confirms that the absence of effective state institutions, even when an oppressive coercive apparatus is removed, will not bring about democracy. "To anchor democracy in the region, political reformers must focus on building effective, impartial state institutions, nurturing associations that reach across ethnic lines and unite people around common economic and cultural interests as well as fostering economic growth."[15] This is a tall order of tasks, and yet a challenge that many countries around the world face, bringing an end to the "exceptional" discourse surrounding the Middle East and particularly Egypt.

James C. Scott invites us to expand our view beyond institutions and our political focus on who is in power and the elite around power in order to understand the dynamics of political change. He argues,

> So long as we confine our conception of the political to activity that is openly declared we are driven to conclude that subordinate groups essentially lack a political life or that what political life they do have is restricted to those exceptional moments of popular explosion.[16]

However, subordinate or marginalized groups are another form of resistance to domination, and that is where the unorganized workers outside the formal state structures reside. Workers, due to the nature of their conditions, have the ability to organize even under the most difficult of conditions and restrictions. We have seen this phenomenon under Communist rule, such as in Poland and elsewhere. Workers can make a "political life" and create "organized explosions" to challenge the regime for freedom of association—a fundamental need for workers and their unions.

Political participation in an authoritarian environment is difficult to identify, since it is a concept used to analyze activism in democratic environments. Holger Albrecht presents the view that there is political participation in every political system, even in authoritarian regimes.[17] These forms of political participation in

an authoritarian regime are diverse and have to be viewed in an inclusive manner. So, having an expansive broad view helps us better understand the state-society relations through the diverse forms of political participation. Clearly, autocrats do not want to be held accountable by their people; however, they still need a modicum (even if it is a sham) level of support. Albrecht uses the broad yet simple definition of political participation by S. Huntington and J. Nelson. Political participation is an "activity by private citizens designed to influence governmental decision-making" (1976:4).[18] Asef Bayat has observed six types of activism in the Middle East: "urban mass protest, trade unionism, community activism, social Islamism, non-governmental organizations (NGOs), and quiet encroachment."[19] This supports the view that political institutions that are meant for political participation in an authoritarian regime do not play that role and are not channels for political participation. State institutions and political parties play an imitation role that gives the façade of political participation. However, Albrecht does conclude that there are three ways of political participation that does take place despite authoritarian controls: political participation within the confines of the authoritarian institutions usually through populist or corporatist endeavors (for example, the Egyptian trade unions); political participation through informal social networks; and political participation through oppositional political institutions that are autonomous from the state control.[20] We can refer to this type or context for political participation as "imagined political participation."

Another facet of "imagined political participation" can be seen in Egypt's economic structures (workplaces), which often resembled or mirrored the existing stagnant political authoritarian structures. Samer Shehata's extensive ethnographic research has concluded that what is acted out in the factory on the shop floor, i.e. the relations between the workers and the supervisors and managers, easily resemble or mimic the relationship between the state, the society, and the citizens. Workers' experiences at the workplace not only contribute to the process of class formation but also reflect the state-society relationship.

> The culture of the shop floor plays an important role in the process of class formation. Workers differentiated themselves, whether intentionally or not, and were differentiated by others through a distinctive culture that emerged out of the material conditions of the work hall.[21]

The workers in this particular illuminating study help inform us of the overall relations between workers and their employers. Resistance is present whenever there is power (as Foucault writes, "Where there is power there is resistance"), then the workers in their own inimitable manner managed to resist the employer's new work rules. Shehata gives us several examples of worker/employer resistance vignettes where each side was trying to change the behavior of the other.[22] This show of resistance is evidence that workers banded together even in an authoritarian regime (workplace) can resist and even win with getting some grievances resolved.

E. P. Thompson's moral economy informed many of the worker resistance practices that Shehata describes. However, Thompson wrote about a moral economy based on "traditional views of social norms and obligations"—custom and traditional rights that existed in England's eighteenth century. This type of moral economy informed certain market transactions, mainly the sale of bread.

So when the food riots of eighteenth-century England took place, they were not unruly events but direct popular action, disciplined and with clear objectives.[23] So Thompson wrote about a moral economy of provision, and what Shehata reports witnessing in the garment and textile factory was "a moral economy surrounding the exchange of labor power for a wage; ideas, sometimes explicitly formulated but most often implicitly held, about equivalency, fairness, reciprocity, and justice in the wage-labor relation."[24] This moral economy of exchange informed many of the resistance practices that Shehata accurately described in his study.

The nature of work and the workers takes place within a context and informs us about the organizational culture that exists at the workplace. In Egypt, well over one million workers were employed in public sector factories/workplaces from the 1960s until 1990s. Until the 1990s, most large manufacturing took place in public sector (owned by the government) companies. The culture within public sector companies reflects the relationship between the state and society. According to Shehata, organizational culture implies shared meanings, understanding, and norms, including managerial ideology and practices found within organizations.[25] Shehata found that these factories in which he worked were highly hierarchical and authoritarian in their management relations with the workers, reflecting the nature of governance found outside the factory. "The exercise of power was arbitrary and seemingly unlimited. Employees of different rank were intensely conscious of their respective positions and inequality; how they were treated depended entirely on where they stood within the hierarchy."[26] So we can implicitly deduce that workers who were at the bottom of the hierarchical chain were the subjects of arbitrary and unlimited power practiced by those higher up on the ladder—the managers?

> If superiors do not treat their subordinates with respect and dignity, why should people treat those below themselves any differently? This becomes the norm—the expected and acceptable behavior. So being authoritarian becomes an assertion of one's dignity, equality and power.[27]

Rigid hierarchy and arbitrary authority led to sycophantism, fear, and obeisance[28]—very reflective of the Egyptian society at large.

The realm of the everyday practices, whether at work or in society, is not trivial or unimportant. It is also political and therefore should not just be relegated to the world of sociology or psychology and discounted as being not serious. In a multi-faceted disciplinary research, these concepts/perspectives contribute to political and economic behavior. In this realm is where we can understand how society relates to the state and how society can resist the state, especially a repressive authoritarian state. Shehata has

> attempted to integrate political economy and interpretative approaches to the human sciences by demonstrating how "economic relations" are simultaneously relations of signification and meaning and by showing how the production of things is at the same time, the production of identity, patterns of interaction and understanding of the self and the other.[29]

The nature of how the workplace relationships are organized have an impact on how workers/managers interact, thus reflecting the society at large.

Egyptian society's manifestation of political activity was found in the few legal avenues of political participation that existed.

> Egypt presents an example of politics despite authoritarian rule in an area of the world where so many stereotypes about passivity, fatalism, repression, corruption, fanaticism, and terrorism still reign. [. . .] The *sha'b* [the common people or the popular sector in Egypt] are still portrayed as the *objects* of political rule rather than as the *architects* of political change and struggle.[30]

Scott reminds us that "bread and butter issues" are the heart of lower-class politics and resistance. This is fusing self-interest and resistance, which is the main force animating the resistance of the proletariat and the peasants.[31] Workers' bread and butter issues were key motivators in the era of protests starting in 2000 until 2011 January uprising. Subordinate groups (those who are not in power) like workers create alternative ways to express their views and even participate in the political discourse. Scott wrote, "Every subordinate group creates, out of its ordeal, a 'hidden transcript' that represents a critique of power spoken behind the back of the dominant."[32] What are these hidden transcripts by Egyptian workers and the rest of society as a topic of this chapter?

These hidden transcripts included revolt against the state's full-fledged implementation of neoliberal economic reforms. In addition, there was an overall crisis in representation and human agency that has emerged after decades of repression and co-optation. One prime example is the workers who were repressed by the state trade union organizations, including the national federation, the ETUF, that was supposed to protect and defend them. Corporatist arrangements continue to stifle action in many workplaces, beating down on workers who are truly exposed to the full weight and burden of the state's neoliberal economic policy. Meanwhile, a minority of Egyptians have been enriched by the state through its official policy of privatization of the public sector. "Such are the extremes of inequality in today's Egypt," notes Marfleet.[33] Despite these conditions, the workers and their independent network of trade unions acting as a social movement have challenged Mubarak's authoritarian regime. So the "combination of repression, apathy and political demobilization which sustained autocracy in Egypt for over a half of a century has been challenged, making it unlikely that the Mubarak regime will be able to continue indefinitely with business as usual,"[34] wrote Beinin in 2009. Beinin and others writing in this collection of essays edited by El Mahdi and Marfleet were indeed prophetic by laying down the markers for the events of January 2011 to take place. The January 2011 uprising was not a surprise to Egyptians, including the workers; it was inevitable. It was not a surprise as well for the scholars who were carefully watching and methodically documenting the changes and events taking place over the last decade.

Starting in 2004, democracy activists began to contest the uncomfortable and disturbing thought of Mubarak's son, Gamal, becoming president after his father.

> The Egyptian Movement for Change, known by its popular name and slogan—Kifaya (Enough),[35] and its sister groups together known as Harakat al-Tageer حركات التغيير (Movements for Change), attracted much attention in Egypt and abroad. They broke many taboos, bringing to the scene new people, and new activists, who were new to politics and challenging the widespread view that Egypt was immune to democratic activism.[36]

These movements began and subsided within a couple of years, leaving the mantle of democratic activism to be picked up by the independent workers' movement. The workers' movement had reached a tipping point due to the abuses and injustices of the neoliberal economic reforms. Enter the workers—a new wave of activism developed and this time among workers and professionals. Industrial workers began a series of protests and strikes, which included every area of economy, public and private. Rabab el Mahdi writes, "Although the democracy movement cannot claim direct links to workers' activities through organizational coalitions, overlapping constituencies or shared personnel, the rise of the workers' movement cannot be dissociated from its influence."[37] Even though the democracy movement embodied in Kefaya and its affiliates fizzled, it did give a lifeline to the workers who continued the struggle against the regime. Thus, an organic relationship developed between the two—a group mostly rooted in activist oppositional intellectual elite and the other being the working class. These two groups rarely coalesced to form opposition to the regime.

Economic, political, and social protests have produced a large, diverse number of Egyptians expressing their discontent. It was just not in the cities where protests took place but also in the towns, villages, and slums where inhabitants demanded improved state services and basics such as access to clean drinking water. El Mahdi points to McAdam et al.'s (2001:4)[38] observations that "a dynamic of contention," in which "different forms of contention—social movements, revolutions, strike waves, nationalism, democratization, and more—result from similar mechanisms and processes" can be seen in action in Egypt.[39] Rising dissent, even if it was through unorganized public expressions of grievances and making consistent demands with a nascent democracy movement, presented the opportunity, the spark that lit the powder keg leading to the January 2011 mass uprising. It is imperative to have a holistic view that includes those who are not necessarily part of the formal political institutions. Workers and their independent organizations are part of the network of social agents that contribute to the strength of the "politics from below" and the engagement of those normally denied a role in the political field: workers and pro-democracy activists.[40]

Popular Culture and Workers

What is popular culture? Popular culture was used by elites and non-elites, the subordinate classes according to Gramsci, and this was the case in Egypt as well. Scholars have been using more expansive definitions; Harold Hinds defines popular culture as "those aspects of culture, whether ideological, social, or material, which are widely spread and believed in and/or consumed by significant number of people and is popular."[41] This popular culture developed and grew to mobilize many, particularly the workers, to revolt.

Egyptian Workers Used Street Politics to Highlight Economic and Political Mobilizations[42]

As the protests and strikes increased, the workers left their factories and workplaces and came to the center of power, the capital city, Cairo. In itself that is a bold move and a political one—facing both the state and the regime at its headquarters.

The Council of Ministers' building on Hussein Higazi Street became a focal point for the workers to express their anger and grievances. Other protest spots were in front of the Shura Council and the Peoples' Assembly (Parliament). Increasingly, the independent and private media outlets (print and television) started to cover these stories. The workers even took their protests to well-known talk shows on private television stations. Out on the streets, the workers were creative in their use of slogans on hand-held signs, large banners, and posters. They added music, primarily drums and whistles, to their repertoire to give cadence to their chants and keep the crowd on cue and energized using hand-held public announcement systems and microphones. Their very clever use of street slang and the Egyptian dialect to emphasize their message was effective and created sympathy with their cause. The use of microphones and public announcement amplifiers became the norm to ensure that the "higher ups" locked in their offices could hear them. In addition, they held marches and role-playing of "death of a workplace/factory" by enacting a funeral procession. Several protests became "sit-ins" for days turning into weeks with tents set up and all the supporting equipment to meet the needs of, at times, hundreds of workers sitting and sleeping. These street protests were also family events, where the workers' families joined in, giving the clear message that these grievances were affecting not just the one person—the worker—but the whole family and in most cases the whole city or region.

The "Soft State" and Impact on Workers and Society at Large

What is a "soft state"?

> A soft state is a state that passes laws but does not enforce them. The elites can afford to ignore the law because their power protects them from it, while others pay bribes to work around it. Everything is up for sale, be it building permits for illegal construction, licenses to import illicit goods [. . .] the rules are made to be broken and to enrich those who break them, and taxes are often evaded.[43]

In the soft state, corruption is generalized and a way of life to get things done and to survive. Yet, corruption weakens the state and pervades all state institutions. It further supports and defends the power of the elite upper class, and their feeling of loyalty is to their class, families, and clan, not to the nation. Legislation is only meant to provide a window dressing for democracy and justice, yet in essence these elites have the full power to evade or ignore these laws.[44] Gunnar Myrdal's three-volume study, focused on the problems of economic underdevelopment, development, and planning for development in South Asia, was published in 1968. He focused on India, Pakistan, Ceylon (present-day Sri Lanka), Burma, Malaysia, Thailand, the Philippines, Cambodia, Laos, Vietnam, and Indonesia. Both Amin and Waterbury refer to his theories of the "soft state" and Amin, in particular, never thought that this would apply to Egypt. The case study presented covers South Asia post-independence countries that pledged the promotion of economic development through planned and coordinated efforts by the government.[45]

Amin wrote that in Myrdal's view, many developing countries suffer from being under the control of what he referred to as the "soft state," and this could be the clue to some of the greatest problems and one of the main reasons for the continued poverty and backwardness.[46] John Waterbury wrote "The 'Soft State' and the Open Door: Egypt's Experience With Economic Liberalization, 1974–1984" in 1985, and he makes an assessment of the Sadat-initiated open door economic liberation called "Infitah." He concludes that the "Infitah" policies were lacking in major aspects due to Egypt having a "soft state," a la Myrdal's definition. It further added to the negative perception and actual liberalization and with a relation to democracy since that was the "packaging" in which it was presented. The notion that democracy brings economic liberalization, yet in a system of a "soft state," it brings further inequality, injustice, and the added cementing of corruption.

Egypt's "Infitah" policies were supposed to save the initial socialist experiment under Nasser and to further progress and develop economically. There were positive aspects, yet the social implications and particularly their impact on the working class were harmful. Waterbury wrote, "Egypt's turn to the open door has produced some positive results: remarkable aggregate growth in the economy, an unfettering of individual initiative with all sorts of possibilities for upward mobility, and the resurgence of the private sector."[47] However, the social contract and the state's financial commitments to welfare programs and consumer subsidies has since been reduced, causing havoc for those dependent on those services and those working in the public sector. The problem is that the "soft state" politically with all its components still continues with no reforms in sight. So the "Infitah" liberalization policies further enriched the elites and impoverished the working class and middle class. There were no provisions made to soften the impact on those dependent on the public sector for employment and survival. There cannot be economic growth without political reform; justice for the masses is not achieved and further adds to their misery. Egypt ultimately was not able to afford paying for the "soft state," and as Samer Soliman[48] wrote in 2011, it was vital to reform the Egyptian state, yet the authoritarian regime's priority was to use public money to impose and maintain political stability.

Egypt's quest for democracy has been stifled by the continued "soft state" and economic liberalization policies—all under a context of an authoritarian regime resorting more and more to heavy-handed tactics. Egypt did witness a significant rise in protest movements in the early 2000s leading up to the January 2011 events. Yet shortcomings of this protest movement have limited its continued expansion and success in achieving real and lasting political reform. Starting with the Kefaya movement in 2004, which exposed the limits of the Mubarak regime's capacity to deal with contestation and introduced new mechanisms to the political process, this pro-democracy movement had a wider impact on popular mobilization than was initially anticipated. "Although Kifaya relatively faded away from the political scene after the 2005 elections, there was a rise of a series of demonstrations and protests throughout 2006–07 by other actors."[49] The judges protested for independence of the judiciary, and the labor movement was reawakened after a decade of hibernation, with a series of strikes involving tens of thousands of workers, starting in December 2006.[50] The political environment and the regime's response, especially in trying to accommodate the workers, gave rise to more emboldened action and protests. "The rising protest movement provided a new channel for politics that can attract potential dissent [. . .] thus the

potential of affecting regime change."[51] The rise of contentious politics in Egypt with the acceptance of the decline of the existing political party system will ensure that these protest movements will continue. It is another form of political action that can achieve results, even if limited in scope or nature.

However, El Mahdi warns that when studying social protest movements in Egypt and elsewhere in the Middle East, it is important to note the local vs. the regional dimensions, structural conditions versus agency, and the need for understanding the mechanisms through which contentious politics in nondemocratic settings can start at the fringes and work their way inside.[52] "That is, the process and mechanisms linking different forms of mobilization, and the democratizing effect that nascent social movements can have on locations of contention. Thus, the impact of social movements can transcend seemingly ghettoized context overtime."[53] Social movements can bring otherwise disparate, far-flung, not organized into one-unit groups of workers (in this case) together, seemingly united under one banner. This supports our contention that despite the disparate nature of the independent workers network, their social movement was united under a set of grievances to enable them to challenge the regime. Was this able to help them traverse towards a full measure of success? The answer is no, and thus was an incomplete challenge to the regime.

The Question of Justice vs. Democracy in Egypt

The slogan that rang through Tahrir Square during those heady days starting on January 25 and leading to when Mubarak stepped down on February 11, 2011, was bread, freedom, and social justice. Those were the demands of the throngs of millions of Egyptians, and frankly, that has not changed since those demands have not been met three years later. Why the focus on social justice and not on democracy? These three important concepts, bread, freedom, and social justice, have roots in the histories of the Arab countries and particularly in Egypt. It is clear that in order to appeal to the masses, one needs to talk about justice عدالة "*adala*"—it is a concept that has deep meaning to which the masses can relate.

> Anyone needing an indication of how much the Arab World has changed in the past year has only to tune in to one of the popular satellite TV music channels. The young artist Ramy Essam's hit song "Bread, Freedom and Social Justice" was beamed several times a day to the four corners of the Arab world. The song was released [in 2011], in the wake of the Egyptian uprising that brought down a regime that punished talk about freedom and social justice with imprisonment and torture. It takes its title from one of the most popular slogans chanted during the 2011 protests, which came after bread riots had shaken Egypt and many surrounding Arab countries in the wake of the 2008 food crisis. In that sense, the song adequately summarizes the main demands of the Arab people. Food security is at the top of that list.[54]

A discussion or a call for democracy leads to a myriad of concepts, ideas, and practices, even misunderstandings. Justice and the implementation of justice is the road to democracy, since Egyptians can more readily relate to and understand the concept of justice.

Justice has been and continues to be the most sought after since the beginning of time by humankind. Justice by one human being to another is the most prized act. The definition of justice

> is originally derived from a Latin word "Justitia." Theologically, it means, "the observance of the divine Law," "righteousness," "the state of being just before God." Ethically, it means "one of the four cardinal virtues, the just conduct or the quality of being just and the principle of just dealing." Legally, it connotes, "exercise of authority or power in the maintenance of right, vindication of right by assignment of reward or punishment, infliction of punishment, legal vengeance on an offender." Sociologically, justice is "to render what is one's due, vindicate one's just claims, to do something in a manner worthy of one's abilities.[55]

Bread (the word for bread in Egyptian dialect is 'ayesh, which means life) and freedom are inseparable;

> Until the uprisings began in 2011, Arab leaders argued that economic reform must precede political reform—the so-called bread before freedom approach. They argued that it was premature and even dangerous to introduce political reform before supplying citizens' basic needs. Only when those needs had been met could people make responsible political decisions. But that strategy, even when conducted in good faith, did not work as planned.[56]

Egyptians were demanding bread (life), freedom, and social justice, and not one before the other—all three.

Social Justice and freedom are rooted in Islam, and the following are references made by Sayid Qutb in his book *Social Justice in Islam*. These references further solidify the important relationship between social justice and Islam thus embedded in Egypt's culture: (1) "the nature of Islamic belief about human life makes social justice essentially an all-embracing justice which does not take account merely of material and economic factors; for Islam does not divide the individual into body and soul, into differing intellectual and spiritual sides."[57] (2) "Islam approaches the question of freedom from every angle and from all points of view; it undertakes a complete emancipation of the conscience [. . .] freedom is one of the cornerstones for the building of social justice in Islam. Moreover, it is the principal cornerstone on which all the others must rest."[58] (3) "Islam legislates for mutual responsibility in society in all shapes and forms—these forms take their rise from the basic principle that three is an all-embracing identity of purpose between the individual and society."[59] Justice for all is ensured through the respect for and the implementation of social justice. Social justice, bread, and freedom—the three main demands were made by Egyptians, including the working class, for decades before January 2011, and they are still continuing to make these demands until the present day.

Concluding Remarks

It is clear that Egypt was ready for an uprising, but a full-fledged revolution was just not possible. The so-called deep state apparatus with the military in full

support of such state apparatus will not allow for a full-fledged revolution leading to a possible change in the political system (the requirements needed for a revolution). Egyptian culture and society have been evolving and becoming more and more aggressive against the ineptitudes of the regime and the lack of respect for, or more accurately, the lack of implementation of social justice, bread (life), and freedom. The workers played a role in this societal evolution and change— they pushed down the barriers of fear. Yet, unless the "soft state" is dismantled and replaced by the respect for the rule of law and other universal fundamental principles of human rights, the workers and any other organized social movement will have little impact in achieving serious and sustainable positive political change.

Notes

1. Amin, Galal A. *Whatever Happened to the Egyptians? Changes in Egyptian Society from 1950 to the Present.* Cairo: American University in Cairo Press, 2000: 7.
2. www.nytimes.com/2013/12/07/world/middleeast/ahmed-fouad-negm-dissident-poet-of-egypts-underclass-dies-at-84.html?_r=0
3. Amin 2000: 7–8.
4. Fahmy, Z. *Ordinary Egyptians: Creating the Modern Nation Through Popular Culture.* Stanford, CA: Stanford University Press, 2011: 3.
5. Ibid.: 167.
6. Ibid.: 173.
7. Marfleet, P. E. and Rabab El-Mahdi. *Egypt the Moment of Change.* London: Zed Books, 2009: 14.
8. Brownlee, Jason. *Authoritarianism in an Age of Democratization.* Cambridge: Cambridge University Press, New York, 2007: 35–37.
9. Marfleet and El-Mahdi 2009: 31.
10. Ibid.: 32.
11. Singerman, Diane. *Avenues of Participation: Family, Politics, and Networks in Urban Quarters of Cairo.* Princeton, NJ: Princeton University Press, 1995: 3.
12. Ibid.: 4.
13. Posusney, Marsha P. and P. Michele. *Angrist, Authoritarianism in the Middle East: Regimes and Resistance.* Boulder, CO: Lynne Rienner Publishers, 2005: 23.
14. Ibid.: 37.
15. Ibid.: 38.
16. Scott, James C. *Domination and the Arts of Resistance: Hidden Transcripts.* New Haven, CT: Yale University Press, 1990: 199.
17. Lust-Okar, Ellen. *Political Participation in the Middle East.* Boulder, CO: Lynne Rienner Publishers, 2008: 15–16.
18. Huntington, Samuel P., and Joan M. Nelson. *No easy choice: Political participation in developing countries.* Cambridge, Mass.: Harvard University Press, 1976, p. 4.
19. Bayat, Asef. "Activism and Social Development in the Middle East." *International Journal of Middle East Studies* 34 (1) (2002): 1–28: 3.
20. Lust-Okar 2008: 28.
21. Shehata, Samer S. *Shop Floor Culture and Politics in Egypt.* Albany: SUNY Press, 2009: 56.
22. Ibid.: 123–124.
23. Thompson, E.P. "The Moral Economy of the English Crowd in the 18th Century." *Past and Present* 50 (1971): 76–136: 78 in Shehata's *Shop Floor Culture*, p. 126.
24. Shehata, 2009: 126.
25. Ibid.: 128.
26. Ibid.: 129.
27. Ibid.: 154.
28. Ibid.
29. Ibid.: 184.

30. Singerman 1995: 5.
31. Scott, James. C. *Weapons of the Weak: Everyday Forms of Peasant Resistance*. New Haven, CT: Yale University Press, 1985: 295–296.
32. Scott 1990.
33. Marfleet and El-Mahdi 2009: 30.
34. Ibid.: 86.
35. More details about the Kefaya movement can be found in Chapter 4.
36. Marfleet and El-Mahdi 2009: 87.
37. Ibid.: 100.
38. Aminzade, Ronald R., Jack A. Goldstone, Doug McAdam, Elizabeth J. Perry, Sidney Tarrow, William H. Sewell, and Charles Tilley. *Silence and voice in the study of contentious politics*. Cambridge University Press, 2001, p. 4.
39. Ibid.: 101.
40. Ibid.: 154.
41. Fahmy 2011: 3.
42. The case study on the real estate tax collectors presents several examples of slogans, etc.; see Chapter 5.
43. Amin, Galal A. *Egypt in the Era of Hosni Mubarak: 1981–2011*. Cairo, Egypt and New York: American University in Cairo Press, 2011: 8.
44. Ibid.
45. Myrdal, Gunnar. *Asian Drama; An Inquiry Into the Poverty of Nations*. New York: The Twentieth Century Fund, 1968: 42–43.
46. Amin 2011: 8.
47. Waterbury, J. "The 'Soft State' and the Open Door: Egypt's Experience with Economic Liberalization, 1974–1984." *Comparative Politics* 18 (1) (1985): 65–83.
48. Sulaymān, Samer. *The Autumn of Dictatorship: Fiscal Crisis and Political Change in Egypt Under Mubarak*. Stanford, CA: Stanford University Press, 2011.
49. El-Mahdi, Rabab. "Enough!: Egypt's Quest for Democracy." *Comparative Political Studies* 42 (8) (2009): 1011–1039: 1034.
50. Ibid.
51. Ibid.
52. Ibid.: 1035.
53. Ibid.
54. Zurayk, Rami. "Bread, Freedom, and Social Justice." *Journal of Agriculture, Food Systems, and Community Development* 2 (2) (2012): 7–10.
55. Qureshi, Tufail Ahmad. "Justice in Islam." *Islamic Studies* 21.2 (1982): 35-51.
56. Muasher, Marwan. "Freedom and Bread go Together." *Finance & Development* 50 (1) (2013): 14–17. *ProQuest*. Web. December 12, 2013.
57. Qutb, Sayid. *Social Justice in Islam*. Oneonta, NY: Islamic Publications International, 2000: 51.
58. Ibid.: 67–68.
59. Ibid.: 92.

Part III
Conclusion

7 The Hope for a Democratic Transition

Post-January 2011 Uprising and the Role of the Independent Labor Movement Leading to the May 2012 Elections and Beyond

Chapter Outline:

Democratic Transition: Political and Economic Lessons

This chapter will review the concept of democratic transition and political and economic lessons. Social capital is the main condition to promote social change through collective action. Michael Edwards, the civil society expert, commentator, and author, notes, "social capital is seen as the crucial ingredient in promoting collective action for the common good."[1] Relating this to the labor movement, workers are social capital and can be interpreted as the collective action of workers. This collective action of workers in a social movement can be an effective mechanism in the quest for democratic transition. How does this apply to Egypt specifically and to the Arab world in general? Or is there a "recession of democracy," and civil society activism cannot deliver change?

Democracy experts and scholars were writing and debating about a "democratic recession." Yet, over recent years (2010–2013), we have witnessed millions of oppressed people standing up against authoritarian regimes and demanding justice through reform of the political system with the goal of establishing a substantive representative democracy. The call for freedom, equality, prosperity (bread), and social justice are at the heart of these mobilizations. These movements for positive political change are coming at a time when democracy appears to be receding, as noted by Larry Diamond in *The Spirit of Democracy* and Joshua Kurlantzick in *Democracy in Retreat*.[2] Diamond wrote,

the democratic boom has given way to recession. Its start may be traced to the 1999 military coup in Pakistan which symbolized the failure of many of the new democracies to perform decently in delivering development, social peace, and good governance.[3]

However, despite the more realist analysis of the state of democracy, there is a renewed sense of hope, yet with many pitfalls. There is an increase in the universal demand for democratic values and aspirations. The recession is receding and opening the door to revitalization, yet the main challenge is whether these new "fragile" governments can deliver what the people need and want. And will the recession sink into a depression when their hopes and dreams remain unfulfilled and even more entrenched authoritarian rulers take over after these uprisings?

Since 1989 and the fall of the Berlin Wall, we have witnessed various "color revolutions" in the former Soviet bloc countries until the early 2000s. Yet these ventures into democratic rule have been challenged by the heavy economic challenges and the fragile institutions in these countries. As Freedom House reports in its *Freedom in the World 2013* report,[4] global levels of freedom have declined, thus the continued talk of a democratic recession.

> This is the seventh consecutive year that *Freedom in the World* has shown more declines than gains worldwide. Furthermore, the report data reflected a stepped-up campaign of persecution by dictators that specifically targeted civil society organizations and independent media.[5]

This trend has continued, and Freedom House's report in 2018 documenting the data from 2017 confirms the continued deterioration of political rights and civil liberties around the world, "to their lowest point in more than a decade in 2017, extending a period characterized by emboldened autocrats, beleaguered democracies, and the United States' withdrawal from its leadership role in the global struggle for human freedom."[6]

So, the nascent democratic openings in the Middle East, especially in Tunisia and Egypt in 2012–2013, were watched carefully, since it could have meant a reversal in the democratic recession. Yet there are many hurdles along the way, and

> many countries that once seemed budding with democratic promise now appear mired in political infighting and power grabs by ousted elites, or trapped in downward spirals of poverty and unemployment. History suggests that many transitioning countries will move [very] slowly toward substantive democracy.[7]

These countries face tremendous challenges, such as fragile institutions, weak civil society organizations, lack of respect for the rule of law, high levels of unemployment particularly among the youth, and weak economic indicators and performance, in addition to the decline in investment in human resources in terms of providing decent education, security, and health care.

It is critical that nascent democracies consolidate and withstand the significant challenges. Diamond continued to argue that they must become more deeply democratic—more liberal, accountable, and responsive to their citizens. In his book *Developing Democracy: Toward Consolidation* (1999), in which he draws on extensive public opinion research in developing and post-Communist states,

he demonstrates the importance of freedom, transparency, and the rule of law for generating the broad legitimacy that is the essence of democratic consolidation. The book concludes with a hopeful view of the prospects for a fourth wave of global democratization.[8] So are we to conclude that the Arab Spring is ushering in a "fourth wave of democratization"? It presents a mixed picture, with varying positive and negative results and much skepticism.

The January 2011 uprising came as no surprise, since Egyptians on all levels were suffering economically and there was no national vision to unite everyone. The surprise was possibly in the intensity and how quickly the head of the regime buckled. Also, the surprise can be seen in how the masses were not afraid to stand up to the entrenched state security apparatuses. The gradual withdrawal of the state from providing basic services heavily affected the poor and middle classes. The state decreased expenditures on education, health care, social welfare, culture, and the media, and these areas became privatized so they were not easily available to the masses, only to those who could pay. Corruption continued to thrive in all aspects of society and institutions throughout Egypt.

> During the past twenty years a number of powerful elements have thus gathered together to produce a degree of corruption among various sections of Egyptian society the like of which has never been seen in the 1950s, 1960s, or 1970s, nor even in pre-revolutionary Egypt. There was now a weak state that lost both the power and will to punish those transgressing the law, with no commitment to a national project which could unite the people.[9]

Consumerism and material possessions became more valuable than did respect for learning and academic credentials. Pressure by the IFIs in the early 1990s to quickly privatize state-owned lands and factories resulted in shady deals to sell these assets cheaply to foreigners and locals. Workers in these public sector jobs found themselves in a difficult predicament. Many lost their jobs and had to resort to the volatile private sector. The job security of the public sector was not assured anymore. Others found themselves in workplaces in which the state had reduced investments, and the factories were operating on a shoestring budget and with antiquated equipment and were thus not able to compete in a global economy. There was a significant decline in the number of public sector jobs due to the slow but certain privatization program and the lack of reinvestment in the public sector. Another issue was low wages, which

> remain standard for both public and private sector workers. A 2009 report by the Egyptian Organization for Human Rights found that average monthly wages for public sector employees were LE 684 compared with LE 576 in the private sector ($125 and $105 respectively). The report attributed "the crisis in wages and salaries to the government's disregard for social policies that balance between wages and prices."[10]

The large labor mobilization was a result of the significant changes in Egypt's domestic political economy: the speeding up of neoliberal economic reforms, rapidly rising inflation, dramatic increase in daily consumer goods (especially fruits and vegetables), and stagnant wages.[11]

There was a significant decline in the availability of public sector jobs. These jobs were the backbone of Egypt's economy (and social status) since 1952.

The deepening of neoliberal policies in the 1990s stripped the Nasserist state of its social role: privatization transferred hundreds of thousands of workers to private sector employers who did not provide the same kind of workplace-based benefits and job security as their public sector counterparts, while those who remained employed by the state saw the relentless deterioration of their pay and conditions. All that remained of the Faustian pact between workers and the Nasserist state was the authoritarian apparatus of coercion.[12]

Results of the 2006 ETUF trade union elections removed the local leaders who commanded respect at the local level, which in turn made them into the leaders that would lead the revolt and establish new trade unions such as RETA, for example. In many conversations that I had with labor leaders, it is clear that the 2006 elections for ETUF local leaders exceeded all expectations in terms of violations and infringements. These trade union elections came on the heels of the 2005 parliamentary and presidential elections that were relatively decent in terms of turnout and had fewer violations than usual. These were the parliamentary elections, where 82 members of the banned MB were elected as independents. A public report issued by the CTUWS showed that the ETUF was lacking vibrancy and democratic practices. These elections of local leaders and members of the General Council were marred by restrictions (not stipulated in the law) imposed on who could run for office; violations of the candidates' right to openly communicate with his/her constituency to discuss the candidate's trade union mission; favorable treatment of some candidates close to the ETUF leadership and who were good NDP members; and violations of trade union freedom of choice. The ETUF had become so weak due to the decline in public sector jobs that the official structures had to resort to extreme measures just to keep the organization somewhat functioning.

However, these economic grievances were not the only impetus for collective action, according to Shehata, who examines the connections between workers on the shop floor (at the workplace) in the public sector:

> These ties were, in part, the outcome of lifetime public sector employment and limited employment opportunities elsewhere. The trust, familiarity, and repertoire of quotidian practices that marked class boundaries and developed as a result of long years of working together, arguably provided the social capital necessary for effective collective action.[13]

The economy was increasingly becoming a servant for the elite's enrichment and not for the collective good of the masses. The poor were getting poorer and standing in lines in front of bakeries to buy more expensive, smaller-sized bread. "The middle class in Egypt today is a defeated and humiliated class. No wonder it also has little enthusiasm for national issues and its productivity is low in both the economic and cultural spheres."[14] The deterioration of the middle class is apparent in the decline in their living conditions. It is the middle class upon which hopes are usually pinned for national revival, since the poor do not have the means and the rich do not have the inclination or motivation for such a revival.

The middle class plays an important role in the support for democratic practices. It tends to play a much more important role in its country's economic, political, and cultural development than that played by the lower and upper classes. Today, the same daily living frustrations are shared by the poor and the middle

classes in Egypt.[15] The rest of Egyptian society was not spared: the consistent attack on intellectuals; the increase in the fanaticism of the religious discourse; and the increased marginal independence of the press while losing its moral compass added to the alienation of Egyptians. The reasons for disillusionment came from being in one's own country yet not recognizing the surroundings—that is what was taking place for average Egyptians.

> This was just what one would expect from a regime with no political vision and, even if it did have such a vision, no power to implement it; a regime devoid of both talent and vitality, that confines its role to implementing the directives coming from IFIs and super powers like the US. All of this was bound to strengthen the feeling of alienation among Egyptians, in general.[16]

Amin lamented, "A gloomy climate of great alienation." He compares the different nature of the jokes during the Nasser, Sadat, and Mubarak eras and how they reflected the different types of discontent. "The discontent in the Nasser era was closely associated with fear; in the Sadat era, with anger; and in the Mubarak era, with depression,"[17] particularly the feeling of lack of a national project, lack of talent and ability, and most detrimental, no hope for a better future.

The Mubarak regime and all its tentacles lived in fear of a serious opposition. It worked very hard on providing attractive window dressing with a façade of democracy. This was for public consumption to the point that some Egyptians began to believe the charade. It was also provided for international consumption, particularly to those Western nations that continued to provide Egypt with aid in the form of cash, educational and training programs, technical assistance, and military assistance. "Fear was embodied in local proverbs, such as 'walk quietly by the wall (where you cannot be noticed),' 'Mind your own business and focus on your livelihood,' and 'Whosoever is afraid stays unharmed.' "[18] The regime's uncompromising control also covered workers and all state institutions, including civil society organizations.

The previous chapters have outlined the details of the independent workers' movement of protest starting in earnest from 2006 onward. So, the events of January 2011 should not be a surprise—a mass uprising against the regime as a result of the accumulation of the many years of anger, fear, and depression since the 1960s.

> From 1998 to 2010, well over two million workers participated in at least 3,400 strikes and other collective actions—the largest social movement in the Arab world in six decades, except for the Algerian War of Independence (1954–1962). These collective actions were largely motivated by the threat or actual loss of jobs or social benefits after privatization of public sector enterprises, low wages, and delays or nonpayment of bonuses, incentive pay, and other wage supplements critical to bringing income to a level that can sustain survival.[19]

The workers had the motive and the organization to challenge the regime, yet carried much historical and political baggage that weakened their effectiveness.

The Establishment of Independent Labor Federations in Egypt Post January 2011

After those heady days starting on January 25, 2011, the workers' independent movement and networks, i.e. social movement, began to organize into institutions

while still carrying the baggage of the past. However, these organizations did not last; it was a still-birth. The first independent trade union federation was founded in Tahrir Square. Egyptian workers united to form the Egyptian Federation for Independent Trade Unions (EFITU) (the website for this organization is available "for sale"), effectively attempting to destroy the state-controlled ETUF.

> Its existence was announced at a press conference on January 30, 2011, in Cairo's Tahrir Square—the epicenter of the popular movement. The independent unions of Real Estate Tax Authority workers, healthcare technicians, and teachers established since 2008 initiated the new federation. They were joined by the 8.5 million-member retirees' association, which has just received permission to reorganize itself as a professional syndicate, as well as representatives of textile, pharmaceutical, chemical, iron and steel, and automotive workers from industrial zones in Cairo, Helwan, Mahalla al-Kubra, Tenth of Ramadan, and Sadat City.[20]

Then, when the regime gave all the public sector workers in Egypt that first week of February 2011 as time off, this further brought more workers to protest in the main squares and streets around the country, and many traveled to Cairo to be in Tahrir Square. Tactically, that government action of giving the workers time off was not the most strategic decision and actually added to the protesting masses.

Two independent labor federations of several unions were established within days and months of the January 2011 uprising. While the state-controlled ETUF ordered workers to stay at their jobs, the first new federation led them to strike and to join the protests that ultimately brought about Mubarak's downfall.

> The *Egyptian Federation of Independent Trade Unions (EFITU)* was founded in March 2011 within days of the end of the Mubarak regime. It claims an affiliated membership of around 1.4 million workers with a membership of 200 independent unions. Its president is Kamal Abu Eita, the leader of the [Real Estate] Tax Collectors' Union, the first independent union to emerge [in 2008] before the revolution.[21]

The second independent trade union federation is the smaller Egyptian Democratic Labor Congress (EDLC). EDLC

> claims the affiliation of 246 unions with 149 [were] present during the founding press conference on 16th October 2011. Leading figures in the EDLC are affiliated to an NGO, the Center for Trade Union and Worker Services (CTUWS) established by former steel-worker Kamal Abbas. Abbas with his allies withdrew from the EFITU in the summer of 2011 after a bitter controversy over the role over NGO employees in the democratic decision-making bodies of the new federation.[22]

Therein continues the historic baggage that divides workers' leaders and organizations, leading to less effective behavior and a reduction in the ability to truly influence national policies.

Within eight months of the downfall of the Mubarak regime, two independent trade union federations were established that brought together about 1,000 new

independent unions from various sectors of the economy and different professions. Forming these umbrella federations, bringing hundreds of independent unions together, has been an idea that independent labor-focused non-governmental organizations (NGOs) contemplated for many years. The establishment of these federations broke the effective monopoly on labor activity and representation held for over fifty years by the government-controlled ETUF. However, the government that established ETUF back in 1957 did not dissolve the ETUF. It continued to exist and attempted to exert pressure and control over workers.

After February 2011, workers and their leaders believed in the coming of a new era with respect for the fundamental internationally recognized freedoms and rights for workers. It was a time when everything was possible; when there was hope and change in the air and everyone believed in a new Egypt brought about by a "revolution." Wael Ghonim wrote, "the power of the people is greater than the people in power [. . .] the revolution successfully achieved its first objective, removing the key regime figures from power; thus paving the way for opportunity and hope."[23] However, revolutions are a process and not just events, and the path to a democracy is long and full of many challenges, trials, and tribulations. Nevertheless, something has deeply changed within the Egyptian psyche and presence; they are now more connected to each other, whether via social media or by removing the barrier of fear; the social networks that already existed are fully empowered.

The "Egyptian Spring" = Dashed Hopes?

The revolution, or more correctly, the uprising of January 2011 was different in that there was not one charismatic leader. Ghonim referred to it as the "Revolution 2.0" model, since it did not follow the revolutions of the past that have usually had charismatic leaders.[24] He believed that the revolution was truly spontaneous, led by the wisdom of the crowd. I will contest this assertion since there was such a large build-up of protests fueled by serious grievances leading up to January 2011. The previous chapters have made this point in a variety of different ways. Also, it was a revolt against a political system that was inherited by Mubarak, a system that began over fifty years ago. Egyptians revolted against Mubarak, "that is true, but not entirely accurate. They revolted against a regime—a political order—that he led, but that Mubarak inherited from Sadat who inherited it from Nasser."[25] Cook writes that Egyptians cracked open the regime, ushered Mubarak out of power, and now have the opportunity in many years to determine what kind of government they want and to define Egypt as they wish and not how those in power want to define Egypt.[26] Those were assessments made within months of the January 2011 uprising, when hopes and expectations for change were high. Eight years later, Egypt continues to be in a state of turmoil with a deeply polarized and divided populace. The hope of constructing a new political system seems now to be even more ephemeral.

Let us return to the labor movement and its role between February 2011 and May 2012. After Mubarak stepped down on February 11, 2011, the Supreme Council for the Armed Forces (SCAF) became the caretaker government until elections for president were held in May 2012. A spate of protests took place soon after February 11, in which "thousands of workers, including ambulance

drivers, airport and public transport workers, and even police took to the streets, demanding higher pay, three days after Mubarak's resignation."[27] Street protests became the only way that workers could influence the decision-makers, since they were not being represented by "recognized" unions or part of the negotiations with the military.

The SCAF banned demonstrations and strikes that "disrupted production" and called for calm.

> Only three days after Mubarak's resignation [on 11 February 2011], [on February 14, 2011] the Supreme Council released Communiqué 5, which outlines the negative impact of continuing protests on the economy and calls on labor and professional syndicates to help bring about a return to normalcy in everyday life. A few days later, an army statement described '*fi'awi* demands' as illegitimate, pledging to deal with the agitators through legal means in the name of "protecting the security of the nation and its citizens." [On] March 23 2011, the government of Prime Minister 'Isam Sharaf approved a law banning protests, assemblies and strikes that impede private and public business, and rendering such actions punishable with up to a year in prison and a fine that could reach a half-million Egyptian pounds.[28]

The workers have long been branded fi'awi, i.e. group, or the more maligned term used in American politics, special interest, which is used to denigrate the American labor movement among other socio-economic advocacy groups. These are not just "groups" that are removed from society—they are workers who encompass a good majority of the population.

On March 24, 2011, a revised version of Military Decree 34 became Law 34 and set a fine of up to EGP 50,000 (about $8,333) for anyone participating in or encouraging others to join a sit-in or any other activity that "prevents, delays or disrupts the work of public institutions or public authorities." The penalty increases to EGP 500,000 (about $83,333) and at least a year's imprisonment in the event of violence or property damage that may lead to "destruction of means of production" or harm "national unity and public security and order."[29]

Anne Alexander distinguishes three phases in the development of these workers' protests between February and October 2011. Phase 1 is "between February and early March the revolution entered the workplaces on a mass scale. Hundreds of thousands, possibly millions, of workers took strike action, and organized sit-ins and demonstrations against the 'little Mubaraks' in their workplaces."[30] There was a drop in March due to the SCAF's banning of public protests, so "from March the number of workers' strikes and protests dropped in comparison to the explosion of February, and steadied at roughly 65,000 participants per month in all forms of workers' protests."[31] The second phase was between March and August 2011, and the third phase was in September and October 2011.

Alexander clearly outlines the details of the three phases with an analysis of the shift in the workers' consciousness and demands. There was an atmosphere of freedom after the revolution/uprising and the removal of the barriers of fear that had been built and bolstered for over sixty years.

> The growth and consolidation of workers' organisations both within and between individual workplaces during March to August laid the foundations

for the mass strikes of September and October. The same period also saw important shifts in workers' consciousness, as the focus of their protests shifted from the "little Mubarak" in their workplace, to higher up the institutions of the state. September's strike wave marked a seismic shift in both independent organisation and consciousness among Egyptian workers. Around 500,000 workers participated in strikes and protests that month alone, a significantly higher figure than the entire previous six months. While the numbers of participants were probably lower than February, the significance of September's strikes lay in the qualitative shift towards coordinated national and sector-wide strikes.[32]

National and sector-wide strikes were indeed a shift from the past five years, since the strikes that took place were mostly factory/workplace based. During that period, there was a nationwide teachers strike in addition to a sector-wide strike of sugar refinery workers and nationally coordinated strikes and protests by postal workers. The coordination within sectors and ongoing national or sector-wide strikes/protests were a major change in addition to their demands:

> these were mass strikes articulating generalised social demands with a degree of common purpose which in itself constituted a formidable political challenge to the ruling military council. Moreover, the teachers' strike, which mobilised 250,000 to 500,000 strikers, explicitly demanded the resignation of the minister of education, a Mubarak appointee, and other strikes, such as the Cairo Public Transport Authority workers' strike, began to raise similar demands.[33]

Alexander used data from the Awlad el Ard (Sons of the Land Association for Human Rights[34]) NGO in addition to other labor-oriented NGOs. The strikes prior to January 2011 contributed to an overall malaise and expressed the challenges being faced by average Egyptians. Workers brought social justice issues to the forefront of the national stage with the help of the independent media that regularly reported on these incidents of social movement repertoires. The regime dealt with these strikes and protests in a strategic manner, trying not to completely alienate the working class. In addition, there were professional (white-collar) classes of workers that also joined this wave and went on strike protesting working conditions, wages, and the decline in basic benefits. It was difficult to continue the practice of "insulation" of the workers from the rest of the society. It was impossible to consider workers as just a special interest, particularly as their discourse of grievances touched the daily lives of so many Egyptians.

The strikes and protests after January 2011 continued and the

> broadening of this strike wave still served to "disorganise" the regime, dispelling the illusion of a rapid return to "normality," and forcibly placing the social demands of the working class and wider layers of the poor on the political agenda. The inability of the ruling Supreme Council of the Armed Forces (SCAF) to re-impose normal labour relations in the workplace (or more accurately, the generals' helplessness as workers dramatically shifted the "frontier of control" between workers and bosses in their favour) was all the more politically important as it coincided with a lull in the mass

street mobilisations, and preceded the constitutional referendum which represented the first serious attempt by the reconfigured regime to use the electoral process to create a new veneer of legitimacy.[35]

Alexander believes, and I concur, that these episodes of contention did indeed "disorganize" the regime, so that it could not respond as harshly as it had in the 1980s and 1990s. Also, post January 2011 there was a change in the POS and the possibility for the workers to focus the national debate on respecting the freedom to organize and establish independent unions legally, giving the right to bargain collectively, improving wages in the public sector to keep up with inflation and high consumer goods' prices, enshrining legally a minimum wage, ending casual temporary work contracts, improving health care, legalizing protests and strikes; dismantling the official government trade union federation (the ETUF), and renationalizing privatized companies.

The data in Tables 7.1 and 7.2 from the Awlad el Ard NGO, which Alexander used in her article, show that after 2011, the same number of protest episodes took place in September 2011 as in all of 2008.

Compared to the pre-revolutionary strike wave, September 2011 also marks a dramatic shift: around the same number of workers took part in collective action that month as did during the whole of 2008. Coordination of strikes and protests also increased sharply in September compared not only to previous months, but also to the pre-revolutionary strike wave. The overall

Table 7.1 Estimated number of workers involved in collective action

March	82,000
April	65,000
May	57,000
June	57,000
July	33,000
August	65,000
September	500,000–750,000

Source: Reports by Awlad al-Ard NGO and press reports, 2011

Table 7.2 Number of episodes of collective action

March	123
April	90
May	107
June	96
July	76
August	89
September	56

Source: Awlad al-Ard NGO, 2011

number of episodes was significantly fewer but the increased numbers participating points to the consolidation of the strike wave into fewer, coordinated disputes.[36]

September's strike wave was dominated by the national teachers' strike, which was itself the single largest episode of coordinated strike action in Egypt since the 1940s. Estimating the number of striking teachers is extremely difficult. The Ministry of Education claimed that only 1,400 schools, or 4.3 percent of the total, were affected by the strike, but reports in the independent media suggested a far wider impact, with possibly half of Egyptian schools shut down. However, if the teachers' strike is discounted, September still shows a significant shift towards large, coordinated strikes. Seven strikes and workers' protests involving more than 10,000 workers have been reported since March, with five of these occurring in September.[37]

According to Freedom House's *Freedom in the World 2012 Report* on Egypt,

In March [2011], the SCAF instituted a ban on strikes and demonstrations, and repeatedly used excessive force, including live ammunition, in attempts to disperse protests. Security forces, and in some cases pro-government thugs, engaged in prolonged street battles with demonstrators in June, October, November, and December.[38]

The tide turned quickly against the rule by the military, and in the summer of 2011 Egypt witnessed many large protests against Field Marshall Tantawi and the SCAF in defiance of the new anti-protest law. Egyptians, including workers, defied the restriction on large mass protest. "Yet workers' collective defiance of new laws criminalising strikes and protests, the continued ferment in the workplaces and the hundreds of workers' demonstrations during this period played a vital role in keeping open spaces to organise from below."[39] The spaces to organize have indeed expanded despite SCAF restrictions and the following Morsi-MB rule, which continued the same restrictions.

The workers continued to put pressure on the authorities and did not back down on social justice demands, which expanded to the notion of "*tathir*," i.e. the cleansing of corrupt factory managers leading up to corrupt government bureaucrats. The Freedom House report concurs with my thesis in terms of the labor movement's important contributions, especially during and after the 2011 uprising.

The labor movement made important advances during and after the 2011 uprising, as workers and strikes played a significant role in increasing pressure on Mubarak to step down. Workers were granted the right to establish independent unions and formed an independent trade union federation, ending the long-standing monopoly of the state-run federation. However, the government criminalized protests that disrupt the economy, a clear effort to limit the power of strikes, and initial investigations into corruption at the state-dominated labor movement foundered.[40]

In the post-January 2011 period, there was a rapid growth of independent trade unions, which came as a result of open grassroots organizing at the workplaces

without the restrictions that were felt and practiced before January 2011. The ETUF leadership was either under house arrest or in prison or in a very precarious position. The organization that already was discredited in the eyes of average Egyptians and particularly workers was further being marginalized, yet was not yet disbanded. In addition to this incredible feeling of freedom to practice open independent trade unionism, there were additional elements that contributed to the increase in independent trade unions and the formation of federation organizations such as EFITU and EDLC.

> A number of other factors have shaped the development of workers' organisation so far. They include the actions of different sections of the state, from the Supreme Council of the Armed Forces to the minister of labour, Ahmad al-Borai, to regional governors and the heads of the large public sector combines. Al-Borai's policies have been important in creating a legal space in which the independent unions have been able to operate.[41]

Ahmad al-Borai was appointed minister of manpower shortly after Mubarak stepped down and the SCAF became the caretaker government.

> After the Supreme Council of the Armed Forces (SCAF) came to power on February 11, 2011, Ahmed Hassan Al-Borai was appointed Minister of Labor. Al-Borai was popular with both activists and the international community, as a former member of the International Labor Organization's (ILO) Committee of Experts and lawyer for the independent union movement, newly organized unions outside the ETUF structure that had been agitating for official recognition since 2008.[42]

In March 2011, the former minister of manpower, Ahmed Hassan al-Borai, after consultations with leaders of the independent unions, hosted in Egypt the former Director General of the International Labor Organization Juan Somavia,[43] and together they publicly unveiled the declaration of trade union freedoms[44] that gave life to the creation of independent trade unions in Egypt. This declaration was a first step in putting Egypt back on track in terms of respecting the fundamental international labor standards of freedom of association, the right to organize, and collective bargaining.

Since that declaration, Egyptian workers have been forming hundreds of independent trade unions, though not without resistance. Employers have not always welcomed them with open arms or recognized the validity of the 2011 declaration, in spite of a December 2012 State Council ruling.[45] The test case was in the electrical workers independent union, which petitioned the State Council for their union dues to be deducted legally and go to their new independent union. The State Council ruled on the validity of this action and the recognition of the independent union. In fact, there have been more strikes in the post-2011 period and up until June 2013 than in the several prior years combined, according to Kamal Abbas, coordinator of the CTUWS.[46]

The Egyptian Center for Economic and Social Rights' 2013 report to the United Nations Committee on Economic and Social Rights highlights the increasing need for trade unions in Egypt, "because it is becoming ever more difficult for workers to advocate for their rights. It is not uncommon for both the owners

of private businesses and the government to resort to violence in dealing with the demands of workers." The report details several examples of violations of worker rights from 2012: "For instance, the workers of Faragello, a food and beverages company, and of Titan, a cement company, were assaulted by police and were cornered inside a mosque to be attacked by police dogs before 18 of them were arrested." The report also criticizes the law passed in early 2011[47] banning the right to strike, to which these workers reacted with demonstrations:

> The law, ratified by the SCAF on 12 April 2011, has angered many as it stipulates prison sentences and fines of up to LE 500,000 "for anyone who organizes a protest or an activity which may result in preventing or slowing down the work of a state institution, a general authority or a public or private workplace."[48]

The veteran human rights and labor lawyers

> Ahmed Saif El-Islam and Khaled Ali, on behalf of the plaintiffs: the Real Estate Tax Collectors Union and three other newly-formed, independent unions, told judges that the military council did not have a constitutional right to ban strikes, as it did in Decree 34 of 2011. The lawyers argued that the military council, therefore, could not try workers who decide to strike in military courts as it has done on a number of occasions since it came to power in February 2011.[49]

As of 2012, Egypt's labor force numbered twenty-seven million workers.[50] The independent labor movement will need to insist on a role in the next phase of Egypt's democratic transition. Meanwhile, Egypt has an unemployment rate of 13.2%: this is only the number of people still actively looking for employment as a percentage of the workforce, which can be deceptive[51] in terms of the actual number of those without the means to earn a living. The actual rate of those not working is much higher, so job creation is an essential first step for the interim government. Next, labor representatives need to be included in the drafting of an amended constitution. The right to freedom of association, i.e. the ability to establish independent trade unions and the right to organize, to bargain collectively, and to strike, will have to be included in the constitution as fundamental socio-economic rights.

A Tale of Two Labor Federations: Tensions in the Labor Movement

In June 2012, the Carnegie Endowment for International Peace (CEIP) published a well-documented report by Professor Joel Beinin, "The Rise of Egypt's Workers." The report sums up the following: (1) Workers have been trying to bring about change to the Egyptian system for a long time, yet the independent labor movement found its national voice post January 2011. (2) The workers have not gotten the credit they deserve in bringing down the Mubarak regime. (3) The independent trade unions remain the strongest nationally organized force confronting the autocratic tendencies of the old order. Yet if they can solidify and

expand their gains, according to Beinin, they could be an important force leading Egypt toward a more democratic future.[52] However, problems and challenges persisted and internal divisions within the independent labor movement were a major obstacle to unity and reaching national political goals. Beinin's account of these challenges and persistent internal divisions was supported by conversations with many trade union leaders and members held in May, June, and July 2013 in Egypt during my field research.

On October 15, 2012, the two federations held a press conference with other leftist/progressive political parties to announce a limited alliance to continue the fight for worker rights and against the vicious attacks on the labor movement.

> The goals of the front include the cancellation of the restrictive Trade Union Law 35/1976, the issuing of the draft Trade Union Liberties Law promoting workers' right to free association, protecting unionists and laborers against punitive sackings, confronting labor violations perpetrated by the state and/ or employers, and the establishment of a just pay-scale based on a determined minimum and maximum wage (of no more than 15 times the minimum).[53]

This was a good step forward, yet it was not sustainable and did not last long.

The Ultimate Weakness of the Labor Movement to Mobilize Members for the Elections

The independent workers' movement has made strides despite the challenges on the economic and social front; but, in terms of its political role, there is still much that needs to take place. The divisions between organizations and leaders do not lend themselves to a united political front. Another point is the lack of experience in terms of open electoral politics and the role trade unions can play in that context.

> However, entrenched military and former Mubarak regime forces have attempted, with some success, to maintain their power, reverse the gains of independent trade unions, and block the entry of new and unpredictable forces into the political arena. The democratic labor movement is struggling to present a united front, but is, in fact, divided. And despite their role in over-throwing Mubarak, workers and their interests were not well represented in Egypt's first (and subsequently dissolved) post-Mubarak parliament, nor did they comprise a clearly defined factor in the 2012 presidential election.[54]

After decades of struggles against an authoritarian regime that paid lip service to worker rights, "the removal of some of the repressive constraints of the Mubarak regime gave trade union activists the confidence to assert political demands that they had previously mostly avoided."[55] However, still considered a special interest by the young leaders in Tahrir Square, the independent workers' movement was dismissed as a spokesperson for socio-economic demands during the first few months after the January 2011 popular uprising, when there was much hope for change.

The new independent labor federations did not succeed in mobilizing workers to vote for the one-labor candidate, Khaled Ali, or even to be united to vote for the progressive candidate, Hamdeen Sabahi. Khaled Ali received 0.58% of the vote and Sabahi received 20% representing the Karama (Dignity) Party. Anne Alexander asks, "Can the organised working class in Egypt transform its social leadership into political leadership of the revolutionary movement?"[56] The answer is still "not yet," since the revolutionary left who have traditionally been the vanguard of the movement are a small group with limited outreach. However, the opening of the grassroots space for organizing and for workers' organizations making social demands during this transitional period bode well for a proper place at the "national policy" table. Yet, in terms of a political player role that can mobilize workers at the election polls for a candidate who supports workers' needs, the new independent labor movement is still deficient in that role.

The following statement by Egypt's Freedom House office director, Nancy Okail, sums up the results of the first post-uprising/revolution elections.

> While Morsi ran on an Islamist platform, Okail noted, his victory does not mean that Egyptians desire an Islamist government. "People voted for Morsi to avoid military rule," she said, noting that many non-Islamists voted for Morsi (who won 51.7 percent of the vote) because they viewed his opponent, Ahmed Shafik, Mubarak's final prime minister, as an extension of the ousted political order. Indeed, Okail said, following his victory leftists who voted for Morsi put him on notice, telling him, "Now we go back to the seats of the opposition."[57]

How to translate workers' organizing abilities and successes in creating new independent union into political power is the question at hand.

> Nevertheless, the lessons of the first ten months of the Egyptian Revolution are of immense significance for the left internationally. The rebuilding of independent workers' organisation out of the strike wave and the role of the mass strikes of September [2011] in opening the path to November's second popular uprising provide confirmation once again of the central role played by organised workers in the revolutionary process.[58]

Tahrir square has become a worldwide symbol for a path of change and transition and not just a simple space of gathering. The workers were part of that space and symbol; they were not just an interest group that caused problems and was not concerned with the nation's welfare.

Interesting developments took place after the January 2011 uprising, including the intensification of the overall negative view of workers and their unions.

> By reinforcing the impression that the demands of discontented workers for more humane wages and working conditions are the mere product of parochial employee-management disputes inside various factories and bureaucracies, the term *fi'awi* does more than just stigmatize and dehistoricize these demands. Characterizing so-called *fi'awi* claims as the sum of a variety of disjointed narrow interests masks the serious national economic problems that these demonstrations and sit-ins collectively underscore.[59]

This characterization of fi'awi claims and the perception of the workers' parochial self-interested demands reinforce the divisions within society. In addition, the labor strikes during the last week of Mubarak's rule were considered by many observers, including labor activist and blogger Hossam El-Hamalawy, as the tipping point that forced his resignation. There was a chain of events, and the workers were responsible for many of those events. Yet the SCAF's first action after Mubarak stepped down was to stop strikes. This gives the clear signal that the generals took the workers' contentious protests as a serious threat to any ruling regime.[60]

The first round of elections was held on May 23–24 with thirteen candidates running for president. The second round of elections was held on June 16–17, 2012, between the two highest vote receivers, Mohamed Morsi and Ahmed Shafik. The final results were 51.7% of the votes for Morsi and 48.27% for Shafik. Mohamed Morsi became the first MB president of Egypt. The independent trade union organizations and their members were not supporters of the MB or their candidate. The injustices against workers continued and actually the grievances even increased during Morsi's presidency.

During Morsi's presidency, it became uncomfortably clear that the strategy of the MB was to take control of many of Egypt's major civil society organizations. While everyone's attention was focused on the assault on the constitution and the judiciary, President Morsi strategically revised a trade union law that affected millions of Egyptian workers. This move affected the lives, jobs, and political freedom of millions of Egyptian workers, as well as renewed the ETUF's longstanding role as an enforcer of government labor policy.[61]

ETUF remains in existence despite efforts to dismantle it during the immediate post-Mubarak period.[62] It claims a membership of over four million workers, mostly in the public sector. Under Mubarak, ETUF was notorious for its failure to protect worker rights. In recent years, a courageous—and illegal—independent trade union movement has challenged ETUF's supremacy and dared to press for freedom of association, using strikes and protests in all the major sectors of the economy. First established in December 2008, the independent union movement has grown enormously since the January 2011 uprising. Hundreds of independent trade unions have been established, and Egypt now has two independent trade union federations representing almost two million workers.

Against this background, on November 26, Morsi endorsed revisions to the trade union law ensuring that the MB's Freedom and Justice Party loyalists could be appointed to the ETUF and its affiliated unions' executive boards. This move took place a few days after Morsi's sweeping decree to grant himself immunity against any judicial oversight, basically granting him absolute powers. That decree was withdrawn, and a hastily called referendum on the new constitution was scheduled for December 15.

These political maneuvers have not affected the new labor law, which gives the government the power to fill vacancies on these union governing boards by forcing all who are over sixty years of age to retire. It also extends by six months the time a union member serves on a trade union's executive board. These changes were made without any consultation with the ETUF's current leadership, who remain Mubarak loyalists.

Not surprisingly, the reaction of the ETUF leadership was negative. Chairman Ahmed Abdel Zaher was openly critical of the new law[63] and, with some irony,

now cites the International Labor Organization's core principles on union rights. This was unheard of in 2008, when Egypt was placed on the ILO's black list of countries in violation of the ILO's conventions and when ETUF was in collusion with the Mubarak regime.

For his part, the head of the Egyptian Federation of Independent Trade Unions said that the attitude of the MB and the new government was "even more hostile" to "workers, trade unions and economic and social rights" than that of the Mubarak regime.[64]

In that light, the new independent unions faced the challenge of a Brotherhood-dominated official trade union structure. The new labor law would have enabled the minister of manpower, a member of the MB's political party, to install President Morsi's supporters in the unions' leadership positions. This change would stop any effort by the old guard to use ETUF as an alternative power center, while, ironically, giving renewed life to the ETUF as an instrument of government policy. It was a shrewd and revealing move by Morsi. His government extended its control over an organization that is mass-based and possesses local and regional structures that reach deeply into many sectors of the Egyptian economy. It also appeared to endorse the Mubarak-era rejection of freedom of association—the right of workers to organize their own unions, free of government control.

During the Mubarak era, the MB was never able to gain a strong foothold within the blue-collar trade unions. Historically, the Brotherhood focused on Egypt's professional unions and associations, referred to as "syndicates," although interest in their "working-class cousins sharply rose after the revolution."[65] Within professional unions, politics and political identity have a high profile, and the Brotherhood controls professional syndicates representing doctors, engineers, pharmacists, scientists, and lawyers.[66] There are twenty-two professional syndicates in Egypt with a total of 3.5 million members.

The political implications of Morsi's move were clear. Morsi overreached his power in his attempted usurpation of the right of judicial review, but the changes in the labor law triggered even more unrest. And Egypt's workers have never hesitated to protest over bread and butter issues. This ETUF takeover confirmed suspicions that the MB was seeking to dominate all aspects of government and civil society. It also raised concerns for independent union leaders who continue to occupy a very vulnerable political and legal position. Will they be next?

Finally, this takeover of a major labor organization—however tarnished its past was—created much anxiety within broader civil society. It added to the worries that, in Egypt, authoritarianism looks the same, whether it is military or Islamist rule.

Post-Morsi and Current Egyptian Government's Policies Towards Workers and Their Organizations

The first elected MB president of Egypt, Mohamed Morsi, was removed from power by the military on July 3, 2013. Abdel Fattah el-Sisi, the minister of defense, became the de facto president of Egypt in July 2013, was elected president in May 2014, and was re-elected in March 2018. Egyptian workers and their varied independent organizations supported the removal of Morsi; while this is an absolutist statement, it was indeed the reality. Egyptian society, by

and large, became anti-Morsi and anti-MB and their policies, leading to a highly polarized, tense political atmosphere. Independent workers' unions continued yet with caution, since they were not quite sure of President Sisi's attitude towards independent institutions.

The role of workers and their independent organizations "shaped versus led" the uprisings and included those protests against the Morsi government's policies. Alexander and Bassiouny argued in their book, published in 2014, that the Egyptian revolution was profoundly shaped from the beginning by the role played by workers as a "self-organized force in both the development of the revolutionary crisis"[67] and the process thereafter. They recognize that "shaping" is not the same as "leading," and the contradiction between Egyptian workers' evident collective social power yet their collective political weakness and paralysis were duly noted due to the historical and institutional structures under which they have functioned.[68] Initially, workers gave their support to the military institution that they knew so well in order to fight the MB's influence in their affairs and Morsi's failing economic policies. This support was then paid back by Sisi once he was in full control of all the government levers through more constraints and increased neoliberal economic policies. The protests in the streets were not connected to institutions that could effectively enforce their demands on the state as a whole.[69] There were limitations of reform and liberalization that could take place initiated from below and thus the workers' disjointed struggles. However, Alexander and Bassiouny argue that these attempts did open up new ways of thinking on how to remake the state according to popular revolutionary principles for thousands and thousands of Egyptians.

Egyptian labor has long functioned under a "corporatist" regime of behavior, and this is well described in Kerrissey and Schofer's article about labor unions and political participation. Corporatism integrates unions into the state structures and policymaking, thus producing a mix of political opportunities and constraints that generally dampen union efforts to mobilize participation across a range of actions, and not only strikes.[70] In Egypt's case where there is a corporatist structure in a less democratic state, the "state control de-powers unions as oppositional actors and reinforces their roles as regime supporters."[71] The state has co-opted the Egyptian labor movement and created the official structure in 1957: the Egyptian Federation of Trade Unions, as outlined in Chapter 1. The authors argue "that corporatist structures [. . .] reduce union members' participation, especially contentious extra-institutional acts."[72] So, Egyptian workers had a long and difficult road to engage in contentious politics and to truly represent their members' needs and grievances. In addition, the big difficulty was in their leaders initiating and sustaining a protest movement to advocate against the state and its interests. There was much to surmount in their efforts to create an effective contentious collective-action protest movement—a social movement.

The current anti-independent workers' unions that the Sisi regime is articulating are focused on those workers and their independent unions. Sisi has adopted neoliberal economic policies that are not what a majority of independent workers are calling for, and he has revived the lifeless structure of the ETUF. As mentioned earlier, there was initial support for Sisi to get rid of the MB and President Morsi from government. However, the honeymoon did not last very long, and the two parties became embroiled in the traditional economic bread and butter issues and conflicts. The workers expect the "Nasserist" style of benefits from the old public sector regime, while Sisi is forging ahead with a more neoliberal economic

package of policies, and he has the support of the ETUF. There is increased state control in Egypt today across the board over civil society organizations, including workers; actually, especially workers, since economic reform is a centerpiece in Sisi's government. However, there is still life in the independent labor movement's Egyptian Federation of Independent Trade Unions (*Al-Ittihad al-Masri lil-Naqabat al-Mustaqilla*). Despite increasing repression on NGOs and opposition groups, EIFTU held its biggest meeting in December 2015. In September 2016, EIFTU was still working and, under strict supervision of the state, organizing labor protests and representing workers' rights.[73] Their protest efforts continue despite the lack of space in Egypt today for dissent of any kind.

The ITUC gathers information about worker rights violations around the world. Each year it publishes a report that surveys violations of trade union rights, especially freedom of association, collective bargaining, and the right to strike. In the 2018 survey report on Egypt, there were at least fifteen documented cases of where strikes were averted due to the arrest of their leaders, ban of May Day celebrations (under the pretext of security concerns), arrest of workers who were on strike or at a sit-in protesting bad working conditions or violations of worker rights, state security courts trying arrested workers from the General Trade Union of Petroleum Workers, arrest of workers who were protesting the lack of implementation of environmental safety measures at the Sinmar plant in South Port Said, and much more.[74] "On 3 February [2016], the body of this young Italian PhD student, who was researching the independent trade union movement in Egypt, was found in a ditch on the outskirts of Cairo. He had disappeared on 25 January, the anniversary of the Egyptian revolution. He had just published an article on the Nena News site on strike action in Egypt and the search for trade union unity. His murder sparked international outrage. In a protest letter, the ITUC underlined, 'It is clear from the intensification of measures hostile to freedom and the freedoms of trade unions in particular, that Giulio was considered a threat to the Egyptian government.'"[75]

Overall gains versus individual battles fought at the workplace distinguishes the impact of the independent labor movement. Alexander and Bassiouny wrote, "while workplace strikes by workers and their unions have often won gains at individual workplaces, the workers' movement has been much less successful in implementing its general demands on the state as a whole."[76] And after the uprisings in 2011 and 2013, the state and employers increased the pressure on workers and escalated their offensive against independent unions and their members. In addition, starting with the MB and President Morsi administration, the ETUF was given a second lease on life and revived to counter the wave of independent activist unionism. These efforts continued under the Sisi administration where ETUF plays the "pied piper" role, singing the praises of the current regime. In September 2015, two well-respected researchers and activists wrote for the Carnegie Endowment for International Peace (and it still rings true today):

> the future of Egypt's labor movement—The current situation is unsustainable in the long term. The drivers of the January revolution remain entrenched. Workers are still economically and politically marginalized. Real incomes are declining and previous gains are threatened with future privatizing of state-owned enterprises, downsizing of the government bureaucracy, and increasing informal labor in the private sector.[77]

Egypt is yet again under authoritarian military rule, and the independent labor movement is under its control. The future does not bode well for workers' organizations' independence and agitation for reforms on the political level let alone at the workplace. One is not advocating that collective protest action will not take place—it will yet with much cost in human lives and difficulty in organizing under the watchful eyes of state security.

Concluding Remarks

After Mubarak stepped down, there was much hope that Egypt would be on a new trajectory towards a transition to democracy. However, that "hope" was purely hope without a real basis in terms of reality in the conditions and situation in Egypt. Egypt's authoritarian regime was not dismantled; the January 2011 events were an uprising and not a revolution. Political parties and civil society were hampered by years of control, divisions, and the inability to properly organize and develop grassroots support. However, workers were able to break out from under the statist corporatist control and develop independent organizations and networks. Yet, these organizations were also not able to become that needed social and political driving force within the political arena to influence new policies. The head of the regime, Mubarak, was removed, but the body continued—the deep state was alive and well. Collective action and the social capital that workers developed in this case were not sufficient to bring about the needed political reform.

The SCAF immediately outlawed protests, yet workers' protests from March 2011 until and after the first election in May 2012 increased due to many economic hardships. Workers' independent organizations were not able to "get out the vote" and organize voters for independent socially minded progressive candidates like Khalid Ali or Hamdeen Sabahi. The military candidate and the MB candidate were the only two that had the necessary organization, funding, and networks to compete in an election after so many years of authoritarian rule. The weakness of the political parties and the system overall became painfully clear. The two independent labor federations were not united, and internal divisions due to leadership egos took over to further undermine workers' potential. Once Morsi became president, the conditions continued to deteriorate on all levels—economically, politically, and socially. Morsi's presidency was marred by many missteps and legislative disasters to attempt to control labor and to undermine freedom of association. Egypt was sinking into a political abyss, leading to the military coup disguised in a popular uprising on June 30, 2013 (beyond the scope of this research). The workers were active in supporting the overthrow of Morsi's rule, yet they were still not strong enough to assert their needs to relieve their serious grievances on a state level. Today, under President Sisi, military authoritarian rule has been reinstalled with severe consequences for independent protest actions. Egypt today has more political prisoners than in all the years of Mubarak's rule and is building new prisons to house them at a steady pace. Human rights groups claim that as many as 60,000 political prisoners now languish in Egypt's jails. (At the end of Mubarak's rule, the figure was between 5,000 and 10,000.)[78] Today, there is a grim new nickname for those activists/political prisoners: "Generation Jail," as opposed to "Generation Protest" in 2011 as described by Amnesty International, according to the *New York Times* magazine article by Joshua Hammer (March 14, 2017).

Notes

1. Edwards, Michael. *Civil Society*. Malden, MA: Polity Press, 2013, page 14.
2. Kurlantzick, Joshua. *Democracy in Retreat: The Revolt of the Middle Class and the Worldwide Decline of Representative Government*. New Haven: Yale University Press, 2013.
3. Diamond, Larry J. *The Spirit of Democracy: The Struggle to Build Free Societies Throughout the World*. New York: Times Books and Henry Holt and Co, 2008: 12.
4. www.freedomhouse.org/report/freedom-world/freedom-world-2013
5. Ibid.
6. https://freedomhouse.org/report/freedom-world/freedom-world-2018
7. Coleman, Isobel and Terra Remer (editors). *Pathways to Freedom: Political and Economic Lessons from Democratic Transitions*. New York, NY: Council on Foreign Relations, 2013.
8. Diamond, L. J. *Developing Democracy: Toward Consolidation*. Baltimore: Johns Hopkins University Press, 1999.
9. Amin, Galal A. *Egypt in the Era of Hosni Mubarak: 1981–2011*. Cairo, Egypt and New York: American University in Cairo Press, 2011: 41.
10. Shehata, Samer. *Afterword, Shop Floor Culture and Politics*. Cairo, Egypt: American University in Cairo Press, 2013: 255.
11. Ibid.: 254.
12. Alexander, Anne. "The Egyptian Workers' Movement and the 25 January Revolution" Issue: 133. Posted: January 9, 2012, *International Socialism—A Quarterly Journal of Socialist Theory*. www.isj.org.uk/?s=contents&issue=133.
13. Shehata 2013: 255.
14. Amin 2011: 85.
15. Ibid.: 100.
16. Ibid.: 145.
17. Ibid.
18. Ghonim, Wael. *Revolution 2.0—A Memoir*. Boston: Houghton Mifflin Harcourt, 2012: 3.
19. Beinin, J. "Workers and Egypt's January 25 Revolution." *International Labor and Working-Class History* 80 (1) (2011): 189–196: 191.
20. Ibid.: 189.
21. http://socialistworker.org/blog/critical-reading/2012/03/09/where-egyptian-revolution-goin
22. Ibid.
23. Ghonim 2012: 292.
24. Ibid.: 293.
25. Cook, S. A. *The Struggle for Egypt: From Nasser to Tahrir Square*. New York: Oxford University Press, 2012: 306.
26. Ibid.
27. Sowers, J. L. and Chris J. Toesing. *The Journey to Tahrir: Revolution, Protest, and Social Change in Egypt*. London and New York: Verso, 2012: 106.
28. Sellam, Hesham. "Striking Back at Egyptian Workers." *MERIP Report* #259 41 (2011). www.merip.org/mer/mer259/striking-back-egyptian-workers. The SCAF communique No. 5 can be found on the State Information Service website: www.sis.gov.eg/Ar/Templates/Articles/tmpArticles.aspx?ArtID=44125.
29. Amnesty International. "Egyptian Authorities Must Allow Peaceful Protest and the Right to Strike." April 30, 2011. www.amnesty.org/en/news-and-updates/egyptian-authorities-must-allow-peaceful-protest-and-right-strike-2011-04-30.
30. Alexander 2012.
31. Ibid.
32. Ibid.
33. Ibid.
34. www.anhri.net/egypt/ae, Description of Awlad el Ard: مؤسسة أولاد الأرض لحقوق الإنسان
في خطوة في جادة على طريق تحسين وتعزيز أوضاع حقوق الإنسان في مصر بسائر أنواعها وأخصها الحقوق الاقتصادية والاجتماعية تعلن مؤسسة أولاد الأرض لحقوق الإنسان عن بدء نشاطها في كافة مجالات عملها وذلك بعد التغلب على كافة الصعاب التي واكبتها منذ ظهور فكرة تأسيسها باعتبارها الامتداد الطبيعي والقانوني لمركز الأرض لحقوق الإنسان في إطار توفيق أوضاعه وفقاً لأحكام قانون الجمعيات والمؤسسات الأهلية

"In a serious step on the way to improve and strengthen the human rights situation in Egypt in all its other types, especially economic and social rights, the Children of the Earth (Land) Foundation for Human Rights announces the start of its activities in all areas of its work, after overcoming all the difficulties that have accompanied it since the emergence of the idea of its establishment as the natural and legal extension of the Earth Center in accordance with the provisions of the Law on Associations and NGOs."

35. Alexander 2012: 3.
36. Ibid.: 4–5.
37. Ibid.: 3–4 and Ali, M. "Egypt Teachers Strike for the First Time Since 1951." September 19. http://english.ahram.org.eg/NewsContent/1/64/21568/Egypt/Politics-/Egypt-teachers-strike-for-the-first-time-since-.aspx.
38. www.freedomhouse.org/report/freedom-world/2012/egypt-0
39. Alexander 2012.
40. www.freedomhouse.org/report/freedom-world/2012/egypt-0
41. Alexander 2012: 10.
42. http://muftah.org/labor-unions-under-attack-in-morsis-egypt/
43. www.ilo.org/global/about-the-ilo/newsroom/news/WCMS_153044/lang--en/index.htm
44. www.ctuws.com/results.aspx?item=1266
45. www.shorouknews.com/news/view.aspx?cdate=01022013&id=e80637b5-73c9-4613-926e-0b1f6a1b430d and www.facebook.com/media/set/?set=a.554060801271432.12 6103.152615734749276&type=1.
46. www.ctuws.com/?item=1242
47. http://english.ahram.org.eg/News/17402.aspx
48. www.egyptindependent.com/news/new-labor-day-egypt-independent-unions-plan-celebrations-set-demands
49. http://english.ahram.org.eg/News/17402.aspx
50. www.tradingeconomics.com/egypt/labor-force-total-wb-data.html   www.capmas.gov.eg/pdf/Electronic%20Static%20Book2013/English/labor_force/untitled1/force.aspx
"Rising unemployment: The number of unemployed reached 3.5 million in the first quarter of 2013, equal to 13.2 percent of the labor force. Some 77 percent of the unemployed are between 15 and 29 years old. More than 162,000 Egyptians lost their jobs in the last quarter of 2012 alone, according to government statistics. Overall unemployment stood at 12.6 percent in June 2012 when Morsi took office." www.wilson-center.org/islamists/article/morsi-meter-9427-protests-and-counting-one-year-later
51. www.tradingeconomics.com/egypt/unemployment-rate
52. Beinin, Joel. *The Rise of Egypt's Workers.* Washington, DC: Carnegie Endowment for International Peace, June 2012: 1. www.carnegieendowment.org/files/egypt_labor.pdf.
53. www.egyptindependent.com/news/independent-unions-declare-new-alliance
54. Beinin 2012: 3.
55. Ibid.: 8.
56. Alexander 2012: 15.
57. Sprusansky, Dale. "Post-Election Egypt." *The Washington Report on Middle East Affairs* 31 (6) (2012): 57–58.
58. Alexander 2012: 15.
59. Sellam 2011.
60. Ibid. and "Interview with Hossam El-Hamalawy." *Jadaliyya*, April 9, 2011.
61. El-Shazli, Heba F. "Egypt's Islamist Government Reaches for Control of the Unions." Albert Shanker Institute Blog. http://shankerblog.org/?p=7304.
62. www.theguardian.com/world/2011/aug/05/mubarak-trade-federation-dissolved-egypt
63. www.egyptindependent.com/news/morsy-issues-law-paving-way-brotherhood-control-trade-federation
64. http://english.al-akhbar.com/node/13151
65. http://muftah.org/labor-unions-under-attack-in-morsis-egypt/
66. Fahmy, Ninette S. "The Performance of the Muslim Brotherhood in the Egyptian Syndicates: An Alternative Formula for Reform?" *Middle East Journal* 52 (4) (1998): 551–562.
67. Alexander, Anne and Mostafa Bassiouny. *Bread, Freedom, Social Justice: Workers and the Egyptian Revolution.* London: Zed Books Ltd, 2014: 285.
68. Ibid.

69. Ibid.: 291.
70. Kerrissey, Jasmine and Evan Schofer. "Labor Unions and Political Participation in Comparative Perspective." *Social Forces* 97 (1) (2018): 427–463 (Article). Published by Oxford University Press: 428.
71. Ibid.: 432.
72. Ibid.
73. Acconcia, Giuseppe. "The Shrinking Independence of Egypt's Labor Unions." *Sada* electronic magazine, Carnegie Endowment for International Peace, September 20, 2016. http://carnegieendowment.org/sada/64634.
74. ITUC Survey results: https://survey.ituc-csi.org/Egypt.html?lang=en#tabs-3.
75. https://survey.ituc-csi.org/Egypt.html?lang=en#tabs-3
76. Alexander and Bassiouny 2014: 227.
77. Ramadan, Fatma and Amr Adly. "Low-Cost Authoritarianism. The Egyptian Regime and Labor Movement Since 2013." September 17, 2015, http://carnegie-mec.org/2015/09/17/low-cost-authoritarianism-egyptian-regime-and-labor-movement-since-2013/ihui.
78. Hammer, Joshua. "How Egypt's Activists Became 'Generation Jail'—Six Years After the Arab Spring, the Country's Democracy Activists Live Under Constant Threat of Prison." *New York Times Magazine*, March 14, 2017. www.nytimes.com/2017/03/14/magazine/how-egypts-activists-became-generation-jail.html.

8   Concluding Remarks and Epilogue

Political, Economic, and Social Developments From 2012 to 2018

The workers took many courageous steps, but there were also critical missteps. So, in order to provide lessons learned and best practices, one needs to examine, for example, the leadership characteristics of these disparate workers' groups using the lens of Weber's "routinization" of charisma. Gramsci wrote of a "crisis of authority" when in the short-run the ruling classes are able to reorganize quickly and regain the control that had slipped from their grasp.[1] He wrote about when the ruling class loses the consent of the broad masses—a crisis of authority, the crisis of hegemony, or in general the crisis of the state over those it governs. Over seventy-six years ago, Gramsci gave an appropriate description of the Egyptian situation pre-January 2011. Post-February 2011 and leading to the first presidential elections in May 2012 (when this research endeavor ended), we witnessed simply a reassertion of the deep state's authority through the strong-arm tactics of the military and the security apparatus.

This research presented in detail two case studies of workers' contentious collective action. Several other smaller groups of independent workers took the lead from these workers featured in the two case studies and joined the growing social movement of labor protests. These workers came from various blue- and white-collar professions, holding positions such as bakers, cement workers, steel workers, mechanical engineers, Suez Canal workers, professors, health technicians, sugar processing workers, teachers, food processing and canning workers, electrical appliances manufacturing workers, etc. The broad and varied types of workers show how the grievances were deeply entrenched in terms of touching many if not all professions and workers in Egypt.

The independent Egyptian workers employed social movements' mechanisms (described in Chapter 1), and also took advantage of POS. They consciously examined the political power of the Mubarak regime and assessed its strengths, weaknesses, threats, and opportunities available to them. They repeatedly tested and challenged the regime, bringing confrontation to the brink of violence; thankfully, the state's security apparatus and the regime would retreat to seek negotiations. Then, it was clear to see how the character of the workers' contentious political and economic actions interacted or collided with the regime or even challenged the regime. Did they succeed to get their claims heard? Yes. Did they succeed in getting their grievances resolved? Yes, partially. Did they succeed in politically influencing the process of reform in Egypt? Yes and no; it was an incomplete impact, a limited and qualified victory, and within constraints. Why? The varied reasons were examined in detail in the various chapters of this book.

Undoubtedly, the millions of workers who participated in the repeated forms of protests had an impact and did contribute to the downfall of the Mubarak regime. This was a movement that had been building and growing in earnest over the years since early 2000 and even before. Egyptian workers stepped out into the streets to demand dignity and universally respected rights when it was not in vogue. At times, they were simply asking to be paid their wages and making other such fundamental demands. There was a continuum of protest events, each breaking down bit by bit the wall of fear. This research showed that the fear of retribution by an authoritarian regime waned for the rest of Egyptians thanks to the workers leading the way. Remember the Egyptian worker who exclaimed to me during a meeting with workers in the summer of 2013—"We started the 2011 revolution and the rest of Egypt followed," say Egyptian workers with strong conviction."

> A veteran labour activist, El-Mahalla-based Kamal Fayoumi, declared when we met him late last year, "El-Mahalla is the mother of Tahrir. On April 6, 2008, they said the whole country was in El-Mahalla." On January 25, 2011, they said everyone was in Tahrir. Strikes have been a feature of Egyptian life for well over a century, with unions achieving a major place in the country's life in the years leading up to the end of the monarchy. The Nasser years saw an authoritarian populist regime dramatically increase wages and living standards for workers, even as it banned all but government-controlled unions.[2]

Democratization theories, the process of change and transition towards democracy, and the role of trade unions were examined in this research. The role of workers' organizations in this transition has many precedents, with Poland coming first to mind and then Latin America. With these lessons learned, how do the Egyptian workers' efforts hold up or compare? Where are the major gaffes and how did their efforts to impact political reforms come up short? Is it the historical baggage that the Egyptian labor movement carries? Is it the issue of leadership? Is it the Egyptian society and the "deep authoritarian state" views on labor thus undercutting their efforts? Or is it that no matter how many millions rose up against the authoritarian Mubarak regime, no one group or groups could ever stand up to the entrenched deep state apparatus, the military, the brutal intelligence services, and the highly organized social/political group, the Muslim Brotherhood (MB)? Indeed, it is clear that even if labor was very well organized and did not carry the historic baggage of perception and image, and even if there was no leadership crisis and division into several labor federations, they would not have been able to galvanize the rest of civil society to defeat the deep authoritarian state with the military as its vanguard.

It is clear that the Egyptian labor movement prior to the events of 1952 had played an important role as a social movement expressing the desires and needs of average citizens, including workers. Their claims and advocacy for social justice and decent wages were the driving force, in addition to the fight against colonialism. The labor movement also had a political role in supporting uprisings against the colonial British forces, the governments that came in and out of rule, and the monarchy, leading to the final ousting of the British troops with the Free Officers' coup in 1952. The 1952 coup d'état began a nationalist socialist

era lasting for about thirty years. Before 1952, the labor movement began as a diverse, pluralist, organized, and independent movement that advocated as effectively as possible for workers' rights. However, "[t]he evolving structure of the working class reflected the uneven development of Egyptian capitalism."[3] Workers participated in trade unions, even those who were employed in small, unmechanized workplaces. Workers in the large mechanized industries such as transport and manufacturing eventually became the most active in the labor movement. "The early concentration of large numbers of workers in transport, public utilities, and service enterprises was largely the result of European capital's primary interest in the extraction of cotton from Egypt."[4] As the mechanized industry grew, thanks to investment by locally owned Bank Misr in the large Mahalla el Kubra Spinning and Weaving company, workers in the textile sector became quite the militant leaders.

By the advent of World War II, the numbers of industrial workers increased, including those in oil and tobacco production and those working on the Suez Canal. "It is impossible to deny the leading role of the textile workers in shaping the political character of the postwar workers' movement."[5] It is this activist political history that is still being carried on by the older leaders in Egypt's independent labor movement. This history of struggle and activism needs to be preserved and referred to in order to support today's independent workers' organizations and network.

The role of labor movements in the Arab world, including Egypt, was mainly co-opted and then overtaken and controlled by the state apparatus through a so-called social contract. The goal of the "social contract" was to maintain the state's autocratic rule in the region. In Egypt, this social contract is now defunct with the launching of a new wild world of unbridled capitalism without the checks and balances of a democratic system in place.

> From the late 1950s onward three successive presidents—Nasser, Sadat and Mubarak—have sought to manipulate and control the behavior of Egyptian workers while claiming to represent them and enjoy their unqualified support. The nature of the three regimes in regard to labor has been different, however. Nasser built an etatist economy enshrined in populist rhetoric, which encouraged workers to believe in a system of reciprocal rights and responsibilities between themselves and the government. Sadat and Mubarak launched efforts to retract the state's commitments to labor established under this Nasserist moral economy, while endeavoring to convince workers that orthodox economic reforms are in their best interests.[6]

The manner by which labor was controlled was through repression by a state-controlled trade union federation, the ETUF. Interestingly, however, the lower cadres and local committees could exercise limited democratic practices and independence. There is a debate since the Communist/leftist forces advocated for one central trade union federation, i.e. a centralized structure, as the best way to advocate for workers' interests and needs. At the same time, opponents of this view were able to interact with regime elites and attempt to delay this corporatization, with limited success.[7]

The decline in the state's finances and thus the power to control social actors such as workers directly impacted and strengthened the ability of an independent

labor movement to develop. It is clear that Egypt was heading towards both a fiscal and political disaster, thus empowering political and social opposition to demand for and get reform. The unfortunate element is the lack of effective alliance building, and missed political opportunities, between labor and the political opposition elites. The conditions were ripe for such an alliance that did not materialize, thus obstructing labor's efforts in demanding political reform.

Egyptian workers did indeed play an important role leading up to and during the January 2011 uprising. However, due to the lack of strong organized political parties to advocate for democratic principles and to the historic baggage that labor carries, which includes weak organizational structures, labor was not able to impact the political process and thus contribute effectively to the democratization process. Again, this does not deny the important role labor played, but it was incomplete. I believe that the independent labor movement was and still is a champion of democracy, but it was organizationally weak as a result of government policies and laws to achieve the desired results. Despite the critics of labor who contend that workers' organizations are only interested in their self-interest (a fi'awi group) and that they will support democratization only if democracy helps their cause, independent and democratic trade unions fundamentally need freedom of association, which can only exist in and be respected by a truly democratic government.

Why were the real estate tax collectors successful in organizing an effective contentious social movement and eventually establishing an independent trade union? What were the ingredients of their success? How did they contribute to the overall Egyptian protest movement and inspire other workers to organize independent unions? Can we say that they contributed to the continuum of events that led to the massive uprising in January 2011? What political role did they play? Did they contribute to positive political change using socio-economic arguments?

It seems that what the labor movement has achieved, with limited success, was pushing for and taking large steps towards imposing trade union freedoms and the right to organize. The workers have come very close to achieving these momentous goals, and the government's offer of simply reorganizing the ETUF executive board, for example, is considered an insult. One has to recognize that building a trade union or a federation or tearing it down has to be done by the workers themselves and not by the government. The government's role is to set, protect, and implement the legal framework to enable the workers to form independent democratic trade unions. Mostafa Bassiouny, a noted labor advocate and journalist, confirmed this governmental role in my interview with him (see Chapter 5).[8] The only way to create a true trade union is by the bottom-up grass-roots method.

In examining the labor movement's role in leading up to the Egyptian uprising, it clearly becomes the case of missing the big picture. The bigger story is that workers and their organizations do not make it to the front pages of newspapers or to the leading stories of newscasts anymore.

The case studies of workers' protests presented in this research highlight labor's decisive role in putting pressure on the authoritarian ruler that ultimately brought Mubarak down. However, the opposition political elite did not necessarily consider labor at the forefront of the pro-democracy movement. Labor was also not directly using the democratic and political discourse. First, they used a

socio-economic discourse through their demands for increased wages, improved benefits, better working conditions, and wage parity and their desire to create an independent trade union. I would argue that these are very political actions and demands that were made under an authoritarian regime where any form of opposition is political. Second, these cases also show that organized large grassroots groups or organizations, such as workers, need not have a central coordination of their mobilization in order to be effective.

The question examined is how these mobilizations took place despite their disparate and fragmented nature, i.e. not all coordinated by one umbrella trade union organization. The role of independent NGOs concerned with labor issues is critical in responding to this question. These NGOs played that most important coordinating role. In addition, these workers' protests further added to the breaking down of the barriers of fear and were considered "training schools" for repertoires, mechanisms, and brokers of contention. They used the independent media (newspaper, radio, and television) to further bring their cause into the home of every Egyptian. These workers took the many brave first steps for several years on the road to the January 2011 uprising. They created an effective social movement to highlight many issues that concerned the overall population and not just for an "interest group." However, it was effective initially, but was not necessarily sustainable for the long term.

After the initial 2011 uprising, the 2013 coup against former President Morsi, and now, under the current Sisi regime—Egyptian workers are still struggling for respect of their fundamental human rights and for their dignity. They are still demanding respect for freedom of association, a fundamental human and worker right. Indeed, Egyptian workers did carry out an incomplete, qualified victory. They did challenge the regime and the state of affairs, yet the workers continue to be the victims of undemocratic policies, high levels of corruption, and stringent neoliberal, high-cost economic policies that are plunging their standard of living downwards and reducing the dignity of decent work and life.

Notes

1. Hoare, Quintin and Geoffrey Smith (editors and translators). *Selections from the Prison Notebooks of Antonio Gramsci*. New York: International Publishers, 2010: 210.
2. "The Labour Movement and the Future of Democracy in Egypt." *Opinion*. Al Jazeera, Apr. 2012. Web. 12 Oct. 2014. https://www.aljazeera.com/indepth/opinion/2012/04/20124117523568936.html
3. Beinin, Joel and Zachary Lockman. *Workers on the Nile: Nationalism, Communism, Islam, and the Egyptian Working Class, 1882–1954*. Princeton, NJ: Princeton University Press, 1987: 449.
4. Ibid.
5. Ibid.: 450.
6. Posusney, Marsha P. *Labor and the State in Egypt—Workers, Unions, and Economic Restructuring*. Columbia University Press, 1997: 245.
7. Ibid.
8. Interview with M. Bassiouny in Cairo on June 4, 2013.

Appendix A

The Municipal Real Estate Tax Collectors Case Study Supporting Letters and Documents

Table of Contents:

Public Services International
Internationale des Services Publics
Internacional de Servicios Públicos
Internationale der Öffentlichen Dienste
Internationalen för Stats- och Kommunalanställda

45, avenue Voltaire, BP 9
01211 Ferney-Voltaire Cedex
FRANCE
+33 4 50 40 64 64
+33 4 50 40 73 20 (Fax)
www.world-psi.org
psi@world-psi.org

President:
Ylva Thörn
General Secretary:
Peter Waldorff

Dr. Ahmed Mahmoud Mohammed Nazif
Prime Minister
Arab Republic of Egypt
Magles El Shaab St.
Cairo
Egypt
Fax: ++2(0)2 735 6449
Email: primemin@idsc.gov.eg

File Reference: PW/CK/SS
Contact Name: Chidi King - Tel: +33 4 50 40 11 70

18 August, 2009

Dear Prime Minister,

Interference in the Affairs of the Real Estate Tax Authority Union

Public Services International (PSI) has been informed by our affiliate the Real Estate Tax Authority Union about serious interference with its independence and autonomy by the President of the Egyptian Trade Union Federation.

The Real Estate Tax Authority Union (RETA) was formally constituted on 21 April 2009 in accordance with the Egyptian Constitution and International Labour Organisation Conventions 87 and 98, which have been ratified by the Egyptian government. After protracted negotiations, RETA succeeded in establishing a Social Care Fund, providing retirement benefits for its members. The Minister of Finance's decision No. 425 dated July 2009 approved the establishment of the Fund.

According to our information, considerable pressure is being exerted by Mr Hussein Megawer, President of the Egyptian Trade Union Federation (ETUF) on officials, including officials in the Real Estate Tax Authority and Ministry of Finance, to withdraw the recognition of RETA as an independent trade union and to dissolve or seize control of the Social Care Fund.

This pressure has taken the following forms:

- Shortly after RETA was formally recognised, Mr Megawer attempted to form a new general trade union for employees of the Real Estate Tax Authority; an attempt which was overwhelmingly rejected by the employees.

- ETUF and the National Trade Union of Banks, Insurance and Financial Affairs have written to your government requesting it not to have any dealings with RETA.

- ETUF has filed corruption charges against the RETA leadership, accusing RETA of collecting union dues without authorisation.

- In July 2009, two RETA officials were physically assaulted in Gharibya Governate and Sharkiya Governate.

- RETA officers have been referred for investigation before administrative prosecutors and the legal departments of their workplaces. These officers include **Mr Tarek Mustafa**, the union treasurer and

chairman of the union committee in Kalubiya Governorate; **Mr Abdel Nasser Sayed Mansour**, chairman of the union committee in Beni Suef Governorate; **Mr Hussein Kilany**, chairman of the union committee in Assiut Governorate; **Mr Ezzat Khaled**, chairman of the union committee in Qena Governorate; and **Mr Khaled Mubarak**, treasurer of the union committee in Aswan Governorate.

- RETA members are often called to the State Security offices where they are intimidated.
- RETA leaders are arbitrarily transferred from their job sites to remote places.
- At the instigation of the ETUF, an amendment to decision No. 425 was signed on 5 August 2009 which replaced RETA with the General Trade Union of Banks and Insurances, an ETUF affiliate, as signatory to the Social Care Fund.
- On 10 August 2009, ETUF filed a report with the Public Prosecutor against the President of RETA, Mr Kamal Abu Eita, and against the decision of the Minister of Finance approving the establishment of RETA's Social Care Fund. The report falsely alleges that Mr Abu Eita's election as President was irregular and that RETA is therefore an illegal entity.

PSI urges your government to take swift measures to ensure that RETA can freely exercise its role as an independent trade union organisation; to condemn all acts of intimidation and harassment against the leadership and members of RETA and to condemn all external interference in RETA's activities. We further call on your government to confirm the establishment of a Social Care Fund for RETA members.

Yours sincerely

Peter Waldorff
General Secretary

Cc: H.E. Dr. Youssef Boutros-Ghali, Minister of Finance; H.E. Mrs. Aesha Abdel Hadi Abdel Ghani, Minister of Manpower and Immigration; PSI Arab countries and PSI Africa; Real Estate Tax Authority Union; Centre for Trade Union & Workers Services; Mr Kacem Afiya; ITUC Geneva and Brussels.

Public Services International (PSI) is a global trade union federation that represents 20 million women and men working in the public services around the world. It has some 600 affiliated unions in more than 150 countries. PSI is an autonomous body, which works in association with federations covering other sectors of the workforce and with the International Trade Union Confederation (ITUC). PSI is an officially recognised non-governmental organisation for the public sector within the International Labour Organisation (ILO) and has consultative status with ECOSOC and observer status with other UN bodies such as UNCTAD and UNESCO.

ITUC INTERNATIONAL TRADE UNION CONFEDERATION CSI CONFÉDÉRATION SYNDICALE INTERNATIONALE
CSI CONFEDERACIÓN SINDICAL INTERNACIONAL IGB INTERNATIONALER GEWERKSCHAFTSBUND

ITUC CSI IGB

SHARAN BURROW
PRESIDENT
PRÉSIDENTE
PRÄSIDENTIN
PRESIDENTA

GUY RYDER
GENERAL SECRETARY
SECRÉTAIRE GÉNÉRAL
GENERALSEKRETÄR
SECRETARIO GENERAL

His Excellency Hosni Mubarak
President of the Arab Republic of Egypt
`Abdin Palace
Cairo
Egypt

Via fax: +202-390-1998

HTUR/NT   20 August 2009

Interference in the Affairs of the Real Estate Tax Authority Union

Dear Mr. President,

The International Trade Union Confederation (ITUC), which represents 170 million workers through its 312 affiliates in 157 countries throughout the world, protests along with Public Services International (PSI) the interference by the President of the Egyptian Trade Union Federation with the independence and autonomy of the PSI affiliate Real Estate Tax Authority Union (RETA).

RETA was formally constituted in April 2009 in accordance with the Egyptian Constitution as well as International Labour Standards ratified by the Egyptian Government. A Social Care Fund, providing retirement benefits for its members was established and then approved by the Minister of Finance (decision No. 425 dated July 2009).

According to our information, since then considerable pressure is being exerted by Mr Hussein Megawer, President of the Egyptian Trade Union Federation (ETUF) on officials, including officials in the Real Estate Tax Authority and Ministry of Finance, to withdraw the recognition of RETA as an independent trade union and to dissolve or seize control of the Social Care Fund. Those pressures include among others: physical assault of two RETA officials, intimidation of RETA members, arbitrary transfers of RETA leaders and public prosecution against the President of RETA, Mr Kamal Abu Eita and against the decision of the Minister of Finance approving the establishment of RETA's Social Care Fund.

In December 2008, the ITUC had expressed its concerns when the RETA was experiencing difficulties while establishing the union. We strongly protest once again against interference with the free and independent functioning of the RETA. This interference is

incompatible with the principle of freedom of association and therefore a violation of ILO convention 87.

Along with PSI, the ITUC urges you to take swift measures to ensure that RETA can freely exercise its role as an independent trade union organisation; to condemn all acts of intimidation and harassment against the leadership and members of RETA and to condemn all external interference in RETA's activities.

Yours sincerely,

Guy Ryder

General Secretary

Copy:
- Dr. Ahmed Mahmoud Mohammed Nazif, Prime Minister
- Egyptian Embassy, Brussels

وانـتـصـرنا...

اعتراف دولي ومحلي بأول نقابة مستقلة في مصر

شرعية النقابة بدأت منذ قبول إيداع أوراقها في ٢١ إبريل

وقريبا: انطلاق صندوق الرعاية الاجتماعية

بشرى سارة

بشرى سارة لجميع العاملين بالضرائب العقارية على مستوى الجمهورية من المتوقع أن يتم الإعلان عنها بشكل متزامن مع بدء أعمال الحصر العام الجديد.

ـلم يتم تخفيض الميزة الثانية التي طالبتم بها مليما واحدا ٢٥٠ شهر ، وتم عمل دراسة على أساسه والتي انتهت ، وبإذن الله لن يصدر العدد القادم من جريدتكم إلا ونحن نحتفل بالدفعات الأولى من الزملاء المستفيدين من الصندوق . أبشروا.

يؤكد «نوبة صحيان» لكافة العاملين أن مشروع صندوق الرعاية الصحية والاجتماعية يسير بشكل مضطرد. وخلال أيام قليلة ستنتهي الدراسة مع السادة المسئولين تمهيدا للعرض على السيد. وزير المالية من اجل توفير الاعتمادات المالية اللازمة. وطمأننا ما طالبتم به بلقي استجابة

نوبة صحيان

نوبة صحيان ليست مجرد جريدة دورية لأبناء مهنة واحدة تحتوي على بضعة أخبار و بعض للمعلومات المهنية بالإضافة إلى بعض الزوايا. فهذه الجريدة تطرحها حركة نضالية مستمرة لتعزيز هذا النجاح و تقوية الحركة ودفعها للأمام بهذا المعنى فهي صوت نضالي لموظفي الضرائب العقارية نطرح فيها نحن الموظفين في كل محافظة و مدينة و مركز الإشكاليات و الظلم و التعسف و القلق الذين نعاني منهم أثناء تأديتنا لوظيفتنا.

و نطرح أشكال النضال و المقاومة و التحرك و الرفض الذين نواجه به هذه العقبات كما نطرح الخبرة التي اكتسبناها. إلى جانب احتواء الجريدة على هذه الأخبار و التقارير. يجب أن تكون ساحة للحوار بين جموع موظفي الضرائب الذين عملوا سويا طوال أعوام للحصول على مطالبهم حتى حققوا بعض المكاسب. لنبنوا على هذه المكاسب.

المواقع الإلكترونية الصديقة:

موقع عرباوي:
www.arabawy.org
www.arabawy.org/tax

موقع يساري مصري:
www.gaberism.net

موقع صحوة الضرائب العقارية:
www.sahwaalalakar-
ia.ahlamontada.com

نقابة البنوك «آيلة للسقوط» استقالة هيئة مكتب لجنة الدقهلية

تقدمت هيئة مكتب اللجنة النقابية للضرائب العقارية التابعة لنقابة البنوك والتأمينات بالدقهلية باستقالات من الاتحاد العام لعمال مصر وهم «صلاح محمد عبد السلام نائب رئيس اللجنة، وفؤاد سراج الدين نائب ثان، وجمال السعيد محمد حسن أمين مساعد، ونجلاء فتحي عبد العزيز عضو اللجنة.

وأرسلت الاستقالات لفاروق شحاتة رئيس النقابة العامة للبنوك والتأمينات بالقاهرة.

وجدير بالذكر أن أكثر من ٧٠ عضو بالدقهلية قد تقدموا باستقالاتهم من لجنة الدقهلية البالغ عدد أعضائها حوالي ١٠٠ عضو.ومن المتوقع اتخاذ خطوات مماثلة في محافظات أخرى خلال الأيام القليلة القادمة.

لفتة تستحق التقدير

صرح رئيس مصلحة الضرائب العقارية طارق فراج لجريدة «الدستور» أن التعاون يسير بشكل جيد مع قيادات النقابة المستقلة لاستكمال البيانات الخاصة والإعداد لإنشاء صندوق الرعاية الاجتماعية والصحية . على عكس ما ذكر فاروق شحاتة رئيس نقابة البنوك.

كان فاروق شحاتة قد صرح للعديد من الصحف إنه يتبنى إنشاء الصندوق بالرغم من عدم معرفته عن أية معلومات تخصه.

شعاع نور ابيض يهزم «الفريق الأصفر»

فجأة في ظل هذا الظلام الدامس ووسط الليل البهيم يأتي شعاع نور الأمل ليشق هذا الليل البهيم ، يأتي ليملأ الدنيا بصوت عال وواضح و كأنه صوت زئير الأسد في الغابة مدويا يزلزل كل إرجاء المعمورة ليرهب كل خائب و متهاون و متخاذل وقع فريسة لغرباء فانية كالنصب و الجاه و المكاسب و الأطماع الشخصية فهذا يا كوكبة الشرفاء هو الفريق الأصفر « المعارض لكم و الذي يضع العراقيل في محاولة منه لثني العزائم و تقييد الهمم و لكن هيهات هيهات أني لهم هذا.

جاء هذا النور ليعلن عن بزوغ فجر النصر فجر جديد ممتلئ بنشاط همم عالية و جدية و حيوية و عمل دءوب علي تحقيق أفضل مكاسب جديدة لصالح كل موظفي الضرائب العقارية زملاؤنا الكافحين الشرفاء من اجل حياة أفضل و أحسن لهم.

جاء هذا الفجر ليشد من العزائم و يشحذ الهمم للمضي قدما نحو تحقيق مستقبل أفضل لنا جميعا.

جاء بالإصرار و التأكيد. علي أن الدرب طويل و بالخطى الثابتة ليست به كل طريق صعب.

جاء ليقول لكم يا رفاق الملحمة أن الطريق رغم انه ليس سهلا أو ممهدا!

أو مفروشا بالورود إلا انه لن يغلب عسر يسر وأن النصر مع الصبر و أن بعد العسر يسرا.

و أول بشائر النصر هو نقابتنا المستقلة و صندوق الرعاية الصحية و الاجتماعية للعاملين بالضرائب العقارية.

فأهنئتوا يا رفاق الملحمة أنتم يا كوكبة الشرفاء الكادحين فأنتم علي الحق و هنيئا لكم النقابة و الصندوق و مبروك لكم مجهوداتكم العظيمة و الله ولي التوفيق.

**خالد اميارك حامد
نقيب أسوان**

قصة نقابتنا!!

إخوتي.. أخواتي.. زملائي.. زميلاتي الآن أستطيع أن أقول لكل فرد فيكم ألف مبروك.. نقابتكم التي حلمتم بها على أسفلت شارع حسين حجازي أصبحت الآن حقيقة واقعة.. بإصراركم و نضالكم و تعبكم.. خرجت النقابة و انتزعت الشرعية. كنتم في الإضراب تشكلون مقاومة النقابة لكم و محاولاتهم المستميتة إجهاض إضرابكم المشروع.. بعد أن من اللّه عليكم بالنصر المبين. لن تجد هذه الشكوى طريقها إليكم ففنقابتكم التي صنعتموها بأيديكم ستكون دوماً إلى جواركم.. مدافعة عنكم مطالبة بحقوقكم.. ستكون كجيش الدفاع في أي بلد. ينصرف الشعب للحياة و العمل و الإجهاد.. و يتولى الجيش الدفاع عن الحدود.. و مواجهة أي محتل أو غاصب ستعملون بجد و اجتهاد. و تحنون أنانكم و تزيدون الإنتاج.. و النقابة جنباً إلى جنب تطالب بالحق.. كنا في الماضي نرفع شعار «يد تبني و يد تحمل سلاح» اليوم سنرفع شعار «يد تبني.. و يد تطالب بالحقوق».

نقابتكم لم تخرج بقرار سياسي.. أو إداري.. لم تهبط على الناس من أعلى. نقابتكم صعدت من أسفل. خرجت من أهم أهم إضراب ناجح حقق جميع مطالب.. وزاد عليها. ويزيد كل يوم. فلسفة الإضراب الناجح انه يفتح القنوات المسدودة.. فتتدفق عبرها مطالبكم ويتم الاستجابة لها. وأشهد إنكم الآن بدون الإضراب تحققون مكاسب و تطلبون فيجاب لكم. اشهد بأن القنوات مفتوحة مع كافة المسئولين ولن تنسد بإذن اللّه. و إذا ما سدت في وجه نقابتكم. فأنتم جاهزون و مستعدون لفتح هذه القنوات في أي لحظة.

أعلم كم بذلتم من تعب و مشقة.. و أنتم تبشرون بحلم النقابة المستقلة التي تجمع أشلاء الضرائب العقارية. كنتم كايزيس التي طافت مصر كلها لتجمع أشلاء أوزوريس.. تعرضتم للسخرية و الهجوم و إطلاق الإشاعات.. و أعلنت عليكم جميعاً حرب

قذرة من أعداء الحياة.. وقعت عليكم الجزائرات.. ولم تبالوا.. تم تهديدكم في أرزاقكم ولم تبالوا.. هددتم بالنقل ولم تبالوا.. قطعتم الآلاف من الأميال في الريف و الحضر و حتى في الصحاري.. تجمعون العضوية لنقابتكم تحملتم من جيوبكم وقوت أولادكم كل مصاريف السفر و الانتقال ولم يدفع لكم كائناً من كان مليماً واحداً.. تسلم أيديكم الطاهرة.. وكان النصر جزاء السعي و الصبر و المقاومة. وتماماً كما قالها رجل عظيم رحل عن دنيانا فقيرا مثلكم «إن اللذين يقاتلون يحق لهم أن يأملوا في نصر.. إما اللذين لا يقاتلون فلا ينتظروا شيئاً إلا القتل»

الآن و بعد أن من اللّه عليكم بالنصر.. قولوا لكل من حاربكم و عاداكم «إذ هبوا فأنتم طلقاء» فتحوا أيديكم و صدروكم للعائدين للحق.. لا تصدوا منهم أحدا.. استكملوا العضوية حيث إنكم نجحتم في ضم ٢٢ ألف زميل لنقابتكم.

باقي حوالي ١٣ ألف.. اجتهدوا في ضمهم إلى نقابتكم.. و من كان منهم من جاهلين العمل النقابي أفسحوا له الطريق.. و أعطوه مكانه و قدموه عليكم.. حتى يكون منكم.. انزلوا الناس منازلهم.. نقابتكم تسع للجميع.. خاطبوا زملاءكم بالحسنة من كان منهم في أي تشكيل نقابي آخر «وهم قليل» فليبادر بالاستقالة فوراً وينضم للصفوف.. فالوحدة شرط

أساس من شروط النجاح و الانتصار.. و اعلموا أن كل زميل تتركوه خارج عباءة النقابة سيكون هدفاً سهلاً لأي مؤامرة تحاك ضدكم.

- الوحدة التي نسعى إليها لها شرطان:

١-الديمقراطية: بحيث يدار كل أمر بديمقراطية وعندما تنقد الديمقراطية يصبح الحل قصرياً مفروضاً.. وعندها لا يمكن الحديث عن الوحدة حيث تصبح إجبارية و قصرية.

٢-الاستقلال؛ ويعني عدم خضوع العمل النقابي لإرادة حزب أي حزب في الحكم أو في المعارضة ولا تنظيم أو جماعة سياسية أو سلطة أو جهة إدارية.

الشرطان السابقان هما شرطا للوحدة مع أي نقابة في مصر أو في الوطن العربي و العالم. ولن نقبل بأقل منها وألا «الاستقلال التام أو الموت الذؤوم»

فيا زملائي يا زميلاتي.. أناديكم أناديكم.. أبوس الأرض تحت نعالكم و أقول أفديكم.. فمأساتي التي أحيا نصيب من مأساتكم أناديكم أناديكم

كمال أبو عيطة
النقيب العام
لنقابة الضرائب العقارية المستقلة

مشاكل تطبيق الكتاب الدوري رقم (١٩) لسنة ٢٠٠٢

بورود الكتاب رقم (١٩) لسنة ٢٠٢ من الادارة العامة للشئون القانونية «ادارة الصياغة والفتوى» ملف رقم (٢٣-٤٧/٢) بشأن اعتبار الصراف الذي يتأخر في التوريد في المواعيد المقررة ايام (١٠ و ٢٠ واخر يوم في الشهر) مختلساً اذا خلال تلك الايام متى بلغ النصاب التحصيل (٣٠٠) جنيه بالنسبة لصراف النواحي و (٦٠٠) جنيه بالنسبة لصراف المتنوعة او انتهى بتاريخ دفتر القسائم واليوم السابق للعطلة الرسمية وفي حالة ما اذا كان يوم التوريد المحدد عطلة رسمية واليوم السابق للعطلات الرسمية التي تتجاوز اليوم الواحد (كعيد الفطر وعيد الاضحى) وفي حالة التأخير عن هذه المواعيد يعتبر مختلساً طبقا لحكم المادة (٣٣٠) من كتاب التعليمات والقوانين والاوامر الصادرة من المصلحة طبقا لسنة ١٩٣٤.

وادى ذلك الى ايقاف عدد كبير من الصيارف لتخطي النصاب بعد عمل لجنة الحساب الختامي للصرفيات التي يعملون بها وتنتهي اعمال تلك اللجان في معظم الحالات الى عدم وجود مخالفات او حالات الاختلاس.

ومع ذلك فانه يتم ايقاف هؤلاء الصيارف وعلى الحصيلة وعلى التفتيش والشئون القانونية والعمل بشكل عام.

- وخصوصا ان حالات تعدي النصاب القانوني للتوريد قد تكون بضعة جنيهات قليلة جدا وتكون ناتجة عن ضغط العمل في موسم التحصيل او في حالات الظروف الطارئة خاصة للصراف مثل حالات الوفاة لاحد افراد اسرته او الهارب او المرض المفاجئ او السهو او التجميع الخطأ او قلب الارقام. ويعمل دراسة حالة على مديرية الضرائب العقارية بمحافظة الدقهلية يتضح لنا من خلال ذلك نتيجة تطبيق الكتاب الدوري (١٩) لسنة ٢٠٢ خلال احد الشهور وجود

ما لا يقل عن (١٠) حالات وذلك يؤدي بشكل كبير الى العجز في عدد الصيارف القائمين باعمال التحصيل وذلك بالاضافة الى الندرة حاليا والعجز الفعلي الموجود وتوفير عدم فتح مدرسة الصيارف والقيام بتدريب والتكلفة العالية التي تتكبدها الدولة في تدريب واعداد الصيارف بالاضافة الى وصمة العار التي تلتصق به طوال حياته الوظيفية دون أي ذنب.

- وهناك ثغرة في هذا الموضوع ادت الى قيام بعض الصيارف بافتعال تجاوز النصاب عن عمد بغرض الابتعاد عن اعمال التحصيل والحصول على الحوافز والجهود غير العادية والمكافآت التشجيعية كاملة والحاقه بجهاز الربط بالمأمورية.

- وهناك بعض الصيارف يقومون بالتوريد يوميا وخصوصا في مواسم التحصيل وتحصيل الصرف الحقلي مما قد يدفع بالصراف بالتغيير في التواريخ حتى لا يقع تحت طائلة الاختلاس او شبه الاختلاس لذلك ...

- برجاء اعادة النظر في الكتاب الدوري (١٩) لسنة ٢٠٢ حيث انه يعتمد على كتاب وتعليمات من المصلحة منذ عام ١٩٣٤ فكيف يتم تطبيقه عام ٢٠٠٩ وما بعدها!

- رفع نصاب التوريد بحيث لا يقل عن (١٠٠٠) جنيه لصراف النواحي ومبلغ (٢٠٠٠) جنيه لصراف المتنوعة تفاديا لمسألة تخطي النصاب.

جمال محمود عويضة
مامور ضرائب اول
مديرية الدقهلية

قرارات

قررت مديرية الضرائب العقارية بالجيزة الآتي :
١- استمرار سريان تقديرات القيمة الايجارية المتخذة أساسا لحساب الضريبة وفقا لأحكام القانون ٥٦ لسنة ٥٤ علي ربط الضريبة لعام ٢٠٩.
٢- استمرار نظر طلبات الرفع والخلو.
٣- استمرار لجان مجالس المراجعة في نظر الطعون في تقديرات مستجدات ٢٠٠٧ ربط ٢٠٨، ٢٠٨ ربط ٢٠٩.
٤- تسري أحكام المواد الخامسة والسادسة والسابعة من القانون رقم ١٩٦ لسنة ٢٠٨ باصدار الضريبة علي العقارات المبنية والخاصة بالتصالح في الطعون القائمة لجلس المراجعة والدعاوى المقيدة والمنظورة أمام المحاكم.
٥- اتخاذ إجراءات حصر وتقدير القيمة الايجارية للعقارات المستجدة عام ٢٠٨ ربط ٢٠٩ وفق أحكام القانون رقم ٥٦ لسنة ٥٤ والقانون رقم ٦١ لسنة ٢١ لحين البدء في اتخاذ إجراءات الربط وفق أحكام القانون ١٩٦ لسنة ٢٠٨.
الاستمرار بالعمل بقانون ٥٦ لسنة ٥٤ حيث ان تنفيذ أحكام القانون ١٩٦ لسنة ٢٠٨ اعتبارا من ٢٤-٦-٢٠٨ تاريخ العمل به و علي ان تستحق الضريبة من ٢٠٩/١/١.

أرجوك اعطني هذا الدواء

طلب يتقدم به كل موظف بالضرائب العقارية بالبحيرة بل كل موظفي الجمهورية. فجرعة من هذا الدواء تحي الشباب و تعيده دواء ضمانة بعد فك أغلال الوظيفة المبري، صندوق عظيم خارج من كفاح رجال عظماء صندوق يعطيه مكافأة لعمل دؤوب قضاه في خدمة الضرائب العقارية.

سؤالي لكم يا عظماء مصر يا صورة سعد زغلول و مصطفى كامل و احمد عرابي هل من الممكن أن تضعف عزيمتكم بسبب العناصر الهدامة التي تحاربنا لهدم كل شيء شريف و الرد مني بكل تأكيد و إخلاص «لا لا»
و الأعداد بتزيد بتزيد و العزيمة حديد في حديد ... و النقابة العامة حديد في حديد.

فتحي علي حسين
مأمورية ضرائب كفر الدوار .. بحيرة

نوبة صوبان

جهاز إداري بدون كوادر

راجل مجند للعزاء
أحمد رجب علي
رئيس نقابة العاملة بالضرائب
العقارية - البحيرة

العامل أصبح ينتج في وقت فراغه وبهذه الطريقة يعلم أولاده الممارسة العملية مع توفير المادة الخام من قبل المصنع وتسويق المنتج عن طريق المصنع. أما نحن فنفعل عكس ذلك. نعمل بطريقة خلي السلاح صاحي خلي السلاح صاحي في ذلك كل مهارة مصرية ويحبك بابرنطيقة الخواجة.

ورحمة الله (عزاء واجب) على عمال الغزل والنسيج وإنا لله وإنا إليه راجعون، فقد توفيت المهارة في شركة كفر الزيات للكيماويات وشركة الحرير الصناعي.

ولي صرخة يارب نسمعها فقد كنا أعظم عمال إنتاج في العالم، في ظل نظام الخصخصة بدأت الدولة في تفريغ مصانعنا من ذوي المرتبات المرتفعة أو تفريغ كياننا الاقتصادي من العمال المهرة والاكتفاء بعمال نص لبة (باريت أعيش في الصين).

ولي قصة عن النظام الصيني المطبق في الصين، فالعامل يعين ولا يأخذ أي حافز إلا بعد مرور سنتين وعندما يصبح ذو كفاءة يبدأ في أخذ الحافز ولكن على صورة أخرى وذلك بإعطائه ماكينة مثل العدة التي يعمل عليها بالمصنع. وبهذه الطريقة يزداد حجم الاقتصاد لأن

في يوم من الأيام طرح في مقر الاتحاد العام لعمال مصر اقتراح بتغيير التعاقد مع المعينين الجدد في الجهاز الحكومي ليكونوا بنظام التعاقد المؤقت، وهذا الاقتراح بالتحديد يعمل على تفريغ الجهاز الحكومي من الكوادر المدربة جيداً وذات القدرة على إصدار القرار السليم والحكيم في الوقت السليم.

ورغم أن هذا الاقتراح قد قوبل بالرفض ولكنه تم تطبيقه من الباب الخلفي مما لم يسمح بوجود فترة زمنية كافية لتطبيق دورات إعداد لهذا الموظف.

نقابتنا المستقلة

مجاهد عبد الرحمن مجاهد
أمين عام نقابة الجيزة

في الصحة)، إنشاء صندوق الرعاية الصحية لجميع العاملين بالضرائب العقارية كمرحلة أولى بحيث تشمل المرحلة الثانية أسرهم، وانجزت الانفلاق على بدل انتقال قدرة ١٥ جنية لليوم الواحد بدلا من ٢٢ جنية شهرية.

فالى الامام ايتها الزميلات والزملاء، لا تنتفتوا لعرضين يريدون تشتيت الانظار وافشال الهدف الذى تسعون لانجازه.

وقد تفتحت عيوننا على شرفاء بيننا حملوا على عاتقهم امانة بناء نقابة مستقلة لجميع العاملين فى كل ربوع مصر .

نقابتنا أهدافنا الدفاع عن مصالح العاملين عن مصالح العاملين بالضرائب العقارية، السعى لانشاء صندوق رعاية العاملين بالضرائب العقارية (وهو مطلب جرى الاتفاق علية مع وزير المالية فى الاجتماع الشهير

زميلاتى وزملائى رفاق الكفاح فى سلحمة تضرب بها الامثال «اضرابنا الشهير فى ٣ديسمبر الحى ابدا فى ذاكرة شرفاء هذا الوطن ،ملحمة الحظناها بأخرى و جبنا لاجلها انحاء مصر من الاسكندرية لاسوان ومن العريش لمرسى مطروح ،ولم ينجزها الا التوفيق اللة الذى الف بين قلوبنا فصرنا جمعا على قلب رجل واحد .

خرجنا من هذا الجمع العظيم

إيداع الأوراق = اعتراف الدولة بنقابتنا

المدة سقط حقها في التظلم من تأسيس النقابة أمام القضاء ..أما إذا أبدت الجهة الإدارية ملاحظاتها وأخطرت به النقابة فيكون للنقابة توفيق أوضاعها والرد على تلك الملاحظات فإن لم تبادر النقابة بالرد يجوز للجهة الإدارية خلال ثلاثين يوما من هذا الإخطار التظلم أمام المحكمة الجزئية المختصة من تأسين النقابة.. وبون أن يترتب على أي من الإجراءات السابقة وقف نشاط النقابة ولا يؤثر على شخصيتها القانونية ولا ينتقص من حقوقها لا يلغي وجودها وتستمر في مباشرة نشاطها بشكل طبيعي إلى أن يصدر حكم قضائي بات في تظلم الجهة الإدارية.

العمل فيما يتعلق بقرارات العمل التي تمس مصالح أعضائها. ويجب على صاحب العمل والجهات الإدارية التابعة له معاونة هيئات النقابة وتسهيل أدائها لعملها ومخاطبتها وحدها باعتبارها الممثل الوحيد لأعضائها ويحظر على هذه الجهات تعطيل نشاط هيئات النقابة أو التدخل في شئونها أو معاقبة أي من أعضائها بسبب نشاطه النقابي. ولم يبقى أمام الجهة الإدارية من طريق غير أن تبدي ملاحظاتها على أوراق التأسيس خلال ثلاثين يوما من تاريخ الإيداع. وتخطر النقابة بتلك الملاحظات بخطاب موصى علي بعلم الوصول فإن لم تبدي هذه الملاحظات خلال تلك

النقابة تولد منذ هذه اللحظة تولد منذ هذه اللحظة وتصبح شخص قانوني وتمارس نشاطها دون تدخل من الجهة الإدارية. ويترتب على ذلك أنه يصبح من حق النقابة فتح مقراتها وتنظيم اجتماعاتها واتخاذ جميع الإجراءات القانونية نيابة عن أعضائها أمام القضاء والجهات الإدارية الأخرى دون حاجة إلى توكيل خاص. وتمثيل أعضائها في منازعات العمل الفردية والجماعية وعقد اتفاقيات العمل الجماعية. ولها الحق في أن تعتمد «خاتم» خاص بها تعتمد به وحده أوراقها التي تصبح من الأوراق الرسمية ويكون لهيئات النقابة وحدهم دون غيرهم - الحق في مخاطبة صاحب

النقابة قائمة ومعترف بها. وأصبحت شخصاً اعتبارياً من لحظة إيداع أوراقها في وزارة القوى العاملة...والشخصية الاعتبارية هي شخصية قانونية مستقلة. وتكون لها الحقوق القانونية والدستورية المقررة للشخصية الطبيعية» الإنسان... ويضفي القانون الصفة الشرعية اللازمة على تصرفاتها .فإذا كانت حياة الشخص الطبيعي تبدأ بالاعتراف القانوني بهذا الشخص. وقد حدد القانون طريق هذا الاعتراف في مجال إنشاء النقابات العمالية، بإيداع أوراق التأسيس في الجهة الإدارية المختصة ولم يعلق اكتساب النقابة للشخصية الاعتبارية على قيد أو شرط. أو يترتب على ذلك أن

نوبة صوبان

نوبة سويس · مايو ٢٠٠٩

رجـال الـسـويـس .. حدث ولا حرج

الاختلاف فى الرأى لا يفسد للود قضية والحق احق ان يتبع ولا يحيق المكر السيئ الا بأهله.

كلمات ابدأ بها مقالتى تلك حتى ينسب الحق لاصحابة ,ولا تعرف الرجال الا فى المحن والمواقف .فبعد الشد والجذب والمضايقات من بعض الزملاء لى بصفة خاصة .. مائثار حفيظة السيد المدير العام ودفعة لمجازاتى بخصم ثلاثة ايام من راتبى قبل ان انقدم حيال القرار بتظلم - كأنا السيد المدير العام اعضاء النقابة بالسويس ثلاثة مرات .. لم يستجب للمدعو سامى مباشر ,اعاد حق الزميلة

فاطمة مختلر فى حوافز شهر من العام الماضى كان قد اقتطع بسبب اجازة الوضع ,وقبول التظلم وتغير صفة جزاءة الموظف على ..

واقسم ان كان الجزاء قد زاد الى خمسة ايام مع طرد المدعو سامى مباشر لعددات الامر انتصارا الى وللحق لان الرجل اشترى كذبا على بقولة انرى دعوتة للسويس بعد خروجة منها بقرار محافظ الاسماعيلية بخصم شهر من راتبة.

ومن مير «نوبة صحبان ابعث بأرق التحية والتقدير للسيد المدير العام

الاستاذ عبد المقصود البنا على تلبيتة طلبات اعضاء النقابة العامة المستقلة بقولة « انا تحت امركم فى اى حاجة لمصلحة الموظف.»

كما ارسل تحيتى للاستاذ مصطفى حسين وكيل المديرية الذى قام بدورة على اكمل وجة اطلعنا على اوراق سامى مباشر ولقنة لدرسا لا بنبناء.

لا تبقى الا بعض الرتوش البسيطة امام السيد المدير العام ,ولو فعل فـتصل السويس لمستوى المحافظة التالية.

واهمـ فى اذنة ومن شق على رعيتة شق اللة علية ومن يسر على رعيتة

يسر اللة علية.

ونحن اهل السويس بالضرائب العقارية من ضمن رعاياة. ونتمنى من اللة دوام التوفيق لسيادتة والمصلحة الاولى والاخيرة لنا ولة هى خدمة موظفى السـويس ولاغير ذلك.

لى اقتراح اخير لجائزة لأفضل مدير مديرية فى معاملاتة مع موظفية بنشر بوستر نصف صفحة لة ونبذة عن حياتة تقديرا لة ولجهودة

يا رجال السويس ..يارجال نقابتنا الخير اللى جاى بايديكم وبايدينا

امره السيد
السـويـس

الـظـالـم .. والمظلـوم

يبدأ بعض الموظفين عند تعيينهم فى العمل بداية متواضعة يتقربون الى زملائهم ويتحببون إليهم وكأنهم ملائكة نزلوا من السماء الى الأرض وعندما يصلوا الى منصب كبير فى العمل تجدة وقد انقلب الى شخص اخر غير الذى كان, وقد ملاءه الكبر وحب الظهور. ويأخذ فى محاولة قتل مجهود كل شخص يحاول الاجتهاد فى العمل حتى لا يلفت النظر السئولين الكبار اليه خوفاً على منصبه حتى لا

يأخذ مكانه ويبقى هو المميز الوحيد حتى ولو على حساب الأخرين, فمثلاً فى بعض المحافظات يقوم بعض وكلاء الوزارة ومديرين العموم بإلغاء تخصصات وكيل المديرية والاستحواذ على كل المناصب والتخصصات رغم انه بذلك يخالف قانون العمل الوظيفى ويخالف تعليمات المصلحة التى حددت اختصاصات كل منهم رغم أنه وفى بعض المديريات وكلاء مشهود لهم بالكفاءة والخبرة فى العمل وهم من كبار

الباحثين ولهم خبرة كبيرة فى مجال الضرائب العقارية بجميع أقسامها ويمكن الاستفادة منهم ومن خبراتهم ففيهم من حصل على شهادات تقديرية من وزير المالية على مجهود فى مجال الضرائب وعلى أبحاثه التى ساعدت فى حل مشاكل كثيرة كانت تعوق العمل الضريبى فكانت مكافأته من مدير المديرية هى الغاء مجهوداته ودفن خبراته بدلاً من الاستفادة منها, وكل ذلك حرصا وخوفاً على النصب.

وهناك الكثير من هذه النوعية من مديرى العموم ووكلاء الوزارة يوزعون التخصصات وبعض الأعمال حسب أهوائهم وكأنهم فى عزبة ورثوها عن أبنائهم ويضربون بلوائح العمل وقوانينه وقرارات الصلحة عرض الحائط. فمن ينقذ هؤلاء من الظلم الواقع عليهم.

عبد الناصر سيد
بنى سويف

نوبة سويس

208 *Appendix A*

قصة عيد العمال كل أيام السنة الباقية للأغنياء... وللفقراء أول مايو

«سيعم العالم كلة صوتنا حتى من تحت الأرض» قالها قبل ما يزيد عن ١٢٠ عاما عامل فقير نافي الهزيمة عنة وعن عمال ها مثل فقره تماما يوشكون على لقاء الموت خضوعا لحكم أعناقهم بإعدامهم .

سمع العالم صوته بالفعل حتى نظم فؤاد حداد شاعر العامية الأشهر فيهم قصيدة الأول من مايو- عام ١٩٦٣- مرددا رجع الصدى «أنا اللي تحت الثرى ها قلق مضاجعكم.. ماضي وحاضر ومستقبل ها راجعكم.. أولها من اولة مايو ومواجعكم»

لم يكن أوجحت سبايز قد اقترف مع الآلاف من زملائة في مصنع ما كورميك للجرارات ها شيكـا جو في أمريكا إلا المطالبة بقـط جو من الـيوم ها حقيقة الأمر .دفع مع المقابل مع أربعة من رفاقية حياتة لقاء ذلك.. قصت محكمة متواطئة مع صاحب المصنع بإعدامهم بخلاف الحكم على ثلاثة آخرين بـسجن مدى الحياة، بتهمة إثارة الشغب والعنف. ومن قبل القاضي تواطأ مدير البوليس الذي ألقى بيده قنبلة يدوية على جنود الشرطة الذين واجهوا تظاهرة عمال المصنع في الأول

من مايو عام ١٨٨٦التى رفعوا فيها راية «ثمانية ساعات للعمل... ثمانية للراحة ..ثمانية للراحة»، بحيث يبدو الأمر وكأن العمال قد فعلوها ...مانحا بذلك الجـنود «حق» الدفاع عن أنفسهم بالرصاص الحي الذي أودى بحياة عدد من العمال. وتحولت تظاهرتهم لمذبحة لقت شماتة الصحف الصادرة في اليوم التالي -المملوكة لرأسماليين انحازوا بطبيعة الحال ضد العمال- والتي اتهمت العمال بالعنف والشغب .

مضت إحدى عشر عاما قبل أن يسمع الضمير حقيقة ما حدث،

قبـل لقاء ،اعترف مدير البوليس للقـبس ربما جنت يداه. وخلافا لشريعة الكنيسة فضح رجل الدين ما حدث لتبرئة ساحة العمال الشهداء .

رفع جيم الصغير ابن سبايز رأسة وعرف العالم فحوى رسالة والدة إليه والتي خطها قبل اعدامة ،والتي ودعة فيها مؤكدا براءته ونبل قضيتة . بعدها بعامين تقريبا أعلنت الأممية الاشتراكية الثانية -تجمع الأحزاب الاشتراكية في العالم- الأول من مايو عيدا عالميا للعمال... وصار للكادحين عيدا .

عيد العمال..بأي حال عدت يا عيد؟!

هناك العديد من العمال الذين تم تسريحهم من المصانع والشركات وتشردت أسرهم نتيجة الفشل في ايجاد وظائف أخرى وذلك على مستوى العالم في عام ٢٠٩ وهو العام المشؤوم على العمال بعد فقدهم للعمل هذا من جانب ومن جانب آخر نجد الاضرابات والاعتصامات. فما أن ينتهي عمال مصنع من اضراب الا ونجد عمال مصنع آخر يردون عليهم نجحوا في انتزاع حقوقهم واجبار المسؤلين الكبار على الرضوخ والاستجابة لمطالبهم فكيف سيمر هذا اليوم الأول من مايو (عيد العمال) على عمال يعانوا من ضغوط الحياة بعد تسريحهم وكيف سيشعرون به اذا كانوا في يأخذونه اجازة في حين أنهم الآن في أجازة طويلة جميع أيامهم تشبه بعضها لا يعلمون أول الشهر من آخره حتي يتذكرون الأول من مايو وقصته الجميلة التي كانت سببا في الأحتفال به. ولكن في نفس الوقت نجد من يستعدون للأحتفال بهذه المناسبة السعيدة. فهم العمال والموظفين الذين انتصروا في معركتهم مع عائشة عبد الهادي وحسين مجاور فهم العمال الذين سيحتفلون ليس فقط بعيد العمال ولكن بانتصارهم أيضا فاذا نظرنا سنجد أن الاضرابات لا تنتهي

فقط بانتزاع حق صرف العلاوات أوزيادة المرتبات ولكن بدأت تنتهي بانشاء نقابة مستقلة لم تشم مصر رائحتها منذ ٨٠ عام. فأتيحت تجربةموظفي الضرائب العقارية أن مطالب العمال لم تقتصر على المطالبة بزيادة الحوافز والعلاوات بل أمتدت لتتوسع الدائرة وتخرج نقابة مستقلة ينظر اليها العمال في كل انحاء العالم محاولين الاستفادة منها. فقصص العمال لم تنتهي عند شهداء ماكورملك للجرارات ولن تكون هي القصة الوحيدة المطروحة في الاحتفال فهناك العديد من القصص والروايات التي سيرويها عمال مصر من غزل المحلة وغزل شبين وسائقي السكة الحديد وموظفي الضرائب العقارية الذين لم ينشأوا نقابة مستقلة فقط بل وأصدروا جريدة مثل (نوبة صحيان) لتعبر عن صوت العمال ومطالبهم.

وعلى الرغم من أن العمال هم أكبر وأكثر شريحة تأثرت بلعنة الأزمة العالية الا

أن هذه الشريحة لا تجد عزائها الا في هذا العيد فظروف العمال في العالم كله قاسية وتمر بأسوأ مراحلها فنحن من فوق وظيفته وحتي من لم يفقد وظيفته يعمل في ظل ظروف وضغوط صعبة فنعلم أن أكثر من نصف مليون عامل فقد عمله من قطاعات الغزل والنسيج والبناء والأخشاب والسياحة والكيماويات الصناعات الغذائية وغيرها من القطاعات ولكننا نعلم أن عيد العمال ايضا فرصة لتجمع العمال من جميع

القطاعات ليلاد حركة عمالية تقف ضد الظلم والقهر وتجبر رجال الحكم علي كله الأزمة ليس لصالح أصحاب الأعمال الكبار خوفا علي رأسمالهم بل لصالح العمال الذين بنتجوا والذين تقف البلد دون كدحهم لذلك فعيد العمال سيكون لكل عامل تم فصله تعسفيا وكل عامل تم الاقتطاع من أجره عنوة وكل عامل طالب بحقوقه.سيكون أول من مايو عيد لكل العمال تروي فيه حكايات للأبطال .

نورة سحبان   مايو ٢٠٠٩

أسرار ي

يوم النصر

الثلاثاء ٢٠٠٩/٤/٢١ تذكروا هذا التاريخ جيداً لأنه علامة فارقة في تاريخ الضرائب العقارية وتاريخ الحركة العمالية والنقابية في مصر بأسرها. وما يحمله هذا اليوم في طياته من تبعات على مستقبل الضرائب العقارية خاصة وعلى الوطن بأكمله بصفة عامة. فقد عقد موظفوا الضرائب العقارية العزم على إبداع أوراق أول نقابة مستقلة في تاريخ مصر في مثل هذا اليوم وحضر أعضاء الهيئات النقابية من ٢٦ محافظة من أسوان والأقصر وقنا وسوهاج وكل محافظات الدلتا وخط القناة. من كل ربوع مصرنا العظيمة جاءوا منها وتحملوا مشاق السفر لكي يحضروا بأيديهم مشاق السفر لن يستطيع أحد أن يحضوه. وقد ظلت هذه الوجوه المكافحة على مدى شهور طويلة تعمل بدأب على نشر الفكرة ظلت على مدى شهور طويلة تعمل بدأب على نشر الفكرة وتجميع العضوية وعمل التشكيلات تحت إشراف لجنة في ٢٦ محافظة لكي يقدموا في النهاية عمل محترم لهذا البلد. فلأول مرة في التاريخ يقوم أصحاب الشأن بأنفسهم بعمل تنظيم نقابي لهم دون انتظار أن يختيهم أو مسئول هذا الحق. والفلسفة التي قامت عليها النقابة المستقلة هي أن العمل النقابي ليس ملك أي مسئول في مصر. وما كان

يحدث فيما سبق من إنشاء النقابات من أعلى وهو ما كان يجعلها غير معبرة عن مصالح أعضائها وليس أكثر من خيال ماتة تهرب من حقوق العمال والموظفين. ولكن العمل النقابي يأتي بإرادة أصحاب الشأن، وأن المادة ٥٦ من الدستور المصري تعطي الحق لنا بإنشاء النقابة دون الرجوع لأي جهة إدارية وكذلك اتفاقية العمل الدولية رقم ٨٧ لسنة ٤٨ الموقع عليها من قبل الحكومة المصرية تعطينا الحق في إنشاء النقابة وكذلك القانون المصري في المادة ٤ ينص على أن تنشأ الصفة الاعتبارية للمنظمة النقابية بإيداع الأوراق في الجهة الإدارية المختصة وهي وزارة القوى العاملة، وأن الجهة الإدارية لها حق الاعتراض خلال ثلاثين يوماً من إجراءات التأسيس وليس على التأسيس. أي أن مقولة أن هناك جهة لها حق الموافقة

على النقابة مقولة كاذبة وغير دستورية وغير قانونية، يوجهها أعداء الحقوق في مصر، وبناء عليه زحف موظفوا الضرائب العقارية يوم الثلاثاء، وقد بلغ عددهم ٩٠٠ موظف احتشدوا أمام وزارة القوى العاملة وصعد منهم وفد القادر الأستاذ كمال أبو عيطة وعبد القادر ندا ووجدنا بعض التسويف والمماطلة والحقيقة أن هذه هي المرة الأولى التي يجد موظفوا القوى العاملة أنفسهم في مثل هذه الحالة. ووقعوا في مأزق حول كيفية التصرف في مثل هذا الموقف وبعد مناقشات وشد وجذب وسط هتافات مدوية كان هناك الاتصال الذي تم بين عائشة عبد الهادي وزيرة القوى العاملة وكمال أبو عيطة وطلبت منه تسليم المذكرة وبالفعل سلمها وتم التأشير عليها بالاستلام. وأغلب الظن أن أن الوزيرة كانت تعتقد. أنا جئنا لتسليم

مذكرة فحسب. ولهذا رفض الجميع التحرك من أمام الوزارة إلا بعد مقابلة الوزيرة وقد كان. حضرت الوزيرة ومعها وفد من خبراء منظمة العمل الدولية ووعدت بلقائنا بعد اجتماعها مع الوفد الدولي. وبالفعل قابلت الوزيرة أعضاء النقابة الذين استقبلوها بالهتافات المدوية. وتحدثت الوزيرة مؤكدة التزامها بالاتفاقيات الدولية والدستور المصري وهذا ما سعين إليه بالفعل. واصطحبت معها وفداً من قيادات النقابة. وخلال الحديث معها والذي استغرق ٢٠ دقيقة أمرت باستلام أوراق الإبداع وتم الاستلام بالفعل وشكر أعضاء الوفد معالي الوزيرة وأخذت الصور التذكارية وسط هتافات التحية للوزيرة وهذا هو أول حدث من نوعه يتم بأيدي أصحابه وأن النجاح برغم هجومهم لن يؤثر على المسيرة، ولنتذكر جيداً أن هؤلاء هم أنفسهم من كانوا يشككون في الاعتصام بل كانوا ضد الاعتصام بعد ذلك أرادوا أن يتسببوا في إفشال النجاح هؤلاء هم أعداء النجاح والي الأمام. والهدية القادمة هي الصندوق بزملاء والي نجاح آخر...

طارق مصطفى
أمين الصندوق للنقابة العامة المستقلة للضرائب العقارية،

هتافات مناضل ٠٠٠ عادل بكري

يا بتوع التنظيم الهرمي... بصراحة انا رافض ضمي
يابتوع الوحدة الجبرية... عايزين نقابتنا بحرية
تنظيمكوا الهرمي البطال... ضد مصالح العمال
ضيع أجري و ضيع قوتي... ثلاثين سنة و انا كاتم صوتي
تلاتين الف و فوقهم عشرة... و صاحبهم هيموت بالحصرة

نورة سحبان

ـوم النـصر

أعياد ورا أعياد

سنة أولى عزيمة (٢٠٠٧)

كلاكيت أول مرة خارجي

الزمان: ١١ سبتمبر ٢٠٠٧

المكان: ش ربيع الجيزي أمام مجمع المصالح الحكومية بالجيزة.

الحدث: اختبار عزيمة الموظفين الميري بالضرائب العقارية بالجيزة للتجمع والتظاهر في الشارع حول مطلب المساواة المالية مع المصلحة والضم للمالية ثم تعليق الاعتصام إلى أكتوبر لتلبية المطالب أو معاودة الاعتصام- تلا ذلك اعتصامات بمعظم محافظات الجمهورية.

كلاكيت ثاني مرة:

الزمان: ٢١ أكتوبر ٢٠٠٧

المكان: وزارة المالية في مجلس الوزراء

الحدث: حشد الموظفين الميري بالضرائب العقارية على مستوى مواقع الجمهورية للتظاهر أمام وزارة المالية حول المطلب.

النتيجة: وصلت الرسالة وكان الرد مطلبكم في يد رئيس الوزراء.

حرارة الإرادة تسوق موظفي الميري مخترقين شوارع القاهرة مرحلين من الوزارة للعباسية لعبده باشا فالعتبة فشارع حسين حجازي والتمركز أمام مجلس الوزراء «واحد أثنين ..رئيس الوزراء فين؟» ثم القسم والعهد على

الإضراب.

كلاكيت ثالث مرة:

الزمان: ١٣ نوفمبر ٢٠٠٧، ١٤ نوفمبر ٢٠٠٧

المكان: رصيف ومدخل اتحاد العمال.

الحدث: التمترس و «با تساوونا بالصلحة... يا ندونوا على المشرحة» و.. «قاعدين ..قاعدين ..قاعدين مش ماشيين».

مفاوضات اليوم السابع لم تنل موافقة المعتصمين التجييش الميري- مساندة الرأي العام- مادة ممتازة لوسائل الإعلام.

مفاوضات ناجحة الليلة الحادية عشر تنال قبول المعتصمين.

النتيجة: انتصار الإرادة وجني الثمار أفراح الضرائب العقارية مع وزير المالية في ١٣، ٢١ ديسمبر ٢٠٠٧.

كلاكيت آخر مرة:

الزمان: ٢- ١٣ ديسمبر ٢٠٠٧

المكان: شارع حسن حجازي في مواجهة مجلس الوزراء

الحدث: التمترس و «وبا تساوونا بالصلحة... يا ندونوا على المشرحة».

العقارية والتصويت على تحويل اللجنة العليا للإضراب إلى نقابة مستقلة للعاملين تحت التأسيس.

النتيجة: الموافقة بالإجماع وبداية إجراءات التأسيس على مستوى جميع المحافظات الجمهورية -والحشد- ومعارك تفتعلها النقابة العامة الرسمية للقضاء على الفكرة.

كلاكيتات ثالث ورابع و...

أزمنة متعددة، وأماكن متعددة.

الأحداث: تثقيف، زيارات للمحافظات. احتفالات، استمارات، تأسيس، وعضوية اجتماعات، استشارات قانونية.

النتيجة: توقيعات للعضوية لمواقع الجمهورية بحوالي ٣٣ ألف -تصميم على إنشاء أول نقابة مستقلة بمصر.

كلاكيت قبل الأخير

الزمان: ٢٠ ديسمبر ٢٠٠٨

المكان: نقابة الصحفيين

الحدث: اجتماع أول جمعية عمومية لأعضاء النقابة المستقلة للميد في اختيار أعضاء النقابة العامة ثم انتخاب للجان الفرعية بجميع محافظات المحروسة.

كلاكيت الزلزال

الزمان: ٢١ أبريل ٢٠٠٩

المكان: وزارة القوى العاملة.

الحدث: إيداع أوراق النقابة العامة المستقلة للعاملين بالضرائب العقارية بعد مقابلة وزيرة القوى العاملة.

توابع الزلزال؛

الزمان: ٢٤ أبريل ٢٠٠٩

المكان: جنيف.

الحدث: الاتحاد الدولي لعمال الخدمات يقر بعضوية النقابة المستقلة للضرائب العقارية للاتحاد الدولي وتنضم الى أسرة من ٢٠ مليون عامل عبر العالم.

وله دى يا ما أعياد جايه!!..

عبد القادر ندا
الأمين العام
للنقابة المستقلة للضرائب العقارية.

سنة ثانية بناء واستقلال

كلاكيت أول مرة

الزمان: أول يناير ٢٠٠٨

المكان: سيارة أبو عيطة ومعه، ندا.

الحدث: أحلام بنقابة مستقلة ولخلق بيئة وبداية الإعداد والتثقيف والتواصل مع ذوي الخبرة.

كلاكيت ثاني مرة

الزمان ، أول مارس ٢٠٠٨.

المكان: مقر مؤقت للجنة العليا للإضراب.

الحدث: اجتماع مع ميري الضرائب

نوبة سويلن ٢٠٠٦م ١٠

شـــرعي ولا عـــرفـــي؟!!..

عبد الحميد عقل
عضو نقابة الجيزة

ترددت في الفترة الأخيرة بعض الكلمات التي لا معنى لها إلا في الزواج رغم أننا بصدد النقابات و المطالبة بالحقوق المسلوبة منذ زمن بعيد فلا تجد أن هذه الكلمات لها معنى محدد . و أقول بدلا من أن نتريص ببعضنا البعض و و نسأل في براءة أنت عرفي و أنا شرعي أو أنا معك و أنا عليك هناك كلمة ساخرة و هي متى يرمي بمين الطلاق علي الضرائب العقارية نصيحتي بدلا من هنا فلتسلك طريقك و راني نتيجة هذا الطريق

في أي شبر، بعود بالفع علي الموظف الشريف حتى أن كان بسيطا وعندها ستشكرك جميعا و ذلك بدلا من أن تنتظر الفرصة للنجاح و تحاول دون فهم ... رزق عيالنا أهم و لقد خرج كل منا من بيته وهو ينتظر قرار النصر و عاهدنا الله ألا نعود إلي منازلنا إلا به و لقد تحقق بالفعل بحمد الله و الآن نحن نعاهد أنفسنا علي ألا تغمض لنا عين إلا و نتحسن الأحوال المالية فأين كنت أنت و أين كنت من ذلك . فقد كنت تغلق الأبواب في وجوهنا و تغلق

علي الرصيف أمام مكتب الدكتور أحمد نطليف مطالبا بحقه واذكر في هذه الأيام عبارة رددتها و سمعتها بنفسي هي تهز الأرض وقت أن كنا نهتف « بالروح بالدم ... رزق عيالنا أهم » و لقد خرج
أن عدم فهمك أو علمك سيعود علي الموظف بالخسارة فهناك مثل نسمعه من قديم الزمن و سيكون نتيجة لما تفعله أيها الشخص الذي تعرف نفسك ألا و هو » من تدخل فيما لا يعنيه سمع ما لا يرضيه » و ما لا يعنيك هو المصلحة للموظف الشريف الذي بات عشرة أيام

دورات المياه علينا و تقول لنا « انتوا بتحلموا «و الآن تقول الشرعي لا و ألف لا فنحن رمينا عليك بمين الطلاق و هو طلاق بائن لا رجعة فيه

كفى يا اعداء النجاح

تمت ويمباركة من المولى عز وجل, وابتدينا المشوار وحققنا جزء كبير من مطالبنا التي طال انتظارنا لها بعون الله سبحانة وتعالى .ومازال أمامنا الكثير والكثير حتى يرتاح الصغير قبل الكبير .فما زال الطريق طويل ويحتاج الى تضافر كل الجهود وتكاتف كل الايادي لأجل هدف واحد نسعي جميعا ليعم الرخاء علي جميع الاخوة الزملاء .وعلى الرغم مما تحقق شعر بة أن كل

منا فى الضرائب العقارية. الا ان هناك من يتريص من صعدوا بهذا الجمع من نقطة الصفر الى ما وصلنا الية من نتائج هائلة .نسمي هؤلاء, وبكل اسف «اعداء النجاح» ولنضع تحت هذا المصطلح الف خط .
فالة اختص النجاح باصحابة الذى الذين ولهم لتسير الامر والصالح لعباده ,يضحون بأوقات فراغهم التى هى حق اصيل لعائلاتهم عليهم, فى

سبيل انجاز هدفهم وصولا للعدالة التى سهروا لاجلها الليالي الطويلة طوال ايام الاعتصام العظيم الذى جاءنا بنصر فى مثل عظمتة
وما كدنا نصل لتلك الفراجة بعد طول جهد لنيل المراد ,الاويخرج علينا اعداء النجاح اولئك ,يلوون الحقائق ويزيفون التاريخ ولا يرون فية الانجازات شخصية بعكس لغة الجماعة التى سادت اعتصامنا

وانجحتة.
لا يجب ان يتقدم ركبنا الا من يعمل لاجل الجماعة ,مثلا نحتذى بة ونعلمهن لقيادة
وما الحياة الا صراع بين النجاح واعدائة ولا زال اللة فى عون العبد مادام العبد فى عون اخية

نوال عبد الرازق عبد العزيز
مديرية الضرائب العقارية بالدقهلية

ثـــمــار الـقــوة

أن الإيمان بالله عز وجل ورسوله وكتبه وشريعته هو السبيل الأقوم للحفاظ على هذه القوة بكل معانيها. لذلك يجب ان تكون قوتنا هي الوسيلة التي يجب ان نحافظ عليها من أي عمل خارجي وأن التعاون يجب أن يكون هو الركيزة الأولي لإنشاء هذه النقابة المستقلة.
ويشهد الوقت الحاضر تطورات هائلة ومذهلة في جميع مجالات الحياة صغيرها وكبيرها لذا يجب أن نحافظ على قوة هذه النقابة. والطريق يبدأ بخطوة. وخطوتنا القادمة يجب أن تكون التخطيط الجيد لهذه النقابة حتي تصبح نقابة قوية مستقلة

ويسود اعتقاد بالأمل في بناء جديد وطريقة عمل نقابية جديدة يكون أهم ثمارها هو التواصل الحقيقي بين الجسم النقابي ممثلين للعمال و أعضاء النقابة بحيث يعود في النهاية بعمل عظيم و متواصل بلمسه الموظفين من القضاء علي مشاكلهم و معاناتهم و تقديم خدمات محسوسة و نشاط دؤوب يصب في النهاية في دفع عجلة التنمية و في صالح العمال والموظفين. وفي النهاية نأمل أن تتكاتف الجمع لحماية هذه النقابة.

حسين قرني أحمد
محافظة بني سويف مركز ببا

نوبة سويلن

ما هو الإتحاد الدولى لعمال الخدمات؟

شرعيتـنا و شرعيـتـهم

يثير انضمام نقابة الضرائب العقارية ـ بالتأكيد ـ الى الاتحاد الدولي لعمال الخدمات التساؤلات حول ماهية الاتحاد وماهو دوره وكل ما يتعلق به. ولن لا يعلم نوجز الحديث حول هذا الاتحاد والتعريف به فى كلمات قليلة ولكنها مهمة ليدرك الجميع أهمية ما استطاعوا أن يحققوه فى كفاحهم للخروج بنقابتهم ككيان قوى.

والاتحاد الدولي لعمال الخدمات هو اتحاد لنقابات القطاع العام ويضم نحو ٦٥٠ نقابة واتحاد فى ١٥٠ دولة ويصل أعضاؤه من العمال نحو ٢٠ مليون عامل على مستوى العالم من العاملين فى قطاعات متعددة مثل عمال القطاع العام والخدمات الصحية والاجتماعية وعمال البلديات والخدمات المجتمعية ـ ذات الصلة بخدمة الجمهور ـ العاملون فى خدمات المرافق العامة ببلادهم.

وقد وضع الاتحاد الدولى للخدمات منذ تأسيسه عام ١٩٠٧ مصالح العمال والموظفين فى أهم أولوياته حيث يقوم عادة بتنسيق الخطوات الكفاحية للعمال لضمان حصولهم على حقوقهم وتوفير العدالة الاقتصادية والاجتماعية لهم. وكذلك العمل على توفير الخدمات العامة لهم بشكل كاف ومتكافىء.

ويعرض الاتحاد الدولى لعمال الخدمات قضايا عمال القطاع العام أمام العديد من المؤسسات والهيئات والمنظمات الدولية مثل منظمة العمل الدولية وغيرها من هيئات الأمم المتحدة والبنك الدولي. وصندوق النقد الدولي. ومنظمة التجارة العالمية ، ومنظمة التعاون الاقتصادي والتنمية وغيرها.

كما يعمل الاتحاد الدولى لعمال الخدمات مع العديد من المنظمات المعنية للدفاع عن حقوق العمال وتوفير مطالبهم بما فى ذلك حرية الانضمام الى الاتحاد. والمفاوضة الجماعية وغيرها من الحقوق بما فيها المساواة بين

الجنسين والتكافؤ بينهم. الى جانب عمله بشكل وثيق مع الاتحاد الدولي للنقابات الحرة وغيرها من الاتحادات النقابية. وخاصة المنظمة الدولية للتعليم والاتحاد الأوروبي لعمال الخدمات العامة.

ويعمل الاتحاد أيضا على توفير الحملات المنظمة من أجل الارتقاء بمستوى الخدمات العامة. وهو ما يتحقق عن طريق العمل بشكل وثيق مع المنظمات الدولية والحكومات وجماعات حماية المستهلكين والمنظمات المجتمعية والمنظمات غير الحكومية. إضافة الى توفير الفرص للتدريب الذي يعمل فى مجال بناء القدرات على أرض الواقع. وخاصة فى البلدان التي توجد فيها نقابات يناضل العاملون فيها من أجل الاعتراف بهم.

وقد وضع الاتحاد عدد من الأهداف العامة والتى يتمسك بها ويدافع عنها سعيا لتحقيقها وهى :

- خدمات عامة مناسبة ومحترمة للجميع.

- حق تكوين الاتحادات والنقابات لجميع العاملين فى الخدمة العامة.

- المساواة بين الجنسين والمساواة فى العمل للجميع.

- بدائل «عامة» لكل القطاعات الجماهيرية التى يتم خصخصتها.

- حركة نقابية قوية.

- العدالة الاجتماعية فى مكان العمل.

- الحد من الفقر وتخفيف أعباء الديون.

ويضم الاتحاد الدول لعمال الخدمات فى صفوفه لجان للمرأة على المستويات المحلية والإقليمية والعالمية اضافة الى تواجد دائم للمرأة فى كل دوائر صنع القرار ايمانا من الاتحاد بمبدأ المساواة بين الجنسين.

الاتحاد الدولي لعمال الخدمات اعتبر نقابتكم إضافة للحركة النقابية العالمية فيما رفض قبول الاتحاد الرسمى بعد أن اتهمهم بافتقار الديمقراطية و الشفافية و الاستقلال.

فى الرابع والعشرين من أبريل ٢٠٠٩ كانت الضرائب العقارية على موعد جديد مع يوم من أيامها. ففي هذا اليوم قرر المكتب التنفيذي للاتحاد الدولي لعمال الخدمات قبول عضوية النقابة المستقلة للعاملين بالضرائب العقارية تصبح النقابة عضوا رسميا فى أسرة تضم ٢٠ مليون عامل في شتى أنحاء العالم. لم نكن نسعى بطلب العضوية الذي تقدمنا به إلى اكتساب شرعية أو اعتراف من أحد فشرعيتنا قد انتزعناها من قبل عبر نضالنا على أسفلت شارع حسين حجازي والاعتراف الذي نعتد به هو اعتراف زملائنا وجمعيتنا العمومية. كنا نسعى بطلب العضوية الذي تقدمنا به لأن يأخذ موظفو الضرائب العقارية المناضلون ونقاباتهم المستقلة مكانهم الطبيعي في الحركة النقابية العالمية كنقابة تأسست بإرادة العاملين وليس بقرار من أعلى. لقد تعودنا مع بعضنا البعض دائما علي أعلى درجات الشفافية والصراحة. لذا وجب علينا اليوم أن نتقدم بتقرير تفصيلي عن عضويتنا فى الاتحاد الدولي لعمال الخدمات.

لقد انعقد المؤتمر التأسيسي للنقابة المستقلة فى ٢٠ ديسمبر ٢٠٠٨ فى نقابة الصحفيين واختار لجنة تأسيسية

وكلفها بإتمام إجراءات التأسيس وعمل ما تراه مناسبا من أجل إعلان النقابة في حدود ما كلفت به من قبل جمعيتها العمومية. بما في ذلك السعي للانضمام لاتحادات عمالية محلية واقليمية ودولية تتوافر فيها مبادئ الديموقراطية والشفافية والاستقلال. وقررت اللجنة بناء على هذا التفويض السعي لنيل عضوية الاتحاد الدولي للخدمات واتخذ قرار اللجنة بالإجماع في الاجتماع التالي على انعقاد المؤتمر. وتقدمت اللجنة بالطلب للإتحاد الدولي الذي تلقاها بالترحاب والحفاوة ووافق المكتب العربي والمكتب الإفريقي على طلب العضوية حتى وصل الطلب للمكتب التنفيذي الذي وافق على الطلب بحفاوة واعتبر النقابة المستقلة للضرائب العقارية إضافة للحركة النقابية العالمية. إن النقابة المستقلة لموظفي الضرائب العقارية التي تشكلت بكفاح وصمود أعضائها قد أصبحت اليوم جزءا لا يتجزأ من الحركة النقابية العالمية لقد كسبنا بصمودنا ووحدتنا.

ونحن ٥٠ ألف موظف وموظفة اليوم توحدنا مع ٢٠ مليون من عمال العالم. لقد رفض الاتحاد الدولي للعمال طلب اتحاد نقابات عمال مصر للعضوية لأنه يفتقر للديموقراطية و الشفافية والاستقلال وكانت هذه نفس الأسباب التي رفضنا الانضمام اتحاد العمال الحكومي من أجلها وبعد عضويتنا في الاتحاد الدولي للخدمات عرف كل عمال مصر من هم ممثلو العمال الحقيقيون.

ثورة صبيان　مايو ٢٠٠٦　١٩

نقابه العاملين بالضرائب العقارية
التشكيل النقابي

انتخب أعضاء سكرتارية المحافظات المفوضين من الجمعية العمومية أعضاء الهيئة العامة للنقابة (السكرتارية العامة) الآتي أسماؤهم:

١- كمال محمد رفاعي أبو عيطة.
٢- مديحه مرسي حامد.
٣- عبد القادر ندا.
٤- أحمد أبو اليزيد الشافعي.
٥- أحمد رجب علي عبد الكريم.
٦- أحمد عبد الصبور محمد إبراهيم.
٧- أحمد محمود الرصيص.
٨- أسامة عبد الحفيظ الكومي.
٩- أمرة السيد قطه.
١٠- جمال محمود عويضه.
١١- حسن علي جمعة.
١٢- حسين كيلاني محمد.
١٣- خالد أمبارك السيد.
١٤- خلف السيد مصطفى عطية.
١٥- السيد منصور جاد.
١٦- صلاح صفوت محمد.
١٧- طارق مصطفى عبد الفتاح.
١٨- طنطاوي شحاتة رجب.
١٩- عبد الناصر سيد منصور.
٢٠- عزت خالد حسين.
٢١- فؤاد حلمي بدوي.
٢٢- محمد جهاد قشقوش.
٢٣- محمد عبد الحي محمد.
٢٤- محمد عبد القادر البدري.
٢٥- محمد علي عبد الله كاسب.
٢٦- مصطفى حامد محمد.
٢٧- يحي أحمد قطب.
٢٨- إيمان أحمد موسى.
٢٩- عزيزة رشاد.
٣٠- فادية شوقي.
٣١- أحمد محمد مختار محمود.
٣٢- فاطمة النبوية.
٣٣- كريمة جمعة حنفي.
٣٤- منى أنيس.
٣٥- جمال الصادق.
٣٦- ميرفت قاسم جلال.
٣٧- نجوى عبد الحفيظ محمد.
٣٨- صلاح عبد السلام.
٣٩- محمد سالم محمد.
٤٠- هناء ذكي.
٤١- هويدا سمير مكين.
٤٢- محمود حسن عامر.
٤٣- دلال محمد السيد.

محافظة الشرقية -عضويه ١٨٧٣-
سكرتارية المحافظة:
١- أحمد عبد الصبور محمد إبراهيم

(أبو كبير)
٢- أحمد السيد أحمد عبد العال (كفر صقر)
٣- البهنساوي عبد الحميد (فاقوس)
٤- جمال حسن عبد العال (القنايات)
٥- حسام الدين محمد علي (هيهيا)
٦- حسن محمد حسين (الحسينية)
٧- السعيد أحمد عبد الرحمن (ديرب نجم)
٨- سميح إبراهيم محمد (الإبراهيمية)
٩- طه راشد (أولاد صقر)
١٠- عبد الرازق محمد عبد السلام (أبو كبير)
١١- عبد الرحمن محمود الجمل (الحسينية)
١٢- عبد الناصر عبد الحميد عطية (المديرية)
١٣- علوان أحمد عثمان (منيا القمح)
١٤- عماد محمود إبراهيم (بلبيس)
١٥- محمود محمد عبد الحميد (بلبيس)
١٦- ماجدة حسن جمعة (المديرية)
١٧- محمد الهادي حلمي (ديرب نجم)
١٨- محمد جودة أحمد موسى (كفر صقر)
١٩- محمد محمد عبد العليم (الحسينية)
٢٠- مراد عبد الكريم حسين (فاقوس)
٢١- هشام سلامة الهوبي (المديرية)

محافظة القاهرة -العضوية ٢٤٥،-
سكرتارية المحافظة:

١- أحمد هنداوي خليفة م- بولاق
٢- أشرف أبو اليزيد إبراهيم م- روض الفرج
٣- إمام فوزي إمام م- ملاهي القاهرة
٤- أمل عبد العال محمد م- متنوعة غرب
٥- إيمان أحمد موسى دار السلام والبساتين
٦- أيمن عبد العزيز إبراهيم م- متنوعة جنوب
٧- بخيت عباس عوض عين شمس
٨- جمال محمد عبد الله مصر القديمة
٩- حسن محمد حسان الوايلي
١٠- خالد حسين السيد الساحل
١١- خالد سعد مرزوق الزاوية
١٢- خالد عبد التواب مصر الجديدة
١٣- سامح عبد الفتاح خليفة م- مدينة نصر شرق
١٤- سعيد عبد المحسن عطية م- غرب أول
١٥- سعيد محمد إبراهيم م- المطرية
١٦- سيد عبد العزيز رشوان متنوعة شرق
١٧- شعبان عبد العزيز طلبه م- مدينة نصر غرب
١٩- صبري مسعد مكي الشرابية
٢٠- صلاح الدين محمد أبو المعاطي المديرية
٢١- صلاح الدين محمد عبد المعطي الموسكي
٢٢- عادل ذكي بشارة حدائق القبة
٢٣- عبد الجليل حسن عبد الجليل الشرابية
٢٤- عطا الله عبد عطا الله وسط القاهرة
٢٥- علي عبد الواحد علي المرج
٢٦- فتحية السيد عيمي م- الحجز والتحصيل
٢٧- ماجدة نبيه فهمي متنوعة شمال
٢٨- محمد رجائي رشاد السيدة زينب
٢٩- محمد سيد محمد بكر السلام
٣٠- محمد عبد الحليم عبد الهادي خفاجي الخليفة والقطم
٣١- محمد عطية ذكي النزهة
٣٢- محمد مسلم الشاطر باب الشعرية
٣٣- محمود عبد العزيز علي الأطيان
٣٤- مديحه مرسي حامد المديرية
٣٥- منى محمد علم رمضان م- شبرا

محافظة ٦ أكتوبر-عضوية ٣٤٢-
سكرتارية المحافظة:
١- أدهم شعبان طلبه منشأة القناطر
٢- أكرامي وهبة محمد أوسيه
٣- خالد إبراهيم سيد الحوامديه
٤- رضا عفيف محمد البدرشين
٥- طه فتحي محمد ذكي العياط
٦- عادل فرج النمر البدرشين
٧- عماد يوسف عواد أوسيم
٨- محمد علي عبد الله عبد القادر كاسب الحوامديه
٩- ناصر بيومي محمود أبو النمرس
١٠-هويدا سمير مكين مأمورية ٦ أكتوبر
١١- هيثم محمود عبد القادر الواحات البحرية

محافظة الإسكندرية -العضوية ٧٧-
سكرتارية المحافظة:
١- أحمد رجب احمد محروس العامرية
٢- أحمد محمد متولي نصر برج العرب
٣- أسامة عبد الحفيظ الكومي مأمورية شرق
٤- أيمن محمد عبد اللطيف مأمورية شرق
٥- حسام الدين حافظ مأمورية شرق

ثورة صبيان

٦- سهام خليل إبراهيم علام مأمورية وسط
٧- السيد محمد السيد محمود مأمورية الجمرك
٨- عادل عبد الواحد محمد مأمورية العامرية
٩- فاطمة أحمد السيد مأمورية المنتزة
١٠- محمد علاء الدين موسي مأمورية وسط
١١- ممدوح مرسي عليوة مأمورية غرب
١٢- ميرفت محمد محمد حسن مأمورية العامرية
١٣- ناديه محروس جيد مأمورية غرب

محافظة كفر الشيخ -العضوية ١٤٢-

سكرتارية المحافظة :-

١- السيد منصور جاد السيد.
٢- محمد حسين السيد.
٣- محمد أحمد رشدي.
٤- السيد بيومي على منصور.
٥- الباز محمد الباز.
٦- عماد على محمد.
٧- مظهر محمد حجازي.
٨- ماجدة مصطفى محمد.
٩- محمد إسماعيل جابر.
١٠- علاء أحمد عبد العظيم.
١١- محمد السيد عبد الفتاح.
١٢- أحمد عيد أحمد.
١٣- الشحات أحمد عبد الرحمن.
١٤- عبد المحسن أبو شعيشع.

محافظة حلوان -عضوية ٣٣٤-

سكرتارية المحافظة : -

١- أحمد نفاد أحمد حسين مأمورية الصف
٢- بكار محمد عبد الغنى مصطفى مأمورية أطفيح
٣- حسن شحاتة أحمد جاد مأمورية الصف
٤- حمدي طه شلبي علواني مأمورية الصف
٥- خالد مصطفى ذكي مأمورية أطفيح
٦- سيد يوسف سيد سالم مأمورية أطفيح
٧- فوزي إبراهيم الجوهري مأمورية حلوان
٨- كمال محمد رفاعي مأمورية حلوان
٩- مبروك مبروك خليفة مأمورية أطفيح
١٠- محمد عبد القادر البدري مأمورية حلوان
١١- نور الدين مصطفى علوان مأمورية ١٥ مايو
١٢- هشام محمد عبد الحميد مأمورية المعادي
١٣- وهبي الدسوقي محمد مأمورية التبيين

محافظة قنا

انتخبت أعضاء الجمعية العمومية لنقابة العاملين بالضرائب العقارية في محافظة قنا سكرتارية المحافظة الآتي:

عضويه ١٣٤٧

١- أحمد حسن محمود عبد الغفار المديرية
٢- أحمد شوقي عبد الحميد فرشوط
٣- أحمد محمد إبراهيم أسنا
٤- أحمد محمد أحمد حسين قنا- مال
٥- أحمد يوسف منولي قنا- عوائد
٦- إسماعيل إبراهيم حامد فقط
٧- أشرف مبارك أبو المجد قنا- مال
٨- حسن سليمان حسن المديرية
٩- حسن مصطفى محمد عابدين أبو تشت
١٠- سعيد ناشد حكيم أرمنت
١١- صبري محمد عبد ربه نقاده
١٢- عادل بدوى محمود فقط
١٣- عيد محمد أحمد أبو المجد أرمنت
١٤- عبد القادر محمد أحمد أبو زيد دشنا
١٥- عزت خالد حسين عبد الرحيم أبو تشت
١٦- عصام فخري أحمد نجع حمادي
١٧- عصام محمد على أحمد توحي
١٨- على عبد الشافي حسن نقادة
١٩- على كحول على موسي دشنا
٢٠- محمد عبد المنعم محمد أسنا
٢١- محمود ريان حسين نجع حمادي
٢٢- محمود محمد الأمير قنا - عوائد
٢٣ - محمود محمد على إبراهيم توحي
٢٤- مشرف محمد عبد اللطيف أبو تشت
٢٥- نجاح عبد العاطى حسين فرشوط

محافظة أسيوط -عدد العضوية ٢٣٥٢-

سكرتارية المحافظة : -

١- أحمد محمد أحمد الفتح
٢- حسنى صلاح محمد أحمد حسن ديروط
٣- حسين كيلاني محمد كيلاني المديرية
٤- رجب حسين عبد اللّه منفلوط
٥- رمضان محمد حسين أطيان أسيوط
٦- سيد عبيد سيد ساحل سليم
٧- سيد عوض سيد عوائد أسيوط
٨- على حماد حسانين صدفا
٩- محمود أحمد إدريس الغنايم
١٠- محمود أحمد حسانين مأمورية أسيوط
١١- محمود أحمد محمود أبوتيج
١٢- محمود عزت عبد الحليم البداري
١٣- مصطفى عمر أحمد عمر ديوان المديرية
١٤- نبيل مديح ميخائيل ديوان المديرية
١٥- ياسر بدري منصور أبنوب

محافظة شمال سيناء -عدد العضوية ١٦٢٣-

سكرتارية المحافظة : -

١- أحمد محمد عبد الحميد مزين رفح
٢- سليمان عطوه ناصر بئر العبد
٣- فؤاد حلمي بدوي المديرية
٤- كمال حمادة حسين المديرية
٥- محسن محمد عميش الشيخ زويد
٦- محمد سالم محمد سليمان بئر العبد
٧- محمد عبد المجيد أحمد العريش
٨- محمد محمد إبراهيم الشيخ زويد
٩- محمود عبد الكريم بكري العريش
١٠- مروان عبد العزيز مصطفى المديرية
١١- نضال أحمد حسن رفح

محافظة الغربية -عدد العضوية ١٦٢٣-

سكرتارية المحافظة : -

١- إبراهيم سعد محمود شبل.
٢- أحمد أبو اليزيد الشافعي.
٣- إسماعيل دسوقي الجمصي.
٤- حسن محمد حسن عيد.
٥- رضا النبوى نعمان.
٦- سعيد أحمد محمود بدوي.
٧- سهير محمد عوض.
٨- شعبان عبد النبي السواح.
٩- طارق أبو السعود حامد.
١٠- عبد الرحمن عبد الفتاح حتاتة.
١١- عبد العزيز حسن العطار.
١٢- عزت أحمد عبده الابشيهي.
١٣- فاطمة إبراهيم رمضان.
١٤- محسن السيد خليل سويدان.
١٥- محمد سليمان النحاس.
١٦- محمد شحاته محمد على.
١٧- محمد عبد الوهاب حسن سالم.

محافظة البحر الأحمر -عضويه ٤٣٧-

سكرتارية المحافظة : -

١- محمد عبد الحى محمد عمر لغردقة
٢- محسن على إسماعيل محمد لغردقة
٣- عثمان محمد محمد الغردقة
٤- آمال مصباح السحاوي الغردقة
٥- حمدى حسين صليح الغردقة
٦- محمود عبد الفتاح محمد الغردقة
٧- وهبي محمد إبراهيم أبو الحسن الغردقة
٨- أحمد محمود عباس القصير
٩- عبد الجبار خليل كحلي راس غارب
١٠- ممدوح عبد العزيز محمود القصير
١١- مرقص حليم اسطفينوس راس غارب
١٢- خالد على حسين سفاجا
١٣- عمر حسين محمد جاد المولى سفاجا

محافظة أسوان -عدد العضوية ٤٣٠-

سكرتارية المحافظة : -

١- أحمد محمود حسن السيالية
٢- بدري محمد فضل ادفو
٣- جلال الدين يوسف على المديرية
٤- خالد أمبارك حامد مأمورية أسوان
٥- زينب كامل محمد مأمورية أسوان
٦- سعد اللّه خبرة فاخورى ادفو

٧- سيد عبد الحميد النجار مأمورية أسوان
٨- على فراج على كوم امبو
٩- محمد أسامة حامد جاد كوم امبو
١٠- محمد الطاهر أبو دوح نراو
١١- احمد عبده عباس حمادة المديرية
١٢- محمد مصطفى كمال موسى دراو
١٣- محمود حسين أحمد حسين السباعية

محافظة المنيا -العضوية ١٤٤٣-
سكرتارية المحافظة : -
١- أحمد عبد العزيز محمد ديرمواس - المنيا
٢- ثروت محمد مجاهد أطيان- المنيا
٣- حسن على أحمد أطيان- العدوة
٤- حمدى إدريس على ديرمواس
٥- خالد محمد على منصور مغاغة
٦- حسن على حسن أحمد العدوه
٧- صديق حسين محمد المديرية
٨- عادل لطفى عبد الجواد أطيان- مغاغة
٩- عبد الرحمن أحمد الدردير بنى مزار
١٠- عطية محمود سيد سمالوط
١١- على ثروت عيد لطفى ملوى
١٢- ماهر بشرى نخله أطيان- مطاى
١٣- محسن عبد الرازق حسن عوائد- سمالوط
١٤- محمد حسن محمد المندى عوائد- المنيا
١٥- محمد خلف على مبانى- ملوى
١٦- محمد سعد صالح المديرية
١٧- محمد عبد الحليم محمد عوائد - مطاى
١٨- محمد على محمد حماد أطيان- أبو قرقاص
١٩- محمود حسن عثمان المديرية
٢٠- ناصر محمد على عوائد- بنى مزار
٢١- وائل محمود حميدة مأمورية- أبو قرقاص

لأقصر -عدد العضوية ٢٢٦-
السكرتارية : -
١- أحمد كمال بسطاوى الوحدة الحسابية
٢- جبريل أحمد كامل الحاسب الآلى
٣- لنططاوى شحاتة حسن مأمورية

السياحة
٤- عبدو موسى محمدين الوحدة الحسابية
٥- فليب فكرى ناشد المديرية
٦- منصور محمود همام المديرية
٧- يحيى هاشم يوسف مأمورية السياحة

محافظة المنوفية -عدد العضوية ١٧٤٩-
سكرتارية المحافظة : -
١- أشرف إبراهيم الدسوقى مأمورية قويسنا
٢- أمانى السيد إبراهيم إدارة التفتيش
٣- أيمن على سيد أحمد السادات
٤- حسين محمد إبراهيم بركة الصبع
٥- خالد عبد الرؤوف زهرة ثلا
٦- رشدى غانم دياب سرس الليان
٧- رفعت عبد الجليل فرج الباجور
٨- سيد محمد شوبك شبين الكوم المديرية
٩- سعيد السيد فرج إدارة التفتيش عوائد- شبين الكوم
١٠- صلاح عبد الحميد محمد بكر عوائد- شبين الكوم
١١- عبد الله فتحى عبد الله المديرية
١٢- عبد المرضى محمد العجمى منوف
١٣- عبد الهادى محمد خلف أشمون
١٤- على حسن على الغباشى الشهداء
١٥- محمد جهاد قشقوش عوائد شبين
١٦- محمد عبد الحميد الصاوى إدارة التفتيش
١٧- محمود حسن عامر عوائد شبين
١٨- مرفت مصطفى سويلم المديرية
١٩- هشام نزيه محمد الجمال مال شبين الكوم

محافظة السويس -عدد العضوية ٤٣٤-
سكرتارية المحافظة : -
١- أسامة خليفة حسن مأمورية السويس
٢- أمرد السيد قط مأمورية السويس
٣- سليم أبو القاسم محمد الأربعين

٤- سيد كامل خضر الأربعين
٥- صلاح على محمد الأربعين
٦- عادل كامل خضير الأربعين
٧- كوثر أحمد سعيد مأمورية السويس
٨- محمد الحسينى أحمد مأمورية السويس
٩- محمد محفوظ محمد بور توفيق

محافظة بنى سويف -عدد العضوية ١٥٦٣-
سكرتارية المحافظة : -
١- أحمد محمد فرج حسين مأمورية العوائد
٢- بركات حسن حسين مأمورية الفشن
٣- سيد فرغلى إبراهيم بركة ناصر
٤- عبد الناصر سيد منصور ببا
٥- عبد الناصر عبد الله عبد العزيز المديرية
٦- عمر فهمى أبو الحسن أهناسيا
٧- كمال ماهر عبد العظيم سمسطا
٨- محمد عبد الوهاب طلب مأمورية المال
٩- محمد صلاح محمد موسى المديرية
١٠- مختار أبو العلا فكرى الواسطى
١١- وحيد صوفى محمد المديرية

محافظة مرسى مطروح -عدد العضوية ١١٧-
سكرتارية المحافظة : -
١- إبراهيم رحوق مهلوم النحيلة
٢- أحمد محمود الرصيص مرسى مطروح
٣- رجب حمدان هاشم السلوم
٤- سهير أحمد الرفاعى الحمام
٥- سمير سعد إبراهيم العلمين
٦- صادق صادق عبد الرازق مأمورية مطروح
٧- صبرى عبد اللطيف عبد الله سيدى برانى
٨- عبد المؤمن شعبان أبو زهرة المديرية
٩- محمد عبد الحسن أبو علام سيوه
١٠- محمد حسنى البدوى المديرية
١١- وليد السيد مصطفى عبده

الضبعة
محافظة دمياط -عدد العضوية ٦١٨-
سكرتارية المحافظة : -
١- أحمد عبد العزيز على مأمورية كفر سعد
٢- أشرف فتحى توفيق محمد مأمورية الزرقا
٣- الباز الباز أبو العز المديرية
٤- جمال إبراهيم غازى مأمورية كفر سعد
٥- حسن أحمد عبده حسن مأمورية مركز دمياط
٦- حنان محمد طه زعتر المديرية
٧- رياض عرفه السعيد مأمورية كفر البطيخ
٨- سامية إبراهيم السعيد مأمورية ثان
٩- سعد السيد عبد السلام مأمورية كفر سكور
١٠- سليم حامد هجرس مأمورية كفر البطيخ
١١- السيد أحمد عبد حسن المركز
١٢- شاهيناز أنور أبو الحسن مأمورية المركز
١٣- صلاح صفوت مجاهد مأمورية الزرقا
١٤- طلبه محمود إبراهيم المديرية
١٥- عبد الحليم محمد عبده مأمورية الزرقا
١٦- محمد محمد إبراهيم خليل مأمورية فارسكور
١٧- محمود طاهر أبو على مأمورية أول

محافظة سوهاج -عدد العضوية ٢٠٦٠-
سكرتارية المحافظة : -
١- أحمد محمد هريدى عبد الآخر مأمورية عوائد أول
٢- إسماعيل محمد عبد العال مأمورية المنشأة
٣- إمام راغب على مأمورية البلينا
٤- حمادة عباس على مأمورية دار السلام
٥- خلف السيد مصطفى عطية مأمورية طما

٦- رشاد أحمد حسين المديرية
٧- سمير نصحي شحاتة مأمورية أخميم
٨- السيد محمود عقل مأمورية طهطا
٩- السيد مختار سيد أحمد الجهينه
١٠- صلاح عبد القادر خليفة مأمورية مركز سوهاج
١١- صبري سعد محمود صديق مأمورية ساقلته
١٢- عاطف مصطفى كامل المديرية
١٣- عبد الحميد السيد أحمد المديرية
١٤- عبد الفتاح السيد جاد المديرية
١٥- عزت عبد الباسط بندر جرجا
١٦- محمد عبد الله أحمد ساقلته
١٧- محمد فؤاد محمد علي المديرية
١٨- محمد فكري أبو زيد المراغة
١٩- محمود محمد السيد الكاشف طهطا

محافظة البحيرة -عدد العضوية ١٣٠٠-
سكرتارية المحافظة : -
١- أحمد رجب عبد الكريم.
٢- عبده عبد العزيز سعد شبل.
٣- وجيه محمود عبد العزيز.
٤- الروماني وصفي أيوب.
٥- صلاح زكريا عبد الفتاح.
٦- فتحي عبد الله هيبه.
٧- سيد إسماعيل شحاتة.
٨- صبري عطا الله عبد الكريم.
٩- وحيد حلمي المحلاوي.
١٠- زكريا عبد الفضيل عبد الهادي.
١١- أشرف عبد العزيز جاد.
١٢- محمد حامد درويش.
١٣- عاطف كمال عبد الله.
١٤- عبد المنعم محمود منصور.
١٥- مصطفى عبد الجواد الطنيفي.
١٦- ساهر محمد منير خطاب.
١٧- رمزي شعبان عبد العظيم.
١٨- علي عبد الهادي حسن.
١٩- محمد عبد المنعم أمين حجاج.

محافظة الدقهلية -عدد العضوية ٢٣٠٨-
سكرتارية المحافظة : :-
١- أحمد عوض محمود إبراهيم مأمورية بني عبيد
٢- بكر عوض السيد المهدي مأمورية الحمودية
٣- جمال شعبان أبو صالح مأمورية دكرنس
٤- جمال محمود عويضه المديرية
٥- الحسيني يوسف السيد مأمورية أجا
٦- حمدي الشربيني سليمان مأمورية بلقاس
٧- سراج الدين الأحمدي محمد مأمورية الأمديد
٨- صلاح محمد عبد السلام مأمورية ميت سلسيل
٩- عادل راضي شتا بدوي المنزلة
١٠- عبد الغني السيد عباس المديرية
١١- عبد المولي أبو الخير عبد الفتاح السنبلاوين
١٢- عماد السعيد حسين المديرية
١٣- فتحي علي عز الدين منيه النصر
١٤- فرج محمد الهواش شربين
١٥- المتولي التولي خضر حمصه
١٦- محمد صابر السيد المطرية
١٧- محمد عبد العزيز حسن حي غرب
١٨- محمد منصور معروف الجمالية
١٩- محمود سعد الطناحي طلخا
٢٠- ممدوح محي الدين الشامي المديرية
٢١- موسى أحمد موسى بندر السنبلاوين
٢٢- نجلاء فتحي عبد العزيز مركز المنصورة
٢٣- نوال عبد الرازق عبد العزيز المديرية
٢٤- وائل إبراهيم محمود مأمورية حي شرق
٢٥- ويده نور الدين خليل المديرية

محافظة الجيزة -عدد العضوية ٧٣٤-
سكرتارية المحافظة : -
١- أحمد محمد مختار محمود مركز المعلومات
٢- أسامة عبد العاطي أحمد امبابه ثان
٣- حجازي عبد التواب هرم أول
٤- حسن محمود سليمان بولاق
٥- خالد عبد القادر المديرية
٦- خلف الله أحمد حسن العمرانية
٧- رمضان عبد الغني صادق الوراق
٨- سليمان ربيع عبد الجواد مركز المعلومات
٩- عبد الباسط أحمد حافظ امبابه أول
١٠- عبد الحميد محمد عقل الوراق أول
١١- عبد القادر محمد الطاهر ندا الوراق
١٢- كريمة جمعه حنفي المديرية
١٣- مجاهد عبد الرحمن مجاهد هرم أول
١٤- مرعي يونس مرعي مأمورية الجيزة
١٥- مرفت قاسم هلال الوراق
١٦- وائل عبد الحميد محمود العجوزة
١٧- ياسر وحيد مصطفى المديرية

محافظة الفيوم -عدد العضوية ٤٠٥-
سكرتارية المحافظة : -
١- بكري فاضل بكري مأمورية يوسف الصديق
٢- حسين محمد الشيمي مأمورية أبشواي
٣- خالد السيد سلطان مأمورية بندر ثاني الفيوم
٤- خالد محمد زكري مأمورية طامية البندر
٥- صلاح عبد الغني الفيوم أول
٦- علي فاروق إبراهيم بندر أول الفيوم
٧- عويس محمود أحمد المديرية
٨- قرني عبد الجليل عثمان الفيوم أول
٩- مجدي السيد محمود المديرية
١٠- محمد أبو الفتوح محمد مأمورية سنورس
١١- محمد عبد الوهاب الجبجي سنورس
١٢- محمد مصطفى سيد الفيوم أول
١٣- محمود سيد الراعي طامية
١٤- مصطفى عبد العال أحمد أبشواي
١٥- نور أحمد مسعود إطسا
١٦- ممدوح بشر أحمد إطسا
١٧- يحي أحمد قطب المديرية

محافظة القليوبية -عدد العضوية ٨٤١-
سكرتارية المحافظة :-
١- إبراهيم رمضان مرسي قها
٢- إبراهيم محمود إبراهيم الخصوص
٣- أبو الريش أحمد علي الخانكة
٤- أحمد محمد عوض القناطر
٥- جيهان مصطفى أحمد عوايد بنها
٦- حسام الدين أحمد عبد الحليم المديرية
٧- حسن محمد محمود قليوب
٨- سامي حلمي إبراهيم طوخ
٩- السيد محمد سالم الخصوص
١٠- طارق مصطفى عبد الفتاح المديرية
١١- عبد الفتاح السيد عبد القاطر
١٢- محمد زكريا شبرا الخيمة
١٣- محمد زكريا سليمان كفر شكر
١٤- محمد عبد الحميد عبد اللطيف كفر شكر
١٥- محمود إسماعيل محمود بنها
١٦- نجوى عبد الحفيظ محمد المديرية
١٧- ولاء محمد السيد بهتيم

محافظة الإسماعيلية -عدد العضوية ٩٨٧-
سكرتارية المحافظة : -
١- أحمد صادق أحمد.
٢- أحمد فاضل محمود حسن.
٣- أشرف كامل محمد.
٤- خالد يوسف محمد.
٥- سعد الدين يوسف قاسم.
٦- سعيد عبد الله محمد.
٧- السيد حسان علي.
٨- عادل سليم حسن.
٩- عبد الرحمن عبد الرازق رضوان.
١٠- عربي حامد ذكي.
١١- علي سليمان علي.
١٢- علي مصطفى عبد الله.
١٣- عماد فتحي الكاشف.
١٤- ماجد أحمد الشيخ.
١٥- ماجد علي السيد.
١٦- محمد عبد الغني عطية.
١٧- محمد فتحي عبد القوي.
١٨- محمد مصطفى كمال.
١٩- محمد مصطفى عبد الراضي.
٢٠- مريم عبد النور غبريال.
٢١- مصطفى حامد محمد.

ثورة صديان ٢٠٠٩ ١١

أول نقابة مستقلة في مصر تضع نظامها الأساسي

يجري العمل في ظل النظام المعمول به في قانون النقابات العمالية رقم ٣٥لـــــ٧٦ على أن يضع الاتحاد العام للعمال نظاما نموذجيا للمنظمات النقابية المختلفة تتخذه هذه المنظمات أساسا لوضع نظمها الأساسية وتلتزم بالهيكل العام الموضوع فيها..ثم تصدر هذه اللوائح بقرار من الوزير المختص (وزير القوى العاملة. بما يعني ذلك من أن اللوائح الداخلية لهذه المنظمات قد تمت مناقشتها وإقرارها بعيدا ويمعزل عن المخاطبين بأحكامها عن العاملين أعضاء تلك النقابات أصحاب المصلحة المباشرة من إنشاء تلك النقابات وأصحاب الحق الأصيل في وضع النظام الأساسي الذي يرتضونه لنقابتهم. فالقانون ١٥ سم مناقشته وإقراره بمجلس الشعب دون أن يعرض عليهم. ولم تشير مواد إصداره -حتى - إلى اشتراك اتحاد العمال في إقراره. ولأن نقابة العاملين بالضرائب العقارية لم تقبل. ولم يكن بإمكانها أن تؤسس لعدل نقابي حقيقي مستقل. ويعبر عن إرادة العاملين ومدافع عن مصالحهم. أن تعتمد هذا القانون أو هذا النظام مرجعيتها. لكون هذا القانون وذلك النظام متناقضا أولا .مع مبادئ الحرية النقابية وقواعد الديمقراطية العمالية التي ارتضتها لها الجمعية العمومية للنقابة ومخالفة هذا القانون، وهذا التنظيم النقابي لمبادئ الدستور

المصري ومقتضيات الاستقلال النقابي - في طريقة آلية ممارسة الديمقراطية الداخلية عند مناقشتهم لائحة النظام الأساسي. التي تمت مناقشتها مادة مادة. وفقرة فقرة..من قبل أعضاء الجمعية العمومية للنقابة. والذين أظهروا ممارسة ديمقراطية حقيقية للعمل النقابي. ومعرفة قانونية وفهم واسع للمواثيق الدولية. فأكدوا وأقروا إنهم أي الجمعية العمومية للنقابة هم السلطة العليا التي تحدد السياسة العامة للنقابة.والتي تضع الخطط والبرامج وتنتخب جميع هيئات النقابة في المحافظات وعلى المستوى المركزي. وهم وحدهم أصحاب الحق في محاسبة هذه الهيئات. وسمي "٥٥ة منها.وأكدوا رفضهم للنظام المعمول به في النقابة

العامة للبنوك واللجان التابعة لها..حيث تباشر هذه النقابة ما وضعه لها الاتحاد العام من برامج وخطط وتلتزم بالحدود التي يرسمها لها..الرقابة من الهيئات الأعلى على الهيئات الأدنى فالاتحاد يراقب ويحاسب النقابات العامة والنقابات العامة التي تحاسب اللجان.. وذلك كله في غياب الطرف الأصيل وهو العمال عن ممارسة أي دور في مراقبة أو محاسبة تلك المستويات النقابية. واعتمدوا مبدأ توسيع المشاركة القاعدية في العمل النقابي ..وانعكس ذلك في لائحتهم التي توجب تمثيل كل مواقع العمل الإدارية في هيئات النقابة ..وتمثيل الوظائف النوعية كذلك حتى يكون التنظيم النقابي معبرا عن إرادة

أعضاؤه..وتأكيدا للمشاركة القاعدية. ومبدأ المراقبة من أسفل . قروا إنشاء مؤتمر يسمى مؤتمر المفوضين - يتم انتخابهم من مواقع العمل مباشرة لتمثيل الوظائف النوعية المختلفة.. بواقع ٢ أعضاء عن كل موقع في حوالي ٤٠٠ موقع عمل على مستوى الجمهورية يقوم هذا المؤتمر بمتابعة نشاط وهيئات النقابة ويطلب منها ويناقل إليها رغبات ومطالب العاملين في مواقع العمل المختلفة ويعقد مؤتمر سنوي قبل انعقاد الجمعية العمومية بشهرين..يتم خلاله مناقشة أحوال النقابة والعمل النقابي وأداء الهيئات النقابية ويرفع تقريره إلى اجتماع الجمعية العمومية السنوي. وحرصا منهم. على "٥.ة.ير الدوري.. وفي ز واختيار القيادات النقابية المنتخبة جعلوا مدة الدورة النقابية عامين. يتخللهما مؤتمر المفوضين واجتماع الجمعية العمومية بكل ما يعنيه ذلك من مراقبة دائمة من قواعد النقابة لهيئاتها ..

باختصار خرجت لائحة النظام الأساسي لنقابة العاملين بالضرائب العقارية..تعبيرا عن إرادة الأعضاء وخياراتهم وتعكس احتياجا مباشرا لمطالبهم وحاجاتهم الملحة.. وأعادوا العمل النقابي إلى أصله واضعين الأساس السليم لبناء النقابات المستقلة.

عاجل إلى وزير المالية

شكوى عاجلة الي معالي وزير المالية و السيد الأستاذ وكيل أول الوزارة و رئيس مصلحة الضرائب العقاري بالقاهرة

يتقدم جميع العاملين بمأمورية الضرائب العقارية بمياي و ملاهي ملوي بشكواهم:

أولا : من ضيق المأمورية حيث ان مقر المأمورية لا يتحمل كثرة الدفاتر و المكلفات بالجرائد من عام ١٩٧٩ حتي الآن رغم ان المأمورية تستعد للعمل بالقانون ١٩٦ لسنة ٢٠٨ و الذي سيوجب حضور جميع أصحاب العقارات بمدينة ملوي و ما يتبعها من قري لتقديم إقرارات ضريبة العقارات التابعة لهم و لا يوجد مكان للمواطنين من ضيق المكان حني استراحة لهم.

ثانيا : يأمل الموظفون النظر لهذا الموضوع خاصة ان المقر لا يوجد به سوي دورة مياه واحدة لا تصلح للاستعمال الأدمي رغم وجود موظفات حيث ان

مقر المأمورية هو شقة من شقق المساكن الشعبية التابعة لمجلس مدينة ملوي بالدور الأرضي و لسوء الصرف في هذه العمارة تكون الدورة بالمأمورية مهبا للروائح الكريهة و التي تسبب الإمراض الخطيرة للموظفين فنرجو من معاليكم التدخل الفوري من اجل حل هذه المشكلة الخطيرة حيث ان مواعيد العمل الرسمية تبدأ من الساعة الثامنة صباحا و تنتهي الساعة الرابعة مساء و هذه الفترة ستوجب استعمال دورات مياه لتكون صالحة للاستعمال الأدمي و ذلك خلاف الفئران و الثعابين و الصراصير المقيمة مع الموظفين بسبب الزراعة المجاورة .

جعلكم الله عونا للموظفين ووفقكم لما فيه الخير

عنهم : محمد خلف علي
اللجنة الفرعية لنقابة العاملين بالضرائب العقارية بملوي

نائب الشعب حمدين صباحي يكتب، عن: النقابة المستقلة

«أتخيل جموعا من المصلين يتوجهون بصلاتهم إلى القبلة الخاطئة ويداومون على صلواتهم المشكوك في صحتها سنوات وسنوات، وحده كمال أبو عيطة يرفع رأسه من سجود ويلتفت حوله ويدرك بيقين أن هذه القبلة خاطئة، ولكنه لا يجادل المصلين حول صحيح القبلة وصحيح الصلاة، في صمت يرفع سجادة الصلاة ويضعها في اتجاه القبلة الحق مستكملا صلاته في هدوء وخشوع وتواضع المؤمنين».

هذه فاتحة رسالة جعلتني أبكى فرحا، تلقيتها وأنا أكتب مقالي عن عبد العمال أحيى في انتصار الضرائب العقارية، وانتهاء الاستجداء على طريقة «المنحة يا ريس»، لصالح النضال الجاد من أجل «أجر عادل ونقابة مستقلة»، ولأخي لأخي كمال أبو عيطة عن بعض ما يليق به من تقدير مستحق، رسالة الدكتورة ماجدة غنيم تعبير عميق وصادق عن رؤية مصرية راقية الوعي والوجدان، قد لا تتطابق معي فيبعض التفاصيل لكنها جديرة بأن تكملوا قراءتها

«كنت أتحدث مع أحد المثقفين عن نقابة الضرائب العقارية فرد بخليط من الأسى والعطف والازدراء؛ لكنها حركة فئوية لا تحمل أهدافا سياسية واضحة.

هذا الموقف يوضح أصل الداء في معظم حركات المعارضة المصرية، فهي مثلها مثل الحكام لا تؤمن بالقاعدة، وتتصور أن التغيير لا يأتي إلا من أعلى، فترفع الشعارات الفوقية عن الدستور والتوريث والائتلافات والجمعيات الوطنية التي لا تأتي في أفضل الحوال إلا بتعديلات هامشية وممكنات.

«التغيير الحقيقي يبدأ من أسفل ضيقا في أهدافه، ثم يتسع

وينمو ويتقاطع في مساحات مشتركة، وتتسع الرؤى باتساع الدوائر، وتتبلور الأهداف باتساع الرؤى، حتى ينصهر الجميع في حركة واحدة ذات مطالب سياسية واضحة تمثل القاسم المشترك.

ورغم أن الحركات الاحتجاجية لم تتوقف طوال السنوات القليلة الماضية، إلا أن الضرائب العقارية تختلف جذريا في سعيها نحو تنظيم نفسها في شكل مؤسسي، وهو الفارق الحاسم.

• نقابة الضرائب العقارية هي أول نقابة مستقلة منذ أممت الدولة حق الجماهير في التنظيم المستقل ولهذا فهي شوكة في جنب النام، ولكن الغريب هو موقف المعارضة منها، فالمتتبع للجرائد المستقلة والمعارضة سيكتشف كم التجاهل والاهتمام الهزيل من باب ذر الرماد في العيون أو «برو العتب» الذي أبدته تجاههالتناول الإعلامي لها أبدا لم يعطها جزءا من ألف مما تستحقه، بل والأدعى للتعجب أن الاهتمام بها وتسليط الضوء عليها كان أقوى كثيرا حين كانت مجرد حركة احتجاجية وتضاءل كثيرا حين تحولت إلى نقابة مستقلة.

• هذا الموقف الذي يبدو غير مفهوم لأول وهلة يصبح منطقيا تماما بعد شئ من التمعن في مغزاه، فالحركات النقابية التي تتبنى مطالب الطبق العاملة هي المحك الفارق الذي سيضطر معه اليمين الإسلامي والليبرالي إلى الإفصاح عمليا عن موقفه الطبقي بلا مواربة أو مراوغة أو شعارات مزوعة المضمون الاجتماعي.

• أما المعارضة اليسارية والقومية بمختلف أطيافها فمن المفترض منطقيا أن تحتفي بالنقابة الوليدة وأن تتبنى الحركة والقائمين عليها بكل ما أوتيت من قوة أوضعف، غلا إذا تشكيل النقابة يواجهها بعجزها ويكشف طبيعة الحركة في المكان الذي أدمنته عبر عقود (وهو ما لا يتناقض مع نبل مقصد الكثيرين من تلك الحركة).

أكثر من ذلك فتشكيل النقابة المستقلة يمثل تحديا لها إذ يدعوها أن تودع أسلوب «نضال» بالكلمات لا تدفع لقاءه إلا بعض الاضطهاد الذي بدونه لا يستقيم السيناريو، و تتبنى إسلوب نضال بالأفعال ليس له سبيل سوى الالتحام بالجماهير و الإنصهار في كتلتهان وهو نضال لم

يعد أغلب المعارضين قادرين على تحمل وطأته ولا قابلين لدفع ثمنه الذي ولا شك سيكون فادحاً.

• إن موظف الضرائب العقارية شارك في الإضراب و ساهم في تأسيس أول نقابة مستقلة لن يساق بعد اليوم للتصويت في إنتخابات مزيفة ولن يشارك في مؤتمر هلامي مطالباً بالمنحة السنوية، ولن يطلب فتوى شرعية حول حقة في الإضراب و التنظيم. وموظفة الضرائب العقارية التي باتت لها على الرصيف مطالبة بحقها لن يمكن إقناعها بعد اليوم بأنها مواطنة ناقصة الأهلية و السيحيون و المسلمون الذين ضمهم نقابة ناضلوا من أجل إنشائها لن يتقاتلوا على الديانة الأفضل. هكذا يضرب الزلزال كل المباني امشوهة.

• تتجسد أمام عيني صورة تلاميذ أذكياء أصحاب منتهين مصطفين في فصل نظيف مشرق، في يوم ليس ببعيد، يدخل عليهم مدرس التاريخ ويكتب بخط واضح عنوان الدرس: أول نقابة حرة في مصر، تأسست في ٢٠٠٩، ثم يحكي للتلاميذ حكاية أبو عيطة وزملائه صانعي هذا التاريخ. فلا شك لدي أن هذه النقابة حتى لو أجهضت لا قدر الله، قد حجزت مكانها المرموق في صفحات تاريخ.

• حمدين صباحي كتب منذ عام يتساءل متى تعزف الحركة الرابعة في السيمفونية. و أعتقد أن نقابة الضرائب العقارية تحت قيادة المايسترو الأعظم كمال أبو عيطة قد جاوبت عن السؤال، فهي تعزف الحركة الرابعة في السيمفونية. و النغمة الأولى في لم يضعها أعداء الحياة. لحن الجماهير، لحن الخلود.

ندى عمرو - الغربية | نديم - الدقهلية | مارينا فاخر - القاهرة | شهد ومحمد عقل - الجيزة | منى محمود - الجيزة | أحمد محمد - القاهرة

تهنئة بالدكتوراه د/ محمد علي القول - الغربية | إيمان صلاح - دمياط | شهد خالد | مريم طارق | محمد أحمد - الفيوم

محافظة الجيزة

زواج سعيد سبهام علام و أسامة إبراهيم

دعوات بالشفاء للزميل صبري لبيب..

تهنئة إسلام حجازي مبروك النجاح

تهنئة بالزواج السعيد، للزميل/ أحمد محمود عبد المعطي من مأمورية الوراق

تمنيات الجيزة بالشفاء للزميله/ هيام

تهنئة للأستاذ/ عبد الرحمن الشريف مناسب لبوغه العاش بصحه جيده

تهنئة للأستاذ/ وحيد حسين نهنئه أن رزق بنجله الأول محمود

الضرائب العقارية بالجيزة تهنئ الزميل السعيد

الضرائب العقارية بالجيزة تهنئ إسلام بالزواج السعيد

الضرائب العقارية بالجيزة تهنئ للزميل/ حمدي سيد أحمد الله لزواجه السعيد

محافظة القاهرة

عيد ميلاد سعيد/ أحمد محمد رؤوف

تهنئة لبلوغ العاش وتمنى لهم دوام الصحة الأستاذة/ شناء عبد البازي

الأستاذة/ منيره أحمد علي

الأستاذ/ كمال عبد السبع

محافظة شمال سيناء

أسرة الضرائب العقارية بشمال سيناء تهنئ الأستاذ/ عزت السيد النجار على قيادته الحكيمة

محافظة السويس

تهنئة للزميل/ أحمد مصطفى بنجاح وتفوق نجله/ أحمد حسين تهنئة للزميل/ رضا سليمان لزفاف أبنته

محافظة الشرقية

تهنئة بزواج أبنه الزميل محمد جوده تهنئ محافظة الشرقية/ نورا أحمد بزواج أبنها محمد من العروسه/ ولاء

محافظة دمياط

تهنئة بالزواج للأستاذ/ محمد نجيب مثال الأستاذه/ سوزان فرحات

محافظة سوهاج

أجمل التهاني للعروسين محمد علي شوشه والعروسه منى طلعت مكى زواج سعيد

محافظة القليوبية

الأخوه الزملاء بمأمورية شبرا أول يتمنون الشفاء العاجل للزميل/ أنور سعد

محافظة دمياط

تهنئة بالنجاح الباهر للتلميذه إسراء أشرف فتحى من والدها لحصولها على المركز الثاني على مستوى المدرسه

محافظة المنيا

تهنئة للسيد/ فاروق حكيم لخروجه على المعاش باتم صحه وعافيه

اللجنه النقابية بالمنيا للأستاذ/ رمضان عيد بدوى لتفوق كريمته مروه رمضان

أسره مأمورية مبانى منوى تهنئ نفسها لتولي الأستاذ/ إبراهيم عبد الستار مدير المأمورية

أسره مأمورية مبانى تهنئ الأستاذ/ عبد الرحمن أحمد الدرديرى لاختياره رئيساً للجنه الفرعيه لنقابه الضرائب العقاريه

محافظة الإسكندرية

تهنئة بالخطوبه للزميله/ مها عقل على الأستاذ/ محمد أبو أحمد

محافظة البحيرة

تهنئ للأستاذ/ عبد العاطل رئيس قسم الأطيان لخروجه على المعاش باتم صحه تهنئة بالزواج السعيد للأستاذ أحمد رجب

مأمورية الخليفة والمقطم تهنئ الأستاذ/

نبيل إسماعيل بوصول حفيده

تهنئة من الخليفه والمقطم للزميل/ نبيل إسماعيل

تهنئة بعيد ميلاد سعيد للدكتوره/ مارينا صموئيل أبنه الزميله/ ميرفت لمى عقل

محمد عبد الحليم خلاجى بهنئ الاستاذ/ نبيل إسماعيل حمد الله على سلامه الأبن العزيز محمد من الحادث مع التمنيات بالشفاء العاجل

أجمل التهاني بعيد الميلاد السعيد مع أطيب التمنيات: نجباه موفق لبناته/ الأستاذه/ جورجت جورجى رئيس السجلات بشرا

تهنئة للزميله/ سحر سالم بقسم الكشوف الرسميه على المولود السعيد/ محمد

تهنئة لمحمد عبد الحليم وأسرة مأمورية الخليفه والمقطم تهنئ الأستاذه/ وفاء إبراهيم بخطوبه أبنها إبراهيم

محافظة مطروح

تهنئ أسره الضرائب العقارية بمطروح الزملاء/ سامر وجمعه وسعد وعبد المجيد وأشرف الشربينى بالمولود الجديد

نورة سعيان — مايو ٢٠٠٩ — ١٠

الكـلام فى كـل دار (قصيدة للزميل على شيحة*)

كان طبيعى ان افكر وانشة

واعمل حساب كل الظروف

واليد فى حضنك، بالام

وسلاحة يديح ى خوف

واخد بسيف الحق حقى

وكلمتى ترص الصفوف

كلمة فيها المعنى بوصل

للى فاكرينها تكية

واللى فاهمنى هفية

بينهوا ويضحوا بى وانديح وانا مش خروف

كان طبيعى انى افهمهم واشوف

واسالك ازاى يا صابرة بـتحتوك؟

وانت خبراتك صنوف

بـس فى جيوب الاكابر

والمراكز اللى سيفهم فى الكلى والكبد نافذ

ناس تخلى الجرح نازى

والكلام فى كل دار

حولوا خيرك لبرة

سرقة وف عز النهار

والعجيب باين وانة

شكلهم ماهوش غريب كل يوم

بنشوف صورهم

واحنا فى عز اللهيب

نصرخ غيثونا

يطلعوا لنا بلعبة تانية

ويسرقوك ويسرقونا

وتبقى للمجهول قضية

ياما راح منك يا صابرة

تحت بند الاكرامية

والعمولة والرشاوى المليونية

والعـرـس حامى اللصوص

فية قانون مفتول حبالة

فبركة ومافيهوش خوف ملكهكم مطبخ

30 يونيو 2005

*صدر للشاعر ديوان جديد بعنوان «الكلام فى كل داره»، وهو عضو فى اتحاد كتاب مصر وعضو مجلس ادارة جمعية الادباء بمصر وصدر لة عدة دواوين :اللى جرى كفى، اكتب شهادة وفاتنا ,يا امى يامة ,نبين زين.

اخبطْ دماغَكْ فى الحيطة...!

نقفْ حبايب و قرايبْ
م اسكندرية لحلايبْ
و نحرس المال السايبْ
و نقول كمان «شايب عايبْ»
و حاضرنا بلغ للغايبْ

* * *

و جَولة من ألفين جَولة
أشرار بتـدَهـْشَ و عتاولة
مش إننا ناخدْه مقاولة
مُحاوـلة... والحرْب مـحاوَلةْ!
ولا خافش من بطش الدولة

* * *

اتعلموا الدرس بسرعة
و قبل ما تجف الزُرـعـة
ربك حيمـى لو تـسـعى !
و إيد لوحدها إيد خرَعة
يهزم جنود ابن الفُزـعة

* * *

و رفعوا ليه البريطلة
و أدي الجاروف و البرويطلة
و الغنوة تلحين «أبو عيطلة»!
بيبث سمّه» فى الزَيطلة
«اخبط دماغك فى الحيطة»

حتماً ولزماً ساعة الجد
عزم الضراير،.٠.١. العزم
واقفين نواجه ظلم الليل
للغول نقول «عينك حمرا»
خد النفاق مونة وأجرة

* * *

يا مصر دى لسه بشاير
نقابتنا درعْ نواجه بيه
حب الوطن إننا ندريه
جينا مصر وقدّمنا
عاش اللى شارك فى الإضراب

* * *

يا كل أهل المحروسة
قبل الجحيم ما يطال الكلّ
يا كل مظلوم فى بلدنا
إيد ويّا إيد الإيد تـقوى
إيد ويا إيد نصبح مارد

* * *

عزم الضرايب شد الحيل
بنبنى للحق نقابـة
ماشيين نغنى «تحيا الشمس»
غنوتنا تهزم لو نشاز
غنوتنا نور بيقول للليل؛

جاهز شغلتة طمس الحروف اكتبى
بالحبر الاسود
دول بضاعة بس فاسدة
لاجل ولادك تشوف
يعرفوا اية اللى جارى
م اللى غير فى الحقيقة
واللى زور زر فى الكشوف
واحنا فى الوقت العصيب
اللى فية لابد نحلم بالشفا على ايد طبيب
عارف مشاعرك
لا يدخل غصب عنك جوة بيتك اى ديب
وانت فى حالى انفجار
المروة والشهامة والانتماء
ماشيين فى سكة الاحتضار
وانت ساكتة ومن سكونك ينولد كام الف حية
يشربوا من بحر تانى
وانت عايزة بق مية وفلاحينك والشادوف
عايزة لحظة تجمعى فيها الحروف
تقلع الباطل بجدارة
والى مش شايف يشوف

تمت فى القاهرة 27 / 4 / 2009، 2.00 صباحا
شعر: عبدالرحمن يوسف

موقع الكترونى:www.arahman.net، بريد الكترونى: arahman@arahman.net

Translation of Newsletter Headings:

A Moment of Awakening
The Voice of the General Trade Union of Workers in the Real Estate Tax Collection
(Independent)

May 2009   *A Member of Public Service International (PSI)*   *No. 4*

And We Have Won!
International and Local Recognition of the First Independent Trade Union in Egypt
The Legality of the Union Began With the Acceptance of Our Registration Documents
on 21st April (page 1 of the newsletter)

A shining white light defeats "the yellow team" (page 2 of newsletter)

The Story of Our Union (page 3 of the newsletter)

The Problem of Implementing the Routine Rules number 19 for the year 2002 (page 4 of the newsletter)

Decisions (page 4 of the newsletter)

Please give me this medicine (page 4 of the newsletter)

An Administrative Unit without Staff/Cadre (page 5 of the newsletter)

Our Independent Union (page 5 of the newsletter)

Presenting our papers (documents) = the government's recognition of our union (page 5 of the newsletter)

The Men of Suez … an event without embarrassment (page 6 of the newsletter)

The Victim of Injustice and the Victor (page 6 of the newsletter)

The Story of Labor Day (page 7 of the newsletter)

Labor Day…how can we consider it a holiday/a celebration? (page 7 of the newsletter)

Secrets…. Day of Victory – Chants by an Activist (page 8 of the newsletter)

Day of Victory (page 9 of the newsletter)

Social Issues: Legal or Temporary (page 10 of the newsletter)
Enough those who are enemies of success (page 10 of the newsletter)
The Fruits of Strength (page 10 of the newsletter)

What is the Public Service International (PSI)? (page 11 of the newsletter)
Our legal existence and theirs...(page 11 of the newsletter)

Real Estate Tax Collectors Union – its organization; names of provinces and leaders in each (page 12-15 of the newsletter)

The First Independent Trade Union in Egypt develops its internal structure (page 16 of the newsletter)

Urgent to the Minister of Finance (page 16 of the newsletter)

The People's Representative Hamdeen Sabahi writes about: The Independent Trade Union (page 17 of the newsletter)

Congratulations to our Colleagues (page 18 of the newsletter)

Our Condolences (page 19 of the newsletter)

Poetry – Talk in every house; hit your head against the wall, cartoon (page 20 of the newsletter)

Author Biography

Heba F. El-Shazli is an Assistant Professor at George Mason University's Schar School of Policy and Government, where she teaches undergraduate and graduate courses on International Relations Theory; Politics, Government and Society of the Middle East; Israeli-Palestinian Politics; and Islam and Politics. She is an affiliate faculty to the Ali Vural Ak Center for Global Islamic Studies (AVACGIS) at George Mason University. She is also an Adjunct Faculty at Georgetown University's Master's Degree Program at the Center for Democracy and Civil Society.

At Virginia Tech, she taught (for one academic year) Politics of the Middle East as an upper-class seminar. She was a visiting professor at the Virginia Military Institute (VMI; www.vmi.edu) teaching Politics and International Relations of the Middle East in the Political Science and International Studies Department and Egyptian Arabic language in the Modern Languages department (2010–2011 academic year). She was the Regional Program Director for the Middle East and North Africa (MENA) programs at the Solidarity Center (SC), AFL-CIO (www.solidaritycenter.org) from September 2004 until June 2011. She managed a staff of 25 persons based in Washington, DC, and in five field offices in the MENA region (Morocco, Algeria, Palestine, Qatar, and Lebanon). El-Shazli was the Deputy Regional Director for the Middle East and North Africa at the National Democratic Institute for International Affairs (NDI; www.ndi.org) from 2001 until 2004. During her tenure at NDI, she served as NDI's Resident Representative in Beirut, where she implemented programs to help develop and empower civil society organizations in Lebanon and in the region.

Before joining NDI, El-Shazli worked at the American Center for International Labor Solidarity (the Solidarity Center), the international institute of the American labor movement, the AFL-CIO. From 1994 to 2000, she was the Solidarity Center's regional representative in the Middle East and North Africa, based in Cairo, Egypt. She managed programs in eight Arab countries. She previously served as the Free Trade Union Institute's (FTUI) Senior Program Officer for Central and Eastern Europe from 1987 to 1994, during which time she developed and implemented educational, training, and financial assistance programs for trade unions in the region. During her tenure with FTUI, El-Shazli responded to regional needs with programs addressing worker rights, gender empowerment, communications, training of trainers (TOT), and vocational and leadership skills training.

El-Shazli has 28 years of experience in civic and union organizing, institution building, leadership skills training, labor education and training methodologies,

political advocacy, and development, implementation, and management of international programs. An Egyptian-born, naturalized American citizen, El-Shazli was educated in Egypt, England, and the United States. Her work with trade unions, political institutions, political parties, and NGOs has taken her to Central and Eastern Europe, the Caucases, Iran, South America, Western Europe, the United States, and the Middle East and North Africa. She is a member of the Council on Foreign Relations (www.cfr.org). Fluent in three languages (Arabic, French, and English), El-Shazli holds a PhD in Government and International Affairs from Virginia Tech, Blacksburg, Virginia, and a Master of Arts degree in International Relations from Georgetown University, Washington, DC.

Bibliography

Theory

Aguero, Felipe. *Soldiers, Civilians, and Democracy: Post-Franco Spain in Comparative Perspective*. Baltimore: Johns Hopkins UP, 1995.

Amin, Magdi. *After the Spring: Economic Transitions in the Arab World*. Oxford: Oxford UP, 2012.

Aminzade, Ronald. *Silence and Voice in the Study of Contentious Politics*. Cambridge: Cambridge UP, 2001. Print.

Apter, David E. *Ideology and Discontent*. London: Free of Glencoe, 1964. Print.

Arendt, Hannah. *The Human Condition*. Chicago: U of Chicago P, 1998.

——. *On Revolution*, Introduction by Jonathan Schell. Penguin Classics, 2006.

Bakunin, Michael A. and K. J. Kenafick. *Marxism, Freedom and the State*. London: Freedom Press, 1950. Print.

Bayat, A. "Activism and Social Development in the Middle East." *International Journal of Middle East Studies* 34.1 (2002): 1–28.

Bellin, E. "Contingent Democrats: Industrialists, Labor, and Democratization in Late-developing Countries." *World Politics* 52.2 (2000):175–205.

——. *Stalled Democracy: Capital, Labor, and the Paradox of State-sponsored Development*. Ithaca, NY, Bristol: Cornell U P U Presses Marketing Distributor, 2011. Print.

Berger, S. "Democracy and Social Democracy." *European History Quarterly* 32.1 (1 Jan. 2002): 13–37.

Black, Adam and Charles Black. "Principles of Political Economy by John Stewart Mill." *Edinburgh Review* (1802) 91.183 (1 Jan. 1850): 1.

Bratton, Michael. *Political Participation in a New Democracy. Comparative Political Studies* 32.5 (1 Aug. 1999): 549.

Breiner, Peter. *Democracy Source: Governments of the World: A Global Guide to Citizens' Rights and Responsibilities*. Ed. C. Neal Tate. Vol. 1. Detroit: Macmillan Reference USA, 2006, 301–307.

Briggs, Xavier DeSousa. *Democracy as Problem Solving: Building Democratic Capacity in Communities around the Globe*. Cambridge, MA: MIT Press, 2008.

Brinton, Crane. *The Anatomy of Revolution*. New York: Random House, 1965. Print.

Brown, Nathan. *The Dynamics of Democratization: Dictatorship, Development, and Diffusion*. Baltimore: The Johns Hopkins UP, 2011.

Burke, Edmund, Ira M. Lapidus, and Ervand Abrahamian. *Islam, Politics, and Social Movements*. Berkeley: U of California, 1988. Print.

Burnell, Peter J. and Peter Calvert. *Civil Society in Democratization*. London: Frank Cass, 2004. Print.

Castells, Manuel. *Networks of Outrage and Hope: Social Movements in the Internet Age*. Cambridge, UK: Polity, 2012. Print.

Chakrabarty, Dipesh. *Rethinking Working-class History: Bengal, 1890–1940*. Princeton: Princeton UP, 1989. Print.

Collier, Ruth Berins. *Paths toward Democracy: The Working Class and Elites in Western Europe and South America*. Cambridge, UK: Cambridge UP, 1999. Print.

—— and David Collier. *Shaping the Political Arena: Critical Junctures, the Labor Movement, and Regime Dynamics in Latin America*. Notre Dame, IN: U of Notre Dame P, 2002.

—— and Samuel Handlin. *Reorganizing Popular Politics: Participation and the New Interest Regime in Latin America*. University Park, PA: The Pennsylvania State University Press, 2009. Print.

Crouch, Colin and Wolfgang Streeck, eds. *The Diversity of Democracy: Corporatism, Social Order and Political Conflict*. Cheltenham, UK, Northampton, MA: Edward Elgar, 2006. Print.

Davenport, Christian, Hank Johnston, and Carol McClurg Mueller. *Repression and Mobilization*. Minneapolis: U of Minnesota, 2005. Print.

Davis, Gerald F. *Social Movements and Organization Theory*. New York, NY: Cambridge UP, 2005. Print.

Diamond, Larry J. *The Spirit of Democracy: The Struggle to Build Free Societies Throughout the World*. New York: Holt Paperbacks, 2008. Print.

——, Marc F. Plattner, and Daniel Brumberg. *Islam and Democracy in the Middle East*. Baltimore: The John Hopkins University Press, 2003. Print.

Dickinson, Torry D., Terrie A. Becerra, and Summer B. C. Lewis. *Democracy Works: Joining Theory and Action to Foster Global Change*. Boulder, CO: Paradigm, 2008. Print.

Di Palma, Giuseppe. *To Craft Democracies: An Essay on Democratic Transitions*. Berkeley: U of California P, 1990. Print.

Dunn, John. *Modern Revolutions—An Introduction to the Analysis of a Political Phenomenon*. Cambridge: Cambridge UP, 1972.

Early, Steve. "Democracy Matters." *New Labor Forum* 13.1 (2004): 106–110.

Edwards, Michael. *Civil Society*, 2nd edition, Cambridge: Polity, 2009.

——. *The Oxford Handbook of Civil Society*. New York: Oxford UP, 2011. Print.

Ehrenberg, John. *Civil Society: The Critical History of an Idea*. New York: New York University Press, 1999.

Elliott, Carolyn. *Civil Society and Democracy: A Reader*. Oxford: Oxford University Press, 2006. Print.

Elman, Colin and Miriam Fendius Elman. *Bridges and Boundaries: Historians, Political Scientists, and the Study of International Relations*. Cambridge, MA: MIT, 2001. Print.

Eyerman, Ron. *Social Movements: A Cognitive Approach*. Cambridge: Polity, 1991. Print.

Foley, Janice R. and Michael Polanyi. "Workplace Democracy: Why Bother?" *Economic and Industrial Democracy* 27.1 (Feb. 2006): 173–19.

Ford, Neil. "A Trailblazer for Democracy?" *Middle East Report* 341 (2004): 20–22.

Frege, Carola. "The Discourse of Industrial Democracy: Germany and the US Revisited." *Economic and Industrial Democracy* 26.1 (Feb. 2005): 151–175.

Giugni, Marco, Doug McAdam, and Charles Tilly, eds. *How social movements matter*. Vol. 10. U of Minnesota Press, 1999.

Godard, John. "Beliefs about Unions and What they Should Do: A Survey of Employed Canadians." *Journal of Labor Research* 18.4 (1997): 621–639.

Goldstone, Jack A. *Revolution and Rebellion in the Early Modern World*. Berkeley: U. of California P, 1991.

Goodwin, Jeff and James M. Jasper. *The Social Movements Reader: Cases and Concepts*. Manchester: Wiley-Blackwell, 2012. Print.

Greenberg, Edward S., Leon Grunberg and Kelley Daniel. "Industrial Work and Political Participation: Beyond 'Simple Spillover'." *Political Research Quarterly* 9.2 (Jun. 1996), 305–330.

Gunn, Christopher. "Markets Against Economic Democracy." *Review of Radical Political Economics* 32 (Sep. 2000): 448–460.

——. "Workers' Participation in Management, Workers' Control of Production: Worlds Apart." *Review of Radical Political Economics* 43 (Sep. 2011): 317–327, first published on May 12, 2011.

Gunther, Richard, Hans-Jurgen Puhle, and P. Nikiforos Diamandouros, eds. *The Politics of Democratic Consolidation: Southern Europe in Comparative Perspective*. Baltimore: Johns Hopkins, 1995.

Haggard, Stephan and Robert R. Kaufman. *The Political Economy of Democratic Transitions*. Princeton: Princeton UP, 1995.

Hall, John A. and Frank Trentmann. *Civil Society: A Reader in History, Theory and Global Politics*. New York, NY: Palgrave Macmillan, 2005. Print.

Hardt, Michael and Antonio Negri. *Multitude: War and Democracy in the Age of Empire*. New York: Penguin Books, 2005.

Haynes, Jeff. *Democracy and Civil Society in the Third World: Politics and New Political Movements*. Cambridge, UK: Polity Press, 1997. Print.

Hirschsohn, Philip. "Union Democracy and Shop Floor Mobilization: Social Movement Unionism in South African Auto and Clothing Plants." *Economic and Industrial Democracy* 28.1 (Feb. 2007): 6–48.

Hobsbawm, E. J. *Primitive Rebels: Studies in Archaic Forms of Social Movement in the 19th and 20th Centuries*. New York: W.W. Norton, 1965. Print.

Hodgkinson, Virginia A. and Michael W. Foley, eds. *The Civil Society Reader*. Hanover: UP of New England, 2003.

Honneth, Axel. *The Struggle for Recognition: The Moral Grammar of Social Conflicts*. Cambridge, UK: Polity, 1995. Print.

Huntington, Samuel P. and Joan M. Nelson. *No Easy Choice: Political Participation in Developing Countries*. Cambridge, MA: Harvard UP, 1976. Print.

Hyman, Richard. "G.D.H. Cole and Industrial Democracy: A Review." *Industrial Relations Journal* 5.3 (1974).

Keck, Margaret E. and Kathryn Sikkink. *Activists Beyond Borders: Advocacy Networks in International Politics*. Ithaca, NY: Cornell UP, 1998. Print.

Knudsen, Herman. "Work Environment Quality: The Role of Workplace Participation and Democracy." *Work Employment & Society* 25.3 (Sep. 2011): 379–396.

Kolb, Felix. *Protest and Opportunities: The Political Outcomes of Social Movements*. Frankfurt: Campus Verlag, 2007. Print.

Koukiadaki, Aristea. "Participation and Democracy at Work." *Personnel Review* 34.6 (2005): 729–731.

Lamb, Peter. "G.D.H. Cole on the General Will: A Socialist Reflects on Rousseau." *European Journal of Political Theory* 4 (Jul. 2005): 283–300.

Lenin, Vladimir Il'ich, and Todd Chretien. *State and revolution.* Haymarket Books, 2015.

Leventhal, F.M. "British Socialists: The Journey from Fantasy to Politics by Stanley Pierson; G. D. H. Cole and Socialist Democracy by A. W. Wright." *The Journal of Modern History* 53.3 (Sep. 1981): 542–544.

Lijphart, Arend. "Unequal Participation: Democracy's Unresolved Dilemma." *The American Political Science Review* 91.1 (Mar. 1997): 1–14.

Linz, Juan J. and Alfred Stepan. *Problems of Democratic Transition and Consolidation—Southern Europe, South America and Post-Communist Europe.* Baltimore: Johns Hopkins UP, 1996.

Liu, Eric and Nick Hanauer. *Gardens of Democracy: A New American Story of Citizenship, and Economy and the Role of Government.* Seattle: Sasquatch Books, 2011.

Madrid, Raúl L. "Labouring against Neoliberalism: Unions and Patterns of Reform in Latin America." *Journal of Latin American Studies* 35.1 (2003): 53–88. Print.

Magnusson, Warren. *Politics of Urbanism: Seeing like a City.* Abingdon, OX, New York: Routledge, 2011.

Maksimov, Grigorij P., Bert F. Hoselitz, Rudolf Rocker, and Max Nettlau. *The Political Philosophy of Bakunin: Scientific Anarchism.* Glencoe: The Free Press, 1953. Print.

Mansbridge, Jane. *Beyond Adversary Democracy.* New York: Basic Books, 1980.

Marx, Karl. *Capital,* Vol. 1. New York: Penguin Books, 1967.

——. *Capital,* Vol. 3. New York: Penguin Books, 1981. Print.

——. *A Contribution to the Critique of Political Economy.* New York: International Publishers, 1970. Print.

——. *The 18th Brumaire of Louis Bonaparte.* Rockville, MD: Wildside Press, 2008.

——, Vladimir I. Lenin, and Friedrich Engels. *Anarchism and Anarcho-Syndicalism.* Moscow: Progress Publishers, 1972. Print.

McAdam, Doug, John D. McCarthy, and N. Mayer. *Comparative Perspectives on Social Movements: Political Opportunities, Mobilizing Structures, and Cultural Framings.* Cambridge, England, New York: Cambridge UP, 1996. Print.

——, Sidney G. Tarrow, and Charles Tilly. *Dynamics of Contention.* Cambridge, New York: Cambridge UP, 2001. Print.

Meyer, David S. and Sidney G. Tarrow. "A Movement Society: Contentious Politics for a New Century." *The Social Movement Society: Contentious Politics for a New Century.* Ed. D.S. Meyer and S.G. Tarrow. Lanham, MD: Rowman and Littlefield, 1998, 1–28.

Millen, Bruce. *The Political Role of Labor in Developing Countries.* Washington, DC: The Brookings Institution, 1963.

Moore, Barrington, Jr. *Social Origins of Dictatorship and Democracy. Lord and Peasant in the Making of the Modern World.* Boston: Beacon Press, 1966 and with new Foreword by Edward Friedman and James C. Scott in 1993.

O'Donnell, Guillermo A., Philippe C. Schmitter, and Laurence Whitehead. *Transitions from Authoritarian Rule.* Baltimore: Johns Hopkins UP, 1986. Print.

Olson, Mancur. *The Logic of Collective Action—Public Goods and the Theory of Groups*. Cambridge, MA: Harvard UP, 1971.

Ottaway, Marina and Theresa Chung. "Toward a New Paradigm." *Journal of Democracy* 10.4 (1999): 99–113.

Paczynska, Agnieszka. "Social Movements for Global Democracy." *Peace & Change* 34.4 (2009): 597–600. Print.

Pantham, Thomas. "Thinking with Mahatma Gandhi: Beyond Liberal Democracy." *Political Theory* 11 (May 1983): 165–188, doi:10.1177/0090591783011002002

Pateman, Carole. "Participatory Democracy Revisited." *Perspectives on Politics* 10.1 (31 Mar. 2012): 7–19.

——. *Participation and Democratic Theory*. Cambridge: Cambridge UP, 1970.

Pollack, Detlef and Jan Wielgohs, eds. *Dissent and Opposition in Communist Eastern Europe: Origins of Civil Society and Democratic Transition*. Burlington, VT: Ashgate, 2004.

Pollak, Johannes. "Contested Meanings of Representation." *Comparative European Politics* 5.1 (2007): 87–103.

Porta, Donatella Della. *Democracy in Social Movements*. Basingstoke: Palgrave Macmillan, 2009. Print.

——. *Globalization from Below: Transnational Activists and Protest Networks*. Minneapolis: U of Minnesota, 2006. Print.

Poutsma, Erik, John Hendrickx, and Fred Huijgen. "Employee Participation in Europe: In Search of the Participative Workplace." *Economic and Industrial Democracy* 24.1 (Feb. 2003): 45–76.

Przeworski, Adam. "Proletariat into a Class: The Process of Class Formation from Karl Kautsky's The Class Struggle to Recent Controversies." *Politics & Society* 7.4 (1977): 343–401.

Radcliff, Benjamin and Ed Wingenbach. "Preference Aggregation, Functional Pathologies, and Democracy: A Social Choice Defense of Participatory Democracy." *The Journal of Politics* 62.4 (Nov. 2000): 977–998.

Rich, Louis. "The Economic Doctrines of G.D.H. Cole." *New York Times* (1923–Current file): BR10. ProQuest Historical Newspapers: *The New York Times* (1851–2008) (2 Sep. 1934).

Roberts, Adam and Timothy Garton Ash, eds. *Civil Resistance and Power Politics—The Experience of Non-violent Action from Gandhi to the Present*. Oxford: Oxford UP, 2011.

Rochon, Thomas. *Culture Moves: Ideas, Activism, and Changing Values*. Princeton, NJ: Princeton UP, 1998.

Rueschemeyer, Dietrich, Evelyne Huber, and John D. Stephens. *Capitalist Development and Democracy*. Chicago: U of Chicago P, 1992. Print.

Safri, Maliha and Eray Düzenli. "Dreaming Big: Democracy in the Global Economy, Rethinking Marxism." *A Journal of Economics, Culture & Society* 16.4 (2004): 361–366.

Salama, Mohammad R. Islam. *Orientalism and Intellectual History, Modernity and the Politics of Exclusion since Ibn Khaldun*. London: I.B. Tauris, 2011.

Schweizer, Steven L. "Participation, Workplace Democracy, and the Problem of Representative Government." *Polity* 27.3 (Spring, 1995): 359–377.

Scott, James C. *Domination and the Arts of Resistance: Hidden Transcripts*. New Haven: Yale UP, 1990. Print.

——. *Two Cheers for Anarchism: Six Easy Pieces on Autonomy, Dignity, and Meaningful Work and Play*. Princeton, NJ: Princeton UP, 2012. Print.

——. *Weapons of the Weak: Everyday Forms of Peasant Resistance*. New Haven: Yale UP, 1985. Print.

Seligman, Adam B. *The Idea of Civil Society*. New York: Free, 1992. Print.

Sewell, Jr., William. *A Rhetoric of Bourgeois Revolution: the Abbé Sieyes and What Is the Third Estate*. Durham: Duke UP, 1994.

Shatz, Marshall. *The Essential Works of Anarchism*. New York: Quadrangle Books, 1972. Print.

Sikkink, Kathryn. "Human Rights Principled Issue-Networks, and Sovereignty in Latin America." *International Organization* 47.3 (1993): 411–41.

Sirianni, Carmen. *Investing in Democracy: Engaging Citizens in Collaborative Governance*. Washington, DC: Brookings, 2009.

Skocpol, Theda. *Social Revolutions in the Modern World*. Cambridge: Cambridge UP, 1994. Print.

——. *States and Social Revolutions: A Comparative Analysis of France, Russia, and China*. Cambridge: Cambridge UP, 1979. Print.

Stewart, Charles J., Craig Allen Smith, and Robert E. Denton. *Persuasion and Social Movements*. Prospect Heights, IL: Waveland, 1989. Print.

Stivers, Camilla. *Governance in Dark Times*. Washington, DC: Georgetown UP, 2008.

Therborn, Göran. "The Rule of Capital and the Rise of Democracy." *New Left Review* 103 (1977): 3–41.

——. *What does the Ruling Class Do When it Rules? State Apparatuses and State Power under Feudalism, Capitalism and Socialism*. London, New York: Verso, 2008. Print.

Thompson, E. P. *The Making of the English Working Class*. New York: Vintage Books, 1966.

Tilly, Charles. *Contentious Performances*. Cambridge: Cambridge UP, 2008. Print.

——. *Democracy*. Cambridge: Cambridge UP, 2007.

—— and Sidney G. Tarrow. *Contentious Politics*. Boulder, CO: Paradigm Publishers, 2007. Print.

Turner, L. "Participation, Democracy and Efficiency in the US Workplace." *Industrial Relations Journal* 28 (1997): 309–313. doi: 10.1111/1468-2338.00067

Turner, Victor. *Dramas, Fields, and Metaphors: Symbolic Action in Human Society*. Ithaca: Cornell UP, 1975.

Turner, Victor W. *The Ritual Process: Structure and Anti-structure*. New York: Aldine Transaction; Reprint edition, 1995.

Valls, Andrew. "Self-Development and the Liberal State: The Cases of John Stuart Mill and Wilhelm von Humboldt." *The Review of Politics* 61.2 (Spring, 1999): 251–274.

Van Gennep, Arnold. *The Rites of Passage*, London: Routledge; Reprint edition (18 Nov. 2010).

Verba, Sidney. "Fairness, Equality, and Democracy: Three Big Words." *Social Research* 73.2 (2006): 499–540.

Whitty, Michael. "Co-management for Workplace Democracy." *Journal of Organizational Change Management* 9.6 (1996): 7.

Methodology

Aberbach, Joel and Bert Rockman. "Conducting and Coding Elite Interviewing." *PS: Political Science and Politics* 35.4 (2002): 673–675.

Bennett, Andrew and Colin Elman. "Case Study Methods in the International Relations Subfield." *Comparative Political Studies* 40.2 (2007):170–195.

Berry, Jeffrey. "Validity and Reliability Issues in Elite Interviewing." *PS: Political Science and Politics* 35.4 (2002): 679–682.

Booth, Wayne C., Gergory G. Colomb and Joseph M. Williams. *The Craft of Research*. Chicago: U of Chicago P, 2008.

Diani, Mario and McAdam, Doug. *Social Movements and Networks: Relational Approaches to Collective Action*. NYC & Oxford: Oxford University Press, 2003.

Geertz, Clifford. *The Interpretation of Cultures*. New York: Basic Books, 1977 (Chapter 1).

George, Alexander and Andrew Bennett. *Case Studies and Theory Development in the Social Sciences*. Cambridge, MA: MIT Press, 2005.

Gerring, John. *Case Study Research: Principles and Practices*. New York: Cambridge UP, 2007. Print.

——. "What is a Case Study and What is It Good For?" *American Political Science Review* 98.2 (2004): 341–354.

Godfrey-Smith, Peter. *Theory and Reality*. Chicago: U of Chicago P, 2003.

Gruber, Lloyd. "Power Politics and the Free Trade Bandwagon." *Comparative Political Studies*, 34.7 (2001): 703–741.

Herrera, Yoshiko M., Bear F. Braumoeller, et al., "Symposium: Discourse and Content Analysis." *Qualitative and Multi-Method Research Newsletter* 2.1 (2004): 15–39.

Johnson, Janet. *Political Science Research Methods*. Los Angeles: CQ Press, 2012. Print.

King, Gary, Robert O. Keohane, and Sidney Verba. *Designing Social Inquiry: Scientific Inference in Qualitative Research*. Princeton, N.J: Princeton UP, 1994. Print.

Klandermans, Bert and Staggenborg, eds. *Methods of Social Movement Research*. U of Minnesota P, 2002.

Leech, Beth. "Asking Questions: Techniques for Semistructured Interviews." *PS: Political Science and Politics* 35.4 (2002): 665–668.

Lieberman, Evan. "National Political Community and the Politics of Income Taxation in Brazil and South Africa in the Twentieth Century." *Politics and Society* 29.4 (2001): 55–76.

Mahoney, James and Dietrich Rueschemeyer. *Comparative Historical Analysis in the Social Sciences*. Cambridge, UK, New York: Cambridge UP, 2003. Print.

Maller, Judy. "Worker Participation and Trade Unionism: Case Studies of Workplace Democracy in South Africa." *Economic and Industrial Democracy* 15 (1994): 241–257.

Maxwell, Joseph A. *Qualitative Research Design: An Interactive Approach*. Thousand Oaks, CA: Sage Publications, 2005. Print.

Mednicoff, David M. "Think Locally—Act Globally? Cultural Framing and Human Rights Movements in Tunisia and Morocco." *International Journal of Human Rights* 7.3 (2003): 72–102. Print.

Ragin, Charles C. *The Comparative Method: Moving Beyond Qualitative and Quantitative Strategies*. Berkeley: U of California P, 1987. Print.

Rose, Richard. "Comparing Forms of Comparative Analysis." *Political Studies* 39 (1991): 446–462.

Rosenau, James and Mary Durfee. *Thinking Theory Thoroughly: Coherent Approaches to an Incoherent World*. Boulder: Westview Press, 2000.

Schensul, Jean. *Essential Ethnographic Methods: A Mixed Methods Approach*. Lanham, MD: AltaMira Press, 2013. Print.

Seidman, Irving. *Interviewing as Qualitative Research: A Guide for Researchers in Education and the Social Sciences*. New York: Teachers College Press, 2006. Print.

Stake, Robert. *The Art of Case Study Research*. Thousand Oaks: Sage Publications, 1995. Print.

Van Evera, Stephen. *Guide to Methods for Students of Political Science*. Ithaca: Cornell UP, 1997. Print.

Wallerstein, Immanuel. *The Uncertainties of Knowledge*. Philadelphia: Temple UP, 2004.

Wedeen, Lisa. "Reflections on Ethnographic Work in Political Science." *Annual Review of Political Science* 13 (2010):255–72.

Woliver, Laura R. "Ethical Dilemmas in Personal Interviewing." *PS: Political Science and Politics* 35.4 (2002): 677–678.

Yanow, Dvora and Peregrine Schwartz-Shea. *Interpretive Research Design: Concepts and Processes*. London: Routledge (Chapters 3 and 5), 2010.

Yin, Robert. *Case Study Research: Design and Methods*. Los Angeles, CA: Sage Publications, 2009. Print.

Zerubavel, Eviatar. *The Clockwork Muse: A Practical Guide to Writing Theses, Dissertations, and Books*. Cambridge, MA: Harvard UP, 1999. Print.

Substantive Area (Egypt and Labor Movement)

——. "Admin Court Rules for Minimum Wage." 2010. Print.

——. "Analysis: Egypt Workers Fight for Pay, Not against the State." 2009. Print.

——. "Egypt: Fragile Transition." *Africa Research Bulletin: Economic, Financial and Technical Series* 48.10 (2011): 19297B–98C. Print.

——. "President of Union of Real Estate Tax Authority Employees Summoned for Questioning." 2009. Print.

——. "Real Estate Tax Authority Form Egypt's 1st Independent Union." 2009. Print.

——. "Real Estate Tax Collectors Protest Inclusion in Govt Syndicate." 2009. Print.

——. "Real Estate Tax Collectors to Negotiate with Ministry, Agree to End Strike." 2009. Print.

——. "Reports Criticize Egypt's Violation of Freedom of Expression and Labor Rights." 2009. Print.

——. "The Road to (and from) Liberation Square." *Journal of Democracy* 22.3 (2011): 20–34. Print.

——. "Trade Union Chief Does Not Speak for Workers, Says President of Only Independent Union." 2009. Print.

——. "Workers and Egypt's January 25 Revolution." *International Labor and Working-Class History* 80.1 (2011): 189–96. Print.

Abdalla, Nadine. "Egypt's Workers—From Protest Movement to Organized Labor. A Major Challenge of the Transition Period." Stiftung Wissenschaft und Politik German Institute for International and Security Affairs, Comments 32, Oct. 2012, Berlin, Germany. https://www.swp-berlin.org/en/publication/egypts-workers/

Abbas, Raouf. *Al-Harakat-u-Ummalieya fi Masr 1899–1952* [The Labor Movement in Egypt 1899–1952]. Cairo: Darul-Katib, 1968.

Acconcia, Giuseppe. "The Shrinking Independence of Egypt's Labor Unions," *Sada Electronic Magazine*, Carnegie Endowment for International Peace, Sep. 20, 2016. http://carnegieendowment.org/sada/64634

Agha, H. and R. Malley. "This Is Not a Revolution." *New York Review of Books*, 59.17 (2012): 71–73.

Alexander, Anne. "Leadership and Collective Action in the Egyptian Trade Unions." *Work, Employment & Society* 24.2 (2010): 241–59. Print.

—— and Mostafa Bassiouny. *Bread, Freedom, Social Justice—Workers & The Egyptian Revolution*. London: Zed Books, 2014. Print.

Amin, Galal A. *Egypt in the Era of Hosni Mubarak 1981–2011*. Cairo: The American U in Cairo P, 2012, Print.

——. *Whatever Happened to the Egyptians? Changes in Egyptian Society from 1950 to the Present*. Cairo: American U in Cairo, 2000. Print.

—— and Jonathan Wright. *Whatever Happened to the Egyptian Revolution*. Cairo: The American U in Cairo P, 2013. Print.

Antonius, George. *The Arab Awakening, The Story of the Arab National Movement*. J. B. Philadelphia, PA: Lippincott Company, 1939.

Ari, Paul. "Egypt's Labor Pains: For Workers, the Revolution Has Just Begun." *Dissent* 58.4 (2011): 11–14. Print.

Aswānī, Alā'. *On the State of Egypt: What Made the Revolution Inevitable*. New York: Vintage Books, a division of Random House, Inc, 2011. Print.

Bayat, Asif. *Life as Politics—How Ordinary People Change the Middle East*. Stanford: Stanford UP, 2010.

Beinin, Joel. "Egyptian Workers and January 25th: A Social Movement in Historical Context." *Social Research* 79.2 (2012): 323–48. Print.

——. "Egypt's Workers Rise Up," *The Nation* 292.10–11 (2011): 8–9.

—— and Peace Carnegie Endowment for International. "The Rise of Egypt's Workers." *Carnegie Endowment for International Peace*, Jun. 2012.

—— and Zachary Lockman. *Workers on the Nile: Nationalism, Communism, Islam, and the Egyptian Working Class, 1882–1954*. Princeton, NJ: Princeton UP, 1987. Print.

—— and Frédéric Vairel. *Social Movements, Mobilization, and Contestation in the Middle East and North Africa*. Stanford, CA: Stanford UP, 2011. Print.

Belhaj Hassine, Nadia. "Inequality of Opportunity in Egypt." *The World Bank Economic Review* 26.2 (2012): 265–95. Print.

Bellin, Eva R. "Contingent Democrats: Industrialists, Labor and Democratization in Late-Developing Countries." *World Politics* 52.2 (Jan. 2000): 175–205.

——. *Stalled Democracy: Capital, Labor, and the Paradox of State-sponsored Development*. Ithaca: Cornell University Press, 2002. Print.

Berque, Jacques. *L'Egypte Impérialisme Et Révolution*. Paris: Gallimard, 1967. Print.

Bianchi, David. "The Corporatization of the Egyptian Labor Movement." *Middle East Journal* 40.3 (Summer 1986): 429–444.

——. *Unruly Corporatism: Association Life in Twentieth-Century Egypt*. New York: Oxford UP, 1989.

Cammett, Melani and Marsha Pripstein Posusney. "Labor Standards and Labor Market Flexibility in the Middle East: Free Trade and Freer Unions?" *Studies in Comparative International Development* 45.2 (2010): 250–79. Print.

Candland, Christopher and Rudra Sil. *The Politics of Labor in a Global Age: Continuity and Change in Late-industrializing and Post-socialist Economies*. Oxford, New York: Oxford UP, 2001. Print.

Cook, Steven A. *The Struggle for Egypt: From Nasser to Tahrir Square*. New York: Oxford UP, 2012. Print.

Council on Foreign Relations. *The New Arab Revolt*. Washington, DC & NYC: Council on Foreign Relations, 2011. Print.

Dabashi, Hamid. *The Arab Spring: The End of Post Colonialism*. London, New York, New York: Zed Books Distributed in the USA exclusively by Palgrave Macmillan, 2012. Print.

El-Hamalawy, H. "Unions under Scrutiny." *Al-Masry Al-Youm* 8 Jul. 2009. www.arabawy.org/2009/07/09/govt-unions-under-scrutiny/

El-Mahdi, Rabab and Philip Marfleet. *Egypt: the Moment of Change*. London: Zed, 2009. Print.

Fahim, Kareem. "Strikes Pitting Workers against Military in Egypt." *International Herald Tribune* 18 Aug. 2011, p. 5.

Fahmy, Ziad. *Ordinary Egyptians: Creating the Modern Nation through Popular Culture*. Stanford, CA: Stanford UP, 2011. Print.

Faiola, Anthony. "A Burgeoning Labor Movement in Egypt." *The Washington Post* 26 Sep. 2011, p. A.9. Print.

Farah, Nadia Ramsis. *Egypt's Political Economy Power Relations in Development*. Cairo: American U in Cairo, 2009. Print.

Ghonim, Wael. *Revolution 2.0, The Power of the People is Greater than the People in Power, A Memoir*. Boston: Houghton Mifflin Harcourt, 2012.

Goldberg, Ellis. "The Foundations of State-Labor Relations in Contemporary Egypt." *Comparative Politics* 24.2 (1992): 147–61. Print.

——. *The Social History of Labor in the Middle East*. Boulder, CO: Westview Press, 1996. Print.

——. *Tinker, Tailor, and Textile Worker: Class and Politics in Egypt, 1930–1952*. Berkeley, CA: University of California Press, 1986.

——. *Trade, Reputation, and Child Labor in Twentieth-century Egypt*. New York, NY: Palgrave Macmillan, 2004. Print.

Goldschmidt, Arthur, Amy J. Johnson, and Barak A. Salmoni. *Re-envisioning Egypt 1919–1952*. Cairo: American U in Cairo, 2005. Print.

Hammer, Joshua. "How Egypt's Activists Became 'Generation Jail'—Six years after the Arab Spring, the Country's Democracy Activists live under Constant Threat of Prison." *New York Times Magazine* 14 Mar. 2017. www.nytimes.com/2017/03/14/magazine/how-egypts-activists-became-generation-jail.html

Hanieh, Adam. "Beyond Mubarak: Reframing the 'Politics' and 'Economics' of Egypt's Uprising." *Studies in Political Economy* 87 (2011): 7–27. Print.

Hartshorn, Ian. "Labor Unions under Attack in Morsi's Egypt." *Muftah* e-zine, 30 Nov. 2012. http://muftah.org/labor-unions-under-attack-in-morsis-egypt/—.VJOKW7jo8

Hijab, Nadia. *Womanpower: The Arab Debate on Women at Work*. Cambridge, Cambridgeshire, New York: Cambridge UP, 1988. Print.

Ibrahim, Fouad N. and Barbara Ibrahim. *Egypt: An Economic Geography*. London: I.B. Tauris, 2003. Print.

Kerrissey, Jasmine and Evan Schofer. "Labor Unions and Political Participation in Comparative Perspective." *Social Forces* 97.1 (Sep. 2018): 427–463.

Kester, Gerard and Henry Pinaud, eds. *Trade Unions and Democratic Participation in Europe: A Scenario for the 21st Century*. Aldershot, England: Avebury, 1996.

Khalil, Ashraf. *Liberation Square: Inside the Egyptian Revolution and the Rebirth of a Nation*. New York: St. Martin's, 2012. Print.

Korany, Bahgat and El-Mahdi, Rabab, eds. *Arab Spring in Egypt—Revolution and Beyond*. Cairo: American U in Cairo P, 2012.

Lachapelle, Jean. "Lessons from Egypt's Tax Collectors." *Middle East Report* 264. Middle East Research & Information Project, Washington, D.C., Fall 2012. 38–41. Print. www.merip.org/mer/mer264/lessons-egypts-tax-collectors-0

Langohr, Vickie. "Too Much Civil Society, Too Little Politics: Egypt and Liberalizing Arab Regimes." *Comparative Politics* 36.2 (Jan. 2004): 181–204.

Lesch, Ann. "Egypt's Spring: Causes of the Revolution." *Middle East Policy* 18.3 (2011): 35–48.

Liauzu, Claude. "The History of Labor and the Workers' Movement in North Africa." *The Social History of Labor in the Middle East*. Boulder, CO: Westview Press, 1996. 193–221. Print.

Lockman, Zachary. *Contending visions of the Middle East: the history and politics of Orientalism*. Cambridge, UK, New York: Cambridge UP, 2010.

——. *Workers and Working Classes in the Middle East: Struggles, Histories and Historiographies*. Albany, NY: State U of New York, 1994.

Longuenesse, Elisabeth. "Labor in Syria: The Emergence of New Identities." *The Social History of Labor in the Middle East*. Ed. Ellis J. Goldberg. Boulder, CO: Westview Press, 1996, 99–129. Print.

Looney, Robert. "Labor and the State in Egypt: Workers, Unions, and Economic Restructuring." *Journal of Third World Studies* 16.1 (1999): 287. Print.

Lust-Okar, Ellen and Saloua Zerhouni, eds. *Political Participation in the Middle East*. Boulder, CO: Lynne Rienner Publications, 2008.

Lynch, Marc. *The Arab Uprising: The Unfinished Revolutions of the New Middle East*. New York: Public Affairs, 2012.

Lynch, Sarah. "Key Force in Tahrir Square: Egypt's Labor Movement; Kamal Abu Eitta Endured Years of Torture and Arrest Trying to Build an Independent Labor Movement in Egypt. Now Organized Labor Is Trying to Emerge as a Real Force in Egypt's Transition." *The Christian Science Monitor* (7 Aug. 2011). Web.

Masoud, Tarek. "The Road to (and from) Liberation Square." *Journal of Democracy* 22.3 (2011): 20–34. Print.

Maugiron, Nathalie and Nicholas S. Hopkins. *Political and Social Protest in Egypt*. Cairo, New York: American U in Cairo P, 2009. Print.

McGrath, C. A. M. "Independent Unions Flourish in Post-Mubarak Egypt." *Middle East* 422 (2011): 38–39. Print.

——. "Egypt's New Unions Face Uncertain Future." *The Arab American News* (2012): 4–4. Print.

Minot, Nicholas, et al. "Trade Liberalization and Poverty in the Middle East and North Africa." *International Food Policy Research Institute* (Dec. 2010), 224 pp. Print.

Owen, Roger. *State, Power and Politics in the Making of the Modern Middle East*. London: Routledge, 2004.

Owen, E. R. J. *Cotton and the Egyptian Economy: 1820–1914: A Study in Trade and Development*. Oxford: Clarendon, 1969. Print.

Paczynska, Agnieszka. "Globalization, Structural Adjustment, and Pressure to Conform: Contesting Labor Law Reform in Egypt." *New Political Science* 28.1 (2006): 45–64. Print.

——. *State, Labor, and the Transition to a Market Economy: Egypt, Poland, Mexico, and the Czech Republic*. University Park, PA: Pennsylvania State UP, 2009. Print.

Posusney, M. "Irrational Workers, the Moral Economy of Labor Protest in Egypt." *World Development* 46.1 (1993): 83–120. Print.

Posusney, Marsha Pripstein. *Labor and the State in Egypt: Workers, Unions, and Economic Restructuring*. New York: Columbia University Press, 1997. Print.

—— and Michele P. Angrist, eds. *Authoritarianism in the Middle East—Regimes and Resistance*. Boulder, CO: Lynne Rienner Publications, 2005.

Ramadan, Fatma and Amr Adly. "Low-cost Authoritarianism: the Egyptian regime and Labor Movement since 2013." Carnegie Endowment for International Peace, Middle East Center, 2015. http://carnegie-mec.org/2015/09/17/low-cost-authoritarianism-egyptian-regime-and-labor-movement-since-2013-pub-61321

Rogan, Eugene. *The Arabs: a History*. New York: Basic Books, 2009.

Said, Atef. "Can Workers' Struggle End Mubarak's Dictatorship? Egyptian Labor Erupting." *Against the Current* 24.4 (2009): 11–18. Print.

Said, Mona. "Trade Reform, Job Quality and Wages of the Working Poor in Egypt: Evidence from Manufacturing Panel Data." *The Journal of Developing Areas* 46.2 (2012): 159–83. Print.

Saleh, Heba. "Activists Renew Calls for Union Law in Egypt." *Financial Times* (2012): 11. Print.

——. "Independent Labour Unions Take Shape in Egypt." *Financial Times* (8 Jun. 2011): ABI/INFORM Global. Web. 31 Oct. 2012.

Sallam, Hesham. "Striking Back at Egyptian Workers." *Middle East Report* 259.41 (2011), ME Report (MERIP).

Shehata, Samer. *Shop Floor Culture and Politics in Egypt*. Albany: SUNY Press, 2009. Print.

——. "In the Basha's House: The Organizational Culture of Egyptian Public-Sector Enterprise." *International Journal of Middle East Studies* 35.1 (2003):103–132.

Singerman, Diane. *Avenues of Participation: Family, Politics, and Networks in Urban Quarters of Cairo*. Princeton: Princeton UP, 1995.

Snider, Erin A. and David M. Faris. "The Arab Spring: U.S. Democracy Promotion in Egypt." *Middle East Policy* 18.3 (2011): 49–62. Print.

Sowers, Jeannie and Chris Toensing, eds. *The Journey to Tahrir: Revolution, Protest, and Social Change in Egypt*. New York City, NY: Verso Press, 2012.

Stacher, Joshua. *Adaptable Autocrats: Regime Power in Egypt and Syria*. Stanford, CA: Stanford UP, 2012. Print.

Tarek, Masoud. "Are They Democrats? Does It Matter?" *Journal of Democracy* 19.3 (2008): 19–24. Print.

Tidjani, Bassirou. "Labor and the State in Egypt." *Relations Industrielles* 55.1 (2000): 187–91. Print.

Toth, James. "Labor and the State in Egypt: Workers, Unions, and Economic Restructuring." *Labor History* 41.2 (2000): 250–51. Print.

Totonchi, Emil P. "Laboring a Democratic Spring: The Past, Present and Future of Free Trade Unions in Egypt." *Working USA: The Journal of Labor and Society* 14 (Sep. 2011): 259–283.

Tschirgi, Dan, Walid Kazziha, and Sean F. McMahon. *Egypt's Tahrir Revolution.* Boulder, CO: Lynne Rienner Publishers, 2013. Print.

Valenzuela, J. Samuel. "Labor Movements in Transitions to Democracy: A Framework for Analysis." *Comparative Politics* 21.4 (Jul. 1989): 445–472.

Vitalis, Robert. *When Capitalists Collide, Business Conflict and the End of Empire in Egypt.* Berkeley, CA: University of California Press, 1995.

Waterbury, J. "The 'Soft State' and the Open Door: Egypt's Experience with Economic Liberalization, 1974–1984." *Comparative Politics* 18.1 (1985): 65–83.

Wickham, Carrie R. *The Muslim Brotherhood—Evolution of an Islamist Movement.* Princeton, NJ: Princeton UP, 2013.

Youssef, Carolyn M. "Recent Events in Egypt and the Middle East: Background, Direct Observations and a Positive Analysis." *Organizational Dynamics* 40.3 (2011): 222–34. Print.

Index

For Product Safety Concerns and Information please contact our EU
representative GPSR@taylorandfrancis.com
Taylor & Francis Verlag GmbH, Kaufingerstraße 24, 80331 München, Germany

www.ingramcontent.com/pod-product-compliance
Ingram Content Group UK Ltd.
Pitfield, Milton Keynes, MK11 3LW, UK
UKHW020939180425
457613UK00019B/466